Language Policy

Volume 19

Series Editors
Joseph Lo Bianco, University of Melbourne, Australia
Terrence G. Wiley, Professor Emeritus, Arizona State University, USA

Editorial Board
Claire Kramsch, University of California at Berkeley, USA
Georges Lüdi, University of Basel, Switzerland
Normand Labrie, University of Toronto, Ontario, Canada
Anne Pakir, National University of Singapore, Singapore
John Trim, Former Fellow, Selwyn College, Cambridge, UK
Guadalupe Valdes, Stanford University, USA

The last half century has witnessed an explosive shift in language diversity not unlike the Biblical story of the Tower of Babel, but involving now a rapid spread of global languages and an associated threat to small languages. The diffusion of global languages, the stampede towards English, the counter-pressures in the form of ethnic efforts to reverse or slow the process, the continued determination of nation-states to assert national identity through language, and, in an opposite direction, the greater tolerance shown to multilingualism and the increasing concern for language rights, all these are working to make the study of the nature and possibilities of language policy and planning a field of swift growth.

The series will publish empirical studies of general language policy or of language education policy, or monographs dealing with the theory and general nature of the field. We welcome detailed accounts of language policy-making - who is involved, what is done, how it develops, why it is attempted. We will publish research dealing with the development of policy under different conditions and the effect of implementation. We will be interested in accounts of policy development by governments and governmental agencies, by large international companies, foundations, and organizations, as well as the efforts of groups attempting to resist or modify governmental policies. We will also consider empirical studies that are relevant to policy of a general nature, e.g. the local effects of the developing European policy of starting language teaching earlier, the numbers of hours of instruction needed to achieve competence, selection and training of language teachers, the language effects of the Internet. Other possible topics include the legal basis for language policy, the role of social identity in policy development, the influence of political ideology on language policy, the role of economic factors, policy as a reflection of social change.

The series is intended for scholars in the field of language policy and others interested in the topic, including sociolinguists, educational and applied linguists, language planners, language educators, sociologists, political scientists, and comparative educationalists.

More information about this series at http://www.springer.com/series/6209

Jennifer Rennie • Helen Harper
Editors

Literacy Education and Indigenous Australians

Theory, Research and Practice

 Springer

Editors
Jennifer Rennie
Monash University
Melbourne, VIC, Australia

Helen Harper
University of New England
Armidale, NSW, Australia

ISSN 1571-5361 ISSN 2452-1027 (electronic)
Language Policy
ISBN 978-981-13-8628-2 ISBN 978-981-13-8629-9 (eBook)
https://doi.org/10.1007/978-981-13-8629-9

© Springer Nature Singapore Pte Ltd. 2019
This work is subject to copyright. All rights are reserved by the Publisher, whether the whole or part of the material is concerned, specifically the rights of translation, reprinting, reuse of illustrations, recitation, broadcasting, reproduction on microfilms or in any other physical way, and transmission or information storage and retrieval, electronic adaptation, computer software, or by similar or dissimilar methodology now known or hereafter developed.
The use of general descriptive names, registered names, trademarks, service marks, etc. in this publication does not imply, even in the absence of a specific statement, that such names are exempt from the relevant protective laws and regulations and therefore free for general use.
The publisher, the authors, and the editors are safe to assume that the advice and information in this book are believed to be true and accurate at the date of publication. Neither the publisher nor the authors or the editors give a warranty, express or implied, with respect to the material contained herein or for any errors or omissions that may have been made. The publisher remains neutral with regard to jurisdictional claims in published maps and institutional affiliations.

This Springer imprint is published by the registered company Springer Nature Singapore Pte Ltd.
The registered company address is: 152 Beach Road, #21-01/04 Gateway East, Singapore 189721, Singapore

Foreword

My involvement in improving education for Indigenous students spans more than 50 years, bringing with it a perspective not available to many. This foreword is the third I have written for books reporting on literacy interventions for Indigenous students, in my capacity as the chair of the ACER Indigenous Education Advisory Committee and as emeritus professor with the University of South Australia. In 2011, I wrote the foreword for the Australian Council for Educational Research (ACER) Monograph 65 *Literacy and Numeracy Learning: Lessons from the Longitudinal Literacy and Numeracy Study for Indigenous Students* (Purdie et al. 2011). In 2003, it was for the Australian Council for Educational Research (ACER) Monograph 57 *Supporting English Literacy and Numeracy Learning for Indigenous Students in the Early Years* (Frigo et al. 2003). Prior to that was the publication *Double Power: English Literacy and Indigenous Education* (Wignell 1999).

Seven years since the last publication on this topic, it is time that we once again took stock of the state of research about improving outcomes for Indigenous literacy learners. The field of literacy education continues to be a complex and contested field. Exemplified in this volume are approaches arguing that family and community involvement as well as Indigenous cultural content are foundational; approaches based on the idea that we should follow student interests to maintain engagement in literacy; approaches that go back to the basics of decoding and encoding; and approaches that argue for explicit teaching of the purposes and functions of literacy.

Each of these varied approaches claims evidence of efficacy, claims which may seem bewildering to the observer. Indigenous literacy education is inevitably influenced by these competing literacy approaches, and will continue to do so, as educators seek to find a way to improve outcomes. After all these years, I'm disappointed with the continued difficulties with long-term data collection and therefore evidence-based research. I realise the effort involved in doing this, but without it, it is difficult to find a clear direction. We need evidence, not just about phonics but also about how to effectively develop academic meaning-making across the learning areas.

I welcome this book as an opportunity to keep Indigenous literacy education in the minds of Australian educators and policy makers and as an update of current literacy interventions worthy of our attention. Our task as readers is to identify the qualities of the different approaches which should be sustained and replicated.

University of South Australia   Emeritus Professor Paul Hughes AM, FACE
Adelaide, SA, Australia

References

Frigo, T., Corrigan, M., Adams, I., Hughes, P., Stephens, M., & Woods, D. (2003). *Supporting English literacy and numeracy learning for indigenous students in the early years* (ACER research monograph 57). Camberwell: Australian Council for Educational Research.

Purdie, N., Reid, K., Frigo, T., Stone, A., & Kleinhenz, E. (2011). *literacy and numeracy learning: Lessons from the longitudinal literacy and numeracy study for indigenous students* (ACER research monograph 65). Camberwell: Australian Council for Educational Research.

Wignell, P. (1999). *Double power: English literacy and indigenous education*. Melbourne: Language Australia.

Contents

1 Why a Book About Indigenous Literacy Education in Australia? 1
Helen Harper and Jennifer Rennie

Part I   Examining the Local: Theory and Practice

2 The Evidence of Literacy Learning Through Contemporary Kunibídji Knowledge Systems 15
Lena Djabibba, Glenn Auld, and Joanne O'Mara

3 Sensory Ways to Indigenous Multimodal Literacies: Hands and Feet Tell the Story 33
Kathy A. Mills and Jane Dooley

4 Durithunga Boul: A Pattern of Respectful Relationships, Reciprocity and Socially Just Literacy Education in One Urban School 51
John Davis and Annette Woods

5 Family Story Time in the Ngaanyatjarra Early Years Program 71
Anne Shinkfield and Beryl Jennings

6 Confessions from a Reading Program: Building Connections, Competence and Confidence 87
Jennifer Rennie

7 Talking and Writing to Develop Mathematical Meanings in a Remote Indigenous Context 109
Helen Harper and Bronwyn Parkin

8 Indigenous Doctoral Literacy in the Humanities and Social Sciences 127
Zane M. Diamond and Peter J. Anderson

vii

9 **Preparing Pre-service Teachers to Teach Literacy
in Remote Spaces**.. 147
Jennifer Rennie and Peter J. Anderson

Part II Examining the Systemic: Theory and Practice

10 **A Long Unfinished Struggle: Literacy and Indigenous
Cultural and Language Rights** 165
Janine Oldfield and Joseph Lo Bianco

11 **Embedding Evidence-Based Practice into a Remote
Indigenous Early Learning and Parenting Program:
A Systematic Approach** 185
Louise Cooke and Averill Piers-Blundell

12 **Early Literacy: Strengthening Outcomes Through Processes
of Collaboration and Engagement**........................... 203
Janet Scull and Debra Hannagan

13 **'Just Teach Our Kids to Read': Efficacy of Intensive
Reading Interventions for Both Younger and Older
Low-Progress Readers in Schools Serving Mainly Remote
Indigenous Communities** 221
Kevin Wheldall, Robyn Wheldall, Alison Madelaine,
Meree Reynolds, Sarah Arakelian, and Saskia Kohnen

14 **A Case Study of Controversy: The Cape York Aboriginal
Australian Academy** 247
John McCollow

15 **Good Theory, Good Systems: An Instance of Accelerated
Literacy Pedagogy Implementation** 271
Bronwyn Parkin

16 **'A Strong Belief in the Possibility of a Better Life':
The Pedagogy of Contingency and the Ethic of Solidarity
in the *Yes, I Can!* Aboriginal Adult Literacy Campaign**........... 293
Bob Boughton and Frances Williamson

17 **Afterword: Being Literate in 'Australian': The Future Can** 313
Peter Freebody

About the Editors and Contributors

Editors

Dr. Jennifer Rennie is a senior lecturer in literacy education in the Faculty of Education, Monash University. Prior to working in higher education, she worked as a primary and high school teacher. Her research interests relate to Indigenous literacies, students who are marginalised from mainstream schooling and reading pedagogy for disengaged adolescent readers. She has had a long-standing association with the Australian Literacy Educators Association and was the recipient of the ALEA medal for outstanding service to the association and the profession in 2015. She recently took office as vice president of ALEA. She has been managing editor of the *Australian Journal of Language and Literacy* since 2009.

Dr. Helen Harper has worked as a researcher and lecturer in language and literacy education, as a linguist in remote Indigenous communities, and as a teacher of English as an Additional Language. Currently Helen is a senior lecturer in the School of Education at the University of New England (UNE) where she teaches English language and literacy education. Helen's research interests include pedagogies for educationally marginalised students, pedagogies of literacy, and classroom interactions. Before taking up her post at UNE in 2018, Helen lived for more than two decades in the Northern Territory, where she worked as a researcher and educator.

Contributors

Peter J. Anderson Indigenous Research and Engagement Unit, QUT, Brisbane, QLD, Australia

Sara Arakelian Macquarie University, Sydney, NSW, Australia

Glenn Auld Deakin University, Melbourne, VIC, Australia

Bob Boughton University of New England, Armidale, NSW, Australia

Louise Cooke Gunbalanya School, Gunbalanya, NT, Australia

John Davis Stronger Smarter Institute, Logan, QLD, Australia

Jane Dooley Deakin University, Melbourne, VIC, Australia

Lena Djabibba Elder, Kunibídji Community, Maningrida, Australia
Deakin University, Melbourne, VIC, Australia

Peter Freebody School of Education, The University of Wollongong, Wollongong, NSW, Australia

Debra Hannagan Waardi Limited, Broome, WA, Australia

Helen Harper University of New England, Armidale, NSW, Australia

Paul Hughes University of South Australia, Adelaide, SA, Australia

Beryl Jennings Warburton Community via Kalgoorlie, WA, Australia

Saskia Macquarie University, Sydney, NSW, Australia

Joseph Lo Bianco Melbourne Graduate School of Education, University of Melbourne, Melbourne, VIC, Australia

Janine Oldfield Batchelor Institute of Indigenous Tertiary Education, Batchelor, NT, Australia

Averill Piers-Blundell University of Melbourne, Melbourne, VIC, Australia

Zane M. Diamond Faculty of Education, Monash University, Melbourne, VIC, Australia

Alison Madelaine Macquarie University, Sydney, NSW, Australia

John McCollow TJ Ryan Foundation, Brisbane, QLD, Australia

Kathy A. Mills Institute for Learning Sciences and Teacher Education, Australian Catholic University, Brisbane, QLD, Australia

Joanne O'Mara Deakin University, Melbourne, VIC, Australia

Bronwyn Parkin University of Adelaide, Adelaide, SA, Australia

Jennifer Rennie Monash University, Melbourne, VIC, Australia

Meree Reynolds Macquarie University, Sydney, NSW, Australia

Janet Scull Monash University, Melbourne, VIC, Australia

Anne Shinkfield Monash University, Melbourne, VIC, Australia

Kevin Wheldall Macquarie University, Sydney, NSW, Australia

Robyn Wheldall Macquarie University, Sydney, NSW, Australia

Frances Williamson University of New England, Armidale, NSW, Australia

Annette Woods QUT, Brisbane, QLD, Australia

Chapter 1
Why a Book About Indigenous Literacy Education in Australia?

Helen Harper and Jennifer Rennie

This book brings together diverse perspectives about Australian literacy education for Indigenous peoples. The editors of this volume share a long history of working in Indigenous education, both as classroom teachers and as academics, and in school and tertiary settings. As non-Indigenous (Settler) academics, we acknowledge that Indigenous educational priorities ultimately need to be driven by Indigenous people, and we must enter this space respectfully. As educators we are aware of the disparate voices in literacy education generally, but the more so in the multiplicity of Indigenous contexts. We are motivated by the need to keep nudging the conversations along, as Indigenous people determine their own ways of being literate, and as educators continue to tackle the unfinished business of growing their institutions into places where Indigenous people can come to learn successfully. For any Australian teachers and researchers in the field of education, the topic of Indigenous literacy education should be particularly significant because it concerns many of our most marginalised students. It brings our attention to one of our deepest national educational dilemmas, namely, who gets to participate fully in which education.

Despite the wealth of recent and valuable research in Indigenous education elsewhere in the world, we have constrained our topic here to educational research in Australia. There are certainly comparisons to be made with North American and other Indigenous contexts, and we have a lot to learn from work on Indigenous teacher training (e.g. Huffman 2010, 2018), student identity (Cummins et al. 2005; Reyhner 2017) and research that stresses the interplay between Indigenous learners' cultural, social and cognitive contexts (NASEM 2018; Tharp 1982; Tharp and Gallimore 1988). However, the Australian Indigenous context has its own challenges

H. Harper
University of New England, Armidale, NSW, Australia
e-mail: hharper2@une.edu.au

J. Rennie (✉)
Monash University, Melbourne, VIC, Australia
e-mail: jennifer.rennie@monash.edu

© Springer Nature Singapore Pte Ltd. 2019
J. Rennie, H. Harper (eds.), *Literacy Education and Indigenous Australians*,
Language Policy 19, https://doi.org/10.1007/978-981-13-8629-9_1

that are worth elaborating: its diversity takes unique forms, with settings ranging from our inner cities to the farthest corners of the continent; it encompasses dozens of distinct language groups and social groups with a wide variety of aspirations.

From the start of our journey in assembling this book, we were inspired by a much earlier volume: the 1990 collection edited by Christine Walton and William Eggington, *Language: maintenance, power and education in Australian Aboriginal contexts.* Walton and Eggington's work brought together many different kinds of language and literacy work, with a focus on the local, and on building the status of Indigenous voices in the education space. A shorter collection specifically addressing English literacy was published in 1999 (Wignell 1999). Subsequently as Paul Hughes has outlined in the foreword here, the Australian Council for Education Research (ACER) published two monographs reporting on research into Indigenous literacy and numeracy (Frigo et al. 2003; Purdie et al. 2011). Most recently Devlin et al. (2017) drew together grassroots perspectives of practitioners and researchers who have contributed to the Northern Territory Bilingual Education Program, established in 1973. Their collection offers valuable Indigenous and non-Indigenous accounts that capture the achievements of bilingual education and give us insights into the policy settings of bilingual/biliteracy education and minority language rights in Australia. However, in recent years there has been no collection of writing that addresses the broader perspective of thinking about Indigenous people's relationship to literacy, and how this is addressed in educational settings. The current volume aims to bring together a range of ways to conceptualise literacy in the one space, and in so doing, to tease out the complex ideologies, educational approaches and aspirations that create the rich texture of debates about Indigenous literacy education in Australia.

In the context of these debates, it can be difficult to find common ground amongst the many voices. The imperatives of formal schooling can seem at odds with the many local initiatives in which Indigenous people appropriate literate practices for their own purposes, maintaining traditional forms, and making them flourish as their own societies evolve and as they appropriate new technologies. With such diverse perspectives, the conversation about Indigenous literacy education can seem fractured and incoherent. Are we talking about urban children or children in remote schools? Are we promoting learning through a first language, or are we focused on how students can learn to read and write effectively in Standard English? Do we attend primarily to print literacy as the key to educational success, and/or should we value small, local innovations that challenge more hegemonic notions of literacy? The practical concerns and research activities arising from these questions are so varied that it seems as if the bodies of work will never be able to speak to one another. It can be a difficult and often uncomfortable space to navigate. But the discussions are too important to abandon. This then is the motivation for the current volume: to scope these debates and to bring together at least some of the disparate voices.

Which Literacy and for Whom?

The notion of literacy education is, needless to say, highly contested. First, the term 'literacy' can be understood in different ways. It can be understood as simply 'knowing how to read words on the page': the mastery of skills associated with the encoding, decoding and comprehension of print. In this 'autonomous' model (Street 2006) literacy is a neutral, context-free construct, a set of skills that are transferrable from one context to another. But literacy can also be viewed as a set of social and cultural practices, deriving from the political, social and cultural contexts in which they are learned (Barton and Hamilton 1998; Freebody and Luke 1990; Street 1993). In the social and functional view that underpins much of the thinking about literacy education in Australia, literacy is also seen as a tool for creating meaning (Australian Curriculum, Assessment and Reporting Authority [ACARA] n.d.; Christie 1990; Halliday 1978), serving our large and small communication purposes through multimodal forms of communication, incorporating not only print, but also spoken, visual and other modes and increasingly drawing on digital technologies.

Literacy education is often framed in economic terms as a function of work readiness, in the sense that young people need to be literate in order to be employable. This position is problematic and open to critique, especially in remote Indigenous settings where people's priorities of looking after land, family and culture are not well matched with broader labour market concerns (Altman 2009; Fogarty et al. 2018). At the same time there is no getting around the fact that literacy is a key tool for active, informed participation in a contemporary democratic society. Print literacy in particular occupies a privileged position in education and in twenty-first-century literacy practices more generally. Mastering the language and the written conventions of the academic disciplines allows children to be successful at school and to access higher education. It is empowering. Not learning to master the conventions of print has implications for how children will progress through school.

For the education systems that provide schooling to all Australians, it must be a matter of social justice that Australia's most marginalised students are successful in learning to read and write in English. But recent reports suggest that this is far from being the case. Data from the Australian Curriculum and Assessment and Reporting Authority in 2016 demonstrated that only 73.6% of Indigenous students in Year 9 were at or above reading benchmarks in the National Assessment Program – Literacy and Numeracy (NAPLAN), in contrast to 92.8% of students nationally. In very remote locations, the scores for Indigenous students were much lower, with only 33.9% of Year 9 students reading at or above benchmark (ACARA 2016). These results have barely shifted in the decade since NAPLAN was first introduced (ACARA 2009).

With these kinds of figures circulating in the public sphere, it is easy to construct narratives of failure and crisis (Fogarty et al. 2018), and look for a 'fix' that can be parachuted in to schools, particularly in the remote north. Over the past two decades, responding to the need for 'something that works', a number of systematic approaches to teaching reading and writing skills have been developed or imported and trialled in schools with predominantly Indigenous students. MultiLit, Direct Instruction and Accelerated Literacy are three such programs, and each of these is discussed in this volume, in Chaps. 13, 14 and 15, respectively.

In contrast to these interventionist kinds of approaches, many practitioners have long sought to realise more deeply contextualised and locally driven ways of teaching language and other communication technologies. Local perspectives emphasise the need to promote bi- and multilingualism (Oldfield & Lo Bianco, this volume), and to represent local knowledge and identities through visual and other creative meaning-making systems. There are the voices from communities—urban, rural and remote—that contest non-Indigenous values of what constitutes success (Godinho et al. 2017; Guenther 2013). They see preoccupations with standardised testing as detrimental to a nuanced understanding of the issues faced by Indigenous learners and the communities in which they live. This perspective potentially foregrounds very different concerns, including the role of Indigenous languages in schooling, Indigenous perspectives in the curriculum, how schools can cater for Indigenous ways of talking and thinking, cultural safety and the potential alienating role of mainstream schooling for Indigenous students. Local perspectives also attend more to the relationships between literacy and student identities, as elaborated in several chapters in this volume, notably Davis and Woods (Chap. 4), Rennie (Chap. 6) and MaRhea and Anderson (Chap. 8). Most importantly, local perspectives tend to foreground Indigenous aspirations, and to be comfortable with the fact that these aspirations may or may not match those of the mainstream.

Indigenous Education, Literacy and the Political Imagination

Literacy has not always been at the centre of Indigenous education policy. In fact, it was not until the 1980s that Aboriginal education started to establish a firm place on the educational agenda. The first Aboriginal Education Policy in Australia was developed in NSW (in consultation with the NSW Aboriginal Education Consultative Group and the NSW Teachers Federation) and emphasised, amongst other things, that Aboriginal children should experience success in school (Kerwin and Van Issum 2013). Subsequently, and at the national level, the National Aboriginal Education Policy (1989) was tabled with the stated intention of working towards greater fairness and equity in educational decision-making, access, participation and outcomes.

Over the past two decades, Indigenous education policy has come increasingly to focus on 'measurables', including literacy and numeracy outcomes and pathways to employment. The National Strategy for the Education of Aboriginal and Torres Strait Islander Peoples 1996–2002 promoted training for both teachers and for Indigenous parents and extended culturally inclusive curriculum; it also set literacy, numeracy and employment goals (Ministerial Council on Education, Employment,

Training, and Youth Affairs [MCEETYA] 1996). In 2008, the Council of Australian Governments approved the National Indigenous Reform Agreement, which set out six 'Closing the Gap' targets relating to early childhood, schooling, health, economic participation, healthy homes, safe communities and governance and leadership (Council of Australian Governments [COAG] 2008). This agenda fueled the development of the *National Indigenous Education Plan* (Ministerial Council for Education, Early Childhood Development and Youth Affairs [MCEEDYA] 2010), which had six priorities including pathways to post-school options, school readiness, engagement and connections, attendance, literacy and numeracy, and leadership, quality, teaching and workforce development. Continuing this agenda, chapters in this volume document community involvement in education, from early childhood (Cooke & Piers-Blundell in Chap. 11) to primary (Davis & Woods in Chap. 4) and adults (Boughton and Williamson in Chap. 16).

Currently public discourse about Indigenous education seems dominated by our failure to 'close the gap' between Indigenous and non-Indigenous students, as measured by NAPLAN and other standardised testing regimes, primarily focused on literacy and numeracy. The Northern Territory in particular has seen Indigenous education become 'a politically fraught and controversial space at the sharp end of debates' (Fogarty et al. 2018, p. 185). We don't dispute that the current policy goals of helping students succeed in school are important; but we do suggest that formal education is still not entirely meeting people's needs, as evidenced by the number of reviews, plans and strategies that have been produced and continue to emerge from both state and national levels (see, e.g. Hughes 1988; Yunupingu 1995; Northern Territory Department of Education 1999, and more recently Wilson 2014; Gillan et al. 2017). We also suggest that the increasing government attention on poor outcomes in standardised school assessments is working to narrow the policy focus and reduce the available policy space for the aspirations and innovations of Indigenous people themselves, and for educators who work with longer term perspectives than those allowed by the reactive political funding cycle.

How This Book Is Organised

Organising the chapters in this collection was challenging. The Indigenous and non-Indigenous writers bring a range of expertise and backgrounds to the topic, representing multiple ways of thinking, and the chapters are highly diverse in the types of projects they present, their methodologies and their theoretical views on literacy. The locus for literacy education is usually imagined as a formal institution of learning, and accordingly most, but not all, of the research reported in these chapters is situated in the educational sectors, from early learning (before children go to school), through primary, secondary and adult education. We acknowledge that English language and literacy take a dominant place in this book, reflecting the current research efforts and interests of the contributing authors. We present less work here on creative learning, reading and writing in Indigenous languages. However, a number of chapters remind us of the importance of home and community for providing the context and knowledge that lay the foundations of literacy learning. Some chapters present projects that are locally grown: by communities, but also by schools and groups of individuals working to understand their own educational context. Others present a wider view of educational work that aims to impact in a systemic way. The tension between 'locally grown, working from the inside out', and 'systemic, working from the outside in' was ultimately the thread that we used to define the two sections in this book.

The first section, *Examining the local: Theory and practice*, presents locally developed, situated literacy practices, based on work carried out in within communities, classrooms and other spaces of learning. The chapters in this section foreground knowledge that both children and adults bring to the task of learning to be literate, but literacy is presented in multiple ways. The writers explore literacy practices that Indigenous people have created and appropriated, incorporating accounts of locally driven initiatives. All the chapters in this section address questions of how to work more effectively to bring collective and individual knowledge into spaces of learning. Some of this knowledge is generated in informal contexts by Indigenous people; some is generated within formal educational contexts, as teachers and community members grapple with the challenges of learning and practising literacy. The chapters present a wide spectrum of ways to think about literacy practice and theory, as they may be applied to Indigenous contexts.

The scope of the studies in this section encompasses working with individual students, examining classroom interactions, and whole school approaches. The chapters foreground collaborative approaches between school and community, between student and supervisor, between researchers, between educators and between teacher and researchers. The authors present a variety of research methods, including participatory research, ethnographic fieldwork, classroom discourse analysis, autoethnography, analysis of interview data and a critical self-study. The fine-grained analysis in these chapters, often with transcriptions of interactions, is something that is often missing from accounts of more large-scale literacy projects.

Chapters 2 and 3 challenge our ways of thinking about literacy, exploring forms of knowledge and communication that are valued and practised in two very different Indigenous communities. Both chapters present young people navigating a linguistic and cultural complexity in their own learning spaces, and both chapters argue that there are gaps in school curricula, which typically do not take Indigenous forms of representation into account. In the case of Djabibba, Auld and O'Mara in Chap. 2, these representations are created in a remote Northern Territory community when Kunibídji young people learn literacy by integrating mobile phone technology with locally situated, highly dynamic oral narrative practices and knowledge systems. While their practices might seem a long way removed from most standard constructions of literacy, they carry function and meaning by pushing new digital communication technologies in the most innovative and localised ways. Importantly, the contemporary Kunibídji Knowledge Systems allow young people to navigate a linguistic and cultural complexity that contrasts with the literacy instruction they

1 Why a Book About Indigenous Literacy Education in Australia? 7

receive at school. In Chap. 3, Mills and Dooley explore the multi-sensoriality of Indigenous literacies observed in an Indigenous school in southeast Queensland. They argue for the importance of the sensorial dimensions of the body and its role in literacy practice, and particularly for the role of the hands and feet as central to Indigenous identity and literacies. Their chapter has implications for rethinking the role of the whole body in literacy and the literacy curriculum for Indigenous students, because without a sensing body, we cannot know about or communicate with the world.

Chapters 4 and 5 together demonstrate the importance of working with community, of brokering relationships and of establishing and maintaining connections between home and school. In Chap. 4, Davis and Woods explore what a socially just literacy education can look like when Aboriginal and Torres Strait Islander perspectives are foregrounded in authentic ways. Situating their research in a southeast Queensland school, they present the story of how one locally developed, Indigenous led education community approached an agenda of reform by brokering relationships amongst systems, approaches and researchers. Chapter 5 describes the development of a program to introduce children to schooling and to reading in a very remote Indigenous community in Western Australia. Shinkfield details a process of collaboration with families that led to the successful early learning program. She focuses on the implementation of the family story time activity within this program, emphasising the connections between family and home, the importance of home language and of parents as the first teachers of their children.

Chapters 6 and 7 bring us into the world of schooling for some Indigenous students. Both chapters detail successful interactions between teacher and students, showing us some of the different ways in which print literacy, positive relationships and success in learning may be intertwined. In Chap. 6 Rennie asks how reading instruction can be more effective for Indigenous students who are marginalised at school, noting the difficulty for students who are struggling with their reading in the secondary years. Rennie analyses one reading event with an Indigenous secondary student and describes the importance of connecting to students' interests, experiences and reading histories whilst providing enough support for them to feel competent. In Chap. 7 Harper and Parkin explore classroom interactions in a remote Indigenous school. They examine the role of teacher and student talk, as well as written text, in creating meaningful mathematics lessons. While whole class dialogue is essential for creating shared understandings among the teacher and students, Harper and Parkin highlight the potential for written text to be used as a mnemonic and a critical resource in learning across the school curriculum.

Chapters 8 and 9 take us beyond scenarios of children learning, to questions about how adults can learn to function in the Indigenous literacy space. In Chap. 8 MaRhea and Anderson offer a personal, critical self-study of Anderson's academic literacy development during his time as a PhD scholar under MaRhea's supervision. They note that for Indigenous Australian doctoral students, there is need for supervisors and others involved in doctoral training to consider a pedagogy that engages Indigenous persistence in tertiary study and that does not fall into deficit thinking or political correctness. In Chap. 9, Anderson and Rennie report on their research to learn how we might better plan, implement and prepare preservice teachers for teaching placements in remote Indigenous communities. The project grew from their experience as initial teacher educators, and their observations of preservice teachers who struggled to put their theoretical training into practice and to reconcile their knowledge with the demands of remote teaching, most notably with the implementation of prescribed approaches. They describe how they interviewed preservice teachers, community members and school personnel to understand what kinds of knowledge and skills pre-service teachers need as teachers of literacy.

The final chapter in this section brings us back to the importance of first language in language and literacy education. In Chap. 10 Oldfield and Lo Bianco provide an overview of the history of Indigenous bilingual education in the Northern Territory, through a discussion of policy, culturally informed pedagogy, and school team-teaching practices, highlighting educational outcomes and school persistence rates of the children within these bilingual biliteracy programs. They situate the political struggle to secure support for the programs within a framework of language maintenance and human rights.

The second section of this volume, *Examining the systemic: Theory and practice*, takes a view that is more 'outside in'. The chapters in this section describe larger-scale initiatives aimed at improving Indigenous outcomes. These have been carried out in early childhood and school settings in a range of locations throughout Australia. The concerns are with impact and effectiveness, to move beyond the implementation of localised practices to more systemic approaches that demonstrate measurable levels of success, but that nonetheless still speak to the wide-ranging concerns about the place of indigenous people in Australian society. All the writers present a strong research base whilst simultaneously grappling with specific implementation challenges and highlighting ways of working that can both address the needs and aspirations of Indigenous peoples and can be informed by principled approaches to literacy teaching and practice. The interventions reported in this section include some notable approaches, such as MultiLit, Direct Instruction, Accelerated Literacy and Conversational Reading (from the Abecedarian approach). With the exception of Accelerated Literacy, none of these approaches was initially devised in remote Indigenous communities. They were transported from far afield: from urban Australian settings and from North America. What is notable about the accounts here is the way in which each intervention has had to grapple with context and to seek ways of grounding their practice in the local schools and communities.

Chapters 11 and 12 address children's engagement with early literacy in two remote settings. In Chap. 11 Cooke and Piers-Blundell discuss the critical need to engage and empower Indigenous families and their young children in quality early learning experiences through increasing parent knowledge and skill. The chapter outlines the process and challenges in systematically implementing the Abecedarian Approach Australia (3a) within a Families as First Teachers program, as part of a remote Indigenous parenting support program in the Northern Territory. Cooke and Piers-Blundell clearly demonstrate the complexity of systematically implementing the approach, arguing nonetheless for the importance of embedding evidence-based practice into an early learning and parenting program. In Chap. 12, Scull and

Hannigan report on an empirical study from the Kimberley region of Western Australia. This study aimed to address the literacy achievement of Indigenous students in the early years of schooling. The chapter details implementation processes at three levels of engagement: with the community, with teacher learning and with classroom practice.

The next group of chapters presents three distinct pedagogic approaches to working in schools, specifically targeting literacy outcomes; these are MultiLit (Chap. 13), Direct Instruction (Chap. 14) and Accelerated Literacy (Chap. 15). All of these chapters foreground issues of implementation and sustainability. The three approaches have all had strong champions to get them off the ground in the first instance and high levels of enthusiasm from many early practitioners. As we noted earlier, however, such approaches have invariably also been objects of contention, perceived to be draining funds from an already stretched system, and ignoring established and local knowledge (Fogarty et al. 2018; Luke 2014). Nonetheless, there is much to be learned from the implementation stories of large-scale interventions as they bump up against the realities not only of bush schools, but also of the systems that administer those schools. Ultimately pedagogic design does and will continue to matter for teachers, and if we ignore the histories of past interventions, we leave ourselves stranded in contextual complexities, without clear ways of progressing to the benefit of Indigenous students in the classrooms around the country.

In Chap. 13, Wheldall et al. present research from four schools in Cape York (north Queensland), where they successfully implemented the MultiLit program, reporting the cumulative results for the total sample of students from all sites over the 3-year life of the project. The implementation of MultiLit in Cape York was followed by the introduction of Direct Instruction, discussed by McCollow in Chap. 14. McCollow interrogates the implementation of Direct Instruction program, as it operated in the remote Queensland communities of Coen, Aurukun and Hopevale and in the context of the Cape York Aboriginal Australian Academy. McCollow examines evidence of both success and failure and explores implications for literacy interventions in other Indigenous communities. In Chap. 15 Parkin further examines the impact of context on program implementation. Drawing on the example of the South Australian Accelerated Literacy Program, Parkin presents data to show how the implementation strategies used in this context were able to show a sustained positive effect. However, she discusses the difficulty of evaluating such a program without due and separate regard to the theories that underpin the pedagogy, and to the implementation processes in each context.

In Chap. 16, the final chapter of this section, Boughton and Williamson report on 4 years of an adult literacy campaign deployed in northwestern New South Wales. In doing so they expose the fragile distinction between the two sections of this volume: the teaching model *Yes I Can!* may well be imported from Cuba, but it derives its strength from being embedded in a broader literacy campaign which has been constructed from multiple tiers of local engagement, led by an Aboriginal organisation, with locally recruited facilitators. Boughton and Williamson explain the success of the program by highlighting two aspects of the campaign model: the pedagogy of contingency and an ethic of solidarity.

Lastly, in the Afterword, Freebody sketches some of the themes that arise from this collection, noting that all of our work is built on the work of others. He also addresses questions about the kinds of projects reported here, their conceptual reach and the extent to which they help us learn what literacy education is *for.* Looking to the future, Freebody suggests some general directions for engaging with Indigenous Australian literacy education, not only with powerful institutionalised, standardised ways of teaching but also with the heritage of Indigenous Australian languages, literature, music, dance and art. Freebody's poignant closing vignette offers us a most personal story and invites us to consider the relationship between history, country and expression through traditional, but simultaneously contemporary, literate forms.

We trust this volume will speak to students of literacy in its many forms, to teachers of Indigenous students and to academics. As a collection, the chapters in this book provoke us to account for what counts as literacy in and outside of school. For teachers who often receive confusing or conflicting advice on how to work with Indigenous students, this book can serve to situate the many approaches to practice. Most importantly, we hope that the contributions will create dialogue between theoretical and ideological perspectives that have hitherto been operating in different spaces.

References

Altman, J. C. (2009). *Beyond closing the gap: Valuing diversity in Indigenous Australia (Vol. 54).* Canberra: Centre for Aboriginal Economic Policy Research, ANU.

Australian Curriculum and Assessment Authority (ACARA). (2009). *National assessment program: Literacy and numeracy.* Retrieved from, http://www.naplan.edu.au/

Australian Curriculum, Assessment and Reporting Authority (ACARA). (2016). *NAPLAN achievement in reading, writing, language conventions and numeracy: National report for 2016.* Sydney: ACARA. Retrieved from https://www.nap.edu.au/results-and-reports/national-reports.

Australian Curriculum, Assessment and Reporting Authority [ACARA]. (n.d.) *Australian curriculum: English.* Retrieved from https://www.australiancurriculum.edu.au/f-10-curriculum/english/key-ideas/

Barton, D., & Hamilton, M. (1998). *Local literacies: Reading and writing in one community.* London: Routledge.

Christie, F. (1990). *Literacy for a changing world.* Melbourne: Australian Council for Educational Research.

Council of Australian Governments (COAG). (2008). *Closing the gap. Australian government.* Canberra: Department of the Prime Minister and the Cabinet. Retrieved from, https://pmc.gov.au/indigenous-affairs/closing-gap.

Cummins, J., Bismilla, V., Chow, P., Cohen, S., Giampapa, F., Leoni, L., Sandhu, P., & Sastri, P. (2005). Affirming identity in multilingual classrooms. *Educational Leadership, 63*(1), 38–43.

Department of Employment, Education and Training. (1989). *National aboriginal and Torres Strait Islander Education Policy: Summary.* Canberra: Department of Employment, Education and Training. Retrieved from, https://www.dss.gov.au/our-responsibilities/families-and-children/publications-articles/national-aboriginal-and-torres-strait-islander-education-policy-1989.

Devlin, B. C., Disbray, S., & Devlin, N. R. F. (2017). *History of bilingual education in the Northern Territory.* Singapore: Springer.

Fogarty, W., Riddle, S., Lovell, M., & Wilson, B. (2018). Indigenous education and literacy policy in Australia: Bringing learning back to the debate. *The Australian Journal of Indigenous Education, 47*(2), 185–197.

Freebody, P., & Luke, A. (1990). 'Literacies' programs: Debates and demands in cultural context. *Prospect, 5*(3), 7–16.

Frigo, T., Corrigan, M., Adams, I., Hughes, P., Stephens, M., & Woods, D. (2003). *Supporting English literacy and numeracy learning for indigenous students in the early years* (ACER research monograph 57). Camberwell: Australian Council for Educational Research.

Gillan, K., Mellor, S., & Krakouer, J. (2017). *The case for urgency: Advocating for indigenous voice in education. Australian education review.* Camberwell: Australian Council for Educational Research.

Godinho, S., Woolley, M., Scholes, M., & Sutton, G. (2017). Literacies for remote schools: Looking beyond a one size fits all approach. *Literacy Learning: The Middle Years, 25*(1), 28–40.

Guenther, J. (2013). Are we making education count in remote Australian communities or just counting education? *The Australian Journal of Indigenous Education, 42*(2), 157–170.

Halliday, M. A. K. (1978). *Language as social semiotic* (1st ed.). London: Edward Arnold.

Huffman. (2010). *Theoretical perspectives on American Indian education: Taking a new look at academic success and the achievement gap.* Lanham: AltaMira Press.

Huffman, T. (2018). *Tribal strengths and native education: Voices from the reservation classroom.* Amherst: University of Massachusetts Press.

Hughes, P. (Chair). (1988). *Report of the aboriginal education policy task force.* Canberra: Australian Government Publishing Service.

Kerwin, D., & Van Issum, H. (2013). An aboriginal perspective on education–policy and practice. In *Pedagogies to enhance learning for indigenous students* (pp. 1–20). Singapore: Springer.

Luke, A. (2014). On explicit and direct instruction. *ALEA Hot Topic Newsletter.* Adelaide: Australian Literacy Educators' Association. Retrieved 20 June, 2016 from http://www.alea.edu.au/documents/item/861

Ministerial Council for Education, Early Childhood Development and Youth Affairs (MCEECDYA). (2010). *Aboriginal and Torres Strait Islander Education Action Plan 2010–2014.* Carlton South: Commonwealth Government of Australia. Retrieved from, http://scseec.edu.au/site/DefaultSite/filesystem/documents/ATSI%20documents/ATSIEAP_web_version_final.pdf.

Ministerial Council on Education, Employment, Training, and Youth Affairs (MCEETYA). (1996). *A national strategy for the education of Aboriginal and Torres Strait Islander peoples 1996–2002.* Carlton South: Ministerial Council on Education, Employment, Training and Youth Affairs..

National Academies of Sciences, Engineering, and Medicine. (2018). *How people learn II: Learners, contexts, and cultures.* Washington, DC: The National Academies Press. https://doi.org/10.17226/24783

Northern Territory Department of Education. (1999). *Learning lessons—An independent review of indigenous education in the Northern Territory.* Report, Retrieved 12 November 2018, from https://www.nintione.com.au/?p=5350

Purdie, N., Reid, K., Frigo, T., Stone, A., & Kleinhenz, E. (2011). *Literacy and numeracy learning: Lessons from the longitudinal literacy and numeracy study for indigenous students* (ACER research monograph 65). Camberwell: Australian Council for Educational Research.

Reyhner, J. (2017). Affirming identity: The role of language and culture in American Indian education. *Cogent Education, 4*(1), 1340081, Web.

Street, B. V. (Ed.). (1993). *Cross-cultural approaches to literacy.* Cambridge: Cambridge University Press.

Street, B. (2006). Autonomous and ideological models of literacy: Approaches from new literacy studies. *Media Anthropology Network, 17*, 1–15.

Tharp, R. G. (1982). The effective instruction of comprehension: Results and description of the Kamehameha Early Education Program. *Reading Research Quarterly, 17*, 503–527.

Tharp, R. G., & Gallimore, R. (1988). *Rousing minds to life: Teaching, learning, and schooling in social context*. Cambridge: Cambridge University Press.

Walton, C., & Eggington, W. (1990). *Language: Maintenance, power and education in Australian aboriginal contexts*. Darwin: NTU Press.

Wignell, P. (1999). *Double power: English literacy and indigenous education*. Melbourne: Language Australia.

Wilson, B. (2014). *A share in the future: Review of indigenous education in the northern territory*. Darwin: Northern Territory Department of Education. Retrieved from https://education.nt.gov.au/__data/assets/pdf_file/0020/229016/A-Share-in-the-Future-The-Review-of-Indigenous-Education-in-the-Northern-Territory.pdf

Yunupingu, M. (Chairman). (1995). *National review of education for aboriginal and Torres Strait Islander Peoples: Final Report*. Canberra: Australian Government Publishing Service.

Dr Helen Harper has worked as a researcher and lecturer in language and literacy education, as a linguist in remote Indigenous communities and as a teacher of English as an additional language. Currently, Helen is a senior lecturer in the School of Education at the University of New England (UNE), where she teaches English language and literacy education. Helen's research interests include pedagogies for educationally marginalised students, pedagogies of literacy and classroom interactions. Before taking up her post at UNE in 2018, Helen lived for more than two decades in the Northern Territory, where she worked as a researcher and educator.

Dr Jennifer Rennie is a senior lecturer in literacy education in the Faculty of Education, Monash University. Prior to working in higher education, she worked as a primary and high school teacher. Her research interests relate to Indigenous literacies, students who are marginalized from mainstream schooling and reading pedagogy for disengaged adolescent readers.

Part I
Examining the Local: Theory and Practice

Chapter 2
The Evidence of Literacy Learning Through Contemporary Kunibídji Knowledge Systems

Lena Djabibba, Glenn Auld, and Joanne O'Mara

Abstract This study examines the literacy learning demonstrated by Kunibídji young people of Northern Australia when interacting with mobile phones. Based on ethnographic field work, we analyze the literacy learning in relation to the constructs of Contemporary Kunibídji Knowledge Systems (CKKS) as well as using Green's (1988, Literacy in 3D: an integrated perspective in theory and practice. ACER Press, Camberwell, 2012) 3D model of literacy practices. The literacy learning referenced by these CKKS incorporate historical, virtual, and lived experiences, relational significance to country, family, and friends, and opportunities to construct hybridized narratives in an ethos of humor, risk taking, and turn taking. The narratives produced by the young people highlight the linguistic and cultural complexity they navigate in their own learning spaces which are in stark contrast to the programmatic literacy instruction they receive at school. We argue that evidence of literacy engagement premised on CKKS foregrounds the young people's ontological being-in-relation-to-the-world. The authors argue the standardized literacy programs offered at school for Kunibídji children are not evaluated for the ontological constructs such as country, relationality, and hybridity that are evidenced to support learning out of school.

Introduction

We recognize we are doing this work as literacy researchers while reconciliation in Australia is unfinished business. The approach we have taken in this chapter acknowledges the Kunibídji Nation as the traditional owners of the lands and seas

---

L. Djabibba
Elder, Kunibídji Community, Maningrida, Australia

Deakin University, Melbourne, VIC, Australia

G. Auld (✉) · J. O'Mara
Deakin University, Melbourne, VIC, Australia
e-mail: glenn.auld@deakin.edu.au

© Springer Nature Singapore Pte Ltd. 2019
J. Rennie, H. Harper (eds.), *Literacy Education and Indigenous Australians*,
Language Policy 19, https://doi.org/10.1007/978-981-13-8629-9_2

around Maningrida, and we recognize and pay our respects to their Elders, past, present, and future.

Before we go any further we need to be clear about the limitations of doing this work. We will introduce who we are and the perspective we are taking in this research. We bring an eclectic partnership. Glenn and Jo both identify as non-Aboriginal Australians and have known each other for several years. They bring a deep respect for teachers battling to uphold the rights of children and young people to learn literacy in their preferred languages, mediums, and contexts in neoliberal times where standardization of literacy learning is the norm in school contexts in Australia. Glenn and Lena have taught and researched together for over 25 years. They have a strong working history of upholding the linguistic human rights of Kunibídji children and young people to be educated in their preferred language of communication, Ndjébbana. Lena is a respected elder of the Kunibídji Nation, leading ceremonies, and the community in times of change in Maningrida. She has worked in the school for many years in the Ndjébbana Bilingual program that is no longer operational and also worked for the health centre to develop texts and translations of public health documents and messages. Lena has provided leadership on numerous community development projects with external agencies to the community. As a team, the three of us see literacy occurring through oral and written texts and that textual composition occurs across modalities and languages. We acknowledge that young people's literacies are often happening in a digital modality and agree about the importance of valuing and learning literacy skills and practices in the young people's home language.

In a community in Northern Australia live 300 members of the Kunibídji Nation who speak Ndjébbana as their preferred language of communication. With a population of around 3000 people and approximately 12 languages spoken on a daily basis in addition to English and Kriol, Maningrida is one of the most multilingual communities in the world. As a consequence, most members of the Kunibídji Nation are multilingual, and children often speak English as a third or fourth language when they begin school. This provides for a diverse and complex context for the learning of literacy. Before they attend school, the children's strong oral traditions of learning Ndjébbana are interwoven with their respect, and care for country. Douglas (2015) defines the Aboriginal English word for "country" as referring to "land that people have traditional ties to and that continues to be significant: emotionally, spiritually and culturally" (p. 2).

Contemporary Kunibídji Knowledge Systems (CKKS) combine the traditional and contemporary knowledges young people use to become adult members of the Kunibídji nation. These young Kunibídji people are exposed to experiences of ceremony that provide rich and lasting connections with their family, relatives, country, and dreaming. They also mediate their lives with phones, sport, popular culture, and humor. The CKKS are highly gendered, with young men and young women participating in different ceremonies, experiences, and relationships.

In this chapter, we analyze a video extract of five Kunibídji *djérwarra* engaging with stories around a mobile phone. *Djérwarra* is the coastal Ndjébbana dialect word for male youths and adolescents, boys who are on the journey of transitioning to men. We analyze this interaction through both CKKS and Green's 3-D model of literacy (1988, 2012). In doing this we highlight educational practices and knowledges that have been evolving in the community for thousands of generations. We recognize the intersecting elements of these knowledge systems. Not only are the *djérwarra* demonstrating a variety of understandings in each story, they are drawing on historical, place-based knowledge from around Maningrida and global discourses. The stories are mediated by languages, movies, and popular culture collages of references and ideas (mashups), as the *djérwarra*, like other young people, weave between real and virtual worlds, local and global knowledge, and performed and consumed texts while drawing on a range of identities they hold (Rowsell et al. 2013; Burnett et al. 2014; Auld et al. 2012; Beavis and O'Mara 2010). We have previously analyzed a different extract from this same storytelling event using translanguaging theory (Auld et al. 2018), which considers how multilingual speakers access different linguistic features or modes to maximize communication (García 2009, p. 140). Pennycook (2017) argues for this approach to language as it transcends predefined notions of language in favor of more fluid accounts of linguistic resources (p. 269). The focus on literacy resources in this chapter is understood in terms of the complexity of intersecting discourses, languages, and narrative constructions. We are aiming to show how this learning around digital literacy events speaks back to the deficit constructions of literacy learning of Aboriginal students (Disbray 2015).

Our approach in this paper is to use Lena's knowledge of CKKS as a way of noticing and naming the Kunibídji intellectual traditions and emerging knowledges that are mediated in the game play and talk around the phone, captured in the videos. We recognize that literacy is a colonizing process (Sommerville 2007), and by using CKKS as the framework for the video analysis, we are not molding Kunibídji practices to fit settler and global discourses. We will, however, make links to literacy learnings that have been identified elsewhere to give a sense of where these practices are positioned if they are considered from the perspective of the Australian schooling system. In keeping with the importance of narrative, so articulately represented by the *djérwarra* in the videos, we will give some methodological background to the videos before providing a link to where the videos can be viewed. We have identified the main understandings of CKKS in the analysis of the videos and provided links to constructs of literacy learning published in academic journals. We are not providing a literature review as these ideas from the literature will be drawn into the analysis of the videos where appropriate. In this way, we are foregrounding the CKKS as the conceptual framework in this paper.

The Kunibídji community have a word, *dja-nabíya,* that means "to become." A good example of the usage of this word is the metamorphosis of tadpoles into frogs. For many thousands of years, the Kunibídji community have used the stories of how animals become, as part of growing up, like how tadpoles become frogs, named *klotals* as they undergo their metamorphosis. Just under 100 years ago, Mikhail Bakhtin, a Russian philosopher, wrote about the importance of becoming that has now been associated with the learning of literacy. He wrote "I cannot manage without another, I cannot become myself without another; I must find myself in another by finding another within myself (in mutual reflection and mutual acceptance)" (Bakhtin 1984, p. 287). The Kunibídji idea of *dja-nabíya* and the Bakhtinian concept of becoming are useful ways of ontologically binding the important cultural and literacy learning in the videos that follow.

The 3D Model of Literacy

While we use the understandings that Lena brings to the videos as a way of foregrounding the learning of the *djérwarra*, we also use Bill Green's (1988, 2012) 3D Model of Literacy to analyze the mobile game play and storytelling in the videos. This model of literacy has been successfully used in the study of digital literacies (Durrant and Green 2000). Green proposed a three-dimensional view of literacy, where the *operational*, *cultural*, and *critical* dimensions, or *aspects*, are conceived as working simultaneously in any literacy act. Importantly in this model, the "dimensions work together, rather than being related sequentially, let alone developmentally. In this way, they are to be understood as interlocking and to various degrees overlapping." (2012, p. 4) (Fig. 2.1).

While this is a settler understanding of literacy, this model brings together language, meaning, and context, and when applied to the data enabled us to see the relationships between different aspects of the complex storytelling these *djérwarra* engage in. Within the 3D model, it is important to note that these three aspects of literacy are seen as both interdependent, and integrated. By describing our analysis using this model, we hope to communicate to the reader ways in which the complexity of the CKKS is shaping the narratives, across cultural, critical, and operational aspects, as well as showing the reader the complexity of the stories, and the collaborative nature of the text construction. In doing so we note moves and offers the *djérwarra* make each other and aim to position them as confident and competent textual composers, highlighting their facility with languages and wide repertoires of literacy practices rather than positioning them as literacy failures in the standardized national testing regime (Gutiérrez and Rogoff 2003).

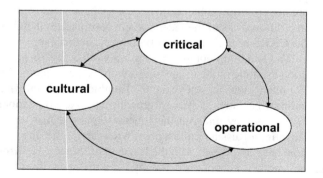

Fig. 2.1 3D model of literacy. (From Green 2012, p. 31)

Limitations of Our Approach

Indigenous knowledges are associated with Aboriginal standpoints that highlight the subjugated positioning of Aboriginal knowledge systems (Nakata 2007) while challenging educational and academic structures to be more receptive to models of Aboriginal political empowerment (Arbon 2008). Lena's standpoint is mediated by English, and the settler worldviews. We do recognize, as Rigney (2003) does, that Aboriginal education in Australia was done really well for thousands of years. Since colonization, the continuity of this education system has been disrupted, first through the disruption of the culture and then through educational intervention. Currently, very few non-Aboriginal people in Australia recognize and acknowledge the strengths and existence of previous successful educational practices in Aboriginal education. Although the Makkassans, Indonesian sea cucumber collectors, had been visiting the area for hundreds of years, the current day settlement began with the establishment of a trading post in 1957. The Ndjébbana Bilingual education program formally started in 1978 (McKay 2017) and closed in 1999. In Maningrida only speakers of Ndjébbana and Burarra had access to a bi-lingual program in their own language as programs were not offered in other languages.

Today, standardized instruments of literacy and numeracy mark these students as deficit, totally ignoring their knowledge and achievements beyond schooling testing in English. Looking at how Kunibídji *djérwarra* interact with their peers in out of school contexts provides some insights into what effective contemporary Aboriginal education might look like, given the extremely long history of Kunibídji continuous occupation of the lands and seas around Maningrida. We recognize these literacy events are still bound by the ongoing colonization of the Kunibídji nation by Aboriginal and non-Aboriginal people, but we also recognize the culture of the Kunibídji people as a dynamic, living culture. We see many similarities across our families—Lena's in Maningrida, Jo's family, and Glenn's family in Melbourne—in which global youth culture influences the ways that young people interact with digital technologies and the texts they create.

Background

Mobile phones are highly valued by Aboriginal people. Members of the Warlpiri Nation use phones to communicate over large distances and also to maintain relationships locally (Vaarzon-Morel 2014). Members of the Lockhart River community use phones for communication, entertainment, and work (Dyson and Bradley 2009; Carew et al. 2015). In Maningrida, phone ownership is seen as communal, with the use based on entertainment and communication framed by the strong relational practices in the community (Auld et al. 2012). In this study, we aim to capture the everyday practices of mobile phone use amongst Kunibídji *djérwarra* to explore the literacy learning in episodes of gaming. We have strong support from the community to do this work as many parents identified mobile phone use as an important part of young people's lives. At the same time people in the community spoke of how the learning on the phones is not clearly identified and that this was a useful project to explore. We entered this project with this community support and the partnership arrangement outlined above.

Data Sources

We collected video evidence of a group of five *djérwarra* interacting around one phone. They are all male between the ages of 9 and 12, *djérwarra* transitioning into men. Lena organized the time and place to collect the video data so the *djérwarra* were comfortable in sharing their practices with Glenn and Lena. Glenn and Lena set the video on a tripod near where the participants were sitting and then moved away. In the 30-minute video, they are focusing on both each other and the imagined audience of the video. The game is being played for themselves, but there is also an element of performance for the viewer through the fourth wall, the space that separates these storytellers from their imagined audience through the video. This is where they are conscious of performing for the person behind the camera, in this case, Lena's son.

For the first 12 min, the interaction was around a motion-controlled racing car game on the phone. The game has an on-screen track, and the car is steered around the track by tilting the phone. As they played the game, each player took on the identity of a racing car driver, making the sounds, dramatically overemphasizing the turning, and providing some narration as they steered the car around the track. After 12 min, however, the battery in the phone died. Rather than stop playing, they indirectly negotiated through a series of offers and acceptances in their play to keep playing the narration game with the blank screen, using the flat phone as a prop in their storytelling. In the next 18 min, the phone was passed around 42 times, with 42 stories composed.

In this chapter, we are presenting only 3 min of the 18 min to allow for in-depth analysis. In this short time, the *djérwarra* composed nine stories. The video can be accessed at https://vimeo.com/294659051/2e8739201f, and we recommend watching the video alongside reading this chapter. We have annotated the video in English, and the notation includes the name and number of each story, the subtitles of the dialog.

The Stories

Dja-marnáwaya You Share (Something) (Story 1–4) (Fig. 2.2)

In this set of stories, the phone has just gone flat, but, without discussion, a shared decision is made to continue the game by pretending the phone is still working. In this sequence of four stories, the stories are still closely related to the actual digital game that was originally being played and narrated to. As these stories progress, the *djérwarra* begin to explore the creative license that is afforded them now they are no longer narrating actual gameplay, but inventing both what the screen might look like and what might be happening as well as their story.

Story 1 tells of two cars going around the racetrack. The cars are racing close together, maybe too close together, and the story is shaped around the anticipation of the crash, and the excitement of this. The *djérwarra* hum the theme song from the *Rocky* movies (Chartoff et al. 1976) and make the sounds of the cars. This creates a sense of anticipation and excitement, with some of the *djérwarra* laughing at the allusion to Sylvester Stallone as *Rocky*. The story ends with the cars crashing, the delighted shrieks and giggles and explosive sounds of the burning wreckage and the phone is passed on and the next story begins. The cars are instantly regenerated, as happens in digital racing car games, and the second story has the car quickly coming to the lead and then winning. The phone is passed, and in the third story the actions of playing a motion-controlled video game are explored and exaggerated, with the phone being moved from side to side in overemphasized gestures that all of the *djérwarra* join in on. The hilarity of this, and the delight in shifting out from the original screen game, sees Story 4 shifts out of the racing car game, and the car is transformed into a boat.

It is important to contextualize the sharing across these stories to understand the Knowledge Systems. The *djérwarra* on the mat have not just come together, they have had years of similar shared experiences. As they transition into men they will

Fig. 2.2 The phone is passed on between story 1 and story 2

build on these shared experiences to learn about gendered ceremonial knowledge. They will one day be the custodians of this male knowledge, probably at the same time as each other. So the interactions around the phone on this mat outside of a house is contextualized by the years of shared experiences they have had together and their recognition of the importance of gendered relationality that contextualizes this learning and sharing. Rose (2007) argues that "gender characterizes country, ceremonies, many sacred sites and many objects and substances" (p. 34). The gendered play in this video aligns with the gendered ontological becoming these *djérwarra* are to perform as an integral learning about Kunibídji Knowledge Systems in the future. Part of the complexity for the *djérwarra* is not referring to this sacred knowledge in dialog with each other in this video, as aspects of this knowledge are restricted and linked to gender and age grading.

The passing on of the phone is both an extension of cultural conventions around turn-taking in conversation and an operational move to enable the game to occur. This type of sharing and turn-taking is seen as positive and rewarded by the Western education system (Cazden 2001). We can see that the students are working across languages and cultures, with the popular culture reference to Rocky Balboa, the usage of the racing car noises, and the interspersing of a few English words as the language of operation shifts in the story. We also see these *djérwarra* operating critically in the ways in which they shape the narrative as a production for non-Indigenous people to view, while simultaneously creating it for their own pleasure. They show their awareness and shaping of the stories for the audience through their acknowledgement of the camera person and the camera itself.

Djalawáya Wiba Knowing About Country (Story 5)

The next storyteller takes up the offer of the boat and transforms the story into something much more than the racing car game, piloting the boat off the racetrack and into the local waterways, where they have a successful dugong (sea cow) hunt and share the meat. This is a significant point in the trajectory of this set of storytelling as it shifts the stories from being closely based on the game screen into a set of narratives freed from this structure, only possible because they are no longer narrating to an actual on-screen game. In terms of Green's model, this move draws on the cultural storytelling forms these storytellers have experienced both as part of their home culture and their connection to global youth culture.

This storyteller and the previous one play significant roles across all of the stories, constantly injecting tensions and hilarity to make the stories more dramatic and funnier. They provide suggestions, sound effects, and new actions. Dunn (1996), in her study of early adolescent dramatic play, noted that some young people play a key role in developing and shaping dramatic play. Their work functions to keep the narrative moving and often, to make it more satisfying, they inject elements of tension and resolution into the play. She termed these young people, "super/dramatists" and noted that when storytelling was sustained, there was usually one or two super-dramatists working to keep things going. The storytellers of Stories 4 and 5 operate in this way, injecting excitement into the framing of the storytelling event by transforming the car into a boat and changing the context (Fig. 2.3).

This story flows from the previous one in that the characters were already traveling in a boat, not a car. The characters also had the tools (the rope) and were positioned in the boat to enact various roles such as to look for the dugong, drive the boat, harpoon the dugong, and bring it into the boat. The *djérwarra* worked together in support of the narrative construction, enacting these characters on the mat and all joining in on the hunting—not just with sound effects, but dialogue such as instructions about where the dugong is and the direction the boat should turn in. The *djérwarra* draw on both operational and cultural repertoires of literacy practice as they operationally co-construct the text, shifting the discourse in the narratives to things that are important to them. Hunting is an important social practice to the Kunibídji nation. Ligtermoet (2016) proposes that customary resources do not only include the species that is hunted but also places of significance and the spiritual importance of these associated sites. So by constructing a narrative about the hunting of a dugong, the *djérwarra* is demonstrating his knowledge about the importance of country and stories associated with these places that can be shared with non-Indigenous people.

An important concept in this narrative is the Kunibídji word *wíba-na'*, meaning *his country*. The scene for this story is one *djérwarra's wíba-na' wib-na*. This is important as the narrative locates the learning to a place and a custom that is very important to the identity and social futures of the five people in the video.

This story ends, and the phone is passed on by the narrator, but one of the other boys, almost as a reminder, begins the process of cutting up the meat, and the others join and share it with the fellow hunters before the next story begins. In this story, knowledge about country is framed by the ontological responsibilities to members of the community as a direct consequence of this knowledge. We see the *djérwarra* performing much of this scene directly to the camera, critically aware of their performance and the act of communicating this knowledge and this story to the viewer.

Fig. 2.3 The car transforms into a boat

24   L. Djabibba et al.

We also see in this the ways in which popular cultural forms of story mash-ups and transformations have been operationalized to enable us to be transported off the racetrack and into the local waterway. In terms of Green's model, we see the three aspects occurring concurrently. The storyteller positions the viewer to delight in the hilarity of the game transformation. Not only has the car transformed into a boat, but it has now been piloted from the track, so we are primed that anything can happen!

Djáwarlbba Djakkarlawa Respecting Elders (Story 6)

In story 6, the *djérwarra* take on the role of a respected elder who is an excellent turtle hunter. The narrator is guiding the boat with the phone, making the noises of the boat engine, when one of the other *djérwarra* offers, "Hey! Slow down! We saw this turtle going there." All of the *djérwarra* then get very excited, screaming and pointing at the turtle, and the boy holding the phone uses it to guide the boat toward the turtle, while the other *djérwarra* yell out instructions to him to slow the boat down and "Turn the boat around this way!" "Slow down and we will spear the turtle!". As he passes the phone on, one of the others finishes the story with, "Cut the meat and finish this story." All the *djérwarra* engaged in the story that reflected the elder's knowledge and achievements in hunting.

Operationally, the *djérwarra* work collaboratively in telling this 30 s story, with all of them acting out the narrative, chasing, spearing, and retrieving the turtle. They draw on cultural forms of acting, miming the activities associated with the hunt and kill. Operationally the pacing of this story adds to the meaning of the text, as the speed of the narrative, the delivery, and the enactment highlight the skill of the elder to get this food, cut it up, and share it with people in such a short time. Adopting this fast pace in the storytelling to communicate speed utilizes both cultural and critical aspects, as the storytelling is employing cultural conventions from western (and possibly also local) storytelling to position the audience to interpret the story from a particular viewpoint, i.e, that this elder is a highly competent and gifted hunter. The story highlights the importance of Kunibídji *djérwarra*'s aspirations to become a respected elder, that is a *djáwarlbba* of their community. An important feature of the story is how they can bring aspirational lives from their real context into the virtual stories they construct to make the story have meaning and purpose. In this sense, this story is representative of the kind of person the *djérwarra* want to become.

Djákkana Djákkana Looking After Others (Story 7)

As the phone is passed on, the next storyteller changes the pace and focus of the narrative with a sound effect and motion—under instruction from the younger boy next to him. He makes the sound of the boat's motor and moves slowly from side to side, slowing down the motor as it slowly halts to a stop and then he dramatically calls for the rope. One of the *djérwarra* offers, "I will fill up the fuel, it is empty." In terms of the construction of the story, operationally, the changing pace of the narrative, the slowing to a stop and refueling, provides drama in the storyline.

Limited resourcing is a feature of Kunibídji life. Running out of fuel on a hunting trip in a boat is a situation that the *djérwarra* would have likely experienced multiple times while growing up. This might seem a dangerous situation to many non-Aboriginal people, broken down on a remote location in a boat. To these *djérwarra*, the context is not remote, there are people about and they know where to go using the resources available to them at the time. This nuanced knowledge about their country coupled with the problem-solving abilities of the participants are important tacit contextual and cultural understandings that the participants use to construct a conclusion to this narrative.

Djarrdjórka Ngúddja Rdórdbalk Telling a Good Story (Story 8)

The *djérwarra* negotiate the direction of this story. They come to a group decision that "the engine was no good." The throttle does not work. The propeller does not work. The propeller then falls off and is missing. One of the super/dramatists suggests, "Let's pretend (our cousin) is in another boat a long, long way away." This suggestion injects drama into the story—here they are, in a stalled boat in crocodile-infested waters and the only help is some distance away. The respected cousin (with superpowers) comes up to the boat and then dives into the water to retrieve the missing propeller. He drags the boat, finds the propeller and, saved, they happily go upstream to see a crocodile (Fig. 2.4).

Knowing they are part of a community that will care for them is an integral part of becoming a member of the Kunibídji community. In the narrative about being

Fig. 2.4 The propeller does not work

rescued the *djérwarra* have drawn on this expectation of reciprocity where members of the community will care for them when their outboard motor is not working. The *djérwarra* constructing this narrative are drawing on hundreds of similar experiences they have had or heard about when growing up in the community. The reciprocity of caring for fellow community members in need is normalized in this narrative. This care is also contextualized by what Martin (2013) identifies as a belonging to country, where country will also look after the spiritual and ontological needs of the custodians of these places.

Culturally, this narrative draws on the reciprocity of caring for other members of the community and highlights the importance of relationships as integral to being a member of the Kunibídji community. In this narrative, the participants normalize this kind of support given to other members of the community by not expecting a reward for doing this kind of work. It also draws on the superhero genre from popular culture, as the cousin has superhuman powers in the rescue operation.

The text builds on the *djérwarra's* cultural knowledge of the superhero genre, and the genre shift to a superhero text provides a different shaping for the next stories as they build on each other. This looking out for one another in a local context relying on communal knowledge is in contrast to the Australian Curriculum that promotes outcomes of individual, global, and commodified knowledge economies. This is part of neoliberal discourse that is aimed at governing the self rather than caring for others as demonstrated in this narrative. This must create a strong tension for teachers of literacy who want to integrate Indigenous Knowledges that are based on epistemological and ontological themes found in Story 5 that appear to be at odds with the standardized literacy learning found in schools.

Djarrdjórka ngúddja Djerriméya Storying for Humor (Story 9 and 10)

The use of humor is used by members of the Kunibídji community to consolidate their insider shared experiences. As illustrated in Story 9, the context shifts and the scene is set for Story 10. The faltering outboard is transformed into a canoe and the storyteller casts himself in role as James Bond. Operationally, this builds on the genre of superheroes set in the story before, where the cousin was described in superhuman terms, able to pull boats quickly, and dive into the water to effortlessly retrieve the propeller. James Bond puts an outboard motor on his canoe. Everyone on the boat then falls asleep and the story ends. In Story 10, James Bond wakes up and takes the canoe upstream. He makes a very strange high-pitched noise and is chased by a lion (Fig. 2.5).

This story traverses the local context of a well-known creek to the global context of being chased by a lion as might happen in another continent. The culturally shared insider experiences of real life and shared movies enable the *djérwarra* to use humor to create a witty and subaltern narrative that engages the immediate

Fig. 2.5 James Bond runs away

audience of young Kunibídji people. Humor is used critically by Indigenous people as a subversive tool to redefine their relationship to non-Indigenous culture and individuals (Farca 2013). In this case the humor comes from juxtaposition of lion and James Bond in the local context. The story highlights the ways in which composing narratives onto the imagined virtual world of phone game provides a space for *djérwarra* to create their own humor and, in the process, develop their sense of purpose and audience in the construction of oral narratives.

Discussion

These *djérwarra* display incredible facilities of narrative construction. They composed the texts quickly and enthusiastically, showing their facility with oral language. We analyzed the video text with the three of us authors together, each bringing a different skill set. This dialogic process enabled the three of us to come to understand the complexity of the interactions from different frameworks of knowing and understanding, testing our ideas about the text with each other as we progressed. There are many levels of dialogue linked to a Bakhtinian notion of becoming, but we can also link this to a Kunibídji understanding of *njarra-ngúddjeya, bárrbarr* (talking together in company) and njarra-nabíya (a group becoming).

When we explore what counts as literacy learning from Contemporary Kunibídji Knowledge Systems, we can see the complex nuanced interactions around phones provide opportunities for young speakers of Ndjébbana to control their storytelling discourse. Their stories weave in and out of virtual and real narratives, the local and global context, as well as traditional and contemporary themes. The *djérwarra* are demonstrating a heightened understanding of audience and purpose as they turn take navigating the consuming and producing of oral narratives that embed hybridized discourses of contemporary Kunibídji knowledge systems.

The *djérwarra* deftly moved their narratives, drawing on a great range of cultural material. We saw the Kunibídji culture of sharing highlighted throughout the stories, emphasizing traditional resource management. Most striking is the act of the *djérwarra* sharing one phone to play the games and turn taking. This approach to resource sharing is also enacted through the insistence that Story 5 is not finished until the meat is shared. As the ending of this narrative highlights, the responsibilities to fellow community members and sharing are key in everyday life.

Drawing on socio-cultural western frames of understanding literacy, Green's (1988, 2012) 3D model provided a framework that enabled us to describe literacy practice using Western educational understandings of knowledge. In the analysis of the 3 min of tape, we have tried to make this complexity transparent to the reader through showing how the *djérwarra* are working across cultural, operational, and critical aspects of literacy, harnessing the range of cultural knowledges they have from their simultaneous trajectories as members and future Elders of the longest living culture in the world, to members of global youth culture.

Other cultural aspects of CKKS weave through the stories, such as the expectations of help and reciprocity through calling for others to come and assist in the propeller story. Practical cultural knowledge such as boat driving and navigating, dugong hunting, and turtle hunting are also present. Popular youth culture, shared with young people around the globe, is embedded throughout the narratives, including the digital racing car game, the reenactment of this digital game, and usage of the Rocky Balboa theme (Chartoff et al. 1976). Across the 18 min of storytelling, many more cultural references are made, including zombies, Punjabi movies, Mad Max, superheroes, and football!

We see a great deal of operational language and literacy facility as the *djérwarra* move between English and Ndjébbana, speech, and sound effects and control the structures of storytelling. The compositional aspects of the story include a range of storytelling genres including recount (Story 1 which is a narrative to the imagined game), adventure story (the superhero propeller rescue), and humor (James Bond and the canoe). Within these stories, we see the *djérwarra* enact their knowledge of the structure of texts, including how to build tension, how to communicate information, how to make people laugh, and the importance of a good ending.

In seeing the ways in which the *djérwarra* skills shift across the literacy dimensions, we would like to emphasize that, as is often found in other cultures, much of the humor in these narratives involves critical literacy skills in examining whose interests are served. In this case, the co-constructed texts serve the interests of all five *djérwarra* sitting on the mat, as they have a great deal of fun with their game. Beyond this, however, their re-presentation of the characters from popular culture in their texts shifts these narratives to include themselves and their countries, as James Bond is stuck up crocodile creek without a paddle. In the construction of the texts, knowing that this is a text that it is to be shared beyond the community, means that all of the *djérwarra* are deliberately not referring to any sacred knowledge.

Teachers and school managers, working in the policy environment of literacy improvement in English, have limited dedicated space and time to capture and describe the kinds of literacy learning highlighted in this chapter. At a structural level, school systems marginalize literacy learning performed by students out of school and compositional skills are valued and assessed mostly through written texts rather than spoken texts. This has important implications when we consider how these *djérwarra* might position and be positioned by the learning of English literacy. In an oral culture, whose languages have only been written down recently, what is the value ascribed to the composition of written text? How might the spoils of literate knowledge be shared more equitably, like it is with dugong hunting? Perhaps there is a need to explore why and who will learn which type of literacy in this closely networked community.

Perhaps one of the most important implications of this chapter is the importance of relationality in literacy learning. The literacy learning of the young people in this chapter was not just based on the epistemological understandings of literacy they brought from home, but also an ontological sense of what it is to be and become a member of the Kunibídji community. This membership carries responsibilities of integrating knowing and being. The young people in this chapter were repeatedly demonstrating that literacy learning for them was underscored by relationships with country, food, family, and peers. They were becoming literate in these relationships while also learning about how oral texts work.

This ontological work highlights for teachers some important limitations of basing literacy learning on "Funds of Knowledge" (Moll et al. 2005) or "Virtual Schoolbags" (Thomson 2002). Such constructs of literacy are predominantly based on epistemological understandings the students bring about literacy into the classroom without really exploring the ontological foundations for the being and becoming that ground the students in the place and people that make this learning meaningful. As the narratives in the videos demonstrate, literacy learning happens in places and with people outside of school. Perhaps teachers might use methodologies of "knocking before entering" (Martin 2008) to ask members of the Aboriginal community to share the intellectual practices where learning is happening outside of school. Perhaps too, the schooling system might open itself to learn from the thousands of generations of connectedness to place.

Conclusions

In the introduction, we paid respects to members of the Kunibídji community by acknowledging their ownership of country. Words similar to those used in the introduction are contextualized for different Aboriginal nations in Australia and are often said at meetings, posted on websites, and used in emails. Looking forward to a post-reconciliation Australia, these words have profound consequences for how literacy researchers might privilege Indigenous Knowledge Systems that were present in Australia before colonization. If we are to acknowledge the traditional owners of the land and pay respects to Elders past, we certainly should be looking at Indigenous knowledge systems relevant to the country on which we are researching as the primary frame of reference for analysis of literacy research. If we don't do this and use settler frames of reference we are not respecting the traditional owners of the land.

The space, time, technology, and language that mediated the learning in the narratives in this research are not counted as core business of teaching the same *djérwarra* at school. Listening to the Aboriginal people, however, is a definitive way to heal past injustices (Cameron 2014). The video in this research is of national significance to policy makers who want to listen to Aboriginal young people expressing the designs of meaning that situate their preferred learning spaces. Changes in policy for teachers to explore and document this learning in these contexts could be critical in closing the gap in literacy attainments of Aboriginal people. In dialogue with members of the community, teachers and school managers could make better informed professional judgments about the why, who, how, and what of literacy learning in schools. In considering this, we wonder how might we better enable these achievements to seep over into the school setting? Or, is it that we need to totally review what school can become?

In this chapter, we have attempted to respect the knowledge of Kunibídji *djérwarra* and make connections to appropriate knowledge in literacy research. Marika-Mununggiritj (1999) warns non-Aboriginal Australians of falling into a trap where reconciliation is an empty word and practicing intellectual terra nullius. Rather than marginalizing Indigenous knowledge systems in a way that assumes Aboriginal frames of reference are constituted as an intellectual terra nullius, we advocate for settler literacy researchers to include these with conceptual frames of literacy understanding. An approach like this would benefit all Australians. When reconciliation is finished business in Australia, perhaps research and teaching of literacy will be framed by Indigenous knowledges that are on the land where schools reside. We hope the evidence and analysis of the literacy learning in this chapter provides an insight into literacy research in post-reconciliation Australia where respectful partnerships between Aboriginal and non-Aboriginal Australians are normalized and Indigenous knowledge systems are used as the primary frame for the analysis of literacy learning, supplemented by settler perspectives.

References

Arbon, V. (2008). *Arlathirnda ngurkarnda ityirnda: Being-knowing-doing: de-colonising indigenous tertiary education*. Teneriffe: Post Pressed.

Auld, G., Snyder, I., & Henderson, M. (2012). Using mobile phones as a placed resource for literacy learning in remote indigenous communities. *Language and Education, 24*(4), 279–296.

Auld, G., Djabibba, L., & O'Mara, J. (2018). Translanguaging across time, space, and generations: ndjébbana djérwarra share 42 stories in 20 minutes. In R. Arber, M. Weinmann, & J. Blackmore (Eds.), *Rethinking languages education: Directions, challenges and innovations*. London: Routledge, Taylor and Francis Group.

Bakhtin, M. M. with Emerson, C. (Trans. & Ed.) (1984). *Problems of Dostoevsky's poetics*. Minneapolis: University of Minnesota Press.

Beavis, C., & O'Mara, J. (2010). Computer games – Pushing at the boundaries of literacy. *Australian Journal of Language and Literacy, 33*(1), 65–76.

Burnett, C., Davies, J., Merchant, G., & Rowsell, J. (2014). *New literacies around the globe: Policy and pedagogy*. London: Routledge.

Cameron, L. (2014). *Bangawarra naa: Ways of making and seeing, creative aboriginal knowledges, An interpretation and reflection of traditional Dharug Aboriginal Australian creative psychological healing practices* (PhD). University of Newcastle, The Wollotuka Institute. Retrieved from http://hdl.handle.net/1959.13/1059928

Carew, M., Green, J., Kral, I., Nordlinger, R., & Singer, R. (2015). Getting in touch: Language and digital inclusion in Australian indigenous communities. *Language Documentation and Conservation, 9*, 307–323.

Cazden, C. (2001). *Classroom discourse. The language of learning and teaching* (2nd ed.). Portsmouth: Heinemann.

Chartoff, A., Winkler, I., & Avildsen, J. (1976) *Rocky*. Chartoff-Winkler Productions. USA: United Artists.

Disbray, S. (2015). Spaces for learning: Policy and practice for indigenous languages in a remote context. *Language and Education*, 1–20. https://doi.org/10.1080/09500782.2015.1114629.

Douglas, J. (2015). *Kin and Knowledge: The meaning and acquisition of Indigenous Ecological Knowledge in the lives of young Aboriginal people in Central Australia*. PhD thesis, Charles Darwin University, Darwin.

Dunn, J. (1996). Spontaneous dramatic play and the 'super/dramatist': Who's structuring the elements of dramatic form? National Association for. *Drama in Education Journal, 20*(2), 19–28.

Durrant, C., & Green, B. (2000). Literacy and the new technologies in school education: Meeting the l(IT)eracy challenge? *Australian Journal of Language and Literacy, 23*(2), 89–108.

Dyson, L. E., & Bradley, F. R. (2009). *Mobile phone adoption and use in Lockhart River aboriginal community*. Paper presented at the 2009 Eighth International Conference on Mobile Business.

Farca, P. A. (2013). Humor in contemporary aboriginal adult fiction. In B. Wheeler (Ed.), *Companion to Australian aboriginal literature* (pp. 125–138). Boydell and Brewer.

García, O. (2009). Education, multilingualism and translanguaging in the 21st century. In T. Skutnabb-Kangas, R. Phillipson, A. K. Mohanty, & M. Panda (Eds.), *Social justice through multilingual education* (pp. 140–158). Bristol: Multilingual Matters.

Green, B. (1988). Subject-specific literacy and school learning: A focus on writing. *Australian Journal of Education, 32*(2), 156–179.

Green, B. (2012). Subject specific literacy, writing and school learning: A revised account. In B. Green & C. Beavis (Eds.), *Literacy in 3D: An integrated perspective in theory and practice* (pp. 174–187). Camberwell: ACER Press.

Gutiérrez, K., & Rogoff, B. (2003). Cultural ways of learning: Individual traits or repertoires of practice? *Educational Researcher, 32*(5), 19–25.

Ligtermoet, E. (2016). Maintaining customary harvesting of freshwater resources: Sustainable indigenous livelihoods in the floodplains of northern Australia. *Reviews in Fish Biology and Fisheries, 26*(4), 649–678.

Marika-Mununggiritj, R. (1999). The 1998 Wentworth lecture. *Australian Aboriginal Studies (Canberra), 1*, 3–9.

Martin, K. (2008). *Please knock before you enter: Aboriginal regulation of outsiders and the implications for researchers*. Tenneriffe/Brisbane: Postpressed.

Martin, B. (2013). Carnal knowledge: Towards a 'new materialism' through the arts. In E. Barrett & B. Bolt (Eds.), *Carnal knowledge: Towards a 'new materialism' through the arts* (pp. 185–204). London/New York: I.B. Tauris.

McKay, G. (2017). The policy framework for bilingual education in Australian indigenous languages in the Northern Territory. In B. C. Devlin, S. Disbray, & N. R. F. Devlin (Eds.), *History of bilingual education in the Northern Territory* (pp. 85–99). Singapore: Springer.

Moll, L. C., Amanti, C., Neff, D., & Gonzalez, N. (2005). Funds of knowledge for teaching: Using a qualitative approach to connect homes and classrooms. In L. C. Moll, C. Amanti, & N. Gonzalez (Eds.), *Funds of knowledge* (pp. 71–87). Mahwah: Lawrence Erlbaum.

Nakata, M. (2007). *Disciplining the savages, savaging the disciplines*. Canberra: Aboriginal Studies Press.

Pennycook, A. (2017). Translanguaging and semiotic assemblages. *International Journal of Multilingualism, 14*(3), 269–282.

Rigney, L. I. (2003). Indigenous education, languages and treaty: The redefinition of a new relationship with Australia. In A. T. S. I. Commission (Ed.), *Treaty – let's get it right!: A collection of essays from ATSIC's treaty thinktank and authors commissioned by AIATSIS on treaty issues* (pp. 72–89). Canberra: Aboriginal Studies Press.

Rose, D. B. (2007). Gendered substances and objects in ritual: An Australian aboriginal study. *Material Religion, 3*, 34–47.

Rowsell, J., Saudelli, M., Scott, R., & Bishop, A. (2013). iPads as placed resources: Forging community in online and offline spaces. *Language Arts, 90*(5), 351–360.

Sommerville, M. (2007). Place literacies. *Australian Journal of Language and Literacy, 30*(2), 149–164.

Thomson, P. (2002). *Schooling the rustbelt kids: Making the difference in changing times*. Crows Nest: Allen and Unwin.

Vaarzon-Morel, P. (2014). Pointing the phone: Transforming technologies and social relations among Warlpiri. *Australian Journal of Anthropology, 25*(2), 239–255.

Lena Djabibba is an elder of the Kunibídji community in Maningrida in Arnhem Land in the Northern Territory. She has spent many years in advisory and consultative roles in projects involving education and health of Aboriginal children. Lena has transformed many educational projects using her Indigenous Knowledge of lands and seas around Nardilmuk and her understandings of respectful relationships.

Dr. Glenn Auld lectures in the Education specializing in language and literacy. His teaching and research span the areas of literacy learning, new media, ethics, and Aboriginal and Torres Strait Islander Education. Glenn was the inaugural winner of the Betty Watts Award for research in Indigenous Education from the Australian Association of Researchers in Education.

Dr. Joanne O'Mara is an Associate Professor in Education at Deakin University, Melbourne, Australia. Her research and scholarship focus on English teaching, learning and curriculum, emergent literacies and new textual practices; digital games; drama teaching; and the spatial, social, and temporal dimensions of teachers' work. A hallmark of her research program has been the focus on establishment of ongoing strategic partnerships with inbuilt benefits to all parties, working in collaboration with key education authorities, professional associations, schools, teachers and students.

Chapter 3
Sensory Ways to Indigenous Multimodal Literacies: Hands and Feet Tell the Story

Kathy A. Mills and Jane Dooley

Abstract This chapter reports original research that asks the question: What are the ways of knowing, being, and communicating that are valued and practiced in Indigenous communities? Literacy curricula, internationally and nationally, typically do not take into account the multi-sensorial dimensions of non-Western forms of representation that go beyond narrow conceptions of print. For example, literacies are often conceived as drawing on print, visual, spatial, gestural, and audio modes, but the role of haptics and locomotion has typically received little attention. This chapter highlights examples of the multi-sensoriality of Indigenous literacies observed in participatory community research with an Indigenous school. It extends recent theories of sensory studies in the history and cultural anthropology of the senses, applying these principles to literacy education. Sensory literacies is a theoretical perspective that gives priority to the sensorial dimensions of the body and its role in communication in literacy practice, because without a sensing body, we cannot know about or communicate with the world. The data demonstrates how the forgotten role of the hands and feet in dominant theories of communication is central to Indigenous identity and literacies. Written by a white academic with an Indigenous researcher, the chapter problematises the privileging of narrow, logocentric, and Western forms of literacy and its implications for rethinking the role of the whole body in literacy and the literacy curriculum for Indigenous students.

K. A. Mills (✉)
Institute for Learning Sciences and Teacher Education, Australian Catholic University, Brisbane, QLD, Australia
e-mail: kathy.mills@acu.edu.au

J. Dooley
Deakin University, Melbourne, VIC, Australia

© Springer Nature Singapore Pte Ltd. 2019
J. Rennie, H. Harper (eds.), *Literacy Education and Indigenous Australians*,
Language Policy 19, https://doi.org/10.1007/978-981-13-8629-9_3

Introduction

This chapter extends recent theories of sensory studies from cultural anthropology (Howes 2014), applying these principles to literacy education. It highlights examples of the sensoriality of Indigenous literacies observed in participatory community research with an Indigenous school. The theory of *sensory literacies* was first outlined by Mills (2016a) to give greater priority to the sensorial dimensions of communication in literacy research and practice. Without a sensing body, we cannot know about or communicate with the world (Mills 2016a).

Sensory studies have demonstrated the importance of the senses across many cultures and historical periods (Howes and Classen 2014), but the potentials of a sensory approach for Indigenous multimodal literacy learning have been under-examined. Indigenous researchers have identified that epistemologies and ontologies of Indigenous groups involve sensing natural entities, such as land, waterways, and animals (Martin 2003), pointing to the need for an approach to schooling that is aligned to these ways of knowing and being. Schooling systems throughout the world have struggled to authentically negotiate literacy practices, and Indigenous cultural identities, including those of Canada (Van de Kleut 2011), Scandinavia (Pietikäinen and Pitkänen-Huhta 2013), New Zealand (Tuhiwai Smith 2006), and Australia (Sarra 2003; Mills et al. 2016).

There is a growing collection of studies that acknowledge the body in encoding and decoding (e.g. Mills 2010; Nespor 1997; Stanton et al. 2001; Stein 2006). Sensory literacy approaches recognise that communication, with or without digital technologies, involves the practical action of the physical body (Mills 2016a). As Scollon and Scollon argue (2003, p. 45), "Our bodies…anchor us in the real, physical world in which we are performing as social actors". At the same time, the mind is not seen as separated from the body, nor the role of the body taken-for-granted; rather, both mind and body are seen as integral to literacy practice. Such a view repositions the body, recognising the primacy of active, sensing beings to all communicative action (Mills 2016a).

There has been a long period of ocularcentrism—the dominance of the visual over other forms of perception—across many disciplines (Howes 1991; Porteous 1990; Stoller 1989). In modern Western societies a widespread empiricist view, that objective truth is what can be observed through the eyes, has persisted. Theorists such as Ingold (2000) and Pink (2009) argue that the visual dimensions of human action should be considered in interrelationship with other senses (Mills 2016a). This is because human action is constituted and experienced multisensorially, including experiences of sight, sound, touch, posture, movement, smell, taste, and other forms of awareness (e.g. response to external temperature).

With regard to some of the non-visual senses, theorists have recently drawn attention to the neglect of haptics or tactility (Paterson 2007). Others, such as Pandya (1993), have demonstrated the power of olfactory senses and identity in culture. In Ongee society of the Little Andeman Islands, individual identity can be defined by distinquishable body odours (Pink 2009; Mills 2016a). Similarly,

Porteous (1990) researched the *smellscapes* and *soundscapes* involved in various human experiences (Mills 2016b). Still others have demonstrated a case for understanding the world perceived through the feet—through human locomotion (Ingold and Vergunst 2008; Mills 2016a). While theorists sometimes focus on one sense or another, the majority are united by a recognition of a "democracy of the senses", not a "hegemony of sight" (Arola and Wysoki 2012, p. 7).

Contributing new understandings of historically and culturally informed literacy practices, this chapter examines sensorial meanings that are valued and practised in an Indigenous[1] school community. Literacy curricula, internationally and nationally, typically do not take into account the multisensorial dimensions of non-Western forms of representation that go beyond narrow conceptions of print (Mills 2016a). For example, even when a broadened view of literacy prevails, such as theories of multimodal literacy, interpreting the meanings of lower limb movement has received less attention than the grammar of images (e.g. Kress and van Leeuwen 2006). While gestures have always been central to communication (Leeds-Hurwitz 1987), there has been renewed research interest in haptics—movement of the hands—in an era of touch-pad technologies and video games (Paterson 2007). Haptics has recently been foregrounded in literacy learning (Walsh and Simpson 2014), while the central role of kinesthetics and locomotion has been researched in children's filming of movies and photography (Mills et al. 2013; Mills 2016a).

Multimodality has become a significant area of research amidst a broadened range of available designs and media forms in digitally networked and globalised textual ecologies. While there are varying definitions of multimodality, this chapter applies a social semiotic perspective that interprets language as fundamentally cultural and social. The term *multimodal literacy* describes communication practices that use two or more modes of meaning (Mills 2011, 2016a). Multimodal literacy is dynamic and able to be modified by users, rather than being a static code (Jewitt 2006). Similarly, the meanings of texts, objects, and events are influenced by the situational context within a culture or community (Mills and Unsworth 2017; O'Halloran 2009).

Language and literacy practices are inherently multimodal—combining two or more modes, including spoken or written words, visual images, gestures, posture, movement, sound, or silence (Mills 2011). Preferences in the use of modes of presentation, such as linguistic, auditory, gestural, and so on, differ according to the uses defined by culture and social context (Mills 2011). The regular pattern of use of modes is called a modal grammar, and these grammars have shared meanings within communities or cultures (Jewitt 2006).

Sensorial approaches to literacy give attention to human experience more broadly than representational forms or texts. While multimodal semiotics explicitly deals with systematic *principles of composition* (e.g. Kress and Bezemer 2008, p. 167),

---

[1] The term *Indigenous* in this research refers to Aboriginal and Torres Strait Islander peoples of Australia. It is acknowledged that there are many First Nations People worldwide, each with their own culture.

and *multimodal metalanguages* (See: Kress 2000), sensorial approaches also attend to the sensory practices of the body in the social process of meaning making.

This research describes the literacy practices observed in an Australian Indigenous school community that is under the care of the Aboriginal Elders. The research was conducted over the course of one year with students in the lower and upper primary school (ages 7.5–11.5 years) in an Indigenous Independent school in South-East Queensland, Australia. The project applied participatory research methods in which the research agenda was negotiated with the cultural community. Indigenous ways of practicing literacies in this school site involved multiple senses, including the use of haptics—being able to touch, feel, and manipulate objects—and locomotion—the position and actions of the limbs.

Indigenous education in Australia has suffered long-term inequality in the interests of Whites, such as limiting Indigenous access to schooling past the third grade during the 1930s and 40s. The first Northern Territory government-funded education for remote Indigenous students did not occur until 1950, and secondary education only became available in remote areas in the 1980s. This was applauded as forward thinking, yet non-Indigenous students had free access to primary and secondary education throughout the entire twentieth century (Ford 2013). Bilingual teaching and education for students who spoke Indigenous languages ended in the 1990s, reinforcing White dominance and monolingual English (Mills and Unsworth 2018). The gross inequality of achievement between Indigenous and non-Indigenous students is currently masked in the reports of the National Assessment of Literacy and Numeracy (ACARA 2016) to downplay the extent of failed political rhetoric that claims to close the Indigenous achievement gap (Ford 2013).

Internationally, research of Indigenous students' counter-storytelling and the use of pedagogies informed by critical race theory has been documented with Chicano students. Using narrative counter-histories, teachers and students have challenged the majoritarian American stories to validate Indigenous epistemologies (Romero et al. 2009). A promising approach for American Indian and Alaskan Indigenous students in US schools has been culturally responsive schooling, which sees that an essential beginning for Indigenous schooling is to provide students with knowledge of their local heritage, language, and culture (Castagno and Brayboy 2008). More research is needed within the politics of school settings to decolonise Eurocentric notions of knowledge and literacy practices, and to embed dynamic ways of communicating through the whole body and the senses in Indigenous schooling. This research is a response to the need for a radically revised approach to literacy pedagogy that follows the dynamic contours and sensory pathways of Indigenous knowledge—central to the decolonising deficit assumptions about Indigenous literacy achievement (Mills et al. 2016).

Research Question

Indigenous people take pride in the valued epistemology (i.e. nature of knowledge) and ontology (i.e. beliefs about existence) of their ancestral history, yet they must continually adapt to the Eurocentric ways of practicing literacies and learning in the institution of schooling (Mills and Dreamson 2015). The mainstream educational practices in many postcolonial societies are not culturally neutral, but are often based by default on the dominant White norms and ways of valuing language and literacy practices. In developing a culturally consistent approach to the multimodal literacy for Indigenous students, the research question asked: What sensory ways of making meaning are valued and practiced in one Indigenous community? It aimed to develop, with Indigenous leaders, an innovative approach to literacy that follows the dynamic contours of Indigenous knowledge and its many forms of expression—central to decolonising Indigenous literacy practices.

Research Context

Participatory research was conducted over the course of one year at an Indigenous independent, suburban school in Queensland, Australia. The students belonged to the Yuggera, Jagera, and Ugarapul language regions of Southeast Queensland and identified as Aboriginal and Torres Strait Islander. The location permitted the researchers to have a sustained presence in the field—an ethical requirement of Indigenous research. Cross-cultural, participatory community research involves genuine collaboration between researchers belonging to a different culture to the research participants. Community leaders address an identified need, rather than the aims being driven by the researcher's own agenda (Stoecker 2005). The researchers have a long-term history of collaboration with the community leaders because outsiders conducting Indigenous research must knock before entering, give rather than take, and build long-term trust (Martin 2008).

The Aboriginal principal and Indigenous Elders identified multimodal literacy as an area of potential development. Aboriginal and Torres Strait Islander students participated in multimodal and arts-based literacy practices, and semi-structured interviews. The research was conducted across Year 3 and Year 5–6 composite primary classrooms (students ages 7.5–11.5 years). The principal and two teachers were involved in the planning of the multimodal literacy practices with the university academic. They were involved with the university in planning meetings, organised the curriculum content, selected resources, and assisted with the collection of ethics consent forms from parents and students.

The first author is an Anglo-Australian university professor of literacy education and a former primary school teacher. The second author is an Aboriginal teacher and Kamilaroi woman who taught a Year 5–6 class and has degrees in both contemporary arts (visual art) and education. Her teaching and research aim to provide frameworks for the Indigenous acquisition of knowledge, values, and skills in culturally inclusive learning environments. This chapter was written with the Indigenous teacher to strengthen the authenticity of the Indigenous perspectives and to respect the ownership of Indigenous knowledge (e.g. Martin 2003). A non-Indigenous teacher of the Year 3 class was from the United Kingdom, who had also taught Aboriginal students in a remote area of the Northern Territory of Australia.

Summary of the Learning Experiences

The learning experiences within the curriculum combined different modes of literacy learning with the teaching of vital cultural knowledge. The integrated literature and history unit for the Year 5 and 6 students (ages 9.5–11.5 years) was based on *The Rabbits*, a graphic novel written by John Marsden and illustrated by Shaun Tan. The novel is simply written using metaphoric language intended to create an empathetic view of the impact of colonisation on First Nations Peoples. The final page of *The Rabbits* asks the question, "Who will save us from the rabbits?" The students were required to script and dramatise a narrative that utilised the symbolism and allegory depicted in the novel. The unit allowed the students to rewrite and act out a new position of Indigenous self-determination and resistance in the face of colonisation and dispossession. The teacher stimulated discussion about the question, "Do we need saving?" The multimodal task involved scriptwriting, papier-mache mask-making, prop-making, speaking, gestures, filming, and digital editing. The students were required to apply dramatic action, empathy, and use of space in improvisations and utilise play-building and scripted drama to develop characters and situations of importance to Indigenous people (ACARA 2017).

The Year 3 students (ages 7.5–8.5 years) created individual tempera paintings of the land, applying Indigenous visual art techniques and colour palettes that were introduced to them by Indigenous Aunties who visited the classroom. The students participated in weekly Aboriginal and Torres Strait Islander dances that were taught by Indigenous young men as part of the school curriculum. The dance group used clapsticks to accompany chants in local Indigenous dialects, while demonstrating the dances. They danced along to video recordings of traditional Indigenous dances performed in the Australian bush, displayed on a large digital television, providing an audiovisual portal between the present and the past. A short video segment of one of many dances practiced by Year 3 students can be viewed by cutting and pasting this link into a browser: goo.gl/6cbTcp.

Methods: Data Collection and Analysis

Three data sets were collected to answer the research question described in section 1 above:

(i) Multimodal artefacts (texts) produced by the Indigenous students—photographs of student paintings, videos of dance performances, and dramatic performances

(ii) Semi-structured interviews with Indigenous students about their multimodal texts and practices

(iii) Semi-structured interviews with teachers about the integration of Indigenous forms of meaning making in subject English and across the curriculum

Data analysis involved attending to the engagement of the senses and embodiment across the range of observed literacy and arts practices, including Indigenous paintings, dances, and dramatic performances (Mills and Dreamson 2015). Focus interviews with students provided understandings of the children's intended meanings for their dances, artwork, and drama. The students' multimodal texts and performances were coded and analysed as sites for embedding Indigenous cultural knowledge, contextualised with reference to the specific cultural meanings in this Indigenous community (Mills et al. 2016).

Semi-structured interviews were conducted with approximately 40 students across three grade levels, using an interview protocol. Example questions included items such as: "Tell me about your painting?"; " Why did you use these symbols/colours?"; and, "What does this song/dance/art mean to you?" Semi-structured interviewing was chosen to be responsive to the content of the students' texts and to allow new ideas to be examined during the interview (Raworth et al. 2012). It enabled the adult researchers to obtain insight into the students' emic or insider cultural frames of reference as Indigenous children and youth (Mills et al. 2016). The coding and analysis of the semi-structured teacher interviews aimed to identify the modes and involvement of the senses in the observed literacy practices, allowing the researcher to learn the viewpoints of the teacher participants. The student and teacher interviews were transcribed and coded for key themes and subthemes that were recurring in the students' talk and multimodal texts, including the participants' own terms (Silverman 2014). Gaining the participants' clarifications of the meanings in their multimodal texts strengthens interpretations of the symbolic meanings intended by the authors.

Findings: Hands and Feet in Indigenous Art, Dance, and Drama

Two Indigenous Aunties prepared paints and materials as they talked to each other and then worked with the students over several hours. They closely guided one student at a time, while observing the whole student group who were absorbed with their painting. The Aunties supplied warm colours for the earth and sky in the background and demonstrated how to mix and blend the paint on the canvas. They allowed the backgrounds to dry during the mealtime. Then the students used vivid, contrasting colours to symbolise birds, animals, and other significant elements of

Fig. 3.1 Eli's painting of Australian animals

Indigenous Country. The instruction of the Aunties is consistent with Oodgeroo's (1990) description of the traditional methods of Aboriginal modes of communication:

> They [Aboriginal ancestors] successfully sustained our people and environment as they talked, sang and danced knowledge to the young, while others used…sticks, stones, ochre, fire and smoke for communication…Messages were shared…through clan and family gatherings, message stick carriers, storytellers, songs, dance and paintings.

The students talked about the cultural significance of the land, waterways, birds and animals, and ceremonial traditions depicted in their paintings. A significant finding was the continuation of an Indigenous legacy for future generations through the use of the hands in their artwork. In the artwork photographed in Fig. 3.1, Eli[2] chose to represent a number of native Australian animals, which are central to Aboriginal ontology and to Eli's cultural heritage and family totems.

The researcher asked Eli about the meanings of the painting:

Researcher: Can you tell me about your painting? What are the different symbols?
Eli: So a turtle. A few snakes, a dingo, a platypus, koala, and an echidna.
Researcher: How did you decide what animals to put in? Are they all special animals to you?
Eli: A few of them—the turtle is one of my totems. The rest, I just thought of them.
Researcher: What about the circles or dots everywhere?
Eli: They represent where they [the animals] go.

Eli's painting featured a variety of native Australian animals, including his family totem animal, the turtle. In this Indigenous community, many of the students were assigned a totem animal at birth, which signifies their ecological and spiritual connectedness to the animals and to place. The totem bird or animals passed on from the

---

[2] All student names are pseudonyms.

mother, father, and clan are often significant to the child. Totems are a vital part of cultural identity in many Australian Indigenous communities and are especially significant in songs, dances, and music. Totems are often depicted on cultural implements, such as through carvings on message sticks used in ceremonial dances. While Aboriginal totemic traditions have many variations, totemism makes significant ontological connections to the period of the Dreaming, describing a vital relation between living humans with ancestral beings and nature, such as plants, animations, and land formations (Monroe 2011). Humans, animals, and natural phenomena find their origin and meanings in the Dreaming period (Mills and Dreamson 2015).

The students shared their familial, historical, and ancestral connections to the creatures in their local sensory ecology and their place on the land. Eighty-three per cent of the children's paintings included Australian native animals of the land, seas, or sky that were either personally significant as totems or are important to Indigenous knowledge and culture. The meanings of multimodal literacy practices were entangled with material and spiritual worlds, which were connected in performative or active ways to their identities (Mills and Dreamson 2015).

A recurring motif in the children's paintings was the handprint—featured in two-thirds of the artworks. Handprints were often integrated into the painted landscape as trees, evoking symbolic connections to the land. For example, Fig. 3.2 is a photograph of Lily's painting of a bird and handprint below.

Lily created the handprint by drawing around the outline of her hand once the red and yellow background had dried. When asked to talk about her painting, Lily explained:

Lily: There's a big bird [in the middle] and little turtles. Those colourful bits [dots] are the feathers, and it's got a tail, but no beak.
Researcher: And what about the dot patterns and other symbols, like the spiral?
Lily: I've seen them in our other art—they are for decoration.
Researcher: Whose is that handprint?
Lily: Mine.

Fig. 3.2 Lily's handprint and bird painting

Lily explained that her dots were for decoration—aesthetic rather than having a corresponding content plane or equivalent meaning (Eco 1976). The practice of successive knowledge is transferred in ways often unseen by normative Western pedagogies. The children's artwork represents an embodiment of practice through observation, conversation, and direct instruction or modelling of art by their Aunties and Elders. Indigenous People teaching Indigenous students is pivotal to this knowledge sharing. Other students similarly indicated that they included dot patterns or other repeated shapes because they had observed these designs in other Indigenous paintings. The use of arts-based pedagogy was part of the transgenerational telling of stories as a cultural heritage practice received from the Elders.

Handprints appear in traditional Aboriginal artwork, forming an embodied symbol or signature of belonging and respect for the place, such as caves or rock walls, where the handprint is marked. In Aboriginal culture, events inextricably belong to places, and places speak through the artwork. The handprint involves using touch or tactile sensation as a connection between the body and the natural world. Unlike some other forms of touch, the embodied practice of Aboriginal handprints made with ochre from the earth has particular meanings, because the hand marks place, and place similarly marks the hands (Mills 2016b).

A third painting is illustrated in Fig. 3.3, which combined a number of visual motifs that were evident across the artworks. In addition to the handprint, totem snake, and Aboriginal flag in Paige's artwork is the circle of respect—a series of concentric circles.

The circle of respect was a significant, repeated visual motif in the children's paintings that symbolised values that were modelled and taught in the broader curriculum and taken up by the students. It was featured on classroom walls and worn on their school uniform. The circle of respect appears in red, white, and black dots, which form concentric circles in the bottom left of Paige's artwork (see Fig. 3.3). Paige explained:

Fig. 3.3 Paige's painting of a hand, totem, flag, and respect circle

Paige:	That's my totem, and that's my family (top right), and that's the but-terflies around us. Then there's the snake, and hands, and then I put the Aboriginal flag. Then I painted what we have on our shirts [school uniform].
Researcher:	Yes, that circle with the larger circles around it.
Paige:	Yeah.
Researcher:	What does it mean, do you know?
Paige:	Respect [Circle of respect].

The symbol of concentric circles—sometimes composed of dotted lines—was used to remind the student to show respect for self, followed by outward movement of respect for family, community, and Country. The pattern of circles is sometimes joined by a pathway to another set of circles, and similar patterns can be observed in Australian Indigenous artwork, rock paintings, and drawings in the sand that are made using touch. Depending on the language region, it can invoke a range of meanings, such as waterholes, campsites, or ancestral connections (Morphy 1991). The Year 3 teacher noted:

I sometimes think, "I wonder how much they identify with their culture? When I see this art I know that the students are being really observant and they're taking things in. Whoa!" [laughs].

The significance of handprints was also observed more widely in the school, such as during a welcoming ceremony. Several of the students dipped their fingers in yellow ochre and water, using touch to physically transfer the earthen mixture from person to person. They painted a pattern of two parallel lines on the arms of each visitor. This symbolised in an embodied, haptic way, a physical co-presence with each other and the encompassing land. We later participated in ceremonial washing to return the soil from our skin to the original earth. This was done to guard against tangibly and symbolically removing the soil from its place of origin. We returned the parti-cles of earth to their physical coherence with the native land and its Indigenous peoples (Mills and Dreamson 2015).

The children's embodied visual art practices became transgenerational flows of Indigenous knowledge from the ancestors, to the Aunties, and to the children. The notion of haptics has been explored in art history and aesthetics across a range of cultures and continues to be an important dimension of the arts, philosophy, and aesthetics (Paterson 2007). Literacy teachers and researchers need to embrace the possibility of attending more consciously to haptics or touch in literacy and the arts, with cultural relevance for Indigenous students (Mills 2016a).

The significance of foot and lower limb movements, synchronised with mean-ingful movements of the whole body, similarly emerged as central in the children's performance of traditional dances, becoming a kind of kinesthetic pathway to children's understanding of Indigenous knowledge and their appreciation of Dreaming narratives. Connections to animals and Country became embodied in their muscle memory and their minds. Aboriginal and Torres Strait Islander knowl-edges were sometimes embodied in the dances through movement, adornments, body paint, and the song lyrics and rhythms of percussion instruments that are associated with storytelling. Many of the students began dancing with their extended families as soon as they were able to walk, while others were first introduced to Indigenous dancing in the school curriculum. The Year 3 teacher explained the centrality of dance for the communities she worked and lived with in the Northern Territory:

> Whenever there were ceremony funerals—and funerals will go for days—they will be dancing every day. The little ones would get up, have a dance for a while and then sit down. Then they get back up, because that's how they learn.

The students explained that the dances they are taught at school come from "Queensland, New South Wales, the Northern Territory…and from the Torres Strait":

Researcher:	So what do the dances mean to you?
David:	It's culture—Aboriginal and Torres Strait…and see those Aboriginal turtles outside? Yeah, they're in the words of one song. And then there's *madin*… [begins to sing] *Kona bodela madin, bodela bodela madin, bodela, madin madin.*
Researcher:	What does that mean?
David:	It means one, two, three…
Researcher:	So it's a counting song.
David:	Yeah. But for NAIDOC, we're doing *Tamila*.

The students pointed to lyrics posted on the classroom walls and explained that they had been taught to sing the songs using a range of Indigenous languages "like Yugumbir"—an important part of their cultural heritage. The students code-switched between several languages and the English translation, a vital communicative resource (Mills 2011), and these linguistic meanings then became embodied through singing, dancing, and playing musical instruments—the didgeridoo for boys and clapsticks for girls.

The boys and girls took turns to dance their respective dance sequences within the same song, based on traditional Indigenous roles for males and females. For example, the dance step *shake-a-leg* is only for the boys, and the boys make their legs into a diamond shape. The girls explained that they don't do "shake-a-leg or play the digeridoo"… "because that's boys' business". The girls' steps are differed by Indigenous tradition, with the feet kept closer to parallel, and the girls play the clapsticks.

Some of the movements in their dances evoke native Australian animals. The students listed the "kangaroo, goanna, eagle, crow, emu, snake, and gecko" as significant, and movements imitate the transit of the animals of the Dreaming. Thus, movements of the feet have specialised meanings that embody Indigenous knowledge. We asked the students about other embodied meanings of traditional dance, such as the way the body is adorned:

Researcher:	Do you ever wear special clothes or paint when dancing?
Jackson:	Yes, we have to wear ochre and lap-laps and like, a red sash around our head, and handprints on our face. We wear no shoes or shirt, but only girls wear shirts, with pants and skirts. When we're performing this dance, we have to wear, like, lap-laps and no shirt on, and that's where we put our paint on [points to chest].

The students explained that the painting of the skin has ceremonial significance—usually "white or yellow ochre from the ground". The "girls wear muu muus" while "boys wear lap-laps, and a red sash around the forehead, sometimes a handprint on the face". The students continued: "The boys wear no shoes or shirt". Thus, the way the body is adorned is as significant as lyrics and dances themselves. Other students explained that the painting of the body can also be used for "medicine" or healing in some ceremonial dances. Spears are sometimes used to symbolise protection of the body. In the children's own words, the dances are "about respecting our Country and community", "respecting the ancestors…and the elders", "connections" to the past, and being "connected to each other dancing".

An imperative expressed by some of the boys was their active engagement in teaching the dances to others—to kindergarten children, to cousins and other family members, to the public, and to future generations. Importantly, students' retellings of Indigenous narratives through their moving feet and bodies provided a platform for the flow and reconstruction of collective memories—through dances that tell the cultural themes of their common ancestral past (Giaccardi 2012). The Year 3 teacher reflected: "The dance and the artworks that they did…they definitely come alive! They know it's serious and they know that it's something that deserves respect".

Similarly, in the upper primary school history and English unit on colonisation and the allegorical, graphic novel, *The Rabbits*, the students' moving bodies were salient.

The groups communicated through a multimodal and sensory ensemble of digitally recorded dramatic performances. A critical reading of the text *The Rabbits* sees the First Nations Peoples positioned as merely passive victims of colonisation. Collins-Gearing and Osland (2010, [no pagination]) note:

> The narrative constructs dichotomous representations of the "coloniser" (Rabbits) and "colonised" (Numbats): strong, weak; modern, ancient; civilised, primitive; centre, peripheral; conqueror, victim. Such binary oppositions are a legacy of pre-Mabo colonialist discourses in Australian children's literature and reveal the text's seemingly neutral colonialist discourses to be rooted in colonialist ideologies and legacies.

The critical retelling of the narrative involved a Welcome to Country ceremony. The students' reinterpretation respected Indigenous cultural protocols and attended to their responsibility as custodian of the land. The students enacted a smoking ceremony that sensorially and symbolically cleared away the wrongdoings of the past, enabling forgiveness and positive direction into the future. The class used branches of gum leaves to gently sweep the white smoke over each other, as the marsupial characters in the book had gently swept the aromatic smoke over the rabbit characters. They bathed the rabbits in cleansing smoke in a kinaesthetic and olfactory ritual. Movements of the feet and hands were salient in the ceremonial practices, involving a historically rich repertoire of meaningful dance movements, chants, aromas, and instrumental rhythms.

Kinesthetics—sensory awareness of the position and movement of the body—has been rarely regarded in theories of literacy learning. The findings in this chapter are significant given the lack of attention to kinesthetics in Western thought in many fields. For example, the exclusion of sensations of the feet in the Western taxonomy of the five senses, has been recognised by a number of scholars, from Descartes, to Dewey, and from Gibson to Merleau-Ponty (Farnell 2012). More recently, Ingold (2000) has forged a number of studies that draw attention to kinesthesis in human action because: "The world of our experience is a world that is suspended in movement..." (p. 242). Without bodily movement, we can experience very little of the world directly (Mills 2016a).

We need to create bridges between Eurocentric and Indigenous knowledges, and an important part of this is acknowledging the power of the body in community practices. For many Indigenous people, schooling has failed if it has not developed a student's cultural identity, and this includes the tangible, corporeal nature of human experience and communication. In Australia, multimodal literacy is also a vital part of the Australian Curriculum, with *multimodal* appearing over 290 times (ACARA 2017). There is scope in Australia to transform the official curriculum to seriously attend to multiple modes that together are more powerful in communication than words alone. We need to challenge Western sensory hierarchies that relegate movements of the hands and feet, and the meanings of aromas, to a lesser plane than sight.

Recommendations for Research, Practice, and Policy

This chapter has problematised the privileging of logocentric, narrow, Western forms of literacy and the need to rethink the integration of multiple senses and the body in multimodal literacy learning. The findings illustrate that the hands and feet, and aromatic burning or smoke, are central to certain Indigenous identities and community practices. This is not to suggest that linguistic forms of literacy, such as writing, are not similarly valued by Indigenous communities; rather, Eurocentric ideologies of literacy practices in education do not respect the deeply sensorial nature of Indigenous ways of communicating, such as through handprint painting, dances, and dramatic performances. These can be much more powerful forms of communication than words alone. Arola and Wysoki (2012) argue that when we teach through varied modes and media we should ask how the media engages with the senses, and how it contributes to the embodiment of Indigenous knowledge (Mills 2016a).

A key recommendation is not that teachers should exclusively offer Indigenous students colourful and highly sensorial practices: all literacy practices engage the senses in some way. For example, even when a seated audience is required to be still and listen, there is always an undercurrent of highly nuanced, subtle gestures, gaze, postures, breathing, and movements. Rather, we need to shift Eurocentric, ocular-centric views of literacy practices to acknowledge the integral role of multiple senses in communication across varieties of cultures. We also need to begin to recognise the biases and limitations of long-held sensory hierarchies in education, and politically blinkered judgements of *what counts* as powerful communication and literacy achievement for all.

Conclusion: Indigenous Multimodal Literacy Through Sensory Ensembles

The sensory literacy practices observed in this research were orchestrated in a way that developed the students' cultural identities through meaning making practices that engaged multiple senses, including touch, movement, and smell. This research has demonstrated how movement in drama, dance, and visual arts were integral to the transgenerational knowledge formation in an Australian Indigenous community through their sensorial reconstruction of collective knowledge. Such responses to the curriculum are aligned with honouring an Indigenous cultural heritage. Teachers were key facilitators of culturally inclusive pedagogy, who continually sought ways to develop relationships with the wider Indigenous community. Teachers can readily become a part of the process of layering Indigenous community experiences of culture in multimodal practices, as successive generations inherit, interweave, and feel cultural stories and maps of their experience through sensory ensembles.

While this participatory research was limited to one Indigenous Australian school community and involved students across 3 years of primary schooling, the research has provided generative examples of multimodal literacy pedagogy that aligns with Indigenous ways of knowing and being. It demonstrates the successful weaving of the senses with Indigenous narratives and histories that were encoded, experienced, and perceived in the students' bodies. The orchestration of multiple senses is important in disrupting the cultural exclusivity that often pervades schooling and ideological views of literacy achievement in colonised countries. This research has demonstrated how authentic Indigenous arts, dance, and dramatic performances can be used for collective cultural remembering through the integration of the senses.

Embodied sensory experiences, including aromatic drama and the movement of the hands and feet, have particular cultural codes that need to be seen as rich resources for representational work in the classroom. This recognition is significant given the regulation of the bodies and the senses in education sites, and the favouring of certain modes that is typically to the detriment of equitable literacy learning. It highlights the need to challenge the idea that the mind is only active when the body is still, and to begin to acknowledge the communicating body in motion. It calls for the transformation of education institutions that uncritically enact a *hegemony of vision* to challenge our sensory ideologies.

References

Arola, K. L., & Wysoki, A. (2012). *Composing media, composing embodiment*. Logan: Utah State University Press.

Australian Curriculum Assessment and Reporting Authority [ACARA]. (2016). *National assessment program: Literacy and numeracy (NAPLAN)*. Syndey: Australian Government.

Australian Curriculum Assessment and Reporting Authority [ACARA]. (2017). *Australian curriculum: Version 8.3*. Canberra: Australian Government. Retrieved December 13, 2017, from: http://www.australiancurriculum.edu.au/?dnsi=1

Castagno, A. E., & Brayboy, B. M. J. (2008). Culturally responsive schooling for indigenous youth: A review of the literature. *Review of Educational Research, 78*(4), 941–993.

Collins-Gearing, B., & Osland, D. (2010). Who will save us from the rabbits? Rewriting the past allegorically. *The Looking Glass: New Perspectives on Children's Literature, 14*(2). Retrieved December 13, 2017, from: http://www.lib.latrobe.edu.au/ojs/index.php/tlg/article/view/227/225

Eco, U. (1976). *A theory of semiotics*. Bloomington: Indiana University Press.

Farnell, B. (2012). *Dynamic embodiment for social theory*. London: Taylor and Francis.

Ford, M. (2013). Achievement gaps in Australia: What NAPLAN reveals about education inequality in Australia. *Race Ethnicity and Education, 16*(1), 80–102.

Giaccardi, E. (2012). *Heritage and social media: Understanding heritage in a participatory culture*. London: Routledge.

Howes, D. (1991). *The varieties of sensory experience: A sourcebook in the anthropology of the senses*. Toronto: University of Toronto Press.

Howes, D. (2014). Anthropology and multimodality: The conjugation of the senses. In C. Jewitt (Ed.), *The Routledge handbook of multimodal analysis* (2nd ed., pp. 225–236). London: Routledge.

Howes, D., & Classen, C. (2014). *Ways of sensing: Understanding the senses in society*. London: Routledge.

Ingold, T. (2000). *The perpection of the environment: Essays in livelihood, dwelling and skill*. London: Routledge.

Ingold, T., & Vergunst, L. (2008). *Ways of walking: Ethnography and practice on foot*. Aldershot: Ashgate.

Jewitt, C. (2006). *Technology, literacy and learning: A multimodal approach*. Abingdon: Routledge.

Kress, G. (2000). Design and transformation: New theories of meaning. In B. Cope & M. Kalantzis (Eds.), *Multiliteracies: Literacy learning and the design of social futures* (pp. 153–161). South Yarra: Macmillan.

Kress, G., & Bezemer, J. (2008). Writing in multimodal texts: A social semiotic account of designs for learning. *Written Communication, 25*(2), 166–195.

Kress, G., & van Leeuwen, T. (2006). *Reading images: The grammar of visual design* (2nd ed.). London: Routledge.

Leeds-Hurwitz, W. (1987). The social history of the natural history of an interview: A multidisciplinary investigation of social communication. *Research on Language and Social Interaction, 20*, 1–51.

Martin, K. L. (2003). Ways of knowing, being, and doing: A theoretical framework and methods for indigenous and Indigenist research: Voicing dissent new talents 21st century, next generation Australian studies. *Journal of Australian Studies, 76*, 203–214.

Martin, K. (2008). *Please knock before you enter: Aboriginal regulation of outsiders and implications for researchers*. Flaxton: PostPressed.

Mills, K. A. (2010). Filming in progress: New spaces for multimodal designing. *Linguistics and Education, 21*(1), 14–28.

Mills, K. A. (2011). *The multiliteracies classroom*. Bristol: Multilingual Matters.

Mills, K. A. (2016a). *Literacy theories for the digital age: Social, critical, multimodal, spatial, material, and sensory lenses*. Bristol: Multilingual Matters.

Mills, K. A. (2016b). *Rethinking Indigenous ways to literacy assessment: Hands that speak, feet that tell the story.* Paper presented at the Research and Innovation in Classroom Assessment Conference, Brisbane, Australia.

Mills, K. A., & Dreamson, N. (2015). Race, the senses, and the materials of writing practices. In J. Turbill, C. Brock, & G. Barton (Eds.), *Teaching writing in today's classrooms: Looking back to look forward* (pp. 298–312). Norwood: Australian Literacy Educators' Association.

Mills, K. A., & Unsworth, L. (2017). Multimodal literacy. In G. Noblit (Ed.), *Oxford research encyclopedia of education.* Oxford: Oxford Univeristy Press.

Mills, K. A., & Unsworth, L. (2018). The multimodal construction of race: A review of critical race theory research. *Language and Education, 32*(4), 331–332. https://doi.org/10.1080/0950 0782.2018.1434787.

Mills, K. A., Comber, B., & Kelly, P. (2013). Sensing place: Embodiment, sensoriality, kinesis, and children behind the camera. *English Teaching: Practice and Critique, 12*(2), 11–27.

Mills, K. A., Davis-Warra, J., Sewell, M., & Anderson, M. (2016). Indigenous ways with literacies: Transgenerational, multimodal, placed and collective. *Language and Education, 30*(1), 1–21.

Monroe, M. H. (2011). *Australia: The land where time began: A biography of the Australian continent.* Retrieved December 13, 2017, from: http://austhrutime.com/geology.htm

Morphy, H. (1991). *Ancestral connections: Art and an aboriginal system of knowledge.* Chicago: University of Chicago Press.

Nespor, J. (1997). *Tangled up in school: Politics, space, bodies, and signs in the educational process.* London: Falmer.

O'Halloran, K. L. (2009). Historical changes in the semiotic landscape: From calculation to computation. In C. Jewitt (Ed.), *The Routledge handbook of multimodal analysis* (pp. 98–113). London: Routledge.

Oodgeroo, N. (1990). *My people.* Sydney: Angus and Robertson.

Pandya, V. (1993). *Above the forest: Andamanese ethnoanemology, cosmology, and the power of ritual.* Delhi: Oxford University Press.

Paterson, M. (2007). *The senses of touch: Haptics, affects and technologies.* Oxford: Berg.

Pietikäinen, S., & Pitkänen-Huhta, A. (2013). Multimodal literacy practices in the indigenous sámi classroom: Children navigating in a complex multilingual setting. *Journal of Language & Literacy Education, 12*(4), 230–247.

Pink, S. (2009). *Doing sensory ethnography.* London: SAGE.

Porteous, D. (1990). *Landscapes of the mind: Worlds of sense and metaphor.* Toronto: University of Toronto Press.

Raworth, K., Sweetman, C., Narayan, S., Rowlands, J., & Hopkins, A. (2012). *Conducting semi-structured interviews.* Oxford: Oxfam.

Romero, A., Arce, S., & Cammarota, J. (2009). A barrio pedagogy: Identity, intellectualism, activism, and academic achievement through the evolution of critically compassionate intellectualism. *Race Ethnicity and Education, 12*(2), 217–233.

Sarra, C. (2003). *Cherbourg state school: Strong and smart. What works program: Improving outcomes for Indigenous students.* Retrieved December 13, 2017, from: http://www.whatworks. edu.au/dbAction.do?cmd=displaySitePage1&subcmd=select&id=111

Scollon, R., & Scollon, S. W. (2003). *Discourses in place: Language in the material world.* London: Routledge.

Silverman, D. (2014). *Interpreting qualitative data* (5th ed.). London: Sage.

Stanton, D., Bayon, V., Neale, H., Ahmed, G., Gahli, A., Benford, S., Cobb, S., Ingrim, R., O'Malley, C., Wilson, J., & Pridmore, T. (2001). Classroom collaboration in the design of tangible interfaces for storytelling. *CHI Letters, 3*(1), 482–489.

Stein, P. (2006). The olifantsvlei fresh stories project: Multimodality, creativity, and fixing in the semiotic chain. In C. Jewitt & G. Kress (Eds.), *Multimodal literacy* (pp. 123–138). New York: Peter Lang.

Stoecker, R. (2005). *Research methods for community change: A project-based approach.* Thousand Oaks: SAGE.

Stoller, P. (1989). *The taste of ethnographic things: The sense in ethnography.* Philadelphia: University of Pennsylvania Press.

Tuhiwai Smith, L. (2006). Choosing the margins: The role of research in indigenous struggles for social justice. In N. K. Denzin & M. D. Giardina (Eds.), *Qualitative inquiry and the conservative challenge* (pp. 151–174). Walnut Creek: Left Coast Press.

Van de Kleut, G. (2011). The whiteness of literacy practice in Ontario. *Race Ethnicity and Education, 14*(5), 699–726.

Walsh, M., & Simpson, A. (2014). Exploring literacies through touch pad technologies: The dynamic materiality of modal interactions. *Australian Journal of Language and Literacy, 37*(2), 98–106.

Kathy A. Mills is a Professor of Literacies and Digital Cultures, at the Institute for Learning Sciences and Teacher Education, Australian Catholic University. She has contributed significant, high-impact publications in the field of literacy education, including five sole-authored books. Her research monograph, *Literacy Theories for the Digital Age*, won the 2016 Edward Fry Book Award of the Literacy Research Association in the United States. *The Handbook of Writing, Literacies and Education in Digital Cultures* won the 2017 Divergent Award for Excellence in twenty-first century Literacies. She has won two Australian Research Council fellowships, including research of Indigenous multimodal literacies for primary school students.

Jane Dooley is a proud Kamilaroi woman and a PhD Candidate at Deakin University, with degrees in both contemporary arts (visual art) and education. Jane's research aims to create educational communities that protect Indigenous knowledge and to provide frameworks for the Indigenous acquisition of knowledge, values, and skills in culturally inclusive learning environments. Her educational practice draws on students' funds of cultural knowledge, to develop positive Indigenous identities, while providing a platform for personal wellness and student engagement.

Chapter 4
Durithunga Boul: A Pattern of Respectful Relationships, Reciprocity and Socially Just Literacy Education in One Urban School

John Davis and Annette Woods

Abstract Systems and schools in Australia continue to be challenged to provide equitable, socially just literacy education for Aboriginal and Torres Strait Islander young people and children in schools. This task seems to continue to be more difficult than might be expected, and this suggests that the current policy approach which relies on a variety of isolated "programs" and new – or old – approaches that layer on top of each other may not be the best way forward. This chapter provides insight into one locally developed, Indigenous-led education community and describes the possibilities created when these educators brokered relationships with other systems, approaches and researchers to reform schooling in the best interests of Aboriginal and Torres Strait Islander students. Details of the variety of strategies taken at one urban school are provided to focus on the important elements of what a socially just literacy education could be when Aboriginal and Torres Strait Islander education perspectives are foregrounded in authentic ways.

Introduction

Research into Aboriginal and Torres Strait Islander education, across a broad range of perspectives, continues to demonstrate that "despite decades of social and educational policy aimed to redress disadvantage, progress toward achieving equality has been slow, at best" (Shay 2016, p. 13). For the past 10 years, the Australian government has measured the nation's success in providing equitable outcomes to Aboriginal and Torres Strait Islander peoples through their *Closing the Gap* strategy

J. Davis
Stronger Smarter Institute, Logan, QLD, Australia
e-mail: john.davis@strongersmarter.com.au

A. Woods (✉)
Queensland University of Technology, Brisbane, QLD, Australia
e-mail: annette.woods@qut.edu.au

© Springer Nature Singapore Pte Ltd. 2019
J. Rennie, H. Harper (eds.), *Literacy Education and Indigenous Australians*,
Language Policy 19, https://doi.org/10.1007/978-981-13-8629-9_4

(Commonwealth of Australia 2018). While there is much to be said about the ideological base of a gap mentality, the strategy itself and the targets set, for this chapter it is enough to say that there has been a sustained and systematic failure to achieve the goals and aims of the strategy. As an example, the 2018 Prime Minister's report on the Closing the Gap Strategy (Commonwealth of Australia 2018) provides details that only two targets related to education are on track to be achieved. There are claims of improvements in some other target areas, and there have also been adjustments made to targets over the years. However, the cruel reality of the situation is that targets for school attendance, and reading and numeracy are not on track. The target to have 95% of Indigenous four-year-olds enrolled in early childhood education is reported as being on track. Additionally, the target to halve the gap between Aboriginal and Torres Strait Islander young people and their non-Indigenous peers in relation to achieving 12 years of schooling by 2020 is claimed as being successful and on track. This claim of success backgrounds the fact that the target only aims to half the gap between these two student groups – and not to achieve parity – and also that statistics on attendance and outcomes suggest that currently achieving 12 years of school continues to be less advantageous to Aboriginal and Torres Strait Islander young people than it may be for their non-Indigenous peers. It is not the point of our chapter to debate these outcomes, but the statistics in these reports, even on the blunt measures detailed in the strategy, demonstrate that the First Australian peoples are not receiving an equitable and just education on a national scale. And this is something that, as educators, we should all be worried about.

So it is fair to claim that our education systems continue to struggle with what it means to provide a high quality literacy education for all students. At this point it is worth considering what we do know about Aboriginal and Torres Strait Islander education and literacy education specifically, and how this plays out for Aboriginal and Torres Strait Islander young people and children in schools in Australia. In the largest review of school education for Aboriginal and Torres Strait Islander students undertaken in Australia to date, Luke et al. (2013) foregrounded several key insights into what our education institutions are offering Aboriginal and Torres Strait Islander children and young people. Statistical analyses of data collected through teacher and leader reports as well as other quantitative and qualitative data sets demonstrated that where the number of Aboriginal and Torres Strait Islander students was greater than 15% in a school, it was more likely that basic skills in literacy would feature as a key emphasis. Similarly, a focus on vocational education, as opposed to academic pathways, was evident in those schools where the population of Aboriginal and Torres Strait Islander students was just more than 11%. Taken with results that demonstrated that this was compounded for schools in communities of high poverty and with teachers with less experience, and based on our understandings about the over representation of teachers with less experience in schools that have a lower ICSEA rating,[1] these findings represent a default mode of providing Aboriginal and

---

[1] ICSEA is an index used in Australia to represent socio-economic advantage and disadvantage for school communities. The average ICSEA is 1000, and taken with the % of children in a school in

Torres Strait Islander students with basic skills in literacy and numeracy and vocational pathways which Luke et al. (2013, p. 258) claim "fits well with a model of deficit and remediation".

In such a context, we believe that telling counter stories is crucial. As such, in this chapter we report on an approach taken in one urban school, which provided spaces for leadership by Aboriginal and Torres Strait Islander educators and students, Elders and community members, and where the focus was on teaching children to be literate as social practice embedded in culturally informed perspectives and approaches. We write this chapter as long-term research partners. John Davis has recently completed doctoral research which investigated Community Durithinga as a process, an alliance of Aboriginal and Torres Strait Islander educators. John is a member of Durithunga and was also a core researcher on the *URL*earning project. The second author, Annette Woods, led the *URL*earning research project and because of partnerships with Community Durithinga members, including John, was able to weave conversations at the school discussed in this chapter toward reform. The *URL*earning project[2] was a school-based reform project in which leaders, teachers, students, their families and communities, Aboriginal and Torres Strait Islander educators, researchers and teachers' union policy makers collaborated to shift curriculum and pedagogical practices; engage Indigenous ways of knowing, doing, being and languaging within core teaching and learning; and capitalise on digital ways of working to improve student outcomes on measures of print-based literacy. John and Annette write together here to provide new insights into positive, locally configured, Aboriginal and Torres Strait Islander-led reform.

Community Durithunga[3] is an alliance of Aboriginal and Torres Strait Islander educators, who meet monthly and work to facilitate and monitor progress in Aboriginal and Torres Strait Islander education in the local area. Durithunga is a method, a set of principles, that engenders success through a strengths-based design and sustainable community modelling. Community Durithunga members built relational weaves with school educators, families and the university team who eventually partnered at the school.[4] Here we use the term "weaves" to connote the deliberate integration of sustainable practices and processes in relationships. The term allows for foregrounding the interlacing of materials, or in this case connections and relationships, that builds up to produce the textures and eventually the product – a

---

low or high bands, this index is used to categorise and compare schools to others and to indicate a general level of advantage for the student populations attending Australian schools.

[2] The *URL*earning project was funded via a partnership between the Australian Research Council under the ARC Linkage Program LP0990289, the Queensland University of Technology and the school that was our research partner.

[3] For a fuller explanation of Community Durithunga, see Davis 2018.

[4] The *URL*earning project team included Annette Woods and John Davis as well as Allan Luke, Karen Dooley, Michael Dezuanni, Kathy Mills, Beryl Exley, Vinesh Chandra, Amanda Levido, Katherine Doyle and Diana Sesay from QUT and John McCollow and Lesley McFarlane from the Queensland Teachers' Union. We acknowledge the many teachers, leaders, children and their families, Elders and Aboriginal and Torres Strait Islander educators who worked in partnership with us on this project.

weave (Davis 2018). Community Durithunga provided the protocols and a toolkit for brokering relationships and developing further sustainable practices and programming through principles of reciprocity. In this chapter, we describe how these principles played out in one school, detailing four key strategies from the very complex, multilayered approach taken to provide equitable access to quality literacy education for the children attending. The case allows for certain claims to be made about what is possible in Aboriginal and Torres Strait Islander education in our current contexts, including discussion about what success looks like; the strength of partnerships based on respect, reciprocity and ethics; and the sustainable impact of foregrounding Indigenous perspectives, cultural ways of knowing, being and doing, and success in literacy reform efforts.

A key point to foreground is that we do not present this case as describing an approach that produces results for Aboriginal and Torres Strait Islander students alone. Rather our purpose in describing a socially just education approach is to claim that all students benefit from learning literacy within a school where all students are able to see that their cultures, languages, backgrounds, experiences and values are recognised and have access to understanding Aboriginal and Torres Strait Islander language, cultural and social practices. In the section that follows we provide some background information about the school and community as the context for this reform case. We then move to define social justice as a term drawing on Nancy Fraser's conceptualisation of social justice (see, e.g. Fraser 2009). We detail the conceptual frame of Community Durithunga before providing insight into how the principles of this approach were framed in the reform work at this urban school. The reform process described is a multi-faceted approach, taken to reform how Aboriginal and Torres Strait Islander education was conducted at the school, and we consider how the locus of control and influence shifted over time and what the sustainable implications of this reform could be.

Thinking About This Urban School Context

The primary school discussed in this chapter is located in a culturally diverse suburb which is part of the urban sprawl of a large capital city in Australia. The area has a rising population and shifting demographics. Along with long-term residents in the area, more recently the location has been targeted as a living option by a diverse range of people including new arrivals to Australia and young families in the search for affordable housing. Numbers of primary school-aged children and those between the ages of 35 and 49 have risen significantly between 2011 and 2016. However, the area does still have a large proportion of more elderly residents (10% in the 70–84 age range). The suburb around this school is relatively densely populated with more than 13 persons per hectare in comparison to an overall population density of just less than 4 persons per hectare in the greater community area within which the suburb is located (http://profile.id.com.au/logan/about/?WebID=480).

The migloo[5] name for the greater community area is Logan City. It is named after Captain Patrick Logan, from the time of invasion. Logan was a tyrant, a murderer, a thief and a leader of his people, and he eventually died at the hands of Indigenous inhabitants of the area (Kirwin 2007). Initially the area of Logan was sourced as a penal outreach. The river was used as a source of transport and for produce. Later a gold mine was founded alongside one of the major creeks – Scrubby Creek (Starr 1988). Outlying areas like Beenleigh became cane and farming communities and thus served as the first port for South Sea Islander labour that came to work the cane fields. German immigrants set up family enclaves in and around the outskirts of this area (Starr 1988), and there remain rich German connections in several locations within the area today.

An extremely diverse immigrant population now shares Logan City's rich historical story. Pacific Islanders represent the largest cultural group in the area and, as such, Pacific Islander children represent significant numbers in schooling institutions. Samoan is the most spoken home language other than English, representing 12.8% of all languages other than English spoken at home (Australian Bureau of Statistics 2011a, b). The human populations are diverse and complex. Logan Central is a mecca for immigrant populations because it is the hub of services as well as the tried and true path of past immigrant families. Overall, however, Logan Central still holds a majority of *migloo* Australians.

Juxtaposed against this backdrop of diversity, the communities in Logan City share a "lower degree" of social advantage. The recognised tool to judge social disadvantage is known as the Socio-Economic Indexes for Areas (SEIFA). The index of relative socio-economic disadvantage is derived from attributes such as low income, low educational attainment and high unemployment, variables that reflect disadvantage. SEIFA has been constructed so that disadvantaged areas have or show low index values. High scores on the index generally indicate that there are few families or households of low income or with unskilled occupations. The SEIFA score ranges from 800 to 1200, so areas of high disadvantage would score in the 800s and areas of low disadvantage would score in the 1000s. ABS (2011a, b) noted that Logan City, according to the SEIFA 2011 data, scored 971, which is higher than some nearby communities, for example, the Ipswich area scores 966.3, but lower than nearby Brisbane at 1047.7 and Logan's closest southerly neighbour, Gold Coast, which scored 1014.2.

The real power of an index such as SEIFA is in providing a fuller picture of the diversity across areas. Logan has areas with a high portion of public housing (e.g. Eagleby, which has a SEIFA score of 865, and Logan Central, which has a SEIFA score of 807) as well as affordable housing estates, and some pockets of communities with high socio-economic status (e.g. Daisy Hill, which has a SEIFA score of 1045, and Logandale, which has a SEIFA score of 1104.9). So what this demonstrates is that while the SEIFA score for Logan City generally is close to 1000, there are communities within this area where disadvantage plays a major part in daily lives.

---

[5] Migloo is a word used to refer to white Australians.

56   J. Davis and A. Woods

These social indicators, coupled with the diverse human demographics, make the city of Logan a highly complex space. One of the authors of this chapter, John Davis (also known as JD in community or authored as John Davis-Warra), has written elsewhere (Davis 2018) that this is what produces the complex but vibrant and rich community that is Logan today:

> Our history, our story is alive and living, vibrant; we come from a complex past and represent today a complex community. This environment provides the rich soil to grow in spite of the diversities, because of these diversities; based on the notion of understanding and responding to the social and cultural context of the learner. **Durithunga Yarning** has evolved in this space, Logan City, as a unique Indigenous practice and process which calls for greater collaboration and recognition of Indigenous processes and principles for learning, and works to fracture the very regimented, often fragmenting, practices of **Migloo** or "mainstream" educational institutions. **Durithunga** does this to reassert the position of Indigenous voice amongst a very diverse and complex social and cultural context – a process of identification, articulation and practice of Indigenous **Ways of Knowing, Being and Doing** that privileges our way, **proper way**, over the dominant **Migloo** or multicultural discourses, and (these) are beginning to emerge and become cemented in this complex learning environment. As is the case for most differential policy or procedures, Indigenous peoples are often contextualised within mainstream settings as a group of "others". (Davis 2018, p.34)

The school that we discuss in this chapter catered to a student population of approximately 500 primary school students, the majority of whom lived in close proximity to the school. Aboriginal and Torres Strait Islander students made up somewhere between 10 and 15%, and there was a further approximately 15% of students from Pacifica backgrounds. Approximately 6% of students were provided with specialised English as an additional language or dialect support, although it is likely that, as is the case in many schools, if more resources had been available more children could have benefited from this specialised instruction. The current Indigenous education leaders within the school chose Community Durithunga as their scaffold and support for Indigenous education program development. Teacher-leaders made the importance they felt noted through Community Durithunga Research responses like, "I feel so supported by the network of teachers; teacher aides; community people to help us move forward in all school programs" (Davis 2018, p221).

During the time that we discuss in this chapter, the school was involved in several phases or steps toward school reform with a focus on improving literacy pedagogy and curriculum at the school. Each of these is presented here as a separate strategy. We do this to provide the opportunity to consider each in its complexity. However, it is important to note that the school reform process was a complex entanglement of many efforts, from a broad range of community members, educators, families and researchers. It is also important to note that while improving literacy education was a key aim of the work done, the reform of literacy education was set within education reform more broadly at the school. Detailing this complexity is difficult, but nevertheless we need to continually push back from the drive to simplify the very complex work of providing equitable schooling for all students in all schools. The Community Durithunga PhD research (Davis 2018) provides another "pushback" or signpost as to the lived educational experience of the Indigenous leaders working within complex school and broader community spaces.

What we report on in this chapter is the work of the Aboriginal and Torres Strait Islander educators at the school who, in partnership with others, took the opportunities made available by the school reform focus and state government mandates to embed Aboriginal and Torres Strait Islander perspectives into the curriculum as the impetus to foreground social justice education as necessarily embedded in the historical, cultural and social practices of Aboriginal and Torres Strait Islander peoples. This provided the spaces required to frame literacy education as a social and cultural practice that could be improved through local curriculum and pedagogical reform.

Defining Social Justice: Thinking About Quality Education for All

It is obvious that there continues to be the need for reform before Australia can claim that it is providing a socially just education for all students. Equity remains as a yet to be attained goal of our education systems. Our claim here is that unless reform practices are grounded in social justice, equity will not be achieved in education systems, schools and classrooms. Having said this, the term "social justice" is so overused in education that it has the potential to stand for everything and at the same time nothing at all. So before we move to provide the theoretical framework for Community Durithunga, we first define the term "social justice" by drawing on the work of Nancy Fraser (1997, 2003, 2009). By this way of thinking social justice is multidimensional and because of this any targets held for social justice must be toward multiple fronts. Attempts to achieve a socially just education need to consider redistributive, recognitive and representational means. When redistribution is discussed it usually refers to ensuring that relevant resources are shifted to redress disadvantage. There are two things to consider here. The first is that redistributive justice is not realised by providing everybody with the same thing. Instead, there is a requirement to shift resources – to *re*distribute in order to tackle past and current inequities. The second is to understand that when this model is taken to literacy education, redistributive justice does not just relate to redistribution of economic resources. We call for the redistribution of those valued and powerful languages, genres, ways and modes of communication that are required to participate in the dominant social practices of any place or society. However, redistribution is just one dimension of a socially just education and, unless matched with recognitive and representative dimensions, has proven over many years to be insufficient. Recognitive justice refers to ensuring that the cultural practices, languages, social repertoires, background and historical experiences of all students are evident, valued and respected in the curriculum, pedagogy and assessment structures of the education system. By this we mean that children can see themselves in the

58   J. Davis and A. Woods

structures and architectures of their school life, and have evidence in these architectures that what they bring from their communities to school is valued, considered useful and worthwhile. The final dimension of social justice put forward by Nancy Fraser is representation. This refers to a requirement that diverse voices and perspectives are evident in the governance and decision making of a school or system.

We move now to present the conceptual framework of Community Durithunga and then to present four key strategies of the approach taken at our one example school.

Community Durithunga

Community Durithunga circle is made of a total of more than 50 members. Regular circles number anywhere from 5 to 15 members.[6] The core Community Durithunga philosophy is related to the concept "to grow". In John Davis' doctoral research, he engaged in yarning with Durithunga members, and growth was the most spoken to and referred to concept used when they were describing Durithunga processes and practices (Davis 2018). By yarning we mean a relational discussion process that involves knowledge exchange (Bessarab and Ng'andu 2010) and is about "sharing through discussion and connecting" (Shay (n.d), p. 2). Yarning is based in the strong oral traditions of Aboriginal and Torres Strait Islander peoples' ways of being and oral traditions. Durithunga lives "growth" through the regular rituals of setting circles and developing relationality through yarning circle processes.

The setting of regular yarning circles supports a focus on action generation or rather seedlings of actions, which are expected to grow. The actions of Durithunga, in developing and sustaining "best practice" models, mirror the theme of sustainability for Indigenous education. This is one of its greatest yet least celebrated strengths. Community Durithunga has been a part of the Logan education context for over a decade, yet no specific funding, apart from in-kind support, has been directed to Durithunga. As a community of practice or Learning Hub, Durithunga has sustained its existence and presence for this time. Policies and directives in Aboriginal and Torres Strait Islander education shift and change with consecutive governments, however the community of practice and the individuals within localised community contexts continue to grow within their contexts. That is the power of a process like Durithunga – it focuses on local leadership and processes for leadership development.

Durithunga represents the power of working from a strengths-based design model (Gorringe and Spillman 2008; Sarra 2012). Durithunga was, and is, an

---

[6]We acknowledge the work of Community Durithunga members in the Logan Community over many years and the fact that this work of others is described by John in this chapter. Author John Davis has been a member of Community Durithunga. Author Annette Woods is a non-Indigenous researcher who led the *URL*earning project, but who is not a Community Durithunga member. She writes this chapter with John as a research partner in the approaches taken at the school.

embedded gift within the community. It is the space that educators and university researchers worked on and out of as part of their relational weave around the school. This was a necessary space to achieve reform, project growth and sustainability, thus supporting the success of other projects, for example, the URLearning project. Durithunga as a process engenders success and as an outcome ensures sustainability of community modelling. Each individual component or strategy, as discussed below, cannot be separated from any other. The system support that enabled the hiring of an Indigenous Languages teacher does not sit as separate from the Indigenous education support of the Indigenous School Support Unit (ISSU) in the State and region, or the insight gained for non-Indigenous colleagues through Stronger Smarter Leadership[7] training, or the strong partnerships built between local and university researchers and educators. The undeniable thread or connection for the sustainable weave in this case were the Community Durithunga members.

Growing and advancing deep and authentic Indigenous education approaches from a community-centric design such as Community Durithunga, creates a high-impact, relatively low-cost model of developing deep, consultative engagement with community. Such a community embedded approach, led by Aboriginal and Torres Strait Islander educators, provides important spaces for learning and professional development and Aboriginal and Torres Strait Islander leadership. The footprint of this Durithunga leadership model is signalled in broader programmatic developments across Durithunga's history. Specifically, these are sites where sustained Aboriginal and Torres Strait Islander education programming has moved beyond the systemic focus on the 4–5 year improvement cycle, instead in many cases marking a decade or generational shift within the reform processes. This is an exciting space which recognises success in a full range of endeavours, including, for example, film making,[8] sustained educational third spaces,[9] leadership[10] and language.[11]

To track and understand the sustainability of the Durithunga approach and the research weave, it is imperative to link into examples of strong partnerships. As an example, when the URLearning project – a project aimed at investigating what could be achieved through connections between leaders and teachers, researchers and local community educators toward improving the quality of literacy education

---

[7] The Stronger Smarter Approach is a part of the Stronger Smarter Institute and based on the original research of Chris Sarra.

[8] See, for example, Footprints in Film – *Nyumba Bugir Anga*, Loganlea, Griffith University, shortlisted Short Film in Cannes International Film Festival and South Coast Regional Showcase Award for Inclusive Education, 2006.

[9] See, for example, *Knowledge House*, Loganlea, Showcase School on Third Cultural Spaces, National Stronger Smarter Leadership Program 2007–2010 and Dare to Lead Showcase school; *Bariebunn Boul*, Waterford West, Premier's Reconciliation Award Winner, 2013; *Dreaming Circle*, Waterford West, Department of Education Showcase Awards, State Winner, 2013.

[10] "Emerging Aboriginal and Torres Strait Islander Educational Leadership", Individual Award, 2014–2015, ACEL.

[11] "Department of Education and Training Indigenous Education Conference 2017. "*Yugambeh* Language Program" Showcase, July 2017.

for all students – came into the research design process for reform at the school, they were leveraging off the advice and links of Community Durithunga, especially through author John Davis as a chief investigator on the funded *URL*earning research project. The critical insight here was the brokerage and relationship of a school community model which was, and is, very proudly community based and kinnected.[12] This idea gets to the heart of an alternative to white race privilege or embedded terra nullius discourses and practices where Indigenous identity is positioned or silenced as other, and most likely in deficit (Fredericks 2015; Moreton-Robinson 2009). To that end the *URL*earning team were supported to embrace the strengths-based approach to research development and direction established well before their entry into the community. The strengths base in this Aboriginal and Torres Strait Islander community context involved the schools who were partnered with Community Durithunga. These schools had been sites where the challenge of addressing deficit policy initiatives had been approached by foregrounding parent voices. This was achieved by creating a regular Yarning Circle to support and develop Aboriginal and Torres Strait Islander education leadership within the local community context. These school sites remain as areas of authentic Aboriginal and Torres Strait Islander education and leadership.

Yarning Circles (Davis-Warra et al. 2011; Mills et al. 2013) are put to work in education in very different ways. They can be spaces of deep listening and learning, or token spaces created only to provide visibility of certain groups in schools. The fact that Durithunga takes a deep approach to yarning is the core to learning and taking authentic Aboriginal and Torres Strait Islander education. There is a deep relational weave and connection, which engenders sustainability and cultural integrity to the environs. This occurs as the process operates with principles of reciprocity, relationships and sustainability – the Durithunga proper way model (Davis 2018). An approach that focuses on recognitive justice and heightened visibility might have its place, but only ever as a component of a broader focus on Indigenous-led reform. And there are significant issues when spaces that encourage visibility of Aboriginal and Torres Strait Islander peoples, but not deep representative engagement and appropriate distribution of funds and resources, are held up as Indigenous education excellence or even as authentic models of Aboriginal and Torres Strait Islander education.

Importantly it was from a space of Aboriginal and Torres Strait Islander leadership that the school has been able to be a part of a deeper authentic Indigenous education circle for a number of years. Community Durithunga is representative of the myriad of strengths-based models currently being successful in Aboriginal and Torres Strait Islander communities all around our country. What Durithunga

---

[12] "Kinnected" is described by John Davis in his doctoral work as "A relational term connecting individuals to specific people and places. Kinnectedness refers to the notion of social mapping and connecting of people to places, names and communities across Australia. For Indigenous Australians this is an integral part of being and living within Indigenous communities – being able to map kinnections – people and families who place you (individually) within context of the broader social or Indigenous community map" (Davis, 2018, p. xi).

processes were able to do on this school site was to provide a clearer blueprint on "how to" engage Aboriginal and Torres Strait Islander community within the business of the school. As is the case in some other schools, and prior to deepening Durithunga relationships, there were challenges and provocations at this school site that could only be healed from within. The school had had real and tangible issues with visibility and program sustainability in its efforts in Aboriginal and Torres Strait Islander education.

As just one example, in times before the reform detailed in this chapter, Aboriginal and Torres Strait Islander education practice, teams and families were located on the school site in a green tool shed, sharing this space with yard maintenance resources. As partnerships developed with real relationships being foregrounded, regular weaves between school leadership, researchers, and Community Durithunga members became important spaces for dialogue of change. There was a foregrounding of Aunty Enid Dirie's leadership and expertise. Aunty Enid is an Indigenous education expert. As these connections were reformed, Indigenous education practices were shifted from the green tool shed to the main Administration block:

> ... our Indigenous workers [were] in a big green shed. Students were never allowed to come near it. Since I've been involved with *Durithunga* [the school] has moved us to the office ... [*Durithunga voices* spoke up and out about this situation] ... Moving us to the office our kids get to see us ... They come in droves and at lunch now our office is full of *jarjums*. (Dirie in Davis et al. 2009)

This is an example of redistribution, in this case of space. Aboriginal and Torres Strait Islander staff were centrally located in this new space, and this was vital in the reconfiguration of recognition of Aboriginal and Torres Strait Islander education at the school. Space matters. Through Durithunga leadership, and collaborative practices, the offices of those entrusted with Aboriginal and Torres Strait Islander education at the school were shifted from the isolated green shed to a central location within the front office administration block. Then the practice of Aboriginal and Torres Strait Islander education was shifted to classrooms facing the oval, and eventually there was a whole new development of an Aboriginal and Torres Strait Islander education space which included a yarning circle and bush tucker gardens. With external support, there has also been a community development of a Family Support Centre on site. The key to this long-term, sustained success and growth has been the community's strengths – the Durithunga approach.

The actions and processes of Community Durithunga are vast and varied. But within a complex learning environment and community context, there grows Aboriginal and Torres Strait Islander communities' own, home-grown response to "proper way" education. In recent research of Community Durithunga, Davis (2018) found that members of the Durithunga research circles brought forward four key strategies or cases within and around this school that they felt had come together, over time, to support positive reform at the school site. In the section that follows we present some insights into these four strategies.

Community Durithunga at This School

Durithunga's power lies in its response and kinnection to local area contexts. New projects and approaches where relationships of reciprocity have been built have a deep relational research well to draw on and foundation strategies to build on. In what follows we present four of these strategies that are relevant to this school. We remind readers that the approach to reform education for Aboriginal and Torres Strait Islander students at this school was multi-faceted and complex. However, these four cases provide some insight to the sustained, "proper way" modelling actioned around the school.

Strategy Element 1: Stronger Smarter (2006–Continuing)

The Stronger Smarter Approach originally comes from the work of Chris Sarra (see Sarra 2011). The strengths-based, high expectations relationship approach to providing Aboriginal and Torres Strait Islander children with access to quality education forms the foundation of a leadership program for school leaders and educators implemented through the Stronger Smarter Institute (Stronger Smarter Institute 2017). The approach aims to improve student outcomes, particularly in literacy and numeracy, and to promote positive cultural identities through high expectations leadership models. Over the course of 2007–2012, the Stronger Smarter Institute continued to grow and invest in its partnership brokerage with Community Durithunga. Initially the entry points for Stronger Smarter were through author Davis, who was a Stronger Smarter Institute facilitator at the time; however, as the national training programs grew so did the scope of program delivery and the need for showcase schools and community groups. Over the course of this time, Community Durithunga, through Stronger Smarter partnerships, toured Canberra, specifically presenting at AIATSIS for the National Indigenous Studies Conference on "Perspectives on Urban Life", in 2009 (see Davis et al. 2009). This experience was shared with touring *jarjum*[13] members, who got to travel interstate and present as part of the national convention.

Community Durithunga members were filmed for the Stronger Smarter Institute forums on Indigenous Education and the video recordings remain online, providing Community Durithunga voices and perspectives on Aboriginal and Torres Strait Islander education in urban environs. These filming activities were augmented by on-the-ground program delivery and facilitation of "Community Durithunga in action" Workshops. Woven into the Stronger Smarter Leadership program, this led to further keynote presentations about the Durithunga principles. These leadership opportunities were not just afforded to one individual representing the larger group; Durithunga's Seedling principle of "rule of three" (Davis 2018) ensured three active

---

[13] Jarjum – young person

Durithunga member voices were sharing yarns and perspectives on what works on an Aboriginal and Torres Strait Islander education front in urban locales at all times.

Through the further development of Stronger Smarter Institute programming came the development of the Stronger Smarter Learning Communities (SSLC) project. Participation in the SSLC led to Community Durithunga being chosen through community consultations as the first site for Stronger Smarter Indigenous Youth Leadership programs to be developed. SSLC partnered with the Department of Education, specifically the Indigenous Schooling Support Unit (ISSU) and Durithunga, to co-create "Logan Indigenous Student Leadership Projects". This leadership program created a *jarjums*-centred learning approach, which developed jarjums' focus on challenges that they could control, and then challenges where they wanted to see change. This weave of activity was the foundation for the award-winning Aboriginal and Torres Strait Islander Homework Hub run at the school, which encouraged a focus on cultural recognition and academic excellence (see Davis-Warra et al. 2011 for further detail).

Strategy Element 2: Embedding Aboriginal and Torres Strait Islander Perspectives Across Schools (EATSIPs), (2010–Continuing)

Again, a major legacy or lasting footprint of Community Durithunga has been in the approach to EATSIPs. At this school the institutional authority of the EATSIPs movement was utilised to foreground visibility and distribution of resources. The EATSIPs policy documents have been the Queensland State Government's influential public document on Aboriginal and Torres Strait Islander education program development and support over some years. Through the steps taken to EATSIPs at the school, Community Durithunga has been an active knowledge creator, facilitator and consultant in the development and delivery of EATSIPs throughout the state. The Queensland EATSIPs approach wove a three-pronged process to deliver on its commitment to Reconciliation. The three prongs of EATSIPs were:

(i) The EATSIPs document – a text designed by Aboriginal and Torres Strait Islander educators from around the state. Initially framed through the work of Mayrah Drieise and then compiled by Penny Hamilton.
(ii) The EATSIPs Principal Project Officers – hired across the seven state education regions and program managed centrally through ISSU. These officers provided professional development for regions and developed EATSIPs project documents for regional cluster schools.
(iii) EATSIPs Online – refers to the "Modular" program for education staff to compete to gain certification in core EATSIPs processes (shared regionally through professional developments).

Community Durithunga's active involvement in the EATSIPs processes is aptly referenced and referred to in the EATSIPs document. Over the years, Durithunga has created a symbiotic and influential relationship with and between peak bodies related to Indigenous education. In the school discussed here, the EATSIPs framework called on the expertise of the Principal Project Officers to foreground visibility of Aboriginal and Torres Strait Islander children and the strengths of their cultures:

> The EATSIPs framework was a powerful tool in providing the shared/common language needed to address the complex issues that existed within Aboriginal and Torres Strait Islander education. The framework could have been likened to a map, a set of instructions or a recipe that schools could utilise to embed Aboriginal & Torres Strait Islander perspectives in schools in a respectful, authentic and non-tokenistic way. (Previous Principal Project Officer Liz Kupsch, 2018, Personal Communication)

This not only strengthened recognitive social justice but provided an interesting space of learning for all teachers in the school, many of whom had limited knowledge and understandings of Indigenous ways of knowing, being and doing before the program's introduction. This is an example of how important it is for staff within schools to be well connected into system-based policy so that these links can be put to work in the best interests of the children attending the school.

Strategy Element 3: Indigenous Languages (2008–Continuing)

Durithunga through its very inception has woven in the concept of strengthening and revitalisation of Indigenous languages. The use of the word *Durithunga* is deeply contextualised in the local area and provides an educational building block to develop and deepen further curricula. Yugambeh languages' teacher and foundational Durithunga member Aunty Eileen Williams and her sister Aunty Robyn provide the Eldership with Aunty Pat O'Connor to underpin languages development. That said, in 2008–2010, Community Durithunga led a concerted localised campaign through Community Durithunga Yarning Circles to grow Indigenous languages even more. There were a number of significant local area deaths and illnesses, which led to the passing of eons of language knowledge. To deepen learning in and around languages and bolster language holder spaces, Durithunga went on a collective sense-making process to best prepare and develop a localised learning response to Aboriginal and Torres Strait Islander languages. This project work conducted by Community Durithunga ran initially before and then in parallel with work being conducted by the State's curriculum authority, Queensland Curriculum and Assessment Authority (QCAA).

Community Durithunga's Aboriginal and Torres Strait Islander Languages project work focused on the language of the Yugambeh. This language weave centred the languages work in and on the Yugambeh Language Museum. The seed document was gifted to four hub schools, in the area. These schools all had Durithunga members and Durithunga leadership woven into their individual spaces. However, it was the initiative of the Indigenous staff, the principal and leadership team of the school described in this paper that led to the development and delivery of the first whole of Primary Indigenous Languages program in the State. The school used the Languages Other Than English (LOTE) curriculum time to develop local Yugambeh languages. The focus of representative justice at the school over many years meant there were spaces where Community Durithunga could provide the seed programming and leadership support for a successful program. The redistributive justice that had also been a focus at the school for many years meant that leadership were in a position to find ways and means to fund the program – funding agencies like ISSU and the school itself provided the monetary initiative to drive the change and sustain it in the school. The language program increased visibility throughout the school – school signage was included in dual languages as an example, and the yarning space and native gardens became a space of belonging for all to benefit. During school parades and events, the national anthem was sung in two languages, an acknowledgement to the Yugambeh peoples was given in language by student leaders and the *jarjums* danced in impressive moments of cultural recognition and acceptance. The languages teacher Gary Crosby has continued to refine and develop core whole school offerings at the school.

At the time the Queensland Curriculum Authority, QCAA, were developing (and now have completed) a comprehensive Indigenous Languages Syllabus. Principal Policy Officer Will Davis (a Durithunga Foundational Member) led the writing of the Languages Syllabus. The QCAA officially launched the syllabus in 2010. Upon releasing the syllabus to the media, this school was chosen as the "showcase school" for further media attention.

Strategy Element 4: **URLearning (2010–2015)**

*URL*earning was a successful research partnership undertaken and led at the school. The project aimed to improve literacy outcomes for all students at the school through a process of school reform which focused on digital and media arts interventions as a way to reflect on pedagogy and curriculum. The *URL*earning project (see Woods et al. 2014 and Davis-Warra et al. 2011) was a partnership between the leaders, educators, children and their families and communities at the school with Aboriginal and Torres Strait Islander Elders and educators, university researchers and the teachers' union. The aim of this larger school reform project was to foreground teacher professionalism to support redistributive and recognitive justice, while supporting moves for representational justice by diverse groups from the school community.

The school was specifically chosen as the project site because it was a Community Durithunga school. What this meant was that Community Durithunga was the broker of and for the research within the school. The goal of the study was to partake in the school's literacy interventions through multiple entry points, focused on teacher efficacy, collaborative engagement and raising expectations held for teachers and students. Community Durithunga leadership was involved in the conceptualisations, consultations and delivery of programs within and for this research project.

Community Durithunga supported the university and union researchers to engage within the community in respectful, reciprocal relationships and raised the expectations of the researchers' research behaviour – asking regularly what will be left behind for the benefit of the community by this action, approach or plan? What is it that community wants from the opportunity of university engagement?

As an example of what this might look like in practice, the afterschool Homework Hub provides an excellent space to consider this concept of reciprocity. The *URL*earning project's focus on recognitive, redistributive and representational justice as the basis for school reform worked in sync with the deep connections of Indigenous-centred learning approaches in the Yugambeh language as a LOTE class, which then led into the creation of the Homework Hub which was an after-school home-centred learning program (see Davis-Warra et al. 2011 for a more detailed account of this space). A key consultative brokerage of the research project was the concept of "gifting back" (reciprocation) to community. This concept ensured the researchers were grounded in the locale of the community they were researching in and with. A basic foundation principle was that the researchers were required to develop a stream of reciprocal processes that gifted back to the community. A powerful development of and on the club space was the gifting of teacher education students to assist in running the after-school program. The students selected to participate were orientated to the privilege of working in other people's neighbourhoods and with other people's children. And so those involved were provided with an opportunity to learn within an Indigenous-specific context while at the same time, their presence enabled additional volunteer support to deliver the after-school programs in literacies and other areas. The power and impact of the different programs, for example, language education and Homework Hub, developed at the school is recorded as part of the *URL*earning research (see, e.g. Woods et al. 2014).

Conclusion

The targeted strategies above are powerful examples of the "wins" of *Community Durithunga* as they relate to the school reform processes around one urban school. The approach to reform at the school was multifaceted, but the sustained connection to Aboriginal and Torres Strait Islander ways of knowing, being and doing through visibility and recognition; the long-term relationships that raised the awareness of, and supported school leadership to be accountable to, the requirement to ensure equitable distribution of human, material, linguistic and financial resources; and finally the solid, sustained leadership of Aboriginal and Torres Strait Islander people through respectful protocols and long-term brokering practices are all important dimensions of the reform strategies.

The Community Durithunga approach to Aboriginal and Torres Strait Islander education, which includes, for example, practices to set regular yarning circles and following distinct research and data gathering protocols (Davis 2018), is practices which engender and have created a sustainable practice model of reform in the school described in this paper, as well as others in the same area. Reciprocity, for those involved in the reform processes at the school, was built and has been embedded on multiple fronts: firstly, the acknowledgement of each other as respected research and education bases; secondly, the brokering of official relationships through the intent of the different research and policy projects; and finally, by positioning Aboriginal and Torres Strait Islander educators from community as lead supporters and researchers within reform projects such as *URL*earning. Sustainability was grounded in the very design of all that occurred at this school. For example, by brokering relationships with leaders, teachers and parents at the school through Aboriginal and Torres Strait Islander ways of knowing, being and doing, the *URL*earning researchers were supported to create a relational weave that maintained strength in research time and has been sustained well after the project completion more than 5 years ago.

More than a decade since the inception of Durithunga in and around the school, the site remains the regional and state lighthouse school on Indigenous Language within the LOTE space. From this strength, the future shapes as one of continuing development and regrowth in our field of expertise, our site of cultural significance, our centre of well-being education. This suggests an interesting perspective on reform sustainability as being much more than sustaining the project of Durithunga around the school. In a sustainable, "proper way" model, the relational weaves built on reciprocity ensure a longer agency and sustained voice and recognition of and for Aboriginal and Torres Strait Islander peoples. This takes many forms. As an example, Durithunga members who were supported at the school within the LOTE program are now linguistic supports for Yugambeh Museum, for Men's Group members and they also now act as language consultants for local Aboriginal and Torres Strait Islander housing organisations. This is a community commitment and school is a part of the community not an island adrift the sea of socio-economic complexities (Davis 2018).

Community Durithunga is a low-cost, high-impact model of Aboriginal and Torres Strait Islander educational sustainability. It is a leadership circle that remains in 2018, continuing to operate with no financial support from partner or funding bodies. As such Durithunga provides an example of a successful Indigenous-led, community-controlled empowerment model, with demonstrated success of supporting urban schools to reform processes and practices to improve the quality and equity of schooling for Aboriginal and Torres Strait Islander students.

References

Australian Bureau of Statistics. (2011a). *Indigenous profile – Census of population and housing.* Retrieved from http://www.abs.gov.au/websitedbs/censushome.nsf/home/data

Australian Bureau of Statistics. (2011b). *Socio-economic indexes for areas (SEIFA): Getting a handle on individual diversity with areas Sept. 2011: Research paper.* Retrieved from https://www.abs.gov.au/

Bessarab, D., & Ng'andu, B. (2010). Yarning about yarning as a legitimate method in Indigenous research. *International Journal of Critical Indigenous Studies, 3,* 37–50.

Commonwealth of Australia. (2018). *Closing the gap: The Prime Minister's report 2018.* Canberra: Commonwealth.

Davis, J. (2018). *Durithunga – Growing, nurturing, challenging and supporting urban Indigenous leadership in education.* Unpublished Thesis. Queensland University of Technology.

Davis, J., Dirie, E., & Sadler, T. (2009). *Durithunga* [Audio podcast]. Presentation at AIATSIS National Indigenous Studies Conference – "Perspectives on urban life: Connections and reconnections", Canberra. Retrieved from http://www.aiatsis.gov.au/research/conf2009/papers/E4.1.html

Davis-Warra, J., Dooley, K. T., & Exley, B. E. (2011). Reflecting on the "Dream Circle": Urban Indigenous education processes designed for student and community empowerment. *QTU Professional Magazine, 26,* 19–21.

Fraser, N. (1997). *Justice interruptus: Critical reflections on the 'postsocialist' condition.* Cambridge, MA: Cambridge University Press.

Fraser, N. (2003). Social justice in the age of identity politics redistribution, recognition and participation. In N. Fraser & A. Honneth (Eds.), *Redistribution or recognition? A political-philosophical exchange* (pp. 7–109). New York: Versco.

Fraser, N. (2009). *Scales of justice: Reimagining political space in a globalizing world.* New York: Columbia University Press.

Fredericks, B. L. (2015). Of old and new. Messages conveyed by Australian Universities. In F. Foley, L. Martin-Chew, & F. Nicoll (Eds.), *Courting blakness: Recalibrating knowledge in the sandstone university* (pp. 78–87). Brisbane: University of Queensland Press.

Gorringe, S., & Spillman, D. (2008, December). Creating stronger smarter learning communities: The role of culturally competent leadership. In *World Indigenous Peoples Conference-Education,* Melbourne, Australia.

Kirwin, D. (2007). *Aboriginal heroes: Dundalli a "Turrwan" an aboriginal leader: 1842–1854.* Nathan: Griffith Institute for Educational Research, Griffith University.

Luke, A., Cazden, C., Coopes, R., Klenowski, V., Ladwig, J., Lester, J., et al. (2013). *A summative evaluation of the stronger smarter learning communities project: Vol 1 and Vol 2.* Brisbane: Queensland University of Technology.

Mills, K. A., Sunderland, N., & Davis-Warra, J. (2013). Yarning circles in the literacy classroom. *The Reading Teacher, 67*(4), 285–289. https://doi.org/10.1002/trtr.1195.

Moreton-Robinson, A. (2009). Imagining the good indigenous citizen: Race war and the pathology of patriarchal white sovereignty. *Cultural Studies Review, 15*(2), 61–79. https://doi.org/10.5130/csr.v15i2.2038.

Sarra, C. (2011). *Strong and smart: Towards a pedagogy of emancipation: Education for first peoples.* New York: Routledge.

Sarra, C. (2012). *"Good morning Mr. Sarra" – My life working for a stronger, smarter future for our children.* St. Lucia: University of Queensland Press.

Shay, M. (2016). Emerging ideas for innovation in Indigenous education: A research synthesis of Indigenous educative roles in mainstream and flexi schools. *Teaching Education, 28*(1), 12–26.

Shay, M. (n.d.). Extending the yarning yarn: Collaborative Yarning Methodology for ethical Indigenist education research. *The Australian Journal of Indigenous Education*, 1–9. https://doi.org/10.1017/jie.2018.25

Starr, J. (1988). *Logan, the man, the river and the city.* Tenterfield: Southern Cross and Press Services.

Stronger Smarter Institute. (2017). *Stronger smarter approach; Monograph.* www.strongersmarter.com.au

Woods, A., Dooley, K., Luke, A., & Exley, B. (2014). School leadership, literacy and social justice: The place of local school curriculum planning and reform. In *International handbook of educational leadership and social (in) justice* (pp. 509–520). Dordrecht: Springer Netherlands.

John Davis is the chief research officer for the Stronger Smarter Institute. Stronger Smarter focuses on building on strengths of Indigenous identity providing the best education for gundoos Australia-wide. On country JD is a traditional owner of the western sides of Bunya Bunya Mountains Country we call Boobagarrn Ngumminge. "My people are Cobble Cobble kinnected to Warra and Dalby. We have links directly to the Barunggam and Wakka Wakka people".

As an educator he is passionate about Aboriginal and Torres Strait Islander peoples, languages and cultures and working and moving our ways forward as best practice in education and community development.

Annette Woods is a professor in the Faculty of Education at Queensland University of Technology. She teaches and researches in literacies, school reform, social justice and curriculum, pedagogy and assessment. Her recent research includes an analysis of learning to write in the early years, a study of literacy and sustainability prior to school settings and continuing research with teacher researcher colleagues on issues related to imagination as a curriculum concept and the inclusion of digital technologies in classroom pedagogies.

Chapter 5
Family Story Time in the Ngaanyatjarra Early Years Program

Anne Shinkfield and Beryl Jennings

Abstract In this chapter, I tell the story of the evolution of an Early Years program that aimed to get children in the Ngaanyatjarra communities in Western Australia ready for school. In particular, I focus on the story time routines in this program. Very young children learn best through experiences in their home language and within their family, and their experiences around books and stories during their first few years of life provide a foundation for them to learn literacy successfully at school. Using a narrative inquiry approach and personal journals, I describe significant milestones of the development of this program over two decades. Analysis of the data suggests there were four important foundations that were pivotal to the success of this program: first, learning together within family groups; second, activities that are valued require an agreed place, time and purpose within family and community life; third, importance of acknowledging the role of parents and families as the first teachers of children; and finally, using storybooks written in the child's first language.

Introduction

It is about half way through the day's playgroup in a remote Indigenous community and the children and parents are finishing their group activities. The facilitator places two large mats on the floor. No words are needed – everyone knows what this

---

Anne Shinkfield is the primary author of this chapter with Beryl Jennings. The work discussed draws directly from Anne's personal journals and field notes over the history of the program. Beryl Jennings has been included in the authorship of this chapter as she was a pivotal colleague at different times throughout the development of the program. Anne is indebted to her wisdom and input.

A. Shinkfield (✉)
Monash University, Melbourne, VIC, Australia
e-mail: anne.shinkfield@monash.edu

B. Jennings
Warburton Community via Kalgoorlie, WA, Australia

© Springer Nature Singapore Pte Ltd. 2019
J. Rennie, H. Harper (eds.), *Literacy Education and Indigenous Australians*,
Language Policy 19, https://doi.org/10.1007/978-981-13-8629-9_5

means. Some two-year-olds, who are playing in the home corner nearby, drop what they are doing and turn to help straighten the mats, and you can hear the parent saying 'Yilala'/'Pull it'. Then the facilitator positions the crate of children's board books in the centre of the mat. Everything is ready.

The call goes out – 'Story time and morning tea!' There's a scurry of activity. Toddlers and little children, familiar with the daily routine, drop what they are doing and move inside. With little hesitation each child goes to the crate and chooses their first book to look at with their parent. In no time there are many groups of adults and children huddled together over books. Family story time is happening. The chatter of parents talking to children in their home language fills the room. Parents and children excitedly point to pictures and talk about the books. Children move to other family groups to investigate what is being read. During this time, there is a constant ebb and flow of movement and then stillness as the books become the focus of children's attention and interest with their parents. Then the facilitator calls out gently 'Pack away time' and another scurry of activity begins. Children pick up their books and toddle over to put them in the crate – then turn back to their parent, wearing a pleased smile. The facilitator gathers up the books, morning tea is handed out to the children and then the second part of story time begins – Group Story Time. With each adult sitting with their child, a Ngaanyatjarra story is read to the group using a routine that you'd see in junior primary programs anywhere. Someone holds the picture book for everyone to see, reading the words on each page and encouraging parents to talk about the picture on each page with the children, until the story comes to its end – 'Palunya'. It is clear from the focused expressions on the young children's faces as they listen to and watch the story that they know already that stories in books are to be enjoyed and shared with everyone.

The above vignette describes a typical Family Story Time in 2017 in the remote Indigenous communities of the Ngaanyatjarra Lands in Western Australia, a shared early literacy event that is part of the daily routine for children and family adults in their Early Years program – a program that was designed to assist the parents get their children ready for school. These parent-child book-sharing activities and the Group Story Time resemble the early experiences of many children in literate cultures across the world.

However, the children and families of this story are from a remote Indigenous community and, if you were actually sitting on the mat with the families, you would notice that nearly all the talking between the children and parents is in their Ngaanyatjarra language and that most of the books are written in Ngaanyatjarra. Yet, for these children, this literacy event, situated within their own family, language, and cultural ways, is providing the early literacy experiences that are foundational to learning literacy at school. For the first time in these communities, the children are now starting school with their own favourite stories, a love of books and a confidence with story time routines. In this chapter, I discuss the development of the Story time routines over two decades.

Background to This Story: The People, the Setting and the Program

The Ngaanyatjarra people live largely in eight very remote and isolated desert communities with a total population of 1850 people. The communities are situated in the Ngaanyatjarra Lands, an area of Western Australia that covers about 160,000 square kilometres. The Ngaanyatjarra people's culture is strong but health, social and economic problems beset the families. Most children are growing up in welfare dependent families, educational outcomes are minimal and there are limited local opportunities for employment post-schooling (Australian Government Productivity Commission 2016; Australian Curriculum Assessment and Reporting Authority 2015).

Ngaanyatjarra is the main language of most of the communities, and rich traditions of oral language use and storytelling continue (Kraal 2012). Ngaanyatjarra people traditionally used no form of printed language until the establishment of the mission in the late 1930s, and then a few books were written in the Ngaanyatjarra language, such as the Bible and hymn books. Many adults cannot read Ngaanyatjarra, and many also have limited English literacy. Most homes have no books or writing materials in them, and it is rare to find printed material for purchase in the local stores.

Government schools had been established across all the communities by the early 1980s, with instruction in English only, although there is limited use of English elsewhere in the community.

Within the communities there were concerns about the impact of schooling on their children. I remember one day in the mid-1990s, talking with a local older woman while leaning together on a school gate watching the children wander into classes, when she turned to me and said: 'They're going to school but they're not learning anything'. Her concerns were frequently echoed by others in the community. Later that year, women from the community talked with the community manager about developing a program that would help them prepare their children for school, and they invited me to work with them to get their children ready for school.

The Ngaanyatjarra Early Years program began in February 1995. For 2 years, every school morning from start of school until recess time, children aged 0–4 and their caregivers came and participated in early childhood activities, called 'playgroup' or 'little kid's school'. Each day's program began with 'come in and play' activities, followed by a group inside activity (often art or craft), morning tea and then outside play activities before home time. Each adult stayed with their child during all the session, sharing in the experiences and routines together, and nearly all the talking between the children and their caregivers was in Ngaanyatjarra.

'Story Time' as Narrative Inquiry

This chapter focuses on the Story Time activity and its development over two decades within this program. To write this account I draw on my experience as a participant observer, from living in the community and working as facilitator and then coordinator within the program. Narrative methodology – 'a methodology for studying lived experience' (Clandinin 2006; Riessman 2008) – is used to interpret personal journals and reflections about daily experiences in the program over a period of 20 years. The understanding of narrative inquiry as stories 'lived and told' (Clandinin and Connelly 2000, p. 20) is consistent with the oral story telling culture of the Ngaanyatjarra people, whose stories, both 'lived and told', guide every part of their family and community life (Kraal 2012).

Some features of narrative inquiry as the study of 'lived experience' are particularly relevant to this story. Narrative inquiry recognises that every experience has a past, present and future, that shared experiences are social and relational, whether between children and parents or between the researcher and community members, and that the told experiences have their own place and context (Clandinin and Rosiek 2007, p. 69). Additionally, and importantly, narratives are stories that are 'strategic, functional and purposeful' (Riessman 2008, p. 8).

My journals, as personal narratives, reflect on the engagement of the parents and children in each activity, especially focusing on the parents in their new role as the teachers of their children in these activities. I used the daily writing of these reflections as 'a method of inquiry' about observed experiences (Richardson and St. Pierre 2005), often addressing questions emerging from the day's experiences, as I was never quite sure where each day would lead in our shared development of the program.

My journals also frequently described the way my Indigenous colleague, Beryl Jennings, intuitively shaped the development of this program over the years. Beryl, a Wongi woman, who had lived in the Ngaanyatjarra Lands for most of her life, came to live in this community with her family in the second year of the program. Beryl had worked in schools for many years, she had a love of children and was passionate about helping children become 'the future of the community'. We shared the commitment to parents being the teachers of their children and children learning in their home language. There were strong links with her family and mine over many years, and working together each day was a great privilege.

For this chapter, I have selected journal entries and reflections that describe the significant milestones that contributed to making Family Story Time 2017 the rich early literacy event it has become. I use my writings to identify some of the foundational themes that have underpinned this program, leading to its longevity and success. I begin, however, by contextualising my study with the broader literature on children's early years' experiences in relation to family and culture, school readiness and early literacy.

Children's Early Experiences and Their Readiness for Learning at School

Multi-disciplinary research has highlighted the importance of the child's early experiences in both supporting development and shaping further learning (Knudsen et al. 2006; McCain and Mustard 1999; Shonkoff and Phillips 2000). Parents and other close adults are essential. Rogoff (2003, p. 283) describes the parent's role with the child as the provision of 'guided participation in cultural activities'. Hence, children learn within the context of their culture, and the different ways that adults structure learning opportunities for their children are culturally determined (Heath 1983; Shonkoff and Phillips 2000).

The quality of the child's experiences during their first few years of life sets the stage for the experiences that follow, as each new capability builds on earlier learning (Heckman 2008; Heckman and Masterov 2007; Knudsen et al. 2006; McCain and Mustard 1999). Within western cultures, extensive research has focused on the early experiences of children as the foundation for future capabilities, demonstrating the predictive nature of a child's 'readiness at five' or 'non-readiness at five' upon school outcomes. For children growing up in the same culture as the school, the child's early experiences are likely to provide opportunities for the learning and development that is required for 'readiness' at school, as school is the traditional 'next step' in the life of a child within that culture. The time of school entry is a critical transition, when individual differences between children become predictive of later achievement (Shonkoff and Phillips 2000; Heckman 2008; McCain and Mustard 1999; COAG 2009).

Early experiences that are foundational to success in literacy are a part of the 'growing up' of young children within literate home environments. For these children, frequent literacy events such as bedtime story routines and shared book reading happen in the context of homes filled with conversations about stories, books and the paraphernalia of a literate family in a literate society (Heath 1982). There are strong correlations between early book reading and later school language and reading performance (Rogoff 2003; Senechal and LeFevre 2002; Whitehurst et al. 1994). In particular, shared picture book reading between children and close adults are highly significant for children's language and literacy development, with parents having the critical role as they structure their children's interactions with books (Barratt-Pugh and Rohl 2015; Bus et al. 1995; Farrant 2012; Heath 1983; Neumann 1996; Whitehurst et al. 1988). Consequently, by the time these children go to school, they have had years of practice in interactions that are foundational to school language and literacy (Heath 1982).

While 'readiness' seems to be predictive of successful school outcomes, 'non-readiness' has been shown to predict school failure, which in turn has been linked to lifelong negative consequences across social, health, educational and economic outcomes for children, families and the community (Knudsen et al. 2006; Heckman 2008; McCain and Mustard 1999). This is the case particularly for Indigenous children living in remote locations and identified as disadvantaged (Australian

Government Productivity Commission 2016), and who continue to underachieve in school relative to their non-Indigenous peers (Australian Government Productivity Commission 2016; Department of Prime Minister and Cabinet 2016; Australian Curriculum Assessment and Reporting Authority 2015).

However, research suggests that effective interventions for children in their early years of life (0–5 years of age) can modify the outcomes of these early year's experiences, by providing a range of stimulating experiences that will both enhance children's development and enable them to be better prepared for learning successfully at school (Knudsen et al. 2006; McCain and Mustard 1999). This in turn can positively impact on children's life-trajectories (Heckman 2008; COAG 2009; Shonkoff and Phillips 2000). For Indigenous children, early years 'school-readiness' programs are increasingly advocated as key to improved outcomes both at school and in later life (Bowes and Grace 2014; COAG 2009; Harrison et al. 2012; McCain and Mustard 1999; Mildon and Polimeni 2012).

Yet there is evidence that for Indigenous children in remote areas their outcomes are still not improving (Department of Education Western Australia 2016). The cultural shift that many Indigenous children need to make when starting school is well documented (Mason-White 2013; McTurk et al. 2008), and research suggests that low outcomes may reflect differences between the culture of the local families and the dominant culture of the school, rather than 'disadvantage' (Fleer and Williams-Kennedy 2002). Hence, it is important to consider cultural difference in relation to school readiness (Dockett et al. 2010; McTurk et al. 2008) and Early Years program implementation (Bowes and Grace 2014; Sims 2011; Wise 2013).

Like other Indigenous children in remote settings, Ngaanyatjarra children experience the child rearing practices of their family and culture (Hamilton 1981; Lohoar et al. 2014; Warrki Jarrinjaku Project 2002). These early experiences are the foundation for their future development within their culture, but provide little continuity with the learning and schooling of another culture. Within traditional Ngaanyatjarra culture, there is minimal need for printed material (Hamilton 1981; Kraal 2012), and literacy is not integral to adult success – economic or otherwise. Consequently, there is no reason for parents to embed reading and writing in 'the texture of daily life' and in the early experiences of their young children (Rogoff et al. 1998; Rogoff 2003).

Further, Ngaanyatjarra children's language is not the English language of schooling. There is strong evidence that children learn most successfully in their first language (UNESCO 1953; Ball 2011), and that a strong first language serves as a foundation for later learning (Baker and Hornberger 2001), including school literacy. However, the current reality for Ngaanyatjarra children is that, like many children from minority cultures around the world, they will grow up needing to learn, live and work in two languages and cultures, and their daily routines will increasingly relate to the practices of more than one community (Rogoff 2003). In particular, by the age of five they will be expected to adopt the language, behaviours and literacy practices of the Australian schooling system. This means that at school they will encounter the double challenge of learning both a new language and the 'new knowledge contained in that language' (Ball 2011, p. 13).

Research suggests a challenging 'yes...but...' scenario for Ngaanyatjarra children, both for going to school and learning literacy at school. We know that children's early experiences, structured within the cultural environment of the family, provide the foundation for later capabilities, but these experiences will only provide continuity for readiness at school for children of the same culture as that of the school. The literature also demonstrates that successful school literacy for children is built on early literary experiences within their family, but these experiences are also only available to children growing up in literate families within the western culture.

So, the question is, how can children who are not from the western culture, such as children from the Ngaanyatjarra families, where early years experiences around shared reading, books and story time routines are not part of their daily family life, gain these pre-requisite early experiences about books and literacy before going to school in the western culture at 5? This question is rarely asked – and the question is made even more complex when the young child's home language is different to the language of the school.

Rogoff (2003) explains that 'people develop as participants in cultural communities', through 'the cultural practices and circumstances of their communities – which also change' (Rogoff 2003, pp. 3–4, see Shonkoff and Phillips 2000). Western schooling is one of the most significant means of cultural change, and, where western schooling is a new addition to the local culture, Rogoff writes of the need to 'produce novel approaches' so that the community can participate together in developing the different practices that will be required (Rogoff 2003, p. 358).

It is in this space that the shared early literacy experiences of Family Story Time are situated. Within the Early Years program, in the context of their family and community practices, the hope is that Ngaanyatjarra children will learn and develop through the learning opportunities structured by their parents that will create some continuity with school and inform their later school literacy.

1995: Group Story Time Begins

The Early Years program began in 1995. Story time became a regular activity just 4 weeks into the new program, when Dorothy Hackett, one of the regional linguists, visited. She was well known by the families and offered to read a couple of children's storybooks that local community men and women had recently written in the Ngaanyatjarra language.

My journals take up the story:

Early March 1995: Dorothy read two of the Ngaanyatjarra big books to the mothers and children; mothers very interested; children don't know about looking at books. Anna looked at it because she was sitting on her mother's knee. Really good time though. Need to continue this reading, but I may have to read until the parents can read...

Mid March 1995: I read the story and Valerie talked about it with the children. Kathy came in and tried to read the pages and I read with her. We read two big books and the small 'Kamurltu' book – boys very interested in that one…. Need to develop story routine each day?

April 1995: Story time seems to be of great importance to the parents, hearing the stories in their own language, and we have them nearly every day…. Children talk about and point to various things in the pictures. The children are starting to want to look at the books for themselves and some are starting to imitate me pointing to words and saying them…

December 1995: When I read the stories, one or two of the women talk about the pictures and story on each page with the children after I've read the words.

It did not take long for Group Story Time to become a regular part of each day's program for the children and the families. The importance of relationships pervaded each entry in my journals. The families were learning within trusted relationships and the young children were learning within their family. The linguist's offer to add this new experience of storybooks to the program was warmly embraced, especially as the stories were in the home language of the families and were about experiences of their shared life. Similarly, the various ways that I supported the women in the actual task of reading was part of our working together towards the shared goal of enjoying Group Story Time with the children. Although my conversation skills in Ngaanyatjarra were limited, I could read the language fluently, and after the reading, the women talked about each page with the children.

The inclusion of the Group Story Time activity, within the Early Years program, became a daily activity within just 1 month. The journals suggest the importance of having an agreed place and time for such activities. Parents and family appropriated a teaching role by structuring the learning environment in a culturally coherent way and guiding students by 'talking about each page' of the books with the children as they read together. The parents' interest in the storybooks and the story time routines were quickly reflected in the growing interest of their young children, with the children soon 'starting to look at the books for themselves'.

Importantly, the journals recorded frequent observations of parents, family and children using home language, which suggest the value of having stories written in first language. The parents enjoyed these storybooks, hearing and watching them being read in their Ngaanyatjarra language. Following Dorothy's example, the parents and I continued to read books each day in Ngaanyatjarra to ensure the continuation of childrens' storybook experiences in home language. At this time, the community had also begun producing children's books in Ngaanyatjarra. These books became an integral part of the Early Years program.

By the end of the program's first year Group Story Time was firmly embedded in each day's routine. For the first time in this cultural group, we afforded the opportunity for very young children to get to know about books and stories in the context of their family and community life and in their home language, before they went to school. The children were beginning to develop early reading behaviours, such as focusing their gaze on the book and engaging in conversations around texts and relating texts to their personal experiences.

5 Family Story Time in the Ngaanyatjarra Early Years Program   79

Throughout 1996, Beryl and I worked together each day with the families and children. Towards the end of that year, the women were ready to look after the program themselves. At this time, I returned to my role as teacher of the Kindergarten year 2 class at the local school and provided mentoring for the women in the program as needed.

In 1997, my Kindy class comprised the six children who had experienced 2 years of the Early Years/playgroup program. These children were confident with the activities, skills, equipment and routines for school – including story time routines. They had a love of books and stories. During their first year at school, with the Principal also implementing a strong EAL program in the school, these 'playgroup graduates' thrived. Not only were these children ready for Kindergarten, but by the middle of that year, they were ahead of some of the Year 2 children in the class. They could write their names, recognise and write some familiar words, listen to story books being read and experience the pleasure of having 'book time' after morning recess each day.

At the end of 1997, my family and I moved away from the community, and for the next few years Beryl facilitated the program with the families until she moved to another community. Various agencies then assisted with the program's operations, both in the initial community and at other communities. In 2004/2005 I was travelling to and from these communities in a visiting role, and Beryl and I once again began talking and working together around the Early Years program.

2006–2009: Group Story Time Develops

In 2006, I returned to live in the community, and for the next few years Beryl and I travelled together facilitating the playgroup/Early Years programs across the communities, using the same model that was developed with the families in the mid-1990s. Community interest was high, so together we wrote a booklet for the families, which explained how to set up the program and described the purpose of each activity within the program. In the booklet, Beryl explained the importance of reading stories and having storybooks in their own language:

Each day at playgroup: Story telling using Ngaanyatjarra stories.

Why tell stories and read storybooks in Ngaanyatjarra? Because Ngaanyatjarra is important, and the children are listening to a story in their home language. Children use Ngaanyatjarra at home, at play and at playgroup, learning their language well while they are young. While they are listening to the story in their own language they learn good ways of speaking. When they go to school they will get another language – English at school. And then they have two languages'. (Jennings and Shinkfield 2006, p. 13)

The children and their families in the communities enjoyed the program and the activity of Group Story Time. At that time, we had a large set of Ngaanyatjarra children's storybooks, written and illustrated by local adults, which reflected local community activities and experiences.

In my journals I reflected on how these Group Story Time activities might grow:

Early 2008: What will be the next step in the development of print-literacy skills for these children and families? What will be the bridge from participating in the Group Ngaanyatjarra Story Time to the print rich environment of kindy in the foreign culture and language of English? Will they move to children's books in English? Will more local stories need to be written?

The next step turned out to be an increase in the number and diversity of stories written in Ngaanyatjarra. In 2009, the Indigenous Literacy Foundation (ILF) offered to support the development of children's early literacy within the program, by providing board books of classic children's stories such as 'Dear Zoo', 'Where's Spot?' and 'The Very Hungry Caterpillar'. Through discussions with the families, the local women decided to translate 16 of these stories into Ngaanyatjarra, as the importance of children learning in their home language and parents being empowered as the teachers of their children through using their home language was paramount to this community-initiated program. The translations were printed on stickers and added to the original books and the families and children continued their journey into books and literacy within the Group Story Time routine of the program.

2009: Family Story Time Emerges

As the children and parents' confidence, interest and familiarity with the story books increased, and with the greater collection of story books to enjoy in their home language, it quickly became apparent that listening to and watching a few stories being read to the whole group at Group Story Time just wasn't enough for these children. My journals from late 2009 to 2010 take up the story:

September 2009: During morning tea, Beryl read a Ngaanyatjarra story to the group and then she said that she had something else – she had a laminated a small Ngaanyatjarra story book for each mum to read/talk about the pictures with the children…They did this for about 10 minutes – really enjoying it…

Early February 2010: After playdough and hand washing, we put the coloured mats out and everyone sat down … giving each of the mums a laminated Ngaanyatjarra book for them to talk about the pictures with their children – or they could read it if they wanted to... It was great to see about 8 mums/carers talking over the books with their children …some of the children turning the pages too... decided that we wouldn't have a group story today and maybe use this new routine more often...

Early September 2010: The children and adults sat on the mats, looking at stories together – each day becomes a more positive time, with the children looking at the books and turning the pages, and the adults talking about each page with the child in their home language, even if they don't read it…Then morning tea was served and I read 'Dear Zoo – Yanamulpa Pirni..' to the whole group.

Mid September 2010: I read the 'Yultutjarra' story at Group Story Time today, as Trisha (aged 3) was pretending to read it to some children during their Family Story Time –

holding the book like you would for a group of children, pointing to the words and pictures, talking about each page, turning each page carefully – all in her language – it was quite amazing…

These journal reflections describe the significant change in the family practices around storybooks that emerged within the program. Story Time now began with Family Story Time, the shared parent/child experience of 'looking at books together' and was then followed by Group Story Time, the early literacy activity in which families and children had participated since 1995.

Knowing the children and families, and having participated with them in the program over the years, Beryl intuitively initiated this change within the routine at just the right time. Family Story time quickly became embedded into the program's Story Time routine, just as 15 years earlier, Group Story Time had initiated children's literacy experiences within the program. It was clear that this activity was meeting a growing interest of the children and families around books and reading. From the strong foundation of the established family practice of Group Story Time, the movement of the book sharing activities to 'within family' groups happened quite naturally. The families and children looked forward to this activity, and it had become a valued part of our daily routines, as the following excerpt from my journal shows:

> Mid February 2010: Then we had story time – we were sitting on the mats ready to hand out the story books to each family… Dale ran to find his nanna, calling out for her and pulling her by the hand to come to the mat to get a book. The mums talked to each other about how Dale didn't want to miss out on looking at the books with his nanna...

The parents actively encouraged the participation of their children each day in these shared storybook activities – 'talking about each page with the child in their home language' and 'looking at stories together'. Consequently, the growing confidence, interest and enjoyment of both parents and children during these Family Story time activities was evident. Having the books written in their home language was the essential foundation for all of the Story Time activities, as it helped to maintain the family and home language environment of the child.

2010–2017: Story Time Within Family and Community Practices

The Early Years program, and the Story Time routines within the program, continued to grow across the communities, and the place of children's storybooks in their home language began to spill over into home, school and community environments, as described in the following journal entries from 2015:

> In most community homes there aren't any children's story books. However, for the last three years, at a special event, each child has received a gift of their three favourite books from Story Time. These books seem to be treasured and last in the home, perhaps because the books are the child's favourites and they are in their Ngaanyatjarra language. School-aged

siblings have commented that they know and like these books because they had them in the early years' program a few years earlier.

In the school environment, sets of the translated books are given to the Kindy/junior primary class when the 'playgroup graduates' go to school. As the 'graduates' know these books well in their home language they are often keen to 'read' them by themselves or to share them with other children.

As the Ngaanyatjarra Early Years Program is gradually established for children and families in other communities, Story Time, a key part of the program, uses the same books and routines in each community. With the transient nature of many families, these familiar books and routines can be enjoyed within the program by children and families in many more locations.

Conclusion

We return to the question of how children who are not from a western culture, and for whom reading routines are not part of their daily family life, can gain the early experiences about books and literacy, which are desirable for school success. Four strong themes emerged through my journals that suggest the important foundations of the ongoing development of the Story Time activities within the program.

First, learning together within family and relationships were pivotal to the development of the Story Time routines discussed in this chapter. Both the Group Story time and Family Story time routines were consistent with learning collectively within family and community relationships, as it enabled the parents to bring the shared storybook activities into their own family interaction, alongside other families participating in these new activities at the same time. Parents, children and the facilitators collaboratively developed their understandings of book literacy. The parallel between Story Time and home practices helped to facilitate people's uptake of the program.

Second, activities that are valued require an agreed place, time and purpose within family and community life in order for them to become an integral part of a young child's daily experiences (Rogoff 2003). For example, the Early Years program had this 'time, place and purpose' agreement through the initial request of the families to develop a program to help them to get their own children ready for school. This program then created the conditions for the story time routines to develop and grow within the program, and eventually become part of the family practices and routines within the community. Through shared participation in regular story time activities within the program, we created a purpose for young children within their family and community life. Families involved in the program continued to develop their interest and expertise in sharing storybooks with their children in their own language, and there was increased awareness across the communities of the importance of introducing children to books and story time routines before they go to school.

Third, was the importance of acknowledging the role of parents and families as the first teachers of children. Parents willingly took on teaching roles as they facilitated their children's participation in the Group Story Time routines. Within the collectivist culture of the Ngaanyatjarra people, Group Story Time provided the opportunity for parents to model the activity of 'looking at books together' knowing that their children would learn through participation in these family activities (Hamilton 1981). Further, the parents showed confidence in adopting new routines as Family Story Time developed.

Finally, was the creation and use of storybooks written in the children's first language, Ngaanyatjarra. It is well documented that young children learn best in their home language (Baker and Hornberger 2001; Ball 2011). These enabled the children and parents to engage with the stories and the Story Time routines in meaningful ways. It is significant that the use of stories written in the home language is still foundational to Story Time today, with many of the original Ngaanyatjarra books still being enjoyed by the families and children in the program.

Over two decades, Story Time and the community Early Years program have become part of the changing experience of family and community life in the Ngaanyatjarra communities. Indeed, the experiences of Ngaanyatjarra children during the Story Time activities with their parents, in their home language, have much in common with the early literate experiences of children elsewhere (Bus et al. 1995; Farrant 2012; Heath 1983; Neumann 1996; Rogoff 2003).

Story Time therefore seems to fit the description of a 'novel approach' as described by Rogoff (2003), that is providing the starting point for this community to engage collaboratively and successfully with schooling practices.

2017 Postscript

At least 7 of these 1997 'playgroup graduates' are now bringing their own children to the programs across the Ngaanyatjarra communities. No one has to teach these parents how to share picture books with their children – they learnt when they were young themselves and now they are giving their children the same opportunities. These young parents enjoy family story time and are very keen on changing their role from the child of 1995 to being the enthusiastic parent for their child in 2017.

They are comfortable within the familiarity of their community-based program and ready to be the teachers for their children, using their home language. These young parents are bringing up their children in the strong family, linguistic and community context of their culture. However, because of their experiences when they were little children in the community, they also know that there is an identified place and time each day, in the company of families across the community, where they can share in activities with their children in their home language to prepare them for the activities of the additional culture of school.

References

Australian Curriculum Assessment and Reporting Authority. (2015). *NAPLAN achievement in reading, persuasive writing, language conventions and numeracy: National report for 2015*. Sydney: ACARA.

Australian Government Productivity Commission. (2016). *Overcoming indigenous disadvantage: Key indicators 2016*. Retrieved from http://www.pc.gov.au/search/overcoming-indigenous-disadvantage/2016/report-documents/oid-2016#overview

Baker, C., & Hornberger, N. H. (2001). *An introductory reader to the writings of Jim Cummins*. Clevedon: Multilingual Matters Ltd.

Ball, J. (2011). *Enhancing learning of children from diverse language backgrounds: Mother tongue-based bilingual or multilingual education in the early years*. Paper commissioned by the UNESCO education sector. Retrieved from http://www.unesco.org/ulis/cgi-bin/ulis.pl?catno=212270&set=0059E18A2B_3_142&gp=1&lin=1&ll=1

Barratt-Pugh, C., & Rohl, M. (2015). 'Better beginnings has made me make reading part of our everyday routine': Mother's perceptions of a family literacy program over four years. *Australian Journal of Early Childhood, 40*(4), 4–12.

Bowes, J., & Grace, R. (2014). *Review of early childhood parenting, education and health intervention programs for indigenous children and families in Australia* (Closing the gap clearing house issues paper No 8). Canberra: Australian Institute of Health and Welfare; Melbourne: Australian Institute of Family Studies.

Bus, A. G., Van Ijzendoorn, M. H., & Pellegrini, A. D. (1995). Joint book reading makes for success in learning to read: A meta-analysis on intergenerational transmission of literacy. *Review of Educational Research, 65*(1), 1–22.

Clandinin, D. J. (2006). Narrative inquiry: A methodology for studying lived experience. *Research Studies in Music Education, 27*, 44–53.

Clandinin, D. J., & Connelly, F. M. (2000). *Narrative Inquiry: Experience and story in qualitative research*. San Francisco: Jossey-Bass.

Clandinin, D. J., & Rosiek, J. (2007). Mapping a landscape of narrative inquiry: Borderland spaces and tensions. In D. J. Clandinin (Ed.), *Handbook of narrative inquiry: Mapping a methodology*. Thousand Oaks: Sage.

COAG Council of Australian Governments. (2009). *Investing in the early years – A National early childhood development strategy*. Canberra: Commonwealth of Australia.

Department of Education Western Australia. (2016). *Early childhood development in Western Australia: Australian early development census. State report: Western Australia 2015*. Perth: Commonwealth of Australia and WA Department of Education.

Department of Prime Minister and Cabinet. (2016). *Closing the gap: Prime minister's report 2016*. Retrieved from http://closingthegap.dpmc.gov.au

Dockett, S., Perry, B., & Kearney, E. (2010). *School readiness: What does it mean for indigenous children, families, schools and communities?* (Issues paper no. 2 prepared for the closing the gap clearinghouse). Canberra: Australian Institute of Health and Welfare; Melbourne: Australian Institute of Family Studies.

Farrant, B. M. (2012). Joint attention and parent-child book reading: Keys to help close gaps in early language, development, school readiness and academic achievement. *Family Matters, AIFS, 91*, 38–46.

Fleer, M., & Williams-Kennedy, D. (2002). *Building bridges: Literacy development in young indigenous children*. Watson: Australian Early Childhood Association Inc.

Hamilton, A. (1981). *Nature and nurture. Aboriginal child-rearing in North-Central Arnhem Land*. Canberra: Australian Institute of Aboriginal Studies.

Harrison, L. J., Goldfeld, S., Metcalfe, E., & Moore, T. (2012). *Early learning programs that promote children's developmental and educational outcomes* (Resource sheet no 15. Produced for the closing the gap clearinghouse). Canberra/Melbourne: Australian Institute of Health and Welfare/Australian Institute of Family Studies.

Heath, S. B. (1982). What no bedtime story means: Narrative skills at home and at school. *Language in Society, 11*(1), 49–76.

Heath, S. B. (1983). *Ways with Words: Language, life and work in communities and classrooms.* Cambridge, MA: Harvard University Press.

Heckman, J. J. (2008). *Schools, skills and synapses* (Working Paper 14064). Retrieved from http://www.nber.org/papers/w14064

Heckman, J. J., & Masterov, D. V. (2007). *The productivity argument for investing in young children.* Paper presented at the Allied Social Sciences Association annual meeting, Chicago, IL, USA.

Jennings, B., & Shinkfield, A. (2006). *Playgroups: Playing to get ready for school.* Retrieved from www.shinkfield.net/playgroup.html

Knudsen, E. I., Heckman, J. J., Cameron, J. L., & Shonkoff, J. P. (2006). *Economic, neurobiological and behavioral perspectives on building America's future workforce.* Paper presented at the National Academy of Sciences 103, Cambridge, MA, USA.

Kraal, I. (2012). *Talk, text and technology: Literacy and social practice in a remote indigenous community.* Bristol: Multilingual Matters.

Lohoar, S., Butera, N., & Kennedy, E. (2014). *Strengths of Australian aboriginal cultural practices in family life and child rearing* (Child family community Australia paper no. 25). Melbourne: Australian Institute of Family Studies.

Mason-White, H. (2013). *Supporting transition to school for aboriginal and Torres Strait Islander children: What it means and what works.* Melbourne: SNAICC.

McCain, M., & Mustard, J. F. (1999). *Reversing the real brain drain: Early years study final report.* Ontario: Ministry of Children and Youth Services.

McTurk, N., Nutton, G., Lea, T., Robinson, G., & Carapetis, J. (2008). *The school readiness of Australian indigenous children: A review of the literature.* Darwin: Menzies School of Health Research and School for Social Policy Research, Charles Darwin University.

Mildon, R., & Polimeni, M. (2012). *Parenting in the early years: Effectiveness of parenting education and home visiting programs for Indigenous families* (Resource sheet no. 16. Produced for closing the gap clearinghouse). Canberra/Melbourne: Australian Institute of Health and Welfare/Australian Institute of Family Studies.

Neumann, S. B. (1996). Children engaging in story book reading: The influence of access to print resources, opportunity and parental interaction. *Early Childhood Research Quarterly, 11,* 495–513.

Richardson, L., & St. Pierre, E. A. (2005). Writing: A method of inquiry. In N. K. Denzin & Y. S. Lincoln (Eds.), *The Sage handbook of qualitative research* (pp. 959–978). Thousand Oaks: Sage.

Riessman, C. K. (2008). *Narrative methods for the human sciences.* Thousand Oaks: Sage.

Rogoff, B. (2003). *The cultural nature of human development.* New York: Oxford University Press.

Rogoff, B., Mosier, C., Mistry, J., & Goncu, A. (1998). Toddlers guided participation with their caregivers in cultural activity. In M. Woodhead, D. Faulkner, & K. Littleton (Eds.), *Cultural worlds of early childhood* (pp. 225–249). London: Open University Press.

Senechal, M., & LeFevre, J. A. (2002). Parental involvement in the development of children' reading skill: A five-year longitudinal study. *Child Development, 73,* 445–460.

Shonkoff, J., & Phillips, D. (Eds.). (2000). *From neurons to neighbourhoods: The science of early childhood development.* Washington, DC: National Academy Press.

Sims, M. (2011). *Early childhood and education services for indigenous children prior to starting school* (Closing the gap clearinghouse resource sheet no. 7). Canberra/Melbourne: Australian Institute of Health and Welfare/Australian Institute of Family Studies.

UNESCO. (1953). *The use of vernacular languages in education* (Monographs of Fundamental Education, 8). Retrieved from: http://unesdoc.unesco.org/images/0000/000028/002897EB.pdf

Warrki Jarrinjaku ACRS Project Team. (2002). *Warrki Jarrinjaku Jintangkanmanu Purananjaku "Working together everyone and listening". Aboriginal child rearing & associated research: A review of the literature.* Canberra: The Commonwealth Department of Family and Community Services.

Whitehurst, G. J., Falco, F. L., Lonigan, C. J., Fischell, J. E., deBaryshe, B. D., Valdes-Menchaca, M. C., & Caulfield, M. (1988). Accelerating language development through picture book reading. *Developmental Psychology, 24*(4), 552–555.

Whitehurst, G. J., Arnold, D. S., Epstein, J. N., Angell, A. L., Smith, M., & Fischel, J. E. (1994). A picture book intervention in day care and home for children from low-income families. *Developmental Psychology, 30I*(5), 679–689.

Wise, S. (2013). *Improving the early life outcomes of Indigenous children: Implementing early childhood development at the local level* (Issues paper no. 6. Closing the gap clearinghouse). Canberra/Melbourne: Australian Institute of Health and Welfare/Australian Institute of Family Studies.

Anne Shinkfield has worked in the Indigenous communities of the Ngaanyatjarra Lands for many years. With a background in education and training, and years of living in the communities with her family, Anne is keen to enable all parents give their children the best start for life and schooling.

Beryl Jennings is an Indigenous Wongi woman who has lived in the Ngaanyatjarra Lands since 1970. Working in the Early Years program, Beryl has been committed to parents being the teachers of their young children, using their home language. Beryl frequently says that 'children are the future of our community'.

Chapter 6
Confessions from a Reading Program: Building Connections, Competence and Confidence

Jennifer Rennie

Abstract As students move from primary school into their high school years there is an expectation that they can read. Coupled with this expectation are the increasing complex demands that are placed on them as readers. The challenges facing these adolescent readers are many and varied. In this chapter I describe those challenges and report on one case study of an Indigenous reader from a regional school in Queensland who participated in a program designed to improve the reading outcomes of a group of Indigenous students, all of whom were assessed as being from 12 months to 4 years behind their peers in reading comprehension. In the research reported on here in addition to developing various strategies and skills to help these students improve their reading performance there was also work done to build relationships, re-connect these students with the practice of reading, build confidence and help them to understand what it looks like to effectively participate in the discourse of school reading experiences. Through a careful analysis of the discourse in a reading event with one student, I demonstrate the principles that underpin this work, why it requires careful thought and why it is paramount to improving the reading competence of these students.

Introduction

As students move from primary school into their secondary years, there is a growing expectation they can already read. In secondary school, students are required to read increasingly complex texts in the various disciplines, which deal with new and difficult concepts and contain many technical words and sophisticated grammatical constructions that are uncommon in everyday conversation (Cummins 2007; Moje et al. 2000; Whithear 2009). The emphasis on reading to learn in secondary school (in contrast to learning to read in primary years) means that reading support is rarely provided (Shanahan and Shanahan 2012). Students who continue to struggle with

---

J. Rennie (✉)
Monash University, Melbourne, VIC, Australia
e-mail: jennifer.rennie@monash.edu

© Springer Nature Singapore Pte Ltd. 2019
J. Rennie, H. Harper (eds.), *Literacy Education and Indigenous Australians*,
Language Policy 19, https://doi.org/10.1007/978-981-13-8629-9_6

their reading in the secondary years find it almost impossible to cope with the demands placed on them as readers. This was the case for the readers in the study reported on here, which focuses on one Indigenous reader, Millie. Over a period of 12 months, Millie was 1 of a group of 12 students (6 Indigenous and 6 non-Indigenous) who received reading assistance from me and from Lei, an Indigenous teacher working in the school at the time. The reading assistance provided to the students aimed to reconnect them with reading and build their confidence through a program based on understanding and connecting to students' interests, experiences and reading histories with enough scaffolding and support so they felt competent (Rennie 2016). In this chapter, I describe the key ideas that were foundational to the development of this program through an analysis of one reading event with Millie.

Setting the Scene

As discussed in the Introduction to this volume, there has been a number of inquiries at state, territory and Commonwealth levels addressing the gap in literacy outcomes between Indigenous and non-Indigenous school-aged children since the 1970s. Despite a range of initiatives to address this gap, as has been stated elsewhere in this volume, there have only been small improvements in reading literacy according to the National Assessment Program Literacy and Numeracy (NAPLAN). In 2008, 70.7% of Indigenous Year 9 students were at or above national minimum standard compared to 94.2% of non-Indigenous students. In 2016, 73.6% of Indigenous students compared to 94.0% of non-Indigenous students were at or above the minimum national standard (ACARA 2016).

There have been a number of explanations put forward in relation to the gap between the literacy outcomes of Indigenous and non-Indigenous students. Distal factors such as poor school attendance, teacher shortages in remote areas, adequate teaching skills, poverty and the disconnect between Western school systems and Indigenous community life have all been suggested as possible contributing factors (Mellor and Corrigan 2004; Prior 2013; Rennie and Patterson 2010; Purdie et al. 2011; Rennie 2006). In 2010 the Australian Council of Educational Research conducted a study that tracked the literacy and numeracy development of a group of Indigenous students from 13 schools across Australia from sites that had been nominated as demonstrating 'good practice' in terms of Indigenous education. The study found that effective school leadership, parental involvement, access to professional development and good teaching characterised by high expectations, positive relationships, meeting individual student's needs and provision of targeted intervention when required all contributed to positive learning experiences (Purdie et al. 2011, p. 72). In addition to identifying a range of factors that characterised effective practice, the study also reported that whilst Indigenous students generally continued to improve their literacy skills throughout primary school, the gap that existed between

Indigenous and non-Indigenous students at the beginning of Year 3 remained relatively consistent until the final year of primary school (Purdie et al. 2011). The study pointed the need for early intervention and 'quality preschool education' to lay strong foundations for achievement in the later years of school. However, focussing on the early years does little to address the large numbers of Indigenous students who continue to enter high school with reading literacy achievement that is well below their non-Indigenous peers.

There is a growing number of secondary students (Indigenous and non-Indigenous) who need assistance with reading and writing more generally. As has been reported in other chapters, there have been a number of whole school approaches to the teaching of literacy adopted in various primary schools including Accelerated Literacy, MULTILIT and Direct Instruction to name but a few. What has been largely lacking are programs designed specifically for students who struggle with literacy in the secondary school. In *Beyond the Middle*, which reported on a study investigating the perceived efficacy of middle years programs in improving the quality of teaching, learning and student outcomes in literacy and numeracy, Luke et al. (2003) found that many of the 23 secondary schools observed in this study took a 'whatever is available' approach in relation to literacy frameworks and assessment practices. Specific initiatives put in place to assist students who were struggling with reading and writing were at best ad hoc, based on 'deficit' or 'remedial approaches', and were not aligned to the pedagogies of the mainstream classroom. In addition, the schools drew from relatively outdated education materials not designed for adolescent learners. The program discussed in this chapter was developed with the specific needs of these learners in mind.

The Study

The research took a sociocultural view of reading which defines reading as a socially, culturally and historically located practice where readers engage in a range of other practices in addition to decoding as they engage with and make meaning from texts (Bloome 1985; Gee 1996; Heap 1991: Heath 1983; Luke and Freebody 1997; Street 1993). Readers not only need to decode texts using various cognitive skills and strategies, but they also need to make sense of what they read. This involves an understanding of the context of what is being read and how this relates to other things readers know and have experienced. Reading is something that is done for particular purposes, and reading-in-school is a particular kind of reading practice (Rennie and Patterson 2010). Instructional reading practices in school are collaborative and involve complex interactions that occur between the reader, the teacher and the text (Patterson et al. 2012; Ruddell and Unrau 2013).

At the time of this study, participating students were in their first year of a regional Australian secondary school (Year 8). Students were previously assessed as

1 to 4 years behind in their reading age as shown through reading tests of accuracy, comprehension and fluency (Neale 1997). All of the students reported receiving reading assistance throughout their schooling, and all described being with groups of other readers who found reading difficult. Given the students had been struggling with the task of reading for an extended period of time, their reading histories were complex. Research suggests that it is not uncommon for students who present as struggling in the early years of school to continue to struggle throughout their schooling despite being afforded reading assistance (Brozo and Simpson 2007; Sanacore and Palumbo 2009). The reading assistance these students described was highly variable. It ranged from having an adult listen to them read and helping them to decode unknown words to participating in programs such as Reading Recovery, a program designed to develop decoding strategies and comprehension (Clay 1982). This assistance invariably occurred outside of the classroom using texts that were below their level of maturity. Historically, many reading programs have tended to focus on the mechanics of reading and are grounded in cognitive theories of skill acquisition (Allington 1998). Whilst these programs may help in improving various skills associated with reading, they tend to ignore the importance of the social and cultural contexts in which reading occurs.

The program discussed was designed with the reading identities and histories of these young people in mind. Lei (pseudonym), an Indigenous teacher, worked with me to help design, implement and refine the reading program over a 12-month period. I worked with Lei on-site at the beginning, middle and end of the study for a total of 6 weeks. In my absence, she continued the program working with each student two or three times per week.

Lei and I held a series of discussions prior to working with them. During these discussions, we worked to gain a sense of who these readers were. We wanted to understand their personal interests, their reading habits, how they described themselves as readers and their prior experiences of reading both in and out of school. Following the interview we also administered the 'Motivations for Reading Questionnaire' (Wigfield and Guthrie 1997), a student-rated assessment that measures the extent to which each student is motivated to read. Finally, students were tested in terms of their reading rate, comprehension and fluency (Neale 1997). We found that all of these students struggled with many aspects of their reading including monitoring comprehension, vocabulary and reading fluency. We also found that the students generally lacked confidence in their abilities as readers and that most had given up on the task around Year 4. In short, they had made the decision not to read and developed a number of reading avoidance behaviours. With this in mind, we knew that we had to reconnect these students with reading and work on developing both their confidence and competence. We also both knew that building and developing positive relationships with these students would be fundamental to working successfully with these readers.

In the following sections, I will outline some of the principles that underpinned the program: first, the importance of relationship work; second, making connections to students' experiences and interests; and third, the need to develop confidence in order to improve readers' competence.

Laying the Foundation: Building Relationships

Establishing, building and maintaining relationships was at the core of the thinking in the design of this program. Research talks about the importance of relationship work with Indigenous students, families and communities (see for example, Santoro et al. 2011). Of particular significance in this study was the inclusion of the Indigenous teacher, Lei. In the post-program interviews, students commented that Lei made an effort to get to know them and their families and that their families 'trusted her'. One student talked about the fact that having 'anyone' do this work would be a 'bit weird because they don't know about us'. Finally, they all said this aspect of the program made them feel 'comfortable'. The students in this study were confident that their teacher 'knew who they were'. There was a real sense that part of the success of this program was the knowledge and understanding that Lei brought to the program in terms of these student's social and cultural worlds and in the careful relationship work that she did with the students and their families. In this paper, it is argued that relationship work is necessary, foundational, ongoing and pivotal to the success of other pedagogical work such as making connections, building confidence and achieving competence.

Making Connections

Taking a sociocultural view, learning is enhanced when we acknowledge, respect and respond to the various cultural, socio-economic and historical contexts of learners (Boon and Lewthwaite 2016). Making connections to students' lifeworlds and experiences has long been seen as a means to help students to access the mandated curriculum (Moll et al. 1992). Moll et al. (1992) talk about funds of knowledge which are 'historically accumulated and culturally developed bodies of knowledge and skills essential for household or individual functioning and well-being' (p. 133). These funds of knowledge result from people's lived experiences through their social, cultural and working lives. Skilled teachers traditionally recognise and use these family and community resources for teaching as a means to bridge the gap between curriculum knowledge and students' lives. Whilst much of the earlier work in this area tended to focus on the lives of adults, in recent years, there has been more of an interest in children's social worlds at home, school and community and in cyber space (Subero et al. 2017). Subero et al. talk about 'funds of identity', a concept based on the premise that we not only accumulate these households 'funds of knowledge' but that we also partake in a number of life experiences that help to shape and reshape us as individuals. They define 'funds of identity' as 'significant people, institutions, cultural artefacts, geographical spaces and meaningful practices, passions and interests encrusted in a learner's self-definition' (Subero et al. 2017, p. 253). Some suggest that we can enhance the academic achievement of students from diverse groups if we utilise, and build upon, the knowledge, skills and languages they acquire in the informal learning environments of their homes and communities (Moll and González 2004). Llopart and Esteban-Guitart propose the principle of contextualisation as an effective pedagogy for working with diverse learners. This principle states that:

> (a) Academic content should be integrated with other knowledge that the children assimilate in the home, school and community; (b) learners need to be guided and supported so that they can make connections between their personal experiences and previous knowledge, and the knowledge or concepts acquired at school; and (c) learners need to be helped to fully understand academic content through solid personal connections. (Llopart and Esteban-Guitart 2017, p. 256)

Making these connections though is not simply about using topics that might interest students. It is also about understanding the skills and strategies students use and knowing what students know in terms of the knowledge and concepts required at school.

Confidence and Competence

The readers in this study had experienced many years of perceived reading failure. This led to a steady decline in their confidence as was evidenced through their interviews and how they responded to the various questions in the 'Motivations for Reading Questionnaire' (Wigfield and Guthrie 1997). Alvermann (2001) suggests that reading identities are decided for students via the various reading practices they participate in at school. School reading practices help students to understand what reading is and to construct how they might define themselves as readers (Rennie 2004, 2016). These students reported routinely being in groups with like-readers who found reading difficult. They talked about the fact that they were given books that were 'babyish' and well below their level of maturity. They discussed having difficulty with various skills such as 'sounding out', not being to read 'quickly' and about not 'knowing words'. The reading practices these students participated in throughout their schooling were predominantly about learning to read rather than reading to learn. In the first year of high school, these students still self-identified as 'learner readers'. Further, they found themselves in a context where 'learning to read' help was not provided.

I now introduce you to Millie, one of the students who participated in this study, and present an analysis of a 40-min reading session with Millie, to explicate some of the design principles of the program.

Meet Millie

As mentioned earlier, understanding who these students were both in and out-of-school was important in relation to making connections, establishing common knowledge, building confidence and ultimately their achieving competence. Prior to doing any reading work with students, we held discussions with them individually and as a group to help us gain a sense of who they were as 'readers'.

At the time of this study, Millie was a 12-year-old Indigenous student in Year 8 in a regional area in Australia. Millie loved to play sports, in particular rugby league. She told us how she had travelled to other Australian cities to play rugby and that she was in awe of the Indigenous Women's All Stars football team.

Millie described herself as a reader who had always struggled. She talked about receiving assistance throughout primary school and said that her previous teacher put students into groups based on ability for both spelling and reading. Millie explained that there were four groups and that she was in the lowest one. Millie described this reading practice in the following way:

> The smart group would have like eight in it, six in the next group, like four in the next group and there was like five of us in our group and we were all reading the same thing. Miss would sit there and she would read the first paragraph. Then the next person would read the next paragraph. And just go round the big circle. And we used to read about like true stories on Alaska and stuff, like all the ice and stuff.

Millie had difficulty remembering books that she had read for pleasure. However, she did recall reading a book from the Zac Power series (Larry, 2009–2010), chapter books that are specifically designed for lower readers with large print and fewer word counts. She did not enjoy these books. She said she liked Harry Potter books. Her Nan's neighbour, who is a teacher, had all the Harry Potter books, and she could borrow the last two, which she had not yet read. She described JK Rowling as her favourite author and an author whose 'mind was outside the box…she comes out with all these really good ideas. She lets her thinking go.' Millie said she had read the first two books in the series and was looking forward to reading the third, *Harry Potter and the Prisoner of Azkaban* (Rowling 1999). The most recent book she recalled was one they were studying in their English called *Nanberry: Black Brother White*, by Jackie French.

When asked to discuss the things that gave her most trouble with her reading, Millie talked about the fact that she was not very confident and that when she read chapter books, as they were expected to do in high school, she found it difficult to figure out what the book 'was actually about', particularly 'in the first few pages'. The other issue she identified was her lack of vocabulary knowledge. She explained:

> I have trouble with the words. I put the book down, take a deep breath and pick it up again. I'll be reading and it really annoys me cause I don't know the word. Like I'll be reading and then I don't know the word. And I go 'Come on, just figure it out!' And then I start guessing and when I guess it … and then I keep reading, I go 'No, that's not it' and I have to go back to it and keep reading and try again.

Later in our discussion, Millie talked about the fact that her mother felt it was important she learn about her culture. She talked about her clan group and said that she liked 'stories about the Dreamtime and stolen generation and stuff cause it like it gets me a lot more in my culture and my heritage.' She also talked about a number of added responsibilities in the home context such as looking after her siblings due to her mother's work commitments.

94   J. Rennie

Millie was tested for reading accuracy, fluency and reading comprehension (Neale 1997). In reading accuracy, she was 1 year and 6 months below her age level; in reading fluency, she was 4 years and 1 month below her age; and in reading comprehension, she was 1 year and 5 months below her age. Similarly, in 'Progressive Achievement Tests in Reading' (ACER) in a Level 7 test aimed at Year 7 students, she scored a stanine of 2 and was in the fifth percentile which meant she was in the low range compared to her peers. A stanine of 4, 5 or 6 is considered average. Like the other students in this study, Millie also completed the 'Motivations for Reading Questionnaire', a student-rated assessment that measures the extent to which each student is motivated to read (Wigfield and Guthrie 1997). The questionnaire comprised 53 questions designed to reflect 11 different constructs of reading using a Likert scale from 1 to 4 with 1 meaning 'very different to me', 3 meaning a' little different to me', 2 meaning 'a little like me' and 4 meaning 'a lot like me'. Wigfield and Guthrie (1997) reported the reliabilities for all the aspects of the 53-item MRQ ranging from 0.43 to 0.81 (Guthrie 2010). Amongst other things, this revealed that on items that measured the construct of reading efficacy, Millie was low, scoring 1.6 out of 5, and that on items that measured the construct reading avoidance behaviours, she scored high with 4 out of 5. Generally, the results of this testing were commensurate with her other various reading tests and the ways in which she presented and talked about herself as a reader.

With this information in mind, we found an article on the Internet that reported on a successful rugby league game played by the Women's All Stars (Australian Womens Rugby League 2011). The article was 689 words in length and contained some unfamiliar vocabulary. The article was one that a lower secondary student would be able to read with some assistance. The following section analyses the 40-min reading session with Millie.

Pre-reading: Connections, Confidence and Competence

Understanding who these students were, both in and out of school, was important in relation to making connections, building confidence and ultimately their achieving competence as readers. At the beginning of the reading session, I wanted to help Millie connect to the reading we were about to work with. I wanted to understand what she knew about the Indigenous Women's All Stars and the game of rugby more generally.

Transcript 6.1: My Coach 'She's Awesome'

1   R: Tell me what you know about the Women's All Stars.
2   M: My coach plays in it.
3   R: Ah your coach she played for them?
4   M: Yeah
5   R: Do you ever watch them play?

6	M:	Yeah I've watched them play a few times.
7	R:	Yeah
8	M:	Yeah
9	R:	Is your coach good?=
10	M:	=Yes she's awesome
11	R:	Is she?
12	M:	Yes. She don't take no crap from nobody. She just runs at them.
13	R:	She runs at them.
14	M:	Yeah she hits them.
15	R:	Do you take crap from anyone?
16	M:	No not when I play.

In this excerpt from the data, Millie made the connection between her coach and her knowledge of the Indigenous Women's All Stars' team. She explained that she had seen the team 'play a few times' (Line 6) and said how her coach who plays for the team was 'awesome' (Line 10). She then proceeded to tell me how she, also like her coach, isn't deterred by other players (Line 16). In the beginning of the conversation, a link was established between what Millie knew and had experienced and the reading she was about to begin. Further, Millie was given the opportunity to position herself as an expert in relation to what was being discussed. She knew someone who played for this team, and more importantly this person was her coach. Following on from the discussion where she makes the point of saying how 'brave' her coach is, I asked her a question about tackling in women's rugby as a means to give her the opportunity to tell me more about the game.

Transcript 6.2: It's Hard

23	R:	=Do you tackle in women's rugby?
24	M:	Yeah. You have the hooker. It's hard.
25	R:	So what does a hooker do?
26	M:	Hooker. It's like. It's like. You get tackled and you have to play the ball and the
27		hooker picks up and passes to half back ((moves hands like passing a ball))=
28	R:	=Ah=
29	M:	=You pass it to half back and half back passes it to whoever is next to them=
30	R:	=Oh ok=
31	M:	=It can be first row, second row, um or five eight or anyone like that ((demonstrating their positions on the desk by drawing with her hands))

In response to my question, she told me that 'yes' you do tackle in the game and then proceeded to explain the role of the 'hooker' in this tackling process. What was interesting in this whole excerpt and many others during the reading session was how Millie used gesture (Line 27) and drawing on the desk (Line 32) to help me to understand. Through this multimodal explanation, there was a real sense that she was reliving the experience as she explained the different moves of the game.

In the remainder of the pre-reading discussion, Millie talked about her training schedule and about a previous and upcoming trip, her team had to Brisbane.

Transcript 6.3: Playing with the Dolphins

37	M:	=yeah we go away in October for a real big one=
38	R:	That's right Brisbane.
39	M:	Yeah Brissie and Toowoomba=
40	R:	=Toowoomba=
41	M:	=Yeah it's good=
42	R:	=Have you done that before?=
43	M:	=Yeah last year but the year before we went away I think it was in October but
44		we went away for the Brisbane one. It was under 14s that was my one that I
45		got to go into. Like we went away and played at the Dolphins. Do you know
46		Redcliffe?
47	R:	Yeah yes I know where that is=
48	M:	=The Dolphins place that's where we played. It was good. It was good fun.

In Transcript 6.3, Millie was excited to tell me about her interstate trip in October to play a match which was obviously of great importance as it is 'a real big one' (Line 37). In this excerpt, Millie came across as being very articulate. She was very precise and explicit about the information she gave me and also felt comfortable to check for shared understanding (Line 45) demonstrating that she was attentive towards the listener.

Further on in the conversation, I wanted also to understand what she felt made a good women's rugby league player as the text we were about to read made reference to the importance of 'passion, team work and determination'. From a pedagogical point of view, I felt this would further assist Millie to connect to the text we were about to read.

Transcript 6.4: 'Talk Is the Key'

49	R:	So what do you think makes a good rugby league player?
50	M:	You've got to run with all your heart=
51	R:	=run with all your heart. What does that mean?
52	M:	Like you got to put all your effort into the game that you are playing. You can't
53		be side-tracked or anything. And um you have to commit to the game.
54	R:	Mm

55	M:	And=
56	R:	=sounds like you'd be a good coach=
57	M:	=Yeah ((Laughs)) you got to commit to the game and you kind of like (.) you got
58		to talk lots on the field=
59	R:	=talk=
60	M:	=talk=
61	R:	=so how does that work?
62	M:	Talk is the key. If you talk talk about the game and like where there are holes
63		((demonstrates by drawing with her hands on the desk)) and you'll get through.
64		You'll score a try.

Millie's passion, enthusiasm and knowledge about the game were very evident in this short excerpt. Like Millie, who sought clarification from *me* in the previous example at Line 52, in this excerpt, I asked her to clarify what she meant by 'run with all your heart' to ensure I had a shared understanding of the meaning being conveyed. She made the point of repeating and giving greater emphasis to words such as 'commit' and 'talk' (Lines 53 and 62). She also used gestures to help me understand the concept of finding the 'holes' in the play on the desk. Millie was confident and clearly the expert during this exchange. In the entire opening discussion that lasted for approximately 8 min, I deliberately posed questions that I was confident she would be able to respond to and in doing so tried to position Millie as the expert in this space. Her confidence to respond, provide animated descriptions to my questions and lead the discussion in parts clearly showed that she felt competent and comfortable in this space.

Setting Up for Success: Connections, Confidence and Competence

In the next phase of the reading session, I read the rugby league passage to Millie, initiated a discussion around the reading to help her understand unfamiliar vocabulary and grammatical constructions and discussed some of the main ideas in the text. The purpose of these discussions was to continue to develop the relationship with Millie, to make further connections to her experiences and knowledge through the explanation of new and difficult vocabulary, to establish shared understandings around the meanings in the text, to develop her confidence and to set her up for success so that she might develop competence to read the text independently.

When I explained to Millie that we were going to read the text in front of us, she was taken aback by its length, and I had to reassure her she would be able to do this. I began to read the passage to Millie stopping at several points to ask questions as a means to check that she was continuing to make some personal connections to the text as the following excerpt from the data show.

Transcript 6.5: 'Do You Know Her?'

86		With halves kept to twenty minutes the pace of the game was expected to be
87		fast and not surprisingly the first points were scored after just three and half
88		minutes when NRL Women's All Stars centre Lisa Fiola.... Lisa Fiola do you know
89		her? =
90	M:	=Um Mum's talked about her but I don't know her in person=

After I had finished the reading, I asked Millie some general questions about bigger ideas that had been explored throughout the text. For example, we talked about women in sport more generally and how it is represented and reported on in the media. Millie felt that women's sport should receive the same coverage as men, since women can play as 'good a game as the men'. Following this more general discussion, we worked our way through the text discussing vocabulary and ideas to check for understanding. I deliberately chose both parts I felt she would be able to explain and parts that she would find more challenging. I wanted her to both feel confident of her knowledge about what was in the text and to also learn vocabulary that might be new to her. I also wanted to give Millie the opportunity to teach me more about the game so that she could further demonstrate her knowledge and expertise.

Transcript 6.6: Solid Defence

161	R:	OK so let's have a look at this. See in the third paragraph it says,
162		'solid defence from the Indigenous All Stars'. What does that mean?
163	M:	Running up a ( ) line ((uses two fingers to imitate running on the desk))
164	R:	OK
165	M:	Altogether
166	R:	Uh huh
167	M:	And to ( ) tackle
168	R:	OK
169	M:	Um (2) and if they need help like go in and like just hit just like grab them and
170		put them to the ground ((pointing to the desk again)).

Millie's response to my question about what 'solid defence' might mean (Line 162) shows her again demonstrating her deep understanding by providing a specific example of how this might look in a game of rugby. This is something she had obviously experienced whilst playing. In this example, it was clear that Millie's personal

6   Confessions from a Reading Program: Building Connections, Competence…   99

connections to playing rugby helped her to understand and make connections to the meanings in the text.

Transcript 6.7: 'You Need to Help Me Out Here'

171	R:	So if I go to the next paragraph ((points to her page then points to the place on
172		M's page)) You need to help me out here because I don't really know
173		the game that well. So when it says they took advantage of the scrum feed to
174		break the Indigenous All Star's defensive line and find good position. What does
175		that mean?
176	M:	A scrum feed is where like they all like ((puts fingers on both hands to form a
177		circle)) bundle up and like a big thing and then say that the half back all be there
178		and roll it through someone's legs ((tries to show action using hands)) gets out
179		the back and they'll pass it and as it says there ((points to place in text)) they
180		took advantage of the scrum feed ( ) good position. So they might have passed it
181		out to a centre or a wing.
182	R:	So that put them in a better position?
183	M:	Yeah, put them in a way better position because they might not been able to get
184		there fast enough

In Transcript 6.7, I asked Millie a genuine question about the text (Lines 171 and 172) to help with my own understanding of the game which was quite limited. In doing so, I was also able to determine whether Millie had understood this part of the text. Millie began by explaining to me what a 'scrum feed' was (Lines 176–178). Again, she used both words and gestures to do this through a specific example of how it might look in a game (Lines 176–181). During her explanation she also pointed back to the text to show me how her explanation was connected to the meanings in the text and my original question (Line 179) and then read from the text 'they took advantage from the scrum feed…good position' (Lines 179–180). This was evidence that she was clearly engaged in the reading process at this time and focused on the question I had asked her. It was interesting how she was able to move effortlessly between her own experiences and the ideas in the text. I then sought clarification after her explanation (Line 182) to ensure that we had a shared understanding of what she had demonstrated and explained. She said, 'Yeah, put them in a better position because they might not have been able to get there fast enough' (Lines 183–184).

100   J. Rennie

Similar to Transcript 6.6, Millie's knowledge and experiences of playing rugby
helped her to make sense of the meanings in the text, and in this exchange similar to
others, she was strongly and respectfully positioned as the expert in this space.

Transcript 6.8: 'Dogs Are Hard Headed Right'

199	R:	We'll just talk about a few more things. See ((points to text)). 'Solid defence in
200		the second half by the NRL Women's All Stars kept the Indigenous All Stars from
201		scoring despite their <u>dogged</u> determination'. What do you think that means?
202	M:	Dogged determination might mean you know, dogs are hard headed right
203	R:	Yes ((laughs))
204	M:	What they want goes, so they (2)
205	R:	A bit like a bull dog yeah
206	M:	Yeah
207	R:	Determined to do something even if it becomes difficult or dangerous

In the above transcript, I wanted to check Millie's understanding of the phrase
'dogged determination', something that I thought she may have had difficulty with
(Line 201). In this example she used morphological knowledge to figure out what the
word 'dogged' meant making connections to the fact that 'dogs are hard headed' (Line
202) and 'what they (meaning dogs) want goes' (Line 204). I affirmed her explanation
and then provided her with a definition (Line 207). In this instant, I provided information to Millie where she did not have the resources herself. This kind of support is
known as contingent scaffolding (Hammond and Gibbons 2005; Wood 1989).

Transcript 6.9: 'Like a Tablet?'

281	R:	So that's good, is there anything else that might be a bit tricky? Oh there's
282		some words here ((points to text)) 'physical encounter encapsulated so much of
283		what epitomised the women's game'. Passion, you talked about that earlier
284		– passion team work and determination.
285		So what might this this mean?
286	M:	Mmm
287	R:	'Encapsulated so much of what epitomises the women's game'. What do you
288		think that might mean?
289	M:	((reads to herself))
290	R:	Have you seen those words before?

291	M:	No.
292	R:	OK
293	M:	I've seen encounter before.
294	R:	OK see this word here ((points to word encapsulates)) If we take off the
295		beginning we are left with (....). If we take off the ending we have
296		something that looks like capsule. Do you know what a capsule is?
297	M:	Like a tablet?
298	R:	Yes. The word can also mean that it represents everything about something.
299		So much of what 'epitomises' ((points to text)) the women's game. So a perfect
300		example of the game. I guess like altogether in a capsule.

The example in Transcript 6.9 is an exchange where making the connections between Millie's own knowledge and new vocabulary was more challenging for the student. Millie struggled a little during this exchange, and I made the decision to try and reduce the cognitive load for her. After I did a little work around base words (Lines 294–296), she eventually made the link between capsule and tablets (Line 297). This was as far as this exchange went, and I don't believe in this example we had come to a shared understanding. In hindsight, more pedagogical work needed to be done here. I should have probed further in relation to her saying she had seen the word 'encounter' before (Line 293); I needed to help her to move from her knowledge of a 'capsule' to how 'encapsulated' was used in the text, and should have discussed 'epitomises'.

Following on from this exchange, which was more cognitively challenging for Millie, I wanted to reinforce the fact that she did know a great deal about this text as the following excerpt shows.

Transcript 6.10: Passion and Teamwork

299		So much of what epitomises ((points to text)) the women's game. So a perfect
300		example of the game. I guess like altogether in a capsule.
301		That's how you described it to me earlier. Before we started reading
302		the text you said you've got to be passionate=
303	M:	=passionate=
304	R:	=remember I asked you what makes a really good women's rugby league player
305	M:	Yes
306	R:	And what did you tell me?
307	M:	You got to have passion. You got to run with all your heart
308	R:	Run with your heart
309	M:	You got to (1.0) you have to have passion. You have to have team work. You

102   J. Rennie

310   have to have (1.0) lots of different things
311   R: So you talked about team work ((points to the text on the page)) and
             you talked
312   about the passion ((points to text)) So you knew all this before we
             read it. Would
313   you like to have a go at reading it? Now that we've talked about it

In this exchange I pointed Millie back to our opening discussion where she had
talked about what makes a good women's rugby league player (Line 301) and how
this connected with the ideas expressed in this text (Lines 311–313). This occurred
just prior to when I invited Millie to read the text to me. I felt this was important, as
I wanted her to feel confident about her ability to read the text independently.

Reading the Text: Connections, Confidence and Competence

In the next phase of the reading session, Millie read the text to me. During the reading, I offered praise at appropriate points and further discussed the text at particular
points making connections back to our previous discussions around the meanings in
the text and new vocabulary to help consolidate her learning.

Transcript 6.11: A Confident Beginning

317   M: No other male dominated sport in the history of Australia (.5) has
             dared to offer
318   their female counter counterparts an opp opportunity on such a
             public stage.
319   There may not have been the widespread pub-licity of the men's
             games however
320   the female version of (.5) Preston Campbell (1.0) inspired NRL
             versus Indigenous
321   Indigenous All Stars rugby league match took place on Saturday the
             12th
322   February. For the first time in the history of Skilled Park women's a
             women's
323   rugby league game entered the Gold Coast crowd and set the tone
             for a
324   spectacular afternoon of rugby league
325   R: Very good.

Millie attacked the opening paragraph will confidence and ease demonstrating
fluency that was above and beyond what her test scores had revealed. During this
part of the reading, she had difficulty pronouncing only two words (Lines 318 and
319) which she solved independently. This was generally characteristic of the way
in which she read the whole text. In total there were only five words where she used

phonological strategies to help her sound them out, three words where she needed my assistance to help her pronounce words and two instances where she repeated a word that she had already said.

Transcript 6.12: Hard and Soft Sound

392	M:	intercept a risky pass by the NRL All Stars ((turns over page laughs)) and cross
393		the white line. Captain Tracey Thompson added another two points having the
394		Indigenous girls having the indigenous girls chasing (.5) a four point (1)
395	R:	Defic
396	M:	Defic Ohh
397	R:	Deficit
398	M:	Deficit
399	R:	OK sometimes the c has a s sound
400	M:	Yeah yeah it has a hard and soft sound
401	R:	Yes that's exactly right do you remember that from primary school?
402	M:	((nods head))

In Transcript 6.12 Millie has difficulty decoding the word 'deficit' (Line 395). Since this was the second word in the passage containing the soft 'c' sound that she had difficulty with I decided to talk the fact sometimes 'c' sounds like 's'. She then connected this to what she had learned at primary school (Line 399).

Transcript 6.13: Dogged Determination

403	M:	Deficit at the half time break as the NRL Women led ten to six.
404		'Solid defence in the second half by the NRL Women's All Stars kept the
405		Indigenous All Stars from scoring despite their dogged determination'.
406	R:	You remembered that when we talked about it didn't you?
407	M:	((nods head and smiles))
408	R:	Great.
409	M:	'Despite their dogged determination to break the blue defensive line. Taking
410		advantage of a field position with ten minutes remaining five-eight Erin Elliot
411		regathered their own kick to score the third All Stars try and push the lead to
412		fourteen to six following a failed conversion attempt. Fullback Tegan Sullivan (1)
413		crossed the line for the final try of the match seconds of the match with seconds
414		to go. Hancock again converted before adding another two points' (2)

104   J. Rennie

During Millie's reading, I also took opportunities to make connections back to what she had learned earlier. Again the reading here is performed with confidence and fluency. I praised her when she read the sentence containing the phrase 'dogged determination' (Line 405) commenting that she had remembered this from our previous discussions. Millie nodded and smiled.

In addition to referring back to ideas we had previously learned, I also seized opportunities to explore new ideas as the following excerpt shows.

Transcript 6.14: 'Reads the Play Beautifully'

365	R:	Ok what does that mean? You were talking about that before. What does it
366		mean if somebody reads the play beautifully?
367	M:	It means that you can see where holes are ((points out circles on the desk)) you
368		can see where like where they all are and then you like say that someone's
369		getting too far dragged in and this person here's got it they can dummy it and
370		get it in themselves ((showing how it works on the desk)) ((Puts up hands))
371		They're reading the play.
372	R:	Great. We can read lots of things. I've talked to fisherman who say
373		they can read the water
374	M:	Yeah
375	R:	And they can read where the fish are and what is going on. So reading is about
376		understanding?
377	M:	Yeah
378	R:	So when you read the play it's about understanding what's going on?
379	M:	Yeah

In asking Millie what it might mean if someone 'reads the play beautifully', I saw an opportunity to reinforce the idea that we can read other things besides words and that 'reading' is essentially about understanding. This was important for Millie as in previous discussions about her reading it was clear that she often didn't monitor whether she had understood. When I asked what it meant if someone read the play beautifully (Line 365–366), she proceeded to provide me with one of her eloquent examples complemented by her drawing on the desk (Line 367–371). The explanation was complete with her returning to my original question – 'they're *reading* the play' (Line 317). I then made reference to what others had told me about 'reading the water'. We both concluded the exchange in agreement that reading was about 'understanding'. In this exchange, shared understanding was established.

6   Confessions from a Reading Program: Building Connections, Competence…

After Millie had finished the reading, we both reflected on her accomplishments.

Transcript 6.15: They Won't Lose

455	R:	Wow you did really well. You read some really interesting words.
456	M:	Yes
457	R:	Words you hadn't seen before=
458	M:	=It's hard
459	R:	But you did so well you did really well and you knew what it was all about. You
460		understood so that's even better. So what's important when we read?
461	M:	It's about understanding
462	R:	Yes so it's not so much about getting every word right but about understanding.
463		You should be really proud of yourself.
464	M:	Can I take that away and show my Mum what I read. Dad is coming to visit
465		tonight so I could tell him too.
466	R:	Yes. Are you watching the game tonight?
467	M:	Yeah
468	R:	Who barracks for who?
469	M:	All of us barrack for Queensland
470	R:	So if they don't win everyone will be sad
471	M:	Yeah
472	R:	You'll need a box of tissues
473	M:	((laughs)) but they won't lose
474	R:	They won't lose is that what you think?
475	M:	Yes

After the reading, I wanted to let Millie know that I was proud of her achievements. I reinforced that she had learned some new and interesting words and that even more importantly she had demonstrated understanding of the text. It was also clear that Millie was proud of her own achievements evidenced by the fact that she wanted to 'take' the text away and show her parents (Lines 464–465).

Implications

Throughout this 40-min reading session, I have illustrated how making connections can help to develop confidence and achieve competence for Millie. This reading session and subsequent reading sessions with Millie disrupted the ways in which Millie had experienced reading help in the past.

First, I took time to understand who Millie was and what she was knowledgeable about and interested in. Lei and I had deliberately chosen texts that Millie was knowledgeable about and texts that her peers would be expected to be able to read. We set our expectations high for Millie. Further, by using texts that explored content she was familiar with, she was able to demonstrate her expertise through the various discussions we had. She was set up as the expert during the reading, which was counter to her previous experiences of reading. In this reading experience and subsequent experiences, we were reading *with* Millie and discussing ideas both in and outside of the reading. It was not simply a case of Millie reading to us, which was characteristic of the reading help she had previously experienced.

Making connections in these reading experiences however did not simply mean connecting to Millie's interests. Rather, it involved a constant process of making connections throughout the reading. It was also about understanding the skills and strategies students use and knowing what students know in terms of the knowledge and concepts required at school. Connections were made to things she previously knew and had experienced, and connections were made to ideas discussed throughout the reading. Connections were made to ideas to both within and outside of the text. This process also involved continually checking for shared understanding as we did this work. To establish shared understanding of what was being conveyed required a recurrent process of checking and rechecking. Edwards and Mercer (2013) refer to this as establishing 'common knowledge'. This analysis showed that utilising students' funds of identity as resources in the classroom and as a means for learners to make connections to the knowledge and concepts that are required at school is a collaborative process of building of meaning between students and teachers. Throughout the reading, pedagogical work was employed, to ensure that Millie would be successful when reading the text. There were discussions and instruction around the meanings in the text, unfamiliar vocabulary and decoding.

Another interesting insight as I analysed the transcript from this reading event was the number of Millie's literacy strengths, strengths that the previous reading tests had failed to reveal. In this reading event, Millie presented as being very articulate. Further, she was very knowledgeable about and engaged in the reading of this particular text.

Finally, relationship work was foundational to working with Millie and the other Indigenous students in this program. It was important to take time to understand who Millie was as a learner both in and out of school. With greater knowledge about Millie's funds of identity, I was able to make connections to these funds during the reading event I have recounted here in this chapter. And with greater knowledge of Millie's funds of identity, Lei was able to continue to plan reading experiences for Millie that were strongly connected to her knowledge and experiences that she was passionate about outside of the classroom. Millie herself captured the important of this relational and connecting work as she reflected with pride about her improved confidence and competence as a reader:

Miss [Lei] helps us to read better. I am reading about things that I am interested in. I have improved in the way that I look at a book. I can conquer new words. I understand because I want to read it and we talk about what we read. I keep reading on to try and figure out words I don't know or I ask someone or try and sound it out. I am feeling a lot better than I was at the start of the year.

References

Allington, R. L. (1998). *Teaching struggling readers: Articles from "the Reading teacher".* Newark: International Reading Association.

Alvermann, D. (2001). Reading adolescents' reading identities: Looking back to see ahead. *Journal of Adolescent & Adult Literacy, 44*(8), 676–690. Retrieved from http://www.jstor.org.ezproxy.lib.monash.edu.au/stable/40018739.

Australian Curriculum, Assessment and Reporting Authority (ACARA). (2016). *NAPLAN achievement in reading, writing, language conventions and numeracy: National report for 2016.* Sydney: ACARA. https://www.nap.edu.au/results-and-reports/national-reports Accessed 14 Apr 2018.

Australian Womens Rugby League (2011). *Women's all stars a great success.* Retrieved from http://websites.sportstg.com/assoc_page.cgi?client=7-2131-0-0-0&sID=29155&&news_task =DETAIL&articleID=16174508

Bloome, D. (1985). Reading as a social process. *Language Arts, 62*(4), 134–142.

Boon, H. J., & Lewthwaite, B. E. (2016). Signatures of quality teaching for Indigenous students. *The Australian Educational Researcher, 43*(4), 453–471. https://doi.org/10.1007/s13384-016-0209-4.

Brozo, W. G., & Simpson, M. L. (2007). *Content literacy for today's adolescents: Honoring diversity and building competence.* Upper Saddle River: Merrill Prentice Hall.

Clay, M. M. (1982). *Observing young readers.* London/Auckland: Heinemann.

Cummins, J. (2007). *Promoting literacy in multilingual contexts* (Research Monograph No. 5). What works? Research into practice. Ontario. http://www.edu.gov.on.ca/eng/literacynumeracy/inspire/research/Cummins.pdf. Accessed 25 Sept 2015.

Edwards, D., & Mercer, N. (2013). *Common knowledge (Routledge revivals).* Routledge: The Development of Understanding in the Classroom.

Gee, J. (1996). *Social linguistics and literacies: Ideology in discourses.* London: Taylor and Francis.

Guthrie, J. T. (2010). *Motivations for reading questionnaire.* Retrieved from http://www.cori.umd.edu/measures/MRQ.pdf. Accessed 16 May 2016.

Hammond, J., & Gibbons, P. (2005). Putting scaffolding to work: The contribution of scaffolding in articulating ESL education. *Prospect, 20*(1), 6–30.

Heap, J. L. (1991). Reading as cultural activities: Enabling and reflective texts. *Curriculum Inquiry, 21*(1), 11–39.

Heath, S. (1983). *Ways with words.* Cambridge: University Press.

Llopart, M., & Esteban-Guitart, M. (2017). Strategies and resources for contextualising the curriculum based on the funds of knowledge approach: a literature review. *The Australian Educational Researcher, 44*(3), 255–274. https://doi.org/10.1007/s13384-017-0237-8.

Luke, A., & Freebody, P. (1997). The social practices of reading. In S. Muspratt, A. Luke, & P. Freebody (Eds.), *Constructing critical literacies: Teaching and learning textual practice* (pp. 185–226). St Leonards: Allen & Unwin.

Luke, A., Elkins, J., Weir, K., Land, R., Carrington, V., Dole, S., Pendergast, D., Kapitzke, C., Van Kraayenoord, C., Moni, K., McIntosh, A., Mayer, D., Bahr, M., Hunter, L., Chadbourne, R., Bean, T., Alvermann, D., & Stevens, L. (2003). *Beyond the middle: A report about literacy and numeracy development of target group students in the middle years of schooling.* Canberra: Commonwealth of Australia.

Mellor, S., & Corrigan, M. (2004). *The case for change: A review of contemporary research on Indigenous education outcomes* (Australian Education Review, 47). Camberwell: ACER.

Moje, E. B., Young, J. P., Readence, J. E., & Moore, D. W. (2000). Reinventing adolescent literacy for new times: Perennial and millennial issues. *Journal of Adolescent & Adult Literacy, 43*(5), 400–410. Retrieved from https://search-proquest-com.ezproxy.lib.monash.edu.au/docview/216910420?accountid=12528

Moll, L. C., & González, N. (2004). Engaging life: A funds-of-knowledge approach to multicultural education. In J. A. Banks & C. A. M. Banks (Eds.), *Handbook of research on multicultural education* (2nd ed., pp. 699–715). San Francisco: Jossey-Bass.

Moll, L. C., Amanti, C., Neff, D., & Gonzalez, N. (1992). Funds of knowledge for teaching: Using a qualitative approach to connect homes and classrooms. *Theory Into Practice, 31*(2), 132–141.

Neale, M. D. (1997). *Neale analysis of reading ability* (3rd ed.). Melbourne: ACER Press.

Patterson, A. J., Cormack, P. A., & Green, W. C. (2012). The child, the text and the teacher: Reading primers and reading instruction. *Paedagogica Historica: International Journal of the History of Education, 48*(2), 185–196. https://doi.org/10.1080/00309230.2011.644302.

Prior, M. (2013). Language and literacy challenges for indigenous children in Australia. *Australian Journal of Learning Difficulties, 18*(2), 123–137. https://doi.org/10.1080/19404158.2013.840901.

Purdie, N., Reid, K., Frigo, T., Stone, A., & Kleinhenz, E. (2011). *Literacy and numeracy learning: Lessons from the longitudinal literacy and numeracy study for indigenous students* (ACER research monograph 65). Camberwell: ACER.

Rennie, J. (2004). Oral reading: Constructing school readers, learning communities. *The International Journal of Learning in Social Contexts, 1*, 35–44.

Rennie, J. (2006). Meeting kids at the school gate: The literacy and numeracy practices of a remote indigenous community. *Australian Educational Researcher, 33*(3), 123–142. org.ezproxy.lib.monash.edu.au. https://doi.org/10.1007/BF03216845.

Rennie, J. (2016). Rethinking reading instruction for adolescent readers: The 6R's. *Australian Journal of Language and Literacy, 39*(1), 42–53.

Rennie, J. A., & Patterson, A. (2010). Young Australians reading in a digital world. In D. R. Cole & D. L. Pullen (Eds.), *Multiliteracies in motion: Current theory and practice* (pp. 207–223). New York/London: Routledge.

Rowling, J. K. (1999). *Harry Potter and the Prisoner of Azkaban.* UK: Bloomsbury Publishing

Ruddell, R. B., & Unrau, N. J. (2013). Reading as a meaning-construction process: The reader, the text, and the teacher. In D. Alvermann, N. Unrau, & R. Ruddell (Eds.), *Theoretical models and processes of reading* (6th ed., pp. 1015–1068). Newark: International Reading Association.

Sanacore, J., & Palumbo, A. (2009). Understanding the fourth-grade slump: Our point of view. *The Educational Forum, 73*, 67–74.

Santoro, N., Reid, J. A., Crawford, L., & Simpson, L. (2011). Teaching Indigenous children: Listening to and learning from Indigenous teachers. *Australian Journal of Teacher Education, 36*(10), 65–76. https://doi.org/10.14221/ajte.2011v36n10.2.

Shanahan, T., & Shanahan, C. (2012). What is disciplinary literacy and why does it matter? *Topics in Language Disorders, 32*(1), 7–18. https://doi.org/10.1097/TLD.0b013e318244557a.

Street, B. V. (Ed.). (1993). *Cross-cultural approaches to literacy.* Cambridge: Cambridge University Press.

Subero, D., Vujasinović, E., & Esteban-Guitart, M. (2017). Mobilising funds of identity in and out of school. *Cambridge Journal of Education, 47*(2), 247–263., doi-org.ezproxy.lib.monash.edu.au/. https://doi.org/10.1080/0305764X.2016.1148116.

Whithear, J. L. (2009). Slipping through the cracks: Why too many adolescents still struggle to read. *Literacy Learning: The Middle Years, 17*(2), 30–46.

Wigfield, A., & Guthrie, J. T. (1997). Relations of children's motivation for reading to the amount and breadth or their reading. *Journal of Educational Psychology, 89*(3), 420–432.

Wood, D. J. (1989). Social interaction as tutoring. In M. H. Bornstein & J. S. Bruner (Eds.), *Crosscurrents in contemporary psychology. Interaction in human development* (pp. 59–80). Hillsdale: Lawrence Erlbaum.

Dr Jennifer Rennie is a Senior Lecturer in Literacy Education in the Faculty of Education, Monash University. Prior to working in higher education, she worked as a primary and high school teacher. Her research interests relate to Indigenous literacies, students who are marginalised from mainstream schooling and reading pedagogy for disengaged adolescent readers.

Chapter 7
Talking and Writing to Develop Mathematical Meanings in a Remote Indigenous Context

Helen Harper and Bronwyn Parkin

Abstract In this chapter we explore how teacher and student talk, as well as written text, helped to build meaning in a series of mathematics lessons in a remote Indigenous school. The topic of the lessons was telling the time using an analogue clock. In recording and analysing the lessons we identified three overarching purposes for language. First, the teachers used whole-class dialogue to establish shared understandings with their students about the purposes of telling the time and to orient the students to the relevant mathematical thinking. Second, they used language intentionally, in conjunction with symbolic and visual representations, to support the students in developing mathematical concepts. And third, they supported the students to use language, both spoken and written, as a mnemonic to help them remember how to carry out the mathematical processes involved in telling the time. Using writing as a mnemonic is a very basic function of literacy, but our research suggests it is nonetheless a valuable way of helping to make the learning more concrete, particularly when working with students who struggle with both literacy and numeracy. We suggest that, if used within a carefully devised teaching sequence, written text can be a critical resource that contributes to the overall meanings created through the interaction of linguistic, symbolic and visual systems in the classroom.

Introduction: Language Teaching and Mathematics in Indigenous ESL Settings

The role of language in mediating meaning and learning in the curriculum area of mathematics, as in other curriculum areas, is of fundamental importance, particularly in contexts where students are educationally marginalised. In remote

---

H. Harper (✉)
University of New England, Armidale, NSW, Australia
e-mail: hharper2@une.edu.au

B. Parkin
University of Adelaide, Adelaide, SA, Australia
e-mail: bronwyn.parkin@adelaide.edu.au

© Springer Nature Singapore Pte Ltd. 2019
J. Rennie, H. Harper (eds.), *Literacy Education and Indigenous Australians*,
Language Policy 19, https://doi.org/10.1007/978-981-13-8629-9_7

Indigenous schools where students characteristically achieve poorly in standardised measures of both literacy and numeracy (Australian Curriculum, Assessment and Reporting Authority [ACARA] 2016b), the role of language is especially critical. A growing body of literature is beginning to address effective mathematics pedagogy in remote Indigenous contexts, examining pedagogic roles, appropriate activity and classroom arrangements and the choice of the language of instruction and discussion (Grootenboer and Sullivan 2013; Jorgensen et al. 2013a, b). Our contribution to this debate explores the role of teacher and student talk, as well as the role of written text, in building meaning in mathematics lessons.

Our discussion is based on classroom discourse material from a research project investigating the use of academic language at Maningrida, a community in Western Arnhem Land in the Northern Territory. For this project we assisted in planning sequences of mathematics lessons[1] with two teachers and subsequently video-recorded the lessons.[2] The set topic of the lessons discussed here was telling the time using an analogue clock. Teaching students to read an analogue clock may seem to be needlessly complex when digital clocks are so easily accessible, but we were aware that students might read the numerals on a digital clock without any mathematical understanding of the time measurement system that it represents, of base 12 (hour scale) and base 60 (minute scale) increments. Teaching students how to use the analogue clock gave us much more scope for explaining the system of standard time measurement. Further, it can be argued that because the analogue clock represents time as cyclical, it is in some ways more reflective of lived experience within the cycles of the natural world. Nonetheless, it was generally considered in the school that this was a very difficult, if not impossible, topic to teach successfully. Indeed, some staff in the school were incredulous when they learned we had chosen to tackle this topic in the context of a research project. 'I've tried; you can't teach these kids the time', one teacher told us. Others commented that teaching the use of the analogue clock was inefficient and a waste of time, when students already had a digital clock on their phone if they needed it. These sentiments contributed to the challenge accepted by our two teaching colleagues in this research.

Central to the challenge was the question of how the teachers could use language to support learning in the context of a mathematics topic. The material that we present in this chapter illustrates three ways in which the teachers addressed this question. First, they used whole-class dialogue to establish shared understandings with their students about the purposes of the mathematical work (Mercer 2011; Mercer and Sams 2006). Second, they used language intentionally to support the students in developing mathematical concepts, and third, they supported the students to use

---

[1] In this context English was the predominant language of instruction. However, we suggest that nothing precludes teachers using the pedagogic strategies described in this chapter to teach through languages other than English, where this is feasible and appropriate.

[2] The lessons were recorded as part of a larger research project titled *Scaffolding academic language with educationally marginalised students*. The project was a collaboration between the two researchers and four teachers in two schools and was funded by the Primary English Teaching Association of Australia (PETAA).

language, both spoken and written, as a mnemonic in carrying out mathematical processes, maximising the students' chances of internalising this language by making sure they encountered the same language consistently. To this end, in planning with the teachers we crafted the important messages into short statements that we call 'focus texts' (Harper et al. 2018; Parkin 2014; Parkin and Harper 2018). The focus texts became pivotal in planning and teaching the topic.

We begin our account by reflecting on the role of language in mathematics generally. We then bring our attention to the context of schooling at Maningrida, with some discussion of the cultural basis of time measurement in the community. After introducing the class and our teaching aims, we present a number of extracts of whole-class teacher-student dialogue that illustrate the significant role that language, both spoken and written, plays in making meaning in the mathematics classroom.

The Role of Language in Mathematics

Mathematics is the work of finding patterns and relationships. Mathematicians strive to solve problems in efficient and defensible ways, in part to solve problems in the real world, but in part also for the satisfaction of finding elegant solutions (AAS 2013). To do this, mathematicians draw on three interacting systems: language, symbolic and visual (Lemke 2004; O'Halloran 2015). The three systems work together to build complex and abstract mathematical meanings. Ultimately, solutions are recorded through writing, using two-dimensional symbols and diagrams that are full of highly impersonal, abstract, dense meanings and specific relationships. Significantly, in creating solutions, language becomes increasingly implicit or even completely disappears. This phenomenon is well illustrated, for example, in a number of recent films with mathematical themes, such as *A Beautiful Mind, Hidden Figures* and *The Imitation Game*. The dramatisations of mathematicians at work in these films highlight the ways that mathematicians solve problems, *not* through using talk, concrete materials or manipulatives, but by signifying abstract meanings through symbols using chalk and a blackboard, or (to speed up calculations in more modern times) a computer.

Yet in the process of learning mathematical concepts, students still need to be able to retrieve language in order to make sense of, and check for understanding of, those symbols and diagrams. We take the sociocultural position that language is the central mediating tool in learning contexts (Halliday 1993; Vygotsky 1986; Wertsch 1985). We suggest that students who cannot talk mathematically are unlikely to be able to think their way successfully through the mathematical content that they encounter at school. While the Maningrida context felt like light years away from the context of working with pure mathematics, the goal of our project was to help the students develop a new perspective and begin talking, and ultimately thinking, like mathematicians.

In classrooms students are inducted into mathematical ways of thinking and talking in the first instance through teacher-led dialogue. One purpose of this dialogue can be to build alignment between the teacher and students about the underpinning motivations for studying the topic. For students such as those we worked with in Maningrida, it is essential that the teacher creates this shared understanding, or common knowledge (Edwards and Mercer 1987) within the group, because children are unlikely to bring understandings from home that are congruent with the curriculum goals. Once the motivations are established, the teacher can also use dialogue to introduce and explain the mathematical concepts, with the goal of 'handing over' (Bruner and Watson 1983) this same language to the students (Harper et al. 2018). While talking extensively about *how* to tell the time, for example, is not necessarily *of itself* an end goal of lessons about reading clocks, we suggest that practising and remembering the language of these explanations is a productive strategy for students who struggle with the new concepts. When the language is formulated into short focus texts, and is used and practised consistently, it can serve as a kind of a mnemonic, consistent with Vygotsky's (1986) characterisation of children's egocentric speech, or self-talk. We can think of these focus texts as useful words that students can appropriate in the process of internalising complex activity and new language (Parkin and Harper 2018).

Oral language is not the only mode to be useful in the mathematics classroom. One aspect of language use that is rarely considered in mathematics teaching is the role of written words as a powerful resource for learning. In our project we wanted to examine how focus texts in both spoken *and* written form could support students as tools for helping them remember how to perform mathematical tasks. Using both spoken and written language can increase message abundancy (Gibbons 2003; Hammond and Gibbons 2005), so that students have opportunities to engage with meanings through more than one system. But more specifically, we were interested in the mnemonic function of the written text (Olson 1994). The nature of writing is such that it allows for a visual and stable fix on language against which students may check their memory, particularly when they are working on a challenging task. The complexity of reading a clock face potentially creates a high cognitive load (Chandler and Sweller 1991; Kirschner et al. 2006; Van Merrienboer et al. 2003), especially for students who are just beginning to learn to manipulate the various scales of time measurement (days, hours, minutes, seconds) simultaneously. Writing down how to read the clock face in words, in collaboration with the students, meant that students could subsequently use those written words to retrieve language more easily when they needed it.

The Research Context

Maningrida College is a government school that services the coastal town of Maningrida in western Arnhem Land, about 500 km east of Darwin. A former welfare settlement, Maningrida is now one of the largest remote Aboriginal towns in the Northern Territory, with a population of around 2600 people. It is a highly multilingual society with at least 11 Aboriginal languages represented, notably Ndjébbana, the language of the local landowning Kunibidji group, as well as Burarra, Kunwinjku, Rembarrnga, and the Yolngu languages from northeast Arnhem Land, and Kriol (Maningrida College 2016).

7 Talking and Writing to Develop Mathematical Meanings in a Remote Indigenous… 113

The official language of instruction is English, although many children hear little English in their daily interactions and have very little knowledge of English when they first come to school, or if their school attendance is irregular. Further, when students do use English outside of school, it is largely limited to the transaction of goods and services, such as in the store and clinic. Literacy and numeracy levels as measured by the National Assessment Program Literacy and Numeracy (NAPLAN) are low, with more than 80% of Year 5 students scoring in Band 3 or below for reading, compared with just 5% nationally (ACARA 2016c).

Within the community, people are used to measuring time by referring to natural events, rather than by using standard units of time measurement such as hours and minutes. As in the Western world, time is perceived to be cyclical, but the Maningrida calendar is calibrated according to events such as seasons, the winds, the arrival of the magpie goose and when the rain comes (Fig. 7.1).

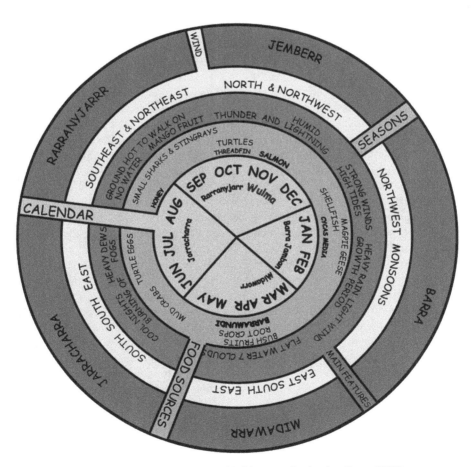

Fig. 7.1 Burarra seasonal calendar. (Maningrida Literature Production Centre 1995)

Days are measured, not by a clock, but by the position of the sun and stars. As an example of a comparable time measurement system, mathematician Pam Harris described the daily cycle of natural events against which time is measured by the Ngaanyatjarra people near Warburton, Western Australia:

> The ground becomes clear / the first light / sunrise / early morning / mid-morning / sun has risen up some distance / midday / not quite afternoon.... (Harris 1984, p. 13)

In Maningrida, although standard units of time are used in some contexts, such as the school, the clinic, the store and the airstrip, significant events are typically also signalled in more concrete ways, such as with a siren or music over the loudspeaker, the plane flying over before it lands or (at school) the lunch arriving, so there is no pressing motivation for being able to tell the time using a clock. It is possible to manage day by day without understanding standard units of time measurement at all. As noted earlier, students have digital time on their phones, but being able to read 4:30 on a digital clock does not necessarily imply a mathematical understanding of this measurement: that those numbers mean *4 h and 30 min (half of 1 h) past midday or midnight*. In addition, there is plenty of scope for confusion, with the English word 'day' meaning both sunlight hours and 24 h beginning at midnight and the 'second' hand on the clock measuring the minutes, while the 'third' hand measuring the seconds.

As noted above, we were confronted with the considerable and understandable frustration experienced by teachers at students' failure to read and use clocks, to engage with timetables and generally to 'be on time'. In this context, there is a danger of essentialising Aboriginal people into a stereotyped explanation in which 'they don't use time', or 'they live in a culture where time is not important'. This kind of account was arguably reinforced by the teachers' feelings of ineffectiveness in teaching what appeared to be basic mathematical concepts.

The classroom material that we discuss here is drawn from a sequence of four lessons that were taught by one of our teacher collaborators, Matt Lotherington. Matt was experienced and skilled in using the scaffolding techniques realised in the Accelerated Literacy pedagogy (Cowey 2007; Gray 2007), an approach to literacy teaching recently used in Northern Territory remote schools. Characteristics of the approach include the use of questioning strategies that help reduce cognitive load, and an emphasis on making explicit the academic literate knowledge that is not readily available to students who do not come from literate backgrounds. Matt's class for these lessons comprised 12 students in Years 5 and 6. All were Aboriginal, all spoke English as an additional language or dialect, and for some students, English was their third or fourth language. They were a high-attending group, averaging 91% school attendance. However, their generally low levels of literacy and mathematics[3] created some challenges for a teacher aiming to work with age-appropriate content.

---

[3] Median scores for both reading and mathematics according to PAT-R and PAT-M (Australian Council for Educational Research [ACER] 2005, 2008) were Year 3, Stanine 4.

7 Talking and Writing to Develop Mathematical Meanings in a Remote Indigenous... 115

The following sections describe the purposes of oral and written language that we identified in Matt's teaching and learning negotiation with his students.

Language Purpose 1: Establishing a Shared Purpose by Inviting Students into a World Where Measuring Time Matters

From the start of the lesson sequence, Matt used language to mediate the shared cultural understandings that provide the rationale for the mathematical knowledge. Matt's first challenge was to find a way of explaining why telling the time with a clock was useful in some circumstances. To do this he needed to make explicit the motivations for using standard units of time measurement. He needed to build on students' existing knowledge, introducing the historical and cultural motivations for telling the time (Grattan 2016), while taking care to avoid an overly laborious and ultimately distracting account. In our planning sessions, we noted some oft-cited reasons for time-telling: that if you cannot tell the time you will be late for events, and you will not be able to function in a workplace. However, while these are valid reasons, they are unlikely to be motivating for children who live in a social context where people are not reliant on clocks and whose families are often not included in the world of regular paid employment. Importantly, we could not assume that students share the value system of a post-industrial culture, in which being on time is implicitly understood as a positive virtue.

After some discussion we settled on an account of time-telling that fit with the social and historical facts and that we thought would carry some weight in the intercultural context of school at Maningrida: that measuring time is most important when groups of people organise themselves to carry out activities together, such as participating in school (as a teacher or a student), or creating and making use of a transport system, or attending any kind of workplace. Because such collective activities require people to be present at the same time, people who do not observe the agreed times disrupt the activity of others. In other words, 'being on time' is a respectful way to interact with others, and it allows organisations to function smoothly.

As we noted earlier, Matt was skilled in constructing dialogue that invites students to participate, even when they began with little shared understanding of the purposes of the lesson (Harper et al. 2018). Extract 7.1 is drawn from the first lesson in the sequence and is an example of this kind of dialogue in the early stages of a teaching sequence. It demonstrates Matt's careful movement from discussing the students' existing knowledge about time measurement to establishing a shared understanding about the purposes of telling the time using standard measures.

Extract 7.1: Using Language to Orient Students to the Social Purpose of Using a Clock (Lesson 1)

T: So nature has its own way of telling time, doesn't it? Okay. And it's pretty good. So we know that at the moment, it's wet season. All right? We know that then, it's gonna be dry season. We know it's daytime, okay? But, people sometimes need to measure time a bit more accurately, don't they? You can't just say, 'Oh, I'll meet you in the daytime.' If I told Michael I'll meet him over at the shops in the daytime, are we gonna get there at exactly the same time?

S: No.

T: We might. But then again, we probably won't. Cause there's a lot of daytime, isn't there? Just cause the sun's up, that's daytime. So people, what we call mankind, okay, people came up with a way of measuring time. [Turns side-on to indicate the images of clocks and calendars on the board.] So we invented some of these things to measure time. So we all know what that is, don't we? [Points and turns back to face class.] What's that a picture of, Tom?

S: Clock, clock.

T: Clock. We've all seen a clock before, haven't we? So mankind invented a clock to measure the time. So yes, it's daytime, but now we can actually measure daytime. Does that make sense? You all are with me, so you know how we measure things?

S: Yeah.

T: We can measure daytime. So instead of saying to Michael, I'll meet him at the shop daytime, I could say I'll meet him at the shop at--

S: 9 o'clock.

T: 9 o'clock

S: 9 o'clock.

T: in the morning. Okay? Just – it's just the way that mankind has tried to make it more accurate. When I say accurate, what's another word for accurate? We've all heard that word. Some of my kids from last year, what's another way of saying accurate? What does that mean, accurate? Mean it's right or wrong? If it's accurate, then it's--

S: Right.

T: Right. And it's more than just right, isn't it? It means that it's really precisely right. It's actually on-the-dot accurate [Taps fingers of right hand on left hand palm repeatedly].

In this extract, Matt first talked about natural measurements of time, aligned to seasons and the rotation of the earth, before moving on to explain how using a clock might be useful. In doing this, he linked the topic to the personal experiences of the students, validating their existing knowledge. At this point in the lesson, however, he also introduced the notions of accuracy and measurement, and this extract demonstrates how he proceeded to elaborate and share the meanings of these terms.

Importantly, he put them into everyday contexts for the students and supported the meaning with visuals to link the idea of measuring time with the physical object of the clock and the familiar language of '9 o'clock'. He checked for understanding from the students of the word 'accurate' by reminding them that this was prior learning ('We've all heard that word') eliciting the more everyday term 'right' and then reinforced its specific mathematical meaning through repetition and gesture. Later in the lesson he would revisit this language, and again in subsequent lessons, thus creating a thread to reinforce the social purpose of mathematics throughout the lesson sequence. In this way, language, as realised through the teacher-led classroom dialogue, was an essential part of setting up the lesson sequence: it not only allowed the teacher to explain what they were going to be doing, but it also served to invite the students to share the motivations of the mathematical activities that would follow.

Language Purpose 2: Using Language to Support the Students in Developing Mathematical Concepts

In planning the lessons, we spent some time discussing the language that Matt would use to represent the mathematical concepts that underpin being able to read an analogue clock face. The Australian Mathematics Curriculum stipulates that students first *tell the time to the quarter hour, using past and to* (ACARA 2016a). This step assumes that students have control of simple fractions (which the students in this study did not have). Furthermore, it complicates the reading of the clock conceptually and linguistically by switching from 'past the hour' to 'to the next hour' when the minute hand reaches 6. We also noted that getting students to understand the equivalence between 'a quarter of the clock face' and '15 min' added another layer of complexity. We knew that most students could skip count by fives, so that is how they read the minutes, and only in a clockwise direction (i.e. 'past', not 'to'). When writing the time, we decided to put the hour first and the minutes second, only reading in a clockwise direction. This sequence afforded the simplest transition between analogue and digital clocks.

To further break down the complexity, we focused on the three discrete time scales that are represented by an analogue clock: one full rotation of the short hand measures half a day, in 12 increments of 1 h; one full rotation of the longer hand measures 1 h in 60 increments of 1 min; and many clocks often have a third, thinner hand which measures 1 min per rotation, in 60 increments of 1 s (hence its potentially confusing name, 'second hand').

Given the available teaching time and the complexity of the content, we decided that Matt should leave the second hand alone and that he should aim to teach the role of the hour hand and the minute hand separately and in sequence, so that students would have the opportunity to consolidate the relevant concepts. We particularly wanted to see how we could use language to mediate meaning so that students could not only say, for example, '5:20', but they would also understand and express that these symbols meant '5 h out of a possible 12 and 20 min out of a possible 60, after midday or midnight, which is 12 o'clock exactly'.

As we planned with the teachers, we determined what important messages or concepts we wanted to establish and how we were going to say them, with a view to creating a shared and consistent language for working with the topic. To represent the movement of the hour hand around a clock face, we devised the following focus text:

> The hour hand takes 12 hours to move around the clock face. Because there are 24 hours in a day, the hour hand moves around the clock face twice each day.

The following extracts illustrate how Matt used this focus text to guide his dialogue with the students and to build their conceptual understanding. In Extract 7.2, Matt began with a simple demonstration of a part of the focus text's meaning: that the hour hand 'goes round twice' in 'one whole day'. He supported his talk by manipulating the hour hand on a model clock.

Extract 7.2: 24 Hours in a Day: It Goes Round Twice (Lesson 1)

T: This thing goes around twice to measure one whole...? Okay, so let's think [moving the hour hand around the clock face]. We got midnight, and we go through. We come to school [moves the hour hand to 8], and we've got our lunchtime [moves the hour hand to 1]. And then, we go home [hour hand points to 3]. And then, we go to bed [moves the hour hand to 8]. Goes around twice. That's one whole what, Polly?

S: Day.

T: One whole day. Okay? But why doesn't it stop?

S: Hm.

T: Why is it important that it's a circle? What happens at the end of one day? What's gonna happen at the end of this day? Does everything just stop?

S: Mm, no.

T: What's gonna happen? At the end of Monday, we click over to...?

SS: Tuesday.

In this extract, the teacher shifted his talk from the abstract to concrete realisations of time. As he moved the hour hand around the clock, he unpacked the abstract notion of '24 hours in a day' as concrete student experiences such as coming to school and unpacked the generalisation of '1 day' to naming specific days Monday and Tuesday.

Later in the same lesson, Matt consolidated the relationship between the number of hours in a day and the number of rotations of the hour hand on the clock face, checking that the students remembered what they had learned about the rotation of the hour hand:

7 Talking and Writing to Develop Mathematical Meanings in a Remote Indigenous…   119

Extract 7.3: 24 Hours in a Day: Checking for Handover (Lesson 1)

T: Did we talk about how many hours there are in a day? Let's see if we can work it out. Hang on, let's ask, and then we'll see if we can prove. Lee?
S: 24 hours in a day.
T: And, who…? You were gonna say 24 hours as well [indicating another student]. Fantastic. So let's see if we can prove that.
T: All right, Cherie. How many times does the hour hand go around the clock in one day? Goes not once, but it goes how many?
S: Twice.
T: Twice, two times around. So it goes 1, 2, 3, 4, 5, 6, 7, 8, 9, 10, 11, 12 [moves the hour hand around the clock face]. That's how many times?
S: One.
T: One. Okay? And then, it goes another 12. 1, 2, 3, 4, 5, 6, 7, 8, 9, 10, 11, 12 [moves the hour hand around the clock face in time with counting]. Two.

In this extract Matt continued to manipulate the hour hand and to ground his meaning in this concrete representation, but he also moved on to make more abstract meanings. While his talk in Extract 7.2 had drawn on shared everyday reference points ('we come to school', 'we've got our lunchtime'), in Extract 7.3, he no longer connected the numbers to everyday events. Instead, he used the clock to support a shift between the algorithmic question, 'How many times?', and the abstracted notion of 24 h in a day. Although the students did not give linguistically extended answers, their responses indicate that they were thinking successfully at this level of abstraction.

Language Purpose 3: Language as Mnemonic to Support Mathematical Processes

By the third lesson, the students were learning to read the clock face for themselves and record the time in numerals. They had made and manipulated their own paper plate clocks to practise reading and recording the time, but before they could practise individually, Matt had some initial work to do in establishing the process for reading the time with the group as a whole and to help students recall the process consistently each time they undertook it.

For this stage of the lesson sequence we had planned an additional focus text, to represent the process of reading the clock and recording the time in numerals:

When we read the time, we read the hour first, and then the minutes past. When we write the time, we write the hour first, and then the minutes past and the divider in between.

The role of this focus text is illustrated in Extract 7.4, which is drawn from Lesson 3. The words had been introduced by Matt in the previous lesson, so it was not the first time the students had heard them. In this extract Matt was revising the language orally to check for handover in preparation for jointly constructing the sentence with the class.

Extract 7.4: Language to Support Mathematical Processes (Lesson 3)

T: So when we write time, what do we put first? What comes first when I'm writing time? Let's have a look at this. This is our time. When we write time, what do we put first? We...

SS Hour.

T: Yeah, we put the hour first. And then what comes next?

T: Then we put the...

SS: Minutes past.

T: That's right. Is there anything else we need to put in there as well?

S: Yes.

T: Didn't we put in the...

S: The div... divider.

T: Yeah. So when we...

S: Divider.

T: ...write the time, we write the hour first and then we write the minutes past. And what do we put in between, Lee? A...

S: Divider.

T: ...divider. So should we write that up as a sentence?

The sentence was then recorded on the whiteboard. Students did not record the sentence for themselves. Rather, it remained as a shared piece of text in the room. Matt revisited it again the next day before giving the students a worksheet with a number of clocks with different times. Their task was to convert the time on the clock to numerals.

In this instance, it was a strategic choice on the teacher's part to record the text as a joint negotiated text (Gray 2007; MacNaught 2015), rather than asking the students to record it for themselves individually. When poor decoders engage independently with text, whether reading or writing, the load of decoding takes precedent over meaning (MacArthur and Graham 2015). If the students had been asked to copy it down from the board, there was a high risk that they would have copied letter by letter, once again overlooking meaning making in the process. By spending time discussing the words, and then taking on the role of scribe, Matt helped keep meaning central to the writing activity.

A further benefit of jointly constructing a written version of the focus text with the students was that the words were now on display for future reference, for whenever students became confused in the high cognitive challenge of reading the clock face. The text served as a scaffold in the sense that, until the understandings were solidly internalised, students could refer to it as a memory aid or mnemonic and as a tool that could potentially help reduce their cognitive load. The role of text as mnemonic was evident in Extract 7.5, which is drawn from the fourth and last lesson that we recorded in this sequence. Here, one of the researchers was sitting with a student working on a worksheet where she had to read a clock face and convert what she read to numbers. Even though the student had successfully completed several of these tasks already, on this particular clock, she had confused the process and had begun by counting the minutes before the hours. The researcher at this point intervened by reminding her:

Extract 7.5: Using Mnemonics for Self-Talk (Lesson 4)

S: 5, 10, 15… [Skip counting the minutes]
T: [Intervening] When we write the time...
S: ... we write the hour first...

That is all that was said. The words had done their job, reorienting the student to the correct process, and she wrote the correct time.

Conclusions

By the end of the teaching sequence, the students in our research classes could say '5:20'. Of course, they could do this before the topic began, but instead of simply reading the numbers with little or no meaning, those two numerals and the colon in between had become place markers in the system of telling the time, encapsulating different time scales. The mediating language had largely disappeared as it should, but instances like that observed in Extract 7.5 suggest that the students could bring the language to consciousness when it was needed.

Arguably, one of the deep failures of Indigenous education is that school can seem to have little relevance to students' lives. Indigenous students in remote communities would survive without Western mathematics. They can continue to rely on the arrival of the school bus to tell them that school is starting soon and the noise of the plane to tell them when to get to the airstrip. They can trust the store workers to give them the correct change, and Centrelink to put the right amount of welfare money in their family bank account each fortnight. But to be without mathematics means being reliant on others to do the mathematical thinking on their behalf and ultimately being without power.

The material we have presented in this chapter highlights the challenge of mediating meaning in mathematics in settings such as Maningrida. In Matt's lessons we noted the time he spent at the outset using classroom dialogue to establish a credible and socially relevant purpose for studying time and to orient students to the mathematical thinking required by the topic. This went beyond simply stating the learning intentions at the start of the lesson, and involved carrying the threads of the salient meanings, such as talking about accuracy and measurement, from one lesson to the next.

In our project, we also set out to demonstrate the usefulness of carefully worded statements, or focus texts, in guiding the teacher to remain purposeful and consistent in the language he used to help students engage with both the concepts and processes of mathematics. The statements gave the teacher a linguistic focus as he built meaning across the lessons and as he managed the complexity of several meaning systems: drawing also on the students' everyday language, the visual and concrete representations of clocks, and the numeric representations of time, while mediating the shift from concrete materials to generalisations and abstractions. The focus texts were designed to help Matt use language consistently so that students had many opportunities to hear it, and they could start to internalise it for themselves.

To be clear, the goal of getting students to remember the wording of the focus texts (Extract 7.4) was not so they would recite the text, parrot-like. Rather, throughout the lesson sequence, Matt continued to remind the students of the meanings they had already constructed together and to create the conditions for the students to practise the wording of the focus texts, while keeping the meanings to the fore of their consciousness. The aim of saying and writing the focus texts was thus to establish a firm link between the representation of time on the clock face and the words that would help the students remember how to conceptualise the meaning system of analogue time-telling. It is likely the students had previously struggled with learning to read the analogue clock largely because of the sheer complexity of taking three scales of time and trying to remember them in their heads. In developing an automatic recall of the language, students could get on with the core business of thinking about decoding a clock face and understanding how telling the time works. The focus texts provided a scaffolding tool to intervene in this difficult process, removing pressure for the students to hold everything in their heads and thereby reducing cognitive load. The texts served as a mnemonic, other people's words that the students could vocalise as self-talk, or a way of mediating the learning process and supporting the shift into abstract thinking. And, as demonstrated in Extract 7.5, once the language was firmly appropriated, the scaffold was no longer required and the self-talk disappeared.

Writing the focus texts as a class activity added another layer to the mnemonic. As well as providing Matt with an opportunity to check for handover, the process of writing the focus text (shifting from the oral to the written mode) served to make the learning more concrete, stabilising the words on the board and creating an object that the class could return to repeatedly. As noted earlier, 'written text as mnemonic' is a very basic function of literacy, but it is nonetheless a very valuable use for the physical product of writing, particularly in the context of teaching students who struggle with both literacy and numeracy. There is thus a role for writing in teaching and learning mathematics that is distinct from the role that writing plays in other curriculum areas, where the writing of distinct genres such as narratives or explanatory reports, for example, is required. If used within a carefully devised teaching sequence, the written text is a critical meaning-making resource that contributes to the overall meanings created through the interaction of linguistic, symbolic and visual systems in the classroom.

As a matter of principle, success in mathematics for students in remote settings will be greatly enhanced by foregrounding language. We see this as a counterbalance to current trends, which, in addressing literacy, prioritise in the school timetable the teaching of constrained skills such as instruction in phonics and decoding (Wilson 2014). We do not dispute the essential nature of these constrained literacy skills; we simply note that the nature of language and literacy instruction needs to be multifaceted if students are to access the full scope of the Australian curriculum. The effective use of language for the purposes we have described here is worthy of more exploration and research, particularly in Indigenous educational contexts.

Acknowledgement We gratefully acknowledge teachers Matt Lotherington and Dan Bell, who participated in this project with us, the Maningrida College Council for supporting our project, Principal Miranda Watt for her assistance in facilitating our work and the Primary English Teaching Association of Australia (PETAA) for their support in funding this research.

References

American Association for the Advancement of Science. (2013). Chapter 2: The nature of mathematics. In *Science for all Americans*. Project 2061: Washington, DC. Viewed 24 May 2018.

Australian Council for Educational Research [ACER]. (2005). *Progressive achievement tests in mathematics* (3rd ed.). Camberwell: ACER.

Australian Council for Educational Research [ACER]. (2008). *Progressive achievement tests in comprehension* (3rd ed.). Camberwell: ACER.

Australian Curriculum, Assessment and Reporting Authority [ACARA]. (2016a). *Australian curriculum mathematics*. Retrieved from https://www.australiancurriculum.edu.au/f-10-curriculum/mathematics/

Australian Curriculum, Assessment and Reporting Authority [ACARA]. (2016b). *National report on schooling in Australia 2016*. Retrieved from https://www.acara.edu.au/reporting/national-report-on-schooling-in-australia-2016

Australian Curriculum, Assessment and Reporting Authority [ACARA]. (2016c). *My school Maningrida College*. Retrieved from https://www.myschool.edu.au/school/50061/naplan/bands/2016

Bruner, J. S., & Watson, R. (1983). *Child's talk: Learning to use language*. Oxford: Oxford University.

Chandler, P., & Sweller, J. (1991). Cognitive load theory and the format of instruction. *Cognition and Instruction, 8*(4), 293–332.

Cowey, W. (2007, July). *Exploring the potential of classroom questioning in the National Accelerated Literacy Program*. Paper presented at Australian Literacy Educators Association National Conference, Canberra, Australia.

Edwards, D., & Mercer, N. (1987). *Common knowledge: The development of understanding in the classroom*. London: Routledge.

Gibbons, P. (2003). Mediating language learning: Teacher interactions with ESL students in a content-based classroom. *TESOL Quarterly, 37*(2), 247–273.

Grattan, K. (2016). A brief history of telling the time. *Conversation*. https://theconversation.com/a-brief-history-of-telling-time-55408. Accessed 7 Nov 2017.

Gray, B. (2007). *Accelerating the literacy development of indigenous students: The National Accelerated Literacy Program (NALP)*. Darwin: Charles Darwin University Press.

Grootenboer, P., & Sullivan, P. (2013). Remote indigenous students' understandings of measurement. *International Journal of Science and Mathematics Education, 11*(1), 169–189.

Halliday, M. A. K. (1993). Towards a language-based theory of learning. *Linguistics and Education, 5*(2), 93–116.

Hammond, J., & Gibbons, P. (2005). Putting scaffolding to work: The contribution of scaffolding in articulating ESL education. *Prospect, 20*(1), 6–30.

Harper, H., Lotherington, M., & Parkin, B. (2018). Carrying the conversation in my head: Classroom dialogue in a remote Aboriginal setting. In P. Jones, A. Simpson, & A. Thwaite (Eds.), *Talking the talk: Snapshots from Australian classrooms* (pp. 75–87). Newtown: PETAA.

Harris, P. (1984). *Teaching about time in tribal communities*. Darwin: NT DET.

Jorgensen, R., Grootenboer, P., & Niesche, R. (2013a). Teachers' beliefs and practices in teaching mathematics in remote aboriginal schools. In R. Jorgensen, P. Sullivan, & P. Grootenboer (Eds.), *Pedagogies to enhance learning for indigenous students: Evidence-based practice* (pp. 75–87). Singapore: Springer.

Jorgensen, R., Sullivan, P., & Grootenboer, P. (2013b). *Pedagogies to enhance learning for indigenous students: Evidence-based practice*. Singapore: Springer.

Kirschner, P. A., Sweller, J., & Clark, R. E. (2006). Why minimal guidance during instruction does not work: An analysis of the failure of constructivist, discovery, problem-based, experiential and inquiry-based teaching. *Educational Psychologist, 41*(2), 75–86.

Lemke, J. (2004). The literacies of science. In E. W. Saul (Ed.), *Crossing borders in literacy and science instruction* (pp. 33–47). Arlington/Newark: International Reading Association/NSTA Press.

MacArthur, C., & Graham, S. (2015). Writing research from a cognitive perspective. In C. MacArthur, S. Graham, & J. Fitzgerald (Eds.), *Handbook of writing research* (2nd ed.). New York: Guilford.

MacNaught, L. (2015). *Classroom talk and the negotiation of academic English*. Doctoral thesis, University of Sydney.

Maningrida College. (2016). *Maningrida CEC manual*. Maningrida: Maningrida College.

Maningrida Literature Production Centre. (1995). *Burarra seasonal calendar*. Maningrida: NT DET.

Mercer, N. (2011). *Thinking together*. Cambridge: School of Education, University of Cambridge. http://thinkingtogether.educ.cam.ac.uk/. Accessed 20 June 2011.

Mercer, N., & Sams, C. (2006). Teaching children how to use language to solve maths problems. *Language and Education, 20*(6), 507–528.

O'Halloran, K. L. (2015). The language of learning mathematics: A multimodal perspective. *The Journal of Mathematical Behavior, 40*, 63–74.

Olson, D. R. (1994). *The world on paper: The conceptual and cognitive implications of writing and reading*. Cambridge: Cambridge University Press.

Parkin, B. (2014). *Scaffolding science: A pedagogy for marginalised students*. Unpublished PhD thesis, University of Adelaide, Adelaide.

Parkin, B., & Harper, H. (2018). *Teaching with intent: Scaffolding academic language with marginalised students*. Newtown: PETAA.

Van Merrienboer, J. G., Kirschner, P., & Kester, L. (2003). Taking the load off a learner's mind: Instructional design for complex learning. *Educational Psychologist, 38*(1), 5–13.

Vygotsky, L. S. (1986). *Thought and language* (A. Kozulin, Trans.). Cambridge, MA: MIT Press.

Wertsch, J. V. (1985). *Culture, communication, and cognition: Vygotskian perspectives*. Cambridge: Cambridge University Press.

Wilson, B. (2014). *A share in the future: Review of indigenous education in the northern territory*. Darwin: Northern Territory Department of Education. Retrieved from https://education.nt.gov.au/__data/assets/pdf_file/0020/229016/A-Share-in-the-Future-The-Review-of-Indigenous-Education-in-the-Northern-Territory.pdf

Dr Helen Harper has worked as a researcher and lecturer in language and literacy education, as a linguist in remote Indigenous communities and as a teacher of English as an additional language. Currently Helen is a senior lecturer in the School of Education at the University of New England (UNE) where she teaches English language and literacy education. Helen's research interests include pedagogies for educationally marginalised students, pedagogies of literacy and classroom interactions. Before taking up her post at UNE in 2018, Helen lived for more than two decades in the Northern Territory, where she worked as a researcher and educator.

Dr Bronwyn Parkin is an adjunct lecturer in Linguistics at the University of Adelaide and a literacy consultant with a long history of working in literacy education with Aboriginal and low socio-economic students. For many years, she was a Literacy Development project officer in the Literacy Secretariat, South Australian Department of Education, and managed the South Australian Accelerated Literacy Program. Together with Dr Helen Harper from the University of New England, she was a recent recipient of a PETAA research grant, 'Scaffolding academic language with educationally marginalised students'.

Chapter 8
Indigenous Doctoral Literacy in the Humanities and Social Sciences

Zane M. Diamond and Peter J. Anderson

Abstract For Indigenous Australian doctoral students, developing the core competencies required for successful completion of their PhD is commonly undertaken at what Nakata has insightfully termed 'the cultural interface' (Disciplining the savages: savaging the disciplines. Aboriginal Studies Press, Canberra, 2007a). While not specifically concerned with doctoral literacy development, Nakata and colleagues (Martin G, Nakata V, Nakata M, Day A, Stud High Educ 42:1158, 2015) develop the theoretical groundwork for considering how the core competency of 'written communication' can be understood at this cultural interface, suggesting that there is a need for supervisors and others involved in doctoral training to consider a pedagogy that engages Indigenous persistence in tertiary study and that does not fall into deficit thinking or political correctness. This chapter examines the multidimensionality of Indigenous doctoral literacy development in the Humanities and Social Sciences. There is a growing body of research about the core competencies associated with doctoral studies. Durette et al. (Stud Higher Educ 41(8):1355–1370, 2016) identify six core competencies developed during a PhD. The most frequently cited competency in their study was 'Transferable competencies that can be formalized' with written communication as a significant element. Murray and Nallaya (Stud Higher Educ 41:(7):1296–1312, 2016: 1298) observe that academic literacy is 'fundamentally a pluralistic concept with each discipline having associated with it a set of literacy practices in which students need to become conversant'.

The authors report here on a critical, self-study of academic literacy development during our time as supervisor and PhD scholar, framed by findings of our analysis of de-identified data drawn from an Indigenous doctoral development program (2002–2008) and embedding our analysis in the Australian higher education policy landscape. Building on Nakata's foundational work, we offer future direction for a

---

Z. M. Diamond (✉)
Faculty of Education, Monash University, Melbourne, VIC, Australia
e-mail: zane.diamond@monash.edu

P. J. Anderson
Indigenous Research and Engagement Unit, QUT, Brisbane, OLD, Australia
e-mail: p21.anderson@qut.edu.au

© Springer Nature Singapore Pte Ltd. 2019
J. Rennie, H. Harper (eds.), *Literacy Education and Indigenous Australians*,
Language Policy 19, https://doi.org/10.1007/978-981-13-8629-9_8

sovereign rights-based approach to academic literacy development in a deimperialised, postcolonial Australian higher education system.

Introduction

For Indigenous Australian doctoral students, developing the core competencies required for successful completion of their PhD is commonly undertaken at what Nakata has insightfully termed 'the cultural interface' (Nakata 2007a, b). It is well-understood in the Humanities and Social Sciences disciplines that there is a particularly high reliance on a PhD candidate having superior English literacy skills and knowledge of English language academic writing conventions of their particular subdiscipline together with a highly competent understanding of English grammatical style and structure (Furneaux 2016). Providing some insight into the issue, a researcher in the English for Academic Purposes field, Turner (2012: 22) provides analysis of some of the academic responses to how they feel about proofreading PhD students' written work, saying:

> The affective discourse of annoyance at the encounter with such errors revealed in words such as 'irritating' and 'expunged', where the choice of 'expunged' seems particularly vehement, pervaded the discourse of my informants. It was apparent also in a discussion about assessment, and the motivation of the reader, when Prof. 1. spoke of: 'nagging issues of presentation that as it dampened the enthusiasm.'

The engagement of a supervisor with the written work of a PhD student is, in general, recognised as being a potential space for troubling conversations, anger, confusion, mistrust and frustration, and there is a small but growing research focus that has attempted to grapple with problems in the 'cultural interface' of the Indigenous and non-Indigenous dyad. Scholarship is emerging in this field (Grant 2010; Harrison et al. 2017; Winchester-Seeto et al. 2014), but except for our small study, there is scant research that tries to understand the 'cultural interface' between an academic supervisor and an Indigenous PhD scholar specifically in doctoral literacy development.

Indeed, most focus in the literature has been firmly about universities creating more culturally inclusive and 'safe' spaces for Indigenous scholars. The technical aspects of doctoral literacy development remain well-buried. Like many others, we recognise the contest between sovereignty and structural racism that continues within Australian universities. In the spirit of the work of Nascimento (2014), we take a sovereign rights-based, deimperialised, Indigenist approach to our analysis finding resonance with Nascimento (2014, 268) where he explains, similar to Australia, that in the Latin American context:

> ...decolonial theoretical perspectives intersected with assumptions from literacy and academic literacy critical studies. In the overall, these discourses point to a naturalization of a racial hierarchical order, consequently, an ontological, epistemological and cultural one, in which mastering certain literacy practices and the authority to use them in the academic context is still a valid criterion for classification of groups as being culturally different. In highlighting an intrinsic relationship between the specific and highly valued textual configurations of academic literacy and the form of knowledge production from an Anglo-

Eurocentric matrix of power, I seek to situate such writing practices in the broader project of modernity, coloniality and, consistent with the framework adopted, I seek for alternatives and viable ways for decolonization of these practices, such as the opening of the academy for new epistemological possibilities and hence to new forms of production and expression of knowledge, especially in intercultural contexts.

We developed our study of our supervisor/student relationship based on Loughran's (2012) logic of effective reflective practice where he argues that to teach about reflective practices requires contextual anchors to make learning episodes meaningful. We developed our self-study with this in mind. In addition, our participation in and analysis of the Indigenous Postgraduate Summer School (IPSS) data highlighted that we needed to pay particular attention to the expectations and anxieties held by first-language, English-speaking Indigenous PhD candidates about writing their PhD in a way that is able to demonstrate a high level of proficiency in academic literacy in the English language. While much attention has been given to how second (third- and fourth-)- language speakers engage in an English language PhD, there is a surprising silence about PhD candidates who are first-language English speakers but are from, '… English speaking backgrounds who may not lack proficiency in the language as such but rather academic literacy' (Read 2008: 181). Read is discussing the New Zealand context where members of the Pacific Nations communities (particularly from Samoa, Tonga, the Cook Islands, Niue and the Tokelau Islands) have 'native proficiency in general conversational English but whose low level of achievement in their secondary schooling would have excluded them from further educational opportunity, had the special admission provision not been available' (Read 2008, p. 181). We extend this point to our small study in two parts: first, we recognise the failure of Australian mainstream schooling to address the education aspirations of Indigenous Australians. This situation is well-understood in policy circles (Commonwealth of Australia 2018; Productivity Commission 2018), and the failures are well-documented in the need of mainstream education systems to address Indigenous educational disadvantage in a manner that properly prepares Indigenous students to continue to tertiary studies. Second, we argue that mainstream schools and universities still operate with a predominantly colonial mind-set that as yet finds little value in Indigenous philosophy and its highly developed skills, knowledge and understanding in and of the Australian continent (Ma Rhea 2015; Ma Rhea and Anderson 2011).

In order to examine the art and craft of Indigenous academic literacy development as part of the Indigenous scholar's research journey as they move into academic careers or other careers where they will use their 'transferable competency' of written communication (Durette et al. 2016), this paper is framed by a pressing need for there to be an exponential increase in the number of Indigenous people who successfully complete a PhD and move into academia as the need is dire. The Australian Government's Department of Education and Training (2016) reports the number of Indigenous Academic Staff currently in full-time employment in Australian universities is 392. This number is a total of all academic levels and function.

Review of Literature

Building on research undertaken in the early 2000s (Ma Rhea and Rigney 2002), this meta-analysis of more recent literature suggests that the *United Nations Declaration on the Rights of Indigenous People* (United Nations 2008; UNDRIPs) has had a profound influence in global policy circles in shaping national responses to provision of education services to Indigenous populations within nation-state boundaries. In this chapter, we will argue for the adoption of an international best practice approach to the development of Indigenous doctoral literacy, recognising that it is not yet possible for Indigenous Australians to achieve a PhD in the language of their ancestors. Indigenous Australians report (see McConvell and Thieberger 2001; Eades 1991, 1988) that at the time of the arrival of the first British settlers in 1788, there were 250–400 living Aboriginal languages being spoken in Australia. In 2017, 229 years later, only 147 of those languages still survive and only 18 of them are considered to be strong and vital, with sufficient speakers of all generations to be presumed to be able to continue to thrive. Because of the impact of colonisation, many potential Indigenous PhD scholars do not speak any other language than English. As Doiz et al. (2013, p.1407) so poignantly explain:

> ...languages, and in particular English, play a role in invading other nations linguistically and culturally (Phillipson 2009). In this sense, globalization cannot be deemed neutral, as the learning of powerful languages becomes a heavily loaded engagement by raising feelings of imposition, cultural occupation and identity loss on those who are forced to learn these powerful languages (Shohamy 2007). Thus, the globalization process may bring about tensions between the different languages involved, be they the local language(s), English as a lingua franca, and/or the home language(s).

We argue for the need to move away from the imposed colonial approach to the acquisition of English language skills towards a sovereign rights-based approach but know that many academic supervisors remain under-skilled in this field, particularly in the use of effective pedagogical approaches in the development of doctoral literacy skills with Indigenous scholars. While this response to colonial higher education is still developing, its main argument is that in order for an Indigenous Australian scholar to engage in deep learning of the level required for doctoral studies, their supervisors must have an understanding and empathy of the Indigenous education experience and the loss of sovereignty that Indigenous peoples experience, in part because of the role played by universities in the colonial project (Ma Rhea 2015). Education, particularly higher education, symbolises the pinnacle of achievement in the Western Education system but it also sits at the centre of the assimilation and dispossession of Australian First Nations people. This is also compounded when non-Indigenous Australians regard this loss and complexity as something in the past, having nothing to do with the legacy which exists today (Anderson and Atkinson 2013).

Australian Higher Education: Why Is There a Problem?

Over the years there has been a quick succession of reports and reviews and recommendations that have identified the absence of Indigenous students in the higher degree by research space. The Indigenous Higher Education Advisory Council Report to the Minister for Education, Science and Training (IHEAC March 2006, p. 11) flagged the urgency of the need to address the situation in 'Priority 3: Improve the level of Indigenous postgraduate enrolment, enhance Indigenous research and increase the number of Indigenous researchers'. Two years later the Behrendt Review (Behrendt et al. 2012) also outlined a number of issues or barriers to a steady growth and completion of Indigenous HDR students. More recently, the review of *Australia's Research and Training System* (McGagh et al. 2016) conducted by the Australian Council of Learned Academies identified 'Indigenous Doctoral participation as poor' (2016, p. 94). The report also identifies the following factors as keys to the successful attraction and completion of Indigenous doctoral students: culturally sensitive supervision, cohort support, cultural awareness within institutions, and financial support. Latest figures released by the Department of Education and Training (2016) show currently that there are 409 doctoral students enrolled across Australia. Across all of this research and policy discussion, there is no indication as to whether or not literacy is an aspect that needs consideration in order to ensure successful doctoral completion.

Our research undertaken for this paper suggests that the absence of attention to Indigenous doctoral literacy development is a socially and politically loaded position. Australian higher education has been staunchly monolingual in its development since the colonisation of the Australian landmass and its waterways by the English since 1788. Initially developed as a system for the administrative elites in the early and mid-colonial years, universities expected a high level of competency in the English language, in its grammar, its conventions and its literature of any aspiring scholar. Of particular note for this chapter, the form of English used for both oral and written communication within the international English-speaking university system was a mark of elite status and was purposefully mobilised as such.

Since 1988, the expansion of the Australian higher education system witnessed significant increases in both domestic and international student numbers in keeping with the general trend towards the globalisation and 'widespread Anglicization of higher education' (noted by Bornman and Potgieter 2015, p. 1). In Australia, this has meant that more Indigenous Australians have also been able to undertake university-level studies. Globalisation has also meant that the conventions governing the use of the English language have become more contested. Whose rules? Whose English? The boundaries that preserved and maintained a particular academic literacy whose conventions mirrored the elite social class of the English colonial system have been somewhat blurred by decolonisation, globalisation, nationalist struggles and recognition of Indigenous peoples' rights in education (Zeegers and Barron 2008; Eades 1988).

Academics and social commentators across the English-speaking university system bemoan the general lack of knowledge of, and proficiency in, the English language found in university students. A headline in a British newspaper, *The Independent* (24/05/2006), reflects the mood well: 'University students: They can't write, spell or present an argument' (cited in Turner 2012, p. 17). Concern for 'falling standards' and criticism of 'special treatment' only intensify when one makes an argument regarding policies and measures to increase Indigenous participation in doctoral studies at universities. Many arguments centre on the perceived inability of Indigenous scholars to become sufficiently proficient in the requirements of what is known as *English for Academic Purposes* (EAP). Turner (2012, p.23) highlights the critical importance of what she calls 'the perfect text' by explaining:

> This point of perfect text as it were, is extremely significant in cultural terms as what is expected of academic writing at the highest level. It is also highly ambivalent. On the one hand, it constitutes a point of no return for the student. It is their responsibility to submit such a text. On the other hand, despite all the possible accolades of strong, interesting, and original research, the student him or herself is not capable of meeting the requirement.

The legacy of colonisation ensures that Indigenous Australians are expected to speak English but are rarely expected to perform it well enough to be granted the privileges of acceptance as being fully proficient in the English language (Martin et al. 2015). Without a sound understanding of the impact of colonial practices on Indigenous Australians, especially attempts to stop Indigenous people speaking their ancestral languages and being made to speak 'English', most academics would not understand how such 'damned if you do, damned if you don't' exclusionary, structurally racist practices in universities actually serve to maintain their role as 'gatekeepers' of the higher status levels of academia through their engagement with students about the development of their doctoral literacy.

Doctoral Literacy

Doctoral literacy is recognised as having a number of core competencies that are developed during the period of doctoral candidacy. Research by Durette et al. (2016, p. 1362; see also, Cryer 1998) demonstrates that:

> The most frequently cited category is 'Transferable competencies that can be formalized' mentioned by 79% of PhDs. In this category, communication skills are most frequently cited (62%) including both written and oral communication skills as core competencies.

Many scholars have focused their research efforts on identifying the skills needed by a PhD graduate (e.g., Bégin and Gérard 2013; Mowbray and Halse 2010; Pearson et al. 2011; and, Sekhon 1989). Within the field of English for Academic Purposes, we have reviewed approaches to the development of specific doctoral literacy skills employing such approaches as Halliday's (1985) systemic functional linguistics. Many others have recognised the complex and often contested nature of this particular work, such as Astorga (2007, p.251) who emphasises 'the social nature of writing and the influence that community and culture have on text processing and production'. Recognising the political nature of such work, Astorga (2007, p.255) provides a framework of 'noticing' that includes 'top-down' and 'bottom-up' noticing and 'output noticing' when discussing the structure of the academic text within, for example, a journal article:

> Top-down noticing calls the student's attention to the social purpose of the text and to the meanings conveyed in each stage of its schematic structure; bottom-up noticing orients the student's attention to the specific lexico-grammatical and discourse features that realize the meanings of the text.

Background to this study: Indigenous doctoral development program 2002–2008

Both authors were involved in a program co-hosted by a group of concerned Indigenous and non-Indigenous academics, Indigenous postgraduate supervision quality, particularly in the Humanities and Social Sciences. Each year, for a week Indigenous postgraduate scholars travelled to an Indigenous Postgraduate Summer School. For the purposes of this paper, we draw from a selection of comments from students and their supervisors which sparked this current self-study.

Overall, 80% of Indigenous participants across 2002–2008 consistently ranked 'writing' as one of their key concerns, with supervisors giving a markedly different ranking of 40%. Some Indigenous scholars and their non-Indigenous supervisors expressed more concern with cultural factors and their skills and confidence to supervise at the 'cultural interface', with one participant writing that:

> IDNO 08 (2007): The biggest issue I have found is fighting to use Indigenous ways of seeing the world in academic work. Creating new models/adapting western ones is where I seem to be putting most of my time (and course reading the great Aboriginal writers in this field). I find the traditional academic approaches don't fit the Indigenous stuff all that well.

Overall, the Indigenous participants were significantly more focused on what participants identified as the highlight of their participation in the development program saying:

> IDNO 06 (2002): I came because I wanted to learn about the nuts and bolts of a Ph.D. …
> IDNO 14 (2005): It hones right in on the nuts and bolts of thesis writing ….
> IDNO 03 (2008): It offered a variety of insights (by both students and supervisors) about thesis writing & research …

General remarks given by participants over the course of this program identified specific needs, with comments such as how to write a proposal, writing tips, styles and approaches, more time on writing, more about writing a thesis, deconstructing colonial writing, more writing workshops, sessions dedicated to actual writing, writing for publication, academic writing, more on writing and editing and more about reading strategies. IDNO 04 (2005) summed up the consistent message about academic literacy development needs saying: 'I don't feel confident about my writing'.

Interesting to note, in our discussions with non-Indigenous academics about their supervision of Indigenous students, most could give examples of 'top-down' noticing as an aspect of their critical pedagogical approach, but most were unable to provide the 'bottom-up' noticing required to explain specific lexico-grammatical and discourse features, for example, external conjunctions, mainly consequential, that signal causal relations between clauses within a sentence; text connectives that link sentences and paragraphs; nominalised processes, that is, using nouns instead of verbs to encode actions; or modality resources (for different degrees of probability, usuality and obligation) that express a position about a specific phenomenon, convey attitudes, temper judgements and make arguments credible (Astorga 2007, p. 256).

Adding to such detailed knowledge requirements, Indigenous PhD scholars bring versions of English to their written work that would be unfamiliar to most academics. As Cumming (2013 p. 131–132) observes:

Multilingual writers tend naturally to use resources from each of their languages while they write, and they inevitably adopt new personal identities as they express themselves while writing in new academic discourse communities.

Cumming goes on to suggest that the PhD supervisor might, 'through reciprocal modeling and dynamic assessment, usefully capitalize on these and other related processes to enhance learners' strategic development of academic literacy abilities' (p. 132). As will be discussed in the following sections, most academics have little knowledge or confidence to employ such methods of doctoral literacy development.

The challenges facing the PhD supervisor are significant when faced with the task of making explicit the rules and conventions of doctoral literacy such that the PhD candidate can learn the necessary skills to produce a thesis in the English language. A daunting task for a well-educated student who comes from the dominant culture, what is the responsibility of the supervisor when the scholar is Indigenous? As noted above, many academics report on research where they have explicitly attempted to make explicit the 'hidden' aspects of English for Academic Purposes at the undergraduate level for both Indigenous (e.g., Rochecouste et al. 2017; Rose et al. 2003, 2008) and international students (Zeegers and Barron 2008). As Murray and Nallaya (2016, p. 1298) explain:

Students need to be made aware of the fact that, unlike generic, context-neutral study skills, literacy practices in their disciplines are socially situated … Students thus need to develop a working understanding of those discourses and to recognize that the genres to which they should strive to conform in their written work … Their written work will be read and assessed by other bona fide members of those communities who will have expectations in relation to the literacy practices that form the norm within their respective disciplines.

While not specifically concerned with doctoral literacy development, Nakata and colleagues (Martin et al. 2015) develop the theoretical groundwork for considering how the core competency of 'written communication' can be understood at this cultural interface, suggesting that there is need for supervisors and others involved in doctoral training to consider a pedagogy that engages Indigenous persistence in tertiary study and that does not fall into deficit thinking or political correctness (see also Pearson and Brew 2002).

Pedagogies for Doctoral Literacy Development

Like Martin et al. (2015), Turner (2012) highlights the role of pedagogy that gives, 'a focus on the socio-political dynamics of EAP [that] situates its pedagogical work within a wider context of institutional politics, policies, and practices, as well as the geopolitical context of English more generally'. In addition, as Murray and Nallaya (2016) explain, PhD scholars need to develop, '… an understanding of language (and specifically academic literacies) as fundamental to the student's integration into their disciplinary community of practice'. In the case of Indigenous PhD scholars, their research would suggest that the PhD supervisor needs to have in place a plan of instructional design involving such elements as, '…modelling, feedback, reinforcement, questioning, task structuring, and direct instruction' (Murray and Nallaya 2016 pp. 1299–1300).

The literature is much more insistent in its arguments for the need for academics to employ various aspects of critical pedagogy. Both Haque (2007) and Zeegers and Barron (2008) deftly summarise the main elements of critical pedagogies that seek to both embed scholars in the academic writing genre that is required and also make explicit the coercive elements of those norms and conventions. Haque (2007, p. 88) cites Pennycook (1997) in making a distinction between:

> …vulgar pragmatism, as an ideological discourse that reproduces an unreflexive acceptance of the status quo valuing efficiency and instrumentality, and critical pragmatism, which is also an ideological discourse, but one that values reflection and a sense of crisis with choices around standards, beliefs, values and discourse practices themselves. (See also Cherryholmes 1988, p. 179)

The problem, broadly, with the critical pedagogy literature is that it gives little direction to a PhD supervisor about how to develop doctoral literacy even while being mindful of the racist, colonial and highly contested context of the work. As Ewald (1999, p. 278) notes 'the exploration of critical pedagogy must move from principles to materials, lesson plans, classroom activities, assessment tools, and course designs'. What is apparent in our analysis of available research is that intentional planning for academic literacy development is an important aspect of the work as is the way in which a sovereign rights-based pedagogy needs to underpin the learning theories held by supervising academics and the pedagogical content knowledge that they bring to this work (Lea 2004; Lea and Street 1998).

Methodology

In order to address what we perceive as a critical gap in research about the development of doctoral literacy with indigenous PhD students in the Humanities and Social Sciences, we have undertaken a critical, self-study of supervision and engagement within our doctoral supervision relationship, embedding our analysis in the Australian higher education policy landscape and offering future direction for research and PhD supervisory skill development into the future.

The methodology of 'self-study' has evolved over the last 30 years emerging out of the field of Teacher Education (Hawley and Hostetler 2017), but they argue for the usefulness of the approach in fields where the researcher/practitioner is:

> The promise of self-study is improved educational practices through inquiry that leverages collaboration and context responsive design features for rich learning in and through practice. (p. 83–84)

In our practice and theorising of our work together as a male, Indigenous PhD scholar and a female, non-Indigenous PhD supervisor, we felt that we needed to focus our study on aspects of the production of a thesis into a literary work where academic literacy requirements and supervisor interventions for literacy development meet colonial impositions and brutal status markers (Petrarca and Bullock 2014). We wanted to examine the potential of our engagement to navigate and understand this collision. We employed a sovereign rights-based approach to our work because we wanted to recognise that Indigenous *sui generis* rights were not extinguished during the period of English colonisation of Australia (Janke 1998) and that the imposition of English as the medium of doctoral supervision and of examination of PhD theses in Australia, by its very nature, highly contested.

Methods

Data Collection

Our focus on the impact of culture on academic literacy development is echoed in the work of authors whose focus has been on the examination of supervisor/PhD student interactions where the student is from an overseas, non-English-background speaking country. Xu (2017) employed a quantitative and then self-reflective approach to her research. As she (2017, p. 240) explains:

> Given the complex rather than unitary nature of supervision, my study is not aiming to be representative or to provide large-scale generalization. Instead, I attempt to offer deep insight into a snapshot of feedback dialogue between a supervision pair, in which I am the student. The author/researcher being the participant makes the study a reflective practice in some way, through which I try to participate consciously and creatively in the process of learning (Zeichner 1999), and to draw supervisors', supervisees' and researchers' attention to the often complex interactions that occur in intercultural supervision.

For this self-study, we adopted a narrative stance for both data collection and analysis (Creswell 2012). We sporadically documented our experiences and thoughts over the period of 8 years and shared our reflections with one another at supervision sessions, held on a fortnightly basis. We 'butcher papered' some of these conversations, mapping thoughts, emotions and connections as we grew our understanding of what we were trying to achieve. In addition to our own data, we examined the literature emerging from the new field of Indigenous rights in education, and we especially followed the work of those seeking to better understand how to work at the interface of a globally changing approach to doctoral work, challenges posed by previously excluded scholars about the 'rules' of the PhD and the 'standards' arguments (Pearson 1999). As discussed previously, our questions were both triggered and framed by our involvement in the Indigenous Postgraduate Summer Schools, and we drew on feedback given by 85 Indigenous postgraduate research students and Australian higher education policy documents to help us to understand the similarities and differences in approach emerging in this field.

Data Analysis

In our critical conversations, we challenged each other to explore more deeply our assumptions and misunderstandings in the cultural interface of academic literacy development. We identified similarities and differences between our experiences. The main focus was to examine the evolution of our own thinking about how to develop a doctoral supervision pedagogy that is able to meet the institutional demands of the task while also engaging in the sovereign rights-based requirements.

We framed our self-study analysis around the feedback from 85 Indigenous PhD students who attended an Indigenous doctoral development program between 2002 and 2008, using manual coding to reveal themes. For this preliminary analysis, we focused on themes that were of particular importance to academic literacy development, examining these data together with our self-study findings.

Findings

Observations from Our Self-Study

At the initial stages of the PhD journey, we found that we were not so much concerned with academic literacy development. Our initial discussions and reflections revolved around the issues noted by others that establishing a respectful relationship founded on a recognition of Indigenous rights in education became our first work together. We give a couple of examples here to highlight the initial work: setting the stage and finding agreement about the political nature of the work.

Setting the Stage

Peter: At the time of my enrolment I was an academic in a university where I had completed my undergraduate degrees. I was also enrolled in a PhD, yet it was in an area that I was not interested, but rather corralled into an indigenous space by my indigeneity which was not motivating at all, so I didn't really think about literacy (my own) at all as I did not want to write at all.

Zane: When you [Peter] approached me to supervise you, I wasn't so much thinking about what literacy skills you had. Indigenous friends had recommended you to me as someone with the potential to lead the development of education in Australia and that they were entrusting you to me to "teach [him] the ropes". I assumed you could write to a high academic standard because you had a good Honors degree.

Finding Agreement About the Political Nature of the Work

Peter: At the time of my enrolment in my personal and professional Indigenous network there was next to no one with a PhD and being somewhat ambitious and having been told at secondary school that I was likely to not succeed, I wanted one and was determined have one, a determined personality trait.

Zane: To me, a PhD is a piece of work that demonstrates that you are able to contribute new knowledge to a field. With you [Peter] it is much more than that. I see it as an act of courage to stay true to who you are and become the best you can be in the western university system. Yes, you could do the more expected Indigenous–related topic and you could find the big issue that really interests you and research that.

Getting Out Grammar Books!

The focus on academic literacy development began to come into focus as the demands of the PhD journey started to require written text for summaries of reading and for the preparation of the PhD confirmation document (Turner 2016). It was at this stage that we began talking about how to write in an academic style. Our discussions and musings ranged across the fact that most Indigenous scholars are monolingual in only speaking English but that the philosophical and contextualisation aspects of their work could be profoundly Indigenous. Both of us being educators, we went to English grammar books and to the literature on how to develop academic literacy. These conversations guided the next stages of the work. We found the work of Cumming (2013, p.132) as particularly helpful in focusing our work on:

1. Heuristic search strategies involving language switching for choices of words and phrases while composing
2. Expressions of personal identity while writing for specific discourse communities

Cumming goes on to suggest that the PhD supervisor might, 'through reciprocal modeling and dynamic assessment, usefully capitalize on these and other related processes to enhance learners' strategic development of academic literacy abilities'. Following Cumming (2013, p.135), we also found Ivanic (1998) helpful in suggesting that university students progressively, but variably, learn to express four aspects of their identities in their writing: (a) an autobiographical self, (b) a discoursal self, (c) a self as an author and (d) possibilities for selfhood.

8 Indigenous Doctoral Literacy in the Humanities and Social Sciences 139

Peter: Looking back on my own journey and supervising Indigenous students particularly who are like I was ... those who are strong and grounded in our cultures ... Yet there was and is with some students an aspect of shyness in outwardly forging an academic identity which of course means some mastery of the English written language. This was something that I sought from my supervisor and our sessions.

Zane: I reflected from what Peter was telling me that he wanted, and needed, confirmation that he could foreground aspects of theory and philosophy that were important to him as an Aboriginal man and that he wanted to be able to write about his ideas in a way that would be understood by an academic audience. He respected my mastery of the genre and wanted me to model my writing style to him in a way that he could then take and develop into his own. This spoke to me of the research that focused on identity formation as an academic writer demonstrating 'reciprocal modeling and dynamic assessment' (Cumming). So I planned to incorporate aspects of all of this into our fortnightly supervision sessions...a bit of modeling of writing from an idea, finding literature, teasing out the important parts, learning to précis the main idea, and then constructing a critical narrative about the idea in relation to the research question. Each time, the matters of Indigenous rights and of identity were there in the middle of these very technical discussions about the elements and mechanics of English language, of grammatical style, and of the art of writing that also involved a lot of discussion about the potential threat to identity and belonging if, as an Aboriginal man, one was to master this genre and succeed in being able to write "like this".

Working Out How

It became clear over the years of our discussions, disagreements, frustrations with and deep respect for each other and the process we were both doing and trying to engage with and change that we needed some technical literacy understanding as Peter began the process of drafting his chapters and developing a writing style that satisfied him. We turned to Astorga (2007) and worked with her suggestions. Zane gave specific feedback about the grammatical categories and labels that Peter found problematic or difficult, providing transparent explanations about a certain linguistic feature in that Peter wanted to use but Zane felt did not communicate his idea properly. Her use of the word 'proper' always raised questions for us about whether it is 'proper' to write in the Aboriginal English style in a PhD. The main aspects of Zane's engagement with giving feedback on Peter's developing chapters were regarding the structure of the thesis and the clear communication of the findings but its foundational challenges were always about punctuation, nominalisation of nouns and grammatical style.

Peter: What really got me through was the level of trust that I had in my supervisor I had learned and watched over the years her successful engagement with HDR students. The key aspect that struck the cord was relationality, a primary foundation that is found in my culture. This came out completely by accident.

Zane: None of this engagement with Peter's writing style was different from my non-Indigenous PhD students. What was different was that I was relying on the strength of the trust that had developed between us over previous years so that when the pressure began to build, and Peter needed to pay attention to the technical aspects of the thesis to convert the writing into a well-edited and proofread piece, that the potential collision at the cultural interface did not destroy the final part of the PhD journey. Different students have different ways of dealing with this final pressure but it is precisely because of the colonial past that the option to walk away and denigrate the process is at its most appealing in these final stages.

At this stage, we employed a technique described by Astorga (2007, p. 265) called 'noticing on output' that she explains is:

> ... to encourage the students to notice features of their texts, not during but after writing, which means that they have to consider the product (or output) of the writing process. The pedagogic objectives of this stage cannot be achieved by simply telling the students "to consider what is right or wrong with your texts." ... I scaffolded the process of self-assessment with guidelines that ... required the students to consider discrete features of their texts first, such as their use of conjunctions, or text connectives, or the syntax of their sentences. As they gained more experience in detecting specific features of their written texts, they began to make integrative observations, thus assessing their texts from various analytical perspectives at the same time.

Discussion of Findings

At issue are a number of matters arising from our self-study, feedback from the Indigenous Postgraduate Summer School (IPSS) data and the broader literature. First, our reflection was that matters relating to writing style and doctoral literacy developed later in the process. This was not reflected in the feedback from the IPSS where most Indigenous scholars wanted a focus on their writing from an early time in their candidature. In our self-study, once Peter started to develop his critical review of literature, Zane felt confident in her doctoral writing skills, and both Peter and Zane were comfortable to get out grammar books and explore the literacy development literature together to support the development of Peter's doctoral writing skills. From the feedback from the IPSS, supervisors mostly did not like to speak about their approach to this aspect of the work but, when pressed, said that they generally knew little about the literacy skills of their Indigenous PhD students, and like the findings of Lockhart (2016), most did not have confidence in their pedagogical skills to engage in culturally appropriate academic literacy development at the PhD level.

Second, Zane and Peter had both been involved over many years in encouraging and supporting universities to offer targeted doctoral-level support to Indigenous postgraduates. In our self-study, we were keenly aware of the lack of such resources at our university. There were many opportunities for undergraduate Indigenous students but markedly less support available to postgraduates. Feedback from the IPSS suggested that most non-Indigenous supervisors were ignorant of the policies and procedures of their universities to either support the needs of their Indigenous students or support for their skills development in being able to effectively engage with Indigenous PhD students, with most commenting that the IPSS was the first time they had been able to get support. Like the literature, those who knew about support services said that the emphasis at their university focuses on creating a culturally safe space for Indigenous students (Grant 2010; Trudgett 2009, 2011). Peter and Zane were keenly aware that there is little specific support given to Indigenous PhD scholars for the development of their academic literacy and that they would need to work it out for themselves.

Third, our self-study highlighted the importance of the non-Indigenous supervisor having an understanding of the cultural needs of the Indigenous doctoral student. While Zane has been involved with the Australian Indigenous community over many years, feedback from other non-Indigenous supervisors suggested that they knew little about Indigenous politics, culture or lifeways and had little understanding of Indigenous *sui generis* rights in education, or the Indigenous world outside the university, but that like for Peter and his Indigenous mentors, this is an important aspect for most Indigenous scholars who want any non-Indigenous supervisors to be knowledgeable at the 'cultural interface'. While possibly of different imports in the early stages of the PhD journey, we found that as the pressure builds for the completion of an examinable PhD in the discipline of, and confidence in, editing written work to a high standard of English academic literacy, this strength of understanding of the multiple pressures on an Indigenous scholar becomes vital in the successful completion of the tome.

Conclusion

This self-study famed by Indigenous higher education policies and an analysis of evaluation feedback from an Indigenous doctoral development program points to the need for further research into the development of a pedagogical approach to Indigenous PhD supervision. Our self-study found that we needed to develop explicitly deimperialised, postcolonial pedagogical skills to engage with the academic literacy demands of the thesis. Zane, as the supervisor, needed to have knowledge of Indigenous rights in education and have an understanding of the historical context of the work. She needed to be able to demonstrate mastery not only of her subject but also of doctoral writing skills. Peter needed to be willing to be inculcated into the conventions of his chosen field without feeling that he had to sacrifice his identity. For that work, we needed together to develop Peter's academic writing identity, including technical aspects of heuristic and expressive literacy such as personhood, autonomy and relatedness within his cultural worldview.

We note that while many universities remain committed to the philosophy of 'creating a safe learning environment for Indigenous students', there appears to be scant attention made to the detailed doctoral literacy development work that is needed (Commonwealth of Australia 2018; IHEAC and DET 2006). Our self-study has revealed some of the possible pedagogical matters that require further attention. We also note that feedback from willing supervisors of Indigenous PhD scholars suggests that many do not feel that they have the skills to undertake this work. This raises the question of whether the doctoral supervision relationship should be the place for this work to be done. Rather is it necessary to investigate the skills and knowledge of literacy support staff in universities to determine their potential contribution in this space?

Certainly, what we can conclude from our small study is that if Australian government higher education policy intends to lead to the acceleration of successful Indigenous doctoral completion rates, then more targeted research must be undertaken to assess the potential impact of poor doctoral literacy development on these slow completion rates.

References

Anderson, P. J., & Atkinson, B. M. (2013). Closing the gap: Using graduate attributes to improve Indigenous education. *International Education Journal: Comparative Perspectives, 12*(1), 135–145.

Astorga, M. C. (2007). Teaching academic writing in the EFL context: Redesigning pedagogy. *Pedagogies: An International Journal, 2*(4), 251–267. https://doi.org/10.1080/15544800701670089.

Bégin, C., & Gérard, L. (2013). The role of supervisors in light of the experience of doctoral students. *Policy Futures in Education, 11*(3), 267–276.

Behrendt, L., Larkin, S., Griew, R., & Kelly, P. (2012). *Review of higher education access and outcomes for Aboriginal and Torres Strait Islander people* (Final report). Retrieved from http://www.innovation.gov

Bornman, E., & Potgieter, P. H. (2015). Language choices and identity in higher education: Afrikaans-speaking students at Unisa. *Studies in Higher Education, 42*, 1–14. https://doi.org/10.1080/03075079.2015.1104660.

Cherryholmes, C. (1988). *Power and criticism: Poststructural investigations in education.* New York: Teachers College Press.

Commonwealth of Australia. (2018). *Closing the gap Prime Minister's report 2018.* Canberra: Department of the Prime Minister and Cabinet.

Creswell, J. W. (2012). *Qualitative inquiry and research design.* Thousand Oaks: Sage.

Cryer, P. (1998). Transferable skills, marketability and lifelong learning: The particular case of postgraduate research students. *Studies in Higher Education, 23*, 207–216.

Cumming, A. (2013, March). Multiple dimensions of academic language and literacy development. *Language Learning: A Journal of Research in Language Studies, 63*(Suppl 1), 130–152. https://doi.org/10.1111/j.1467-9922.2012.00741.x.

Department of Education and Training. (2016). *Indigenous student data 2016.* Department of Education and Training. Online available at: https://docs.education.gov.au/node/45181

Doiz, A., Lasagabaster, D., & Sierra, J. (2013). Globalisation, internationalisation, multilingualism, and linguistic strains in higher education. *Studies in Higher Education, 38*(9), 1407–1421. https://doi.org/10.1080/03075079.2011.642349.

Durette, B., Fournier, M., & Lafon, M. (2016). The core competencies of PhDs. *Studies in Higher Education, 41*(8), 1355–1370. https://doi.org/10.1080/03075079.2014.968540.

Eades, D. (1988). They don't speak an aboriginal language, or do they? In I. Keen (Ed.), *Being black: Aboriginal cultures in 'settled' Australia* (pp. 56–75). Canberra: Aboriginal Studies Press for Australian Institute of Aboriginal Studies.

Eades, D. (1991). Communicative strategies in Aboriginal English. In S. Romaine (Ed.), *Language in Australia* (pp. 84–93). Melbourne: Cambridge University Press.

Ewald, J. D. (1999). A plea for published reports on the application of a critical pedagogy to 'language study proper. *TESOL Quarterly, 33*, 275–279.

Furneaux, C. (2016). Chapter 9: Becoming a post/graduate writer in a social science discipline. In C. Badenhorst & C. Guerin (Eds.), *Research literacies and writing pedagogies for masters and doctoral writers* (pp. 166–183). Leiden: Koninklijke Brill NV.

Grant, B. M. (2010). The limits of 'teaching and learning': Indigenous students and doctoral supervision. *Teaching in Higher Education, 15*(5), 505–517. https://doi.org/10.1080/135625 17.2010.491903.

Halliday, M. A. K. (1985). *An introduction to functional grammar*. London: Edward Arnold.

Haque, E. (2007). Critical pedagogy in English for Academic Purposes and the possibility for 'tactics' of resistance. *Pedagogy, Culture & Society, 15*(1), 83–106. https://doi.org/10.1080/14681360601162311.

Harrison, N., Trudgett, M., & Page, S. (2017). The dissertation examination: Identifying critical factors in the success of Indigenous Australian doctoral students. *Assessment & Evaluation in Higher Education, 42*(1), 115–127. https://doi.org/10.1080/02602938.2015.1085488.

Hawley, T. S., & Hostetler, A. L. (2017). Self-study as an emergent methodology in career and technical education, adult education and technology: An invitation to inquiry. *International Journal of Adult Vocational Education and Technology, 8*(2), 82–92.

Indigenous Higher Education Advisory Council [IHEAC] & Department of Education, Science, and Training. (2006). *Improving indigenous outcomes and enhancing indigenous culture and knowledge in Australian higher education: Report to the Minister for Education, Science, and Training*. Canberra: Department of Education, Science and Training.

Ivanic, R. (1998). *Writing and identity: The discoursal construction of identity in academic writing*. Amsterdam: John Benjamins.

Janke, T. (1998). *Our culture, our future: Report on Australian indigenous cultural and intellectual property right*. Canberra: Australian Institute of Aboriginal and Torres Strait Islander Studies and Aboriginal and Torres Strait Islander Commission.

Lea, M. (2004). Academic literacies: A pedagogy for course design. *Studies in Higher Education, 29*(6), 739–756.

Lea, M., & Street, B. (1998). Student writing in higher education: An academic literacies approach. *Studies in Higher Education, 23*(2), 157–172.

Lockhart, T. (2016). Chapter 20: Flexibility, hybridity, and writing: Theory and practice for developing post/graduate literacies. In C. Badenhorst & C. Guerin (Eds.), *Research literacies and writing pedagogies for masters and doctoral writers* (pp. 371–388). Leiden: Koninklijke Brill NV.

Loughran, J. (2012). *What expert teachers do: Enhancing professional knowledge for classroom practice*. London: Routledge. https://doi.org/10.4324/9780203851470.

Ma Rhea, Z. (2015). Unthinking the 200 year old colonial mindset: Indigenist perspectives on leading and managing Indigenous Education. *International Education Journal: Comparative Perspectives, 14*(2), 90–100.

Ma Rhea, Z., & Anderson, P. J. (2011). Economic justice and indigenous education: Assessing the potential of standards-based and progressive education under ILO169. *Social Alternatives, 30*(4), 25–31.

Ma, Rhea, Z., & Rigney, L. I. (2002). Researching with respect: Supervising aboriginal or Torres Strait Islander students. In J. Sillitoe, G. Crosling, J. Webb, & S. Vance (Eds.), *Assisting beginning research students from non-traditional backgrounds* (pp. 8–19). Melbourne: Higher Education, Research, and Development, HERDSA.

Martin, G., Nakata, V., Nakata, M., & Day, A. (2015). Promoting the persistence of indigenous students through teaching at the cultural interface. *Studies in Higher Education, 42*, 1158. https://doi.org/10.1080/03075079.2015.1083001.

McConvell, P., & Thieberger, N. (2001). *State of Indigenous languages in Australia – 2001* (Australia State of the Environment Second Technical Paper Series (Natural and Cultural Heritage)). Canberra: Department of the Environment and Heritage. http://www.ea.gov.au/soe/techpapers/index.html.

McGagh, J., Marsh, H., Western, M., Thomas, P., Hastings, A., Mihailova, M., & Wenham, M. (2016). *Review of Australia's research training system* (Report for the Australian Council of Learned Academies). www.acola.org.au

Mowbray, S., & Halse, C. (2010). The purpose of the Ph.D.: Theorising the skills acquired by students. *Higher Education Research & Development, 29*(6), 653–664.

Murray, N., & Nallaya, S. (2016). Embedding academic literacies in university programme curricula: A case study. *Studies in Higher Education, 41*(7), 1296–1312. https://doi.org/10.1 080/03075079.2014.981150.

Nakata, M. (2007a). *Disciplining the savages: Savaging the disciplines.* Canberra: ACT: Aboriginal Studies Press.

Nakata, M. (2007b). The cultural interface. *The Australian Journal of Indigenous Education, 36S,* 7–14.

do Nascimento, A. M. (2014). Geopolíticas de escrita acadêmica em zonas de contato: problematizando representações e práticas de estudantes indígenas. *Trabalhos em Linguística Aplicada, 53*(2), 267–297. https://doi.org/10.1590/S0103-18132014000200002.

Pearson, M. (1999). The changing environment for doctoral education in Australia: Implications for quality management, improvement, and innovation. *Higher Education Research & Development, 18*(3), 269–287.

Pearson, M., & Brew, A. (2002). Research training and supervision development. *Studies in Higher Education, 27*(2), 135–150.

Pearson, M., Cumming, J., Evans, T., Macauley, P., & Ryland, K. (2011). How shall we know them? Capturing the diversity of differences in Australian doctoral candidates and their experiences. *Studies in Higher Education, 36*(5), 527–542.

Pennycook, A. (1997). Vulgar pragmatism, critical pragmatism, and EAP. *English for Specific Purposes, 16*(4), 253–269.

Petrarca, D., & Bullock, S. M. (2014). Tensions between theory and practice: Interrogating our pedagogy through collaborative self-study. *Professional Development in Education, 40*(2), 265–281. DOI: 0.1080/19415257.2013.801876.

Phillipson, R. (2009). Linguistic imperialism continued. New York: Routledge.

Productivity Commission. (2018). *Report of government services.* Canberra: ACT: Australian Government. Retrieved from https://www.pc.gov.au/research/ongoing/report-on-government-services/2018/child-care-education-and-training/school-education.

Read, J. (2008). Identifying academic language needs through diagnostic assessment. *Journal of English for Academic Purposes, 7,* 180–190.

Rochecouste, J., Oliver, R., Bennell, D., Anderson, R., Cooper, I., & Forrest, S. (2017). Teaching Australian aboriginal higher education students: What should universities do? *Studies in Higher Education, 42*(11), 2080–2098. https://doi.org/10.1080/03075079.2015.1134474.

Rose, D., Lui-Chivizhe, L., McKnight, A., & Smith, A. (2003). Scaffolding academic reading and writing at the Koori Centre. *The Australian Journal of Indigenous Education, 32,* 41–49.

Rose, D., Rose, M., Farrington, S., & Page, S. (2008). Scaffolding academic literacy with indigenous health sciences students: An evaluative study. *Journal of English for Academic Purposes, 7,* 165–179. https://doi.org/10.1016/j.jeap.2008.05.004.

Sekhon, J. G. (1989). Ph.D. education and Australia's industrial future: Time to think again. *Higher Education Research & Development, 8*(2), 191–215.

Shohamy, E. (2007). Reinterpreting globalisation in multilingual contexts. *International Multilingual Research Journal, 1,* 127–133.

Trudgett, M. (2009). Build it and they will come: Building the capacity of indigenous units in universities to provide better support for indigenous Australian postgraduate students. *Australian Journal of Indigenous Education, 38*, 9–18.

Trudgett, M. (2011). Western places, academic spaces and indigenous faces: Supervising indigenous Australian postgraduate students. *Teaching in Higher Education, 16*(4), 389–399. https://doi.org/10.1080/13562517.2011.560376.

Turner, J. (2012). Academic literacies: Providing a space for the socio-political dynamics of EAP. *Journal of English for Academic Purposes, 11*, 17–25. https://doi.org/10.1016/j.jeap.2011.11.007.

Turner, J. (2016). Chapter 11: The symbolic economy of research literacies: The role of "Writtenness". In the Ph.D. Thesis in C. Badenhorst, & C. Guerin (Eds.) *Research literacies and writing pedagogies for masters and doctoral writers* (pp. 205–220). Leiden: Koninklijke Brill NV.

United Nations. (2008). *United Nations declaration on the rights of indigenous peoples* [UNDRIPs]. Retrieved from http://www.un.org/esa/socdev/unpfii/documents/DRIPS_en.pdf

Winchester-Seeto, T., Homewood, J., Thogersen, J., Jacenyik-Trawoger, C., Manathunga, C., Reid, A., & Holbrook, A. (2014). Doctoral supervision in a cross-cultural context: Issues affecting supervisors and candidates. *Higher Education Research & Development, 33*(3), 610–626. https://doi.org/10.1080/07294360.2013.841648.

Xu, L. (2017). Written feedback in intercultural doctoral supervision: A case study. *Teaching in Higher Education, 22*(2), 239–255. https://doi.org/10.1080/13562517.2016.1237483.

Zeichner, K. (1999). The new scholarship in teacher education. *Educational Researcher, 28*(9), 4–15.

Zeegers, M., & Barron, D. (2008). Discourses of deficit in higher degree research supervisory pedagogies for international students. *Pedagogies, 3*(2), 69–84. https://doi.org/10.1080/15544800801929393.

Professor Zane M. Diamond has worked with Indigenous people over the last 35 years in various capacities. She is recognised internationally for expertise in comparative education and for improving the quality of education and other human services to Indigenous people using a rights-based framework. She supervises students in the fields of Indigenous Education, Leadership, Change Management, Indigenous-Settler Studies and Organisational Development.

Professor Peter J. Anderson is from the Warlpiri and Murrinh-Patha, First Nations in the Northern Territory. He is an Associate Professor at Queensland University of Technology where he is the Director of the Indigenous Research and Engagement Unit. His research theorises the understandings of the organisational value of academic freedom in Australian universities and more broadly the polar south. His current research is in the areas of organisational leadership, indigenous peoples' education and teacher and academic professional development.

Chapter 9
Preparing Pre-service Teachers to Teach Literacy in Remote Spaces

Jennifer Rennie and Peter J. Anderson

Abstract Remote Indigenous communities are often seen as challenging places in which to teach for a range of reasons. Student attendance is erratic, and teachers can feel that their work is not effective. Additionally, remote communities are culturally as well as geographically very isolated, with limited access to services (Price K, Teacher education for high poverty schools. Springer, New York, 2016). Hence, it is often difficult to attract and retain teachers, and those teachers who do take up jobs in remote schools may not feel they have been adequately prepared to work in those settings. In recent years, universities and education departments have put in place a number of initiatives to attract and retain "good" teachers in these communities. For example, several universities offer placement experiences for pre-service teachers to help them develop some understanding of what it means to work and live in remote communities and for them to develop their pedagogical skills to work effectively with Indigenous learners. In this chapter we examine the kinds of knowledge and skills that pre-service teachers need in order to work in the literacy space in remote schools. Our study refers to data from interviews with pre-service teachers, community members and school personnel. It focuses on preparedness for teaching literacy in remote settings, the disconnects between the pre-service curriculum and the expectations of schools and departments and pre-service teachers' expectations versus the realities of their lived experience on community. Data is drawn from a broader study which sought to understand how we might better plan, implement and prepare pre-service teachers for remote teaching placements so that we might provide guidance for universities, jurisdictions and policy-makers.

J. Rennie (✉)
Monash University, Melbourne, VIC, Australia
e-mail: jennifer.rennie@monash.edu

P. J. Anderson
Indigenous Research and Engagement Unit, QUT, Brisbane, OLD, Australia
e-mail: p21.anderson@qut.edu.au

© Springer Nature Singapore Pte Ltd. 2019
J. Rennie, H. Harper (eds.), *Literacy Education and Indigenous Australians*,
Language Policy 19, https://doi.org/10.1007/978-981-13-8629-9_9

Setting the Context

Just over one quarter of Australian Aboriginal and Torres Strait Islander people reside in remote or very remote locations (ABS 2013). Nonetheless, the majority of schools in remote or very remote locations have Aboriginal and Torres Strait Islander enrolments greater than 90%. Remote communities are generally categorised as areas of high socioeconomic disadvantage. For example, in the Northern Territory, 36 out of the 38 schools that are classified "very remote" have an Index of Community Social-Educational Advantage (ICSEA) below 800, well below the average score of 1000 (ACARA 2017). Remote schools are therefore mostly described as high-needs schools and present a number of challenges for both students and teachers (Price 2016). As has been reported elsewhere in this book, students in remote locations in Australia fare worse than their urban peers in standardised tests of literacy and numeracy achievement. Teachers often don't feel effective, and this has attendant problems of stress, anxiety and ultimately teacher turnover.

The difficulty of adequately preparing teachers to work in the remote space has long been recognised. In 2000 the Senate Employment Workplace Relations, Small Business and Education References Committee (2000) said:

> Though Indigenous education represents a significant challenge for teachers and requires high levels of skill and sensitivity to the needs of students, many teachers in Indigenous communities were amongst the most inexperienced and least adequately prepared to meet the challenges of teaching in such demanding and unfamiliar environments. (p. 103)

Almost a decade later in a survey conducted by the Australian Education Union of 1545 teachers, 75% felt their Initial Teacher Education (henceforth ITE) had not prepared them to teach Indigenous students (Labone et al. 2014).

> In recent years a number of initiatives and policy imperatives have been put in place to try and redress the issues of teacher preparedness and retention in remote and very remote communities. The Australian Institute for Teaching and School Leadership has developed professional standards for graduating students, two of which are specifically Indigenous focused. One of these two standards focuses on effective strategies for teaching Aboriginal and Torres Strait Islander students and the other requires teachers to show a respect and understanding of students (AITSL 2011). The standards mean that universities must include relevant content in their courses (Anderson and Atkinson 2014).

A review of Indigenous Education in the Northern Territory (Wilson 2014) put forward a number of recommendations concerning what and how the Department of Education should negotiate with ITE providers. With respect to literacy, the report suggested that ITE should attend to evidence-based approaches (incorporating phonological awareness and phonics, teaching EAL/D learners and assessment), as well as Indigenous languages, cultural awareness and community engagement. Similarly, education departments have been looking seriously at how best to recruit teachers to remote and very remote locations. In 2010 the then Northern Territory Department of Education and Training (DET) launched their Quality Remote Teaching Service Program as a means to recruit teachers for their 82 remote schools. The process involved a number of stages aimed to assess applicants' suitability for working in these contexts (Brasche and Harrington 2013).

One recommendation of the Wilson report was that, where possible, pre-service teachers undertake a practicum in at least one remote school (Wilson 2014). As a result many universities are now offering professional experience opportunities in remote schools. This has been an area of expansion with the emergence of a recent research agenda into the challenges and opportunities for doing this work (see, e.g. Auld et al. 2016; Brasche and Harrington 2013; Moreton-Robinson et al. 2012; Rennie et al. 2018).

Whilst the remote practicum can be a window into life as a remote teacher, planning for and enacting this work is not without its challenges (Osborne 2003). In addition to logistical considerations such as placement planning and coordinating, expense, geographical isolation and challenges of finding suitable accommodation for pre-service teachers, there is also the issue of how well prepared pre-service teachers are to teach and live in remote places (Auld et al. 2016; Sharplin 2002; Yarrow et al. 1999).

Research has highlighted the importance of ensuring that students have the necessary knowledge to interact in a culturally competent way with Indigenous communities and to employ culturally relevant pedagogies. For example, one of the main recommendations of the Indigenous Cultural Competency (ICC) Reform in Australian Universities (2011) project was for all university graduates to "have the knowledge and skills necessary to interact in a culturally competent way with Indigenous communities" (DEEWR 2011, p. 9). This project also noted that Australian universities should aim to produce teaching graduates "who have a comprehensive understanding of … remote education grounded in practical experience and theoretical knowledge" (DEEWR 2011, p. 3). However, it is difficult to know exactly how this should be enacted in the literacy space. Understanding how to prepare pre-service teachers to teach literacy is paramount given the national priority in improving literacy outcomes for Indigenous students (Commonwealth of Australia 2018).

The Study

The data discussed in this chapter was part of a larger project that implemented and evaluated a remote teaching placement funded through a grant received in 2015 from the Indigenous Advancement Strategy (Federal Government). The project was designed to address the national agenda developing a teaching force that is better prepared to work in remote and very remote communities, by providing pre-service teachers with an opportunity to explore career opportunities that they may not ordinarily have considered. In planning the experience we were conscious of the need to adequately prepare teachers, so we worked closely with communities and schools to develop an induction program that was tailored to their specific needs. Further, we used a rigorous selection process to ensure that we sent teachers who were best suited for the experience.

Interviews were used as the primary source of data collection to understand the experiences of various stakeholders in the students' remote placements. Ethics approval was granted by Monash University for the project. We interviewed two principals, two assistant principals, seven mentor teachers, two Indigenous teaching assistants and ten pre-service teachers. With the exception of the pre-service teachers who were interviewed both pre- and post-placement, all of the other stakeholders were interviewed once post-placement. The interview included a number of questions about the development and implementation of the placement, how well we worked with the school and community in this regard and how well prepared our pre-service teachers were to work in this space. We also asked questions specifically about preparation for teaching literacy, and it is this aspect of the study that we focus on here. Transcripts from each of the groups interviewed were analysed using an inductive process, based on assumptions of interpretive qualitative research (Guba and Lincoln 1981). Common themes were identified in relation to what each group thought was important for the planning and implementation of this work. Constant and comparative analysis of the data developed a set of inductive categories that emerged by sorting the data into key themes. The following presents a discussion of these findings.

Findings and Discussion

In the following sections, we first present the data collected from the pre-service teachers, teachers, assistant teachers and principals.

Expectations Versus Reality

All of the pre-service teachers noted that although they had understood that the students they would be working with would have low literacy levels, they had no idea what this actually meant or looked like until they worked with the students.

One pre-service teacher commented,

I guess my expectations going in were in hindsight maybe too optimistic in terms of the education standards I was expecting. I think it's easy for us to read in a text book or be told in a lecture that remote Indigenous communities are facing, really low levels of literacy and numeracy and that it's really not improving, how we need it to improve, and I think even hearing that, I was like, 'Yeah I can understand why that's happening and why it's a problem and why we need to fix it.' But I don't think I pictured in my head exactly what it looked like.

All of the pre-service teachers interviewed were challenged by finding that many students in their class were between 3 and 5 years behind their expected year levels and that the students struggled with their spoken English, reading and writing.

Throughout the interviews it was apparent that the majority of the pre-service teachers felt unsettled by this. This sentiment is summed up in the following comment:

I think it was pretty heartbreaking. I mean, it's heartbreaking hearing it, and having an optimistic expectation, and then being put in a classroom with 15 year olds whose only written English capability is writing their name, their first name, and beyond that not being able to write anything, needing one on one attention to kind of do anything. It was just - I think I probably just didn't realise what kind of issues would result from having such poor literacy and numeracy levels.

Despite this, they were all in awe of what the students could do and felt the students were not well served by the system. One pre-service teacher commented:

I felt that they were being let down (not in the school, but nationally) as I realized that these students didn't get the recognition they deserve. They may not be ranked the highest on tests like NAPLAN but they knew about four languages plus English...... What they could tell me about their land and culture, how they looked out for each other and aided each other in the classroom, I felt they were cheated and these skills need to be recognized.

Similarly, another said:

It was the most eye opening experience I've had since starting university, and it's kind of put me on a bit of a course of motivation to get something done. Like it was depressing and yet so rewarding at the same time, because the kids are amazing and some of those teachers are amazing, and some of the community members are just amazing. But overall it's a really crappy situation and something needs to change. Because it's not good enough for us to be sitting in Melbourne and turning a blind eye to what's going on in our country. Like it's not a different country that we're talking about.

Interviews with mentor teachers and principals were consistent with the pre-service teachers' comments. The teachers and principals talked about their perceptions that the pre-service teachers felt overwhelmed by many things when they arrive on community. These include the literacy and numeracy levels of the students, behaviour management, cultural and language differences and being on community. Many echoed the sentiment that nothing can really prepare them for what they experience and that they have to be willing to watch and learn.

One principal commented:

Because it is a tough gig and we want somebody that's going to be flexible but prepared as well, open minded, definitely culturally competent.

And another teacher said:

Doesn't matter how much you're told, nothing can prepare you. It really is experience and it really is breaking down and going through the hardship and coming up because so much of the learning is relationship building. For these kids to teach literacy and numeracy a good relationship is the foundation.

Teaching Literacy on Community

In the pre-placement interviews the pre-service teachers were asked how prepared they felt to teach literacy. Responses to this question were mixed. Some said that they did not feel that confident as they had limited units in their courses about literacy instruction with some completing two units and others only one. Others said that they would be challenged by working in a community where there were several languages spoken other than English. Three had prior experience working with English language learners in places such as Fiji and they felt this might help them.

During the pre-placement interviews the pre-service teachers made clear that they had little idea how they would go about teaching literacy in the remote classrooms. They all assumed that there would be a focus on the early stages of learning to read and write but found it difficult to talk about key skills and strategies that they might need to use to do this, despite having undertaken studies about approaches to literacy teaching. During the post-placement interviews they echoed similar sentiments. All reflected on how challenging it had been, particularly working in classrooms where there was such a wide range of abilities and where students were often in excess of 4 years below the expected level.

Every pre-service teacher interviewed talked about a need for guidance in their university classes about working with students who have English as an additional language (EAL). One commented:

> When EAL students are really struggling to express themselves to me I need to know strategies to help them to understand better. Sometimes I would talk to the Indigenous kids and I knew they didn't really understand so I needed more strategies to help me with this.

Another similarly said:

> I think I would have benefited from a unit on teaching EAL students because I am sure there are different techniques or strategies that might be more effective for working with these students.

One of the mentor teachers also echoed these frustrations experienced by the pre-service teachers saying:

> Well, my gut feeling is they have the theoretical knowledge but when it comes to practical knowledge sometimes they feel it's an eye-opening experience so when she tries to explain something and the student is not really getting it because her first language is English and this kid's first language is not English.

The pre-service teachers all said they needed much knowledge about teaching early reading and writing. They felt we "brush over this" and don't spend enough time actually understanding what various strategies for working with students look like in practice.

All of the principals and the majority of the teachers in this study agreed that the pre-service teachers would benefit from having more knowledge about how to work effectively with EAL students. One commented:

> Well I think in general, even teachers that we have, there seems to be a lack of knowledge around English as an additional language or dialect (EAL/D) and I think that's something

9 Preparing Pre-service Teachers to Teach Literacy in Remote Spaces

that as a system we need to be working on. I think that definitely with having 98 percent of the students here as English being their third, fourth or fifth language, that's definitely something that they would benefit from.

Others also discussed what they termed "basic EAL pedagogies" such as "scaffolding", "modelling" and "breaking things down" as important for students to understand. Three of those interviewed also commented that it would be useful for pre-service teachers to have an understanding of the Northern Territory ESL levels and the Australian Curriculum EAL/D learning progression. Certainly, many of the teachers were empathetic towards their students, recognising the challenge of learning in English as a second, third or fourth language. One teacher commented:

What these guys [the pre-service teachers] need to know is just because the literacy level is low it is no reflection of the child's intelligence. I think any white fellas who come out here should go through an induction process where it's run by community and they do a whole lesson or they do a whole meeting in language with you and then act like some teachers do, telling people off for not having anything written on their paper, keep them in afterwards and say, 'You're going to do this,' just to understand the world that the kids are coming from.

Finally, teachers talked about other specific techniques that they used in their own classrooms to supplement their literacy teaching such as phonics work, conducting running records and guided reading as being important knowledge for pre-service teachers to have. However, there was often a reluctance to hand over the reins to pre-service teachers when they felt it was a program or technique that they felt required particular expertise or skills as the following comments show:

In my literacy block I start off with guided reading so while I'm doing the guided reading the kids are doing literacy rotations which you saw this morning. That was fine for the pre-service teacher to do the literacy rotations but not the guided reading and really it was difficult to try and find a time for her to start developing that in just one week of full control. She said she'd seen guided reading but she'd never really experienced it.

The collective comments from both pre-service teachers and school personnel raise a number of questions in relation to what kind of preparation might be ideal for students undertaking a practicum in a remote community.

Program Preparation and Perceptions

All of the interviewees talked about whole-school approaches to literacy in their respective schools. At the time of this study one of the schools was using direct instruction (henceforth DI) and the other accelerated literacy (henceforth AL).

Accelerated literacy (AL) pedagogy is an approach to language and literacy instruction that is designed to cater for "educationally marginalised" students (Cowey 2005; Gray 2007). The approach was developed and used extensively throughout remote schools in the Northern Territory from 2004 until 2009, when it received Commonwealth funding under the National Accelerated Literacy Program

(NALP) (Robinson et al. 2009). The approach requires rigorous initial training for teachers and continuing support from mentors or experts who can help teachers plan and can provide feedback on lessons. After the NALP period, only a few remote schools in the Northern Territory continued to invest their own resources in maintaining the level of support required for the program (see Chap. 14).

Direct instruction was developed in the United States in the 1960s (Engelmann and Engelmann 1966). The approach was originally designed to address the needs of children with learning difficulties. Based on behaviourist theories of learning, it breaks each task down into smaller tasks. Students need to master each task before moving on to the next. Students are grouped according to ability and teachers follow carefully scripted lessons. Direct instruction has been implemented in remote Northern Territory schools since 2015, again supported by a grant from the Commonwealth government. Whilst it has been embraced by some teachers who welcome the structure, many others are deeply uncomfortable with the lack of flexibility and the level of scripting required (see Chap. 13).

Preparedness to work in both these programs was a concern to the pre-service teachers and to the school personnel. The principals and mentor teachers noted that it would be useful for pre-service teachers to have some knowledge of their respective whole-school approaches. One principal said:

> I don't know if you want to add the programs into your university courses but you just need to say that we use these programs - AL, Jolly Phonics, Words their Way. This is how we map students against that the ESL band scales. So give them some links to get a bit more information, and get the students to do some homework before they arrive at the school.

Despite this they all understood the complexities and challenges of universities teaching pre-service teachers about particular whole-school approaches. They highlighted that these whole-school approaches often change due to funding no longer being available to support their implementation as was the case with AL. Direct instruction was rolled out in a number of schools once funding support was made available from the Commonwealth government. One principal said:

> But that could all change with a new boss and then AL could go out and something else could come in but I think there are some basic things about modelling and scaffolding and breaking work down that would be really useful. Some basic ESL pedagogies. Because that's all part of AL.

The principal recognised that teaching about specific programs was problematic due to their propensity to change, but also reiterated the importance of teaching some of the important theoretical ideas underpinning AL, especially around modelling and scaffolding children's learning.

Both schools invested heavily in training their teachers for both AL and DI and both programs rely on a level of expertise and consistency in the approach taken by teachers. The pre-service teachers were keen to learn about these programs although the opportunities they had to do this in situ varied. Many talked about the fact that teachers in the school where AL was taught were often reluctant to hand over the reins to the pre-service teachers. The students in the AL school overwhelmingly felt that they were being kept in the dark about the approach and were not being given insight into the basis of the approach. Without a full induction they found it difficult to appreciate the foundations and rationale of the various teaching strategies used. One student commented:

> I taught pretty much everything except AL. They were kind of precious about AL – she said like it takes way too long for you to learn it – you're not going to get your head around it and what I could see her doing I didn't really see how I couldn't have been doing it but maybe she was asking them a lot of questions I wouldn't have thought to ask.

In contrast, the students in the DI school were provided with more opportunities to learn about and teach into the program. At the time of this study, DI was under a process of evaluation so the school was obliged to maintain fidelity and staff were understandably nervous about classes being led by teachers who hadn't been inducted, regardless of their skill level.

One principal described this:

> Well just with our school being a direct instruction school, we have practice sessions which are like staff meetings and PD's twice a week after school for our teachers and we had the student teachers attend those as well. They were also offered coaching and support with direct instruction and practicing their script and working closely, doing team teaching with their mentor teacher, but also working with our direct instruction in school coach.

Despite being to some extent excluded from using the whole-school approaches, the pre-service teachers did their best to make sense of them. Given they had little understanding of the foundations and rationales of these programs, they often used key theoretical ideas that were highlighted as important from their university course to reflect on the programs and their learning. Thus the pre-service teachers at the AL school noted the benefits in a program which relies heavily on scaffolding students' English literacy and related what they learned about scaffolding at university to what they saw in their classrooms. One pre-service also talked about students being familiar with the routines of the AL program and liked the fact that the students were clear about the learning intentions, another concept they had learned as being important in their university classes. They went on to say that they would probably adopt the technique and would like to learn more about the program. On the other hand, they also questioned what they perceived to be the "repetitive" nature of the program and they questioned how students were exposed to limited literature due to the fact that so much time was spent working on one text. One said she tried to find more opportunities to simply "read to the children" as she had learned this was important at university.

The two pre-service teachers in the DI school found less congruence between what they had learned at university and what they experienced in the DI program. They spoke about the structured and repetitive nature of the program which they felt oftentimes "took the joy out of teaching" for them. Both described how students were placed into ability groups for instruction and talked about progressing through various graded teacher manuals and student workbooks. There was a sense that the implementation of DI was much more rigidly structured than that of AL. They talked about scripts that they had to follow to deliver the various lessons and how they were forbidden to go off script. One pre-service teacher talked about a time when she felt the need to try something different and go off the script during a DI maths session. She also reflected on her learning from university but could not match what she experienced in DI and what she had learned at university:

Like you can't deviate from the script. Like when Inge told you she put something up on the whiteboard and thought we're going to get into trouble. I had a moment like that as well. Like there's a maths song called skip counting because we were learning skip counting in DI maths they had a song on 'go noodle' so I asked my mentor teacher if I could use it and she was like that's fine just don't tell anyone. The kids loved it by the end after watching about three times they could skip count. Whereas the first initial DI lesson wasn't working cause they weren't paying attention but they had learned the song and it had movements so it was all kinaesthetic musical learning at the same time so I feel like that's what I learned at University but it was kind of deviating from the script and I wasn't allowed to talk about it.

In contrast to the pre-service teachers who experienced AL, the consensus amongst those who experienced DI was that one would find it difficult to teach in a DI school. One pre-service teacher struggled to find any congruence behind what she had learned about DI and her beliefs about teaching and learning more generally:

I don't think I could teach in a DI school. When delivering the DI, I felt a disconnection between what I believe education should offer students, and what the program offered students. I felt unable to communicate high expectations (except in science where I taught 3 thirty minute sessions at the end of the day) and I felt that the DI positioned me as an 'all-knowing' teacher – and students as empty vessels. I do not believe that DI teaches students to think. It is also questionable that DI would never be *acceptable* for white children, so why is such a program acceptable for Indigenous students? I feel it upholds a deficit view of Indigenous students and their capabilities. Bound by DI, I was not able to design lessons which pertained to student's individual histories, values, interests, aspirations, community values or history.

The pre-service teachers also raised issues around the "buy in" from staff in the school in relation to both AL and DI. Whilst they acknowledged that there would seem to be a majority of teachers who were heavily invested in both programs at their respective schools, two of the pre-service teachers did talk about the fact that their mentor teachers were not so invested. This may be an endemic problem that schools in these contexts face when trying to adopt whole-school approaches to improve literacy outcomes which are significantly lower than the national average.

Communicating on Community

Another theme that emerged from the interviews is related to building relationships and communicating with others. The pre-service teachers were mindful of a unit about Indigenous culture they had studied at university and sought to build their own cultural competence through developing relationships with students, school personnel and community that required cultural competence. However, they were

9 Preparing Pre-service Teachers to Teach Literacy in Remote Spaces   157

unsure what cultural competence might look like in practice and doubted their knowledge in this area. One said:

> The cultural differences worries me as I don't want to offend. If I am not sure I'll ask the teacher first. I'll sit back a lot and listen. It's not really my fault I haven't learned about it. I want to be more culturally competent.

Two of the pre-service teachers expressed a need to learn more about appropriate ways of interacting. One pre-service teacher, herself Indigenous, recalled a moment where she reminded others about paying attention. Throughout the placement they demonstrated more sensitivity in the way they communicated with and engaged with cultural differences than the other students. She commented:

> Like knowing what kinds of language and terminology and words to be using to not be offensive. Things like the word corroboree were thrown around like really flippantly. Like, I just don't know about saying that, and they're like, oh why? It's like just because it's not your word, it's not - their word. And when I kind of mentioned it, not looking for anything other than stop using the word, use gathering, or some other like less specific synonym, it was like oh why can't we? It seems like you're making a big deal about that. I was like oh, I'm not I don't think. Also when to use Aboriginal versus Torres Strait Islander versus both, versus Indigenous. It's a complicated kind of area of study, but it's important that people, especially people going into these communities, are using those words properly and being able to communicate well with both non-Indigenous people and Indigenous people.

All of the pre-service teachers talked about the importance of building relationships with students, the community and school. They discussed how the school was such an integral part of the community and spoke about the numerous coming and going of people:

> The school had strong relationships with community. There were always people coming into the school and meetings going on. A few of the teachers had only been there for a year but a lot of teachers did have very strong connections to community and people.

Many talked about the importance of "stepping back", watching and listening:

> I learned that if you're going to go into a community a similar thing to what I just said you really have to let people come to you. You have to take a step back, listen and watch. I don't think forcing yourself is that great but doing it in a sensitive way where it doesn't look like your trying to force yourself is really important in a quite close knit community.

Finally, one pre-service teacher reflected on how building relationships with students is different to what she has previously experienced. She said that whilst at university and in other practicum placements we do "promote and support positive relationships between teachers and students", relationship building with Indigenous children requires a "mutual understanding and respect, with any ideas of hierarchy and condescension being swiftly replaced with an understanding that both the teacher and the student have knowledge to impart and share with one another". She said it was "confronting" and "unnerving", but "ultimately humbling if you can allow yourself to realise that despite being the teacher, you can learn much from your student yourself".

Like the pre-service teachers, the principals and teachers interviewed also talked about the importance of understanding how to interact in the community and of building relationships with students, school personnel and people in the community.

The two principals praised this group of pre-service teachers for their understanding of the need to sit back, watch and listen and to know when it was appropriate to ask. One teacher said:

> Nobody rushed in and expected they knew everything that they could – I know everything, therefore if I do this, this will happen. Sometimes that happens. Whereas it was quite a bit of sitting back waiting, finding out, rather than being proactive in that space, which is the better way to be. To wait, find out, if you don't know the proactive parties to ask, don't just assume. I don't think we had any issues in terms of any one of them doing something that was not quite right.

The teachers and principals also highlighted the importance of building good relationships whilst working in remote communities. One teacher said it was foundational to teaching and learning:

> It really is experience and it really is breaking down and going through the hardship and coming up because so much of the learning is relationship building. For these kids, to teach literacy and numeracy, a good relationship is the foundation.

Relationships were also very important for the two Indigenous teaching assistants that were interviewed. In addition to discussing the importance of the need for pre-service teachers to understand how to "be" on community, build relationships and have an understanding of cultural rules, they also talked about the need to be able to work collaboratively with the Indigenous community, school community and students. They were clear that there needed to be a reciprocal relationship where all parties learn from each other. One commented:

> Very important to know as soon as when they get into the class, we need to tell them about the rules, if that teacher doesn't know what's in our school. And how to get along with our children. It's very important that we need to see, from other teachers, that they need to show what they have learnt from them and what the students have learnt from them. Like it's just working together. When the students came, they started to talk and sharing. We had lunch together, communicating and working together. That's what I want to see. So she can teach me and I can teach her.

Discussion

Our interviews with the school personnel and pre-service teachers revealed a number of implications for sending pre-service teachers to remote communities for placement experiences in relation to the preparedness to work with Indigenous students and communities in the literacy space. A number of important themes emerged that can inform both universities and schools about what they might do better. Whilst it was clear that preparing students before they embark on their placement was paramount, it was also evident that schools can take steps to support the pre-service teachers.

What Literacy?

Most of the pre-service teachers who embarked on this placement had only completed one of their two compulsory units on literacy and three said that due to the nature of the degree they were enrolled in, they only were required to complete one literacy unit. Overwhelmingly, they said they needed more. Pre-service teachers and school personnel alike mentioned general and specific knowledge about teaching literacy, much of which related to the need to know much more about how to teach early reading and writing.

English as an Additional Language/Dialect

In keeping with the recommendations of the review of Indigenous Education in the Northern Territory (Wilson 2014), the majority of the pre-service teachers and school personnel interviewed spoke of the importance of including content about teaching EAL/D students. The pre-service teachers interviewed voiced their frustrations at not knowing how to make themselves understood by students and they felt that it could have benefitted if they were cognisant of effective EAL/D strategies for working with these students.

Scaffolding and Differentiating Learning

In the interviews the teachers and principals mentioned the importance of pre-service teachers being able to scaffold students' learning and for them to be able to differentiate their teaching. This was highlighted as an important characteristic of teachers in these schools due to the wide-ranging abilities that are often found in each classroom and in one school because of their use of AL which has scaffolding as one of its key principles.

Knowledge About Literacy Programs

Teachers and the pre-service teachers agreed that it would be beneficial for the pre-service teachers to know more about the whole-school approaches used in the respective schools. However, this does raise a number of issues. First, there are practical barriers to investing a lot of effort and time in training university students in specific programs, as history shows that jurisdictions are immensely fickle in their adoption of programs, and there is no guarantee of how "long" any particular approach will be used in a school or jurisdiction. Second, it is important that pre-service teachers understand the underlying philosophies that drive specific programs in order for them to make any informed judgements about the efficacy of a program. The data reported here highlighted that the pre-service teachers often reflected on the theoretical ideas they had explored in their university classes in order to try and connect to and understand and make sense of the literacy programs used by their respective schools. Third, it is almost impossible for students to learn how to teach in a program in a short three-week placement when experienced teachers require hours of professional development to be able to understand and implement a program themselves. Finally, all of this presents another set of issues for pre-service teachers undertaking practicum in these schools. Pre-service teachers are required to demonstrate competency with respect to professional set of standards (AITSL), many of which relate to literacy. In the AL school a number of the pre-service teachers were not afforded the opportunity to teach the literacy lessons and so found it difficult to address these standards. Further in the DI school the pre-service teachers were given little autonomy over the way they planned and implemented their learning experiences, which also made it difficult for them to address many of these standards.

Cultural Competence, Communicating on Community

Another strong theme that emerged from the data was the need for pre-service teachers to have a level of cultural competence and an ability to communicate in effective ways whilst in community. Pre-service teachers and school personnel talked about the importance of being able to "stand back" and not being intrusive. The importance of building and developing relationships was also discussed as being pivotal for effective teaching and learning in schools with school personnel and the pre-service teachers alike frequently making reference to this throughout the interviews.

Conclusion

Findings from this study similarly suggest there is an urgent need for specific content to be included in Initial Teacher Education if we are to adequately prepare pre-service teachers to work in these communities. The data from the interviews clearly showed the need for pre-service teachers to have more literacy in their respective courses due to the focus on literacy teaching in remote schools. In particular, pre-service teachers who undertake professional experience in remote schools need to be provided with course content that focuses explicitly on working with EAL/D students. It would also be useful to consider the various whole-school programs that might be used by schools and at the very least provide students with some background information relating to those programs. Whilst it would not be feasible to know all there is to know about the programs, at the very least we should help them to unpack/critique the programs in relation to what they have learned about effective language and literacy pedagogies for students from diverse linguistic and cultural

9 Preparing Pre-service Teachers to Teach Literacy in Remote Spaces

backgrounds, for example, helping them to understand how and why scaffolding is integral to AL pedagogy. This would provide them with a much more informed base to reflect on literacy programs offered in schools. Schools on the other hand need to be much more willing to allow students to teach into these programs, as observing a program can be very different from actually teaching in a program. This is also important in relation to students fulfilling their requirements to show evidence of meeting the professional standards for teaching. The data also suggests that schools need to be more open to reflective dialogue about the literacy programs and teaching in schools. Finally and most importantly, it is clear that doing work in cultural competence, communicating on community and building relationships are of paramount importance when considering preparing pre-service teachers to undertake this work.

References

ACARA. (2017). *My School*. Australian Government. Retrieved from, https://www.myschool.edu.au/

AITSL. (2011). Australian Professional Standards for Teachers. Retrieved from, https://www.aitsl.edu.au/docs/default-source/apst-resources/australian_professional_standard_for_teachers_final.pdf

Anderson, P. J., & Atkinson, B. (2014). Closing the gap: Using graduate attributes to improve Indigenous education. *International Education Journal: Comparative Perspectives, 12*(1), 135–145.

Auld, G., Dyer, J., & Charles, C. (2016). Dangerous practices: The practicum experiences of non-Indigenous pre-service teachers in remote communities. *Australian Journal of Teacher Education, 41*(6), 165–179.

Australian Bureau of Statistics (ABS). (2013). Retrieved from, http://www.abs.gov.au/ausstats/abs@.nsf/mf/3238.0.55.001

Brasche, I., & Harrington, I. (2013). Promoting teacher quality and continuity. Tackling the disadvantages of remote Indigenous schools in the Northern Territory. *Australian Journal of Education, 56*(2), 110–125.

Commonwealth of Australia. (2018). Department of the Prime Minister and Cabinet, Closing the Gap Prime Minister's Report.

Cowey, W. (2005). A brief description of the national accelerated literacy program. *TESOL in Context, 15*(2), 3–14.

DEEWR. (2011). *Guiding principles for developing indigenous cultural competency in Australian Universities*. Retrieved from https://www.universitiesaustralia.edu.au/uni-participation-quality/Indigenous-Higher-Education/Indigenous-Cultural-Compet#.WbX9BIc0Mbw

Engelmann, S., & Engelmann, T. (1966). *Give your child a superior mind*. New York: Simon & Schuster.

Gray, B. (2007). *Accelerating the literacy development of indigenous students: The National Accelerated Literacy Program (NALP)*. Darwin: Charles Darwin University Press.

Guba, E., & Lincoln, Y. (1981). *Effective evaluation*. San Francisco: Jossey-Bass.

Labone, E., Cavanagh, P., & Long, J. (2014). Critical design features of pre-service education programs to enhance teacher capacity to effectively work in schools with Indigenous students. *The Australian Journal of Indigenous Education, 43*(2), 121–133.

Moreton-Robinson, A. M., Singh, D., Kolopenuk, J., Robinson, A., & Walter, M. (2012). *Learning the lessons? Pre-service teacher preparation for teaching Aboriginal and Torres Strait Islander students* (A report prepared for the Division of Indigenous Education and Training Futures).

Brisbane: Queensland Department of Education, Training and Employment, Indigenous Studies Research Network, and Queensland University of Technology.

Osborne, B. (2003). Preparing preservice teachers' minds, hearts and actions for teaching in remote Indigenous contexts. *The Australian Journal of Indigenous Education, 31,* 17–24.

Price, K. (2016). More Aboriginal and Torres Strait Islander Teachers for Australian High-Needs Schools. In J. Lampert & B. Burnett (Eds.), *Teacher education for high poverty schools* (pp. 95–114). New York: Springer. https://doi.org/10.1007/978-3-319-22059-8_1.

Rennie, J., White, S., Anderson, P., & Darling, A. (2018). Preparing teachers to work with and for remote indigenous communities: Unsettling institutional practices. In D. Heck & A. Ambrosetti (Eds.), *Teacher education in and for uncertain times* (pp. 113–127). Singapore: Springer.

Robinson, G. W., Rivalland, J., Tyler, W. B., Lea, T., Bartlett, C., et al. (2009). *The National Accelerated Literacy Program in the Northern Territory, 2004–2008: implementation and outcomes: Final evaluation report.* Casuarina: School for Social and Policy Research, Charles Darwin University.

Senate Employment, Workplace Relations, Small Business and Education References Committee. (2000). *Katu kalpa: Report on the inquiry into the effectiveness of education and training programs for indigenous Australians* [Parliamentary papers/Parliament of the Commonwealth of Australia, 0727–4181.]. Canberra: ACT.

Sharplin, E. (2002). A taste of country: A pre-service teacher rural field trip. *Education in Rural Australia, 20*(1), 17–23.

Wilson, B. (2014). *A share in the future: Review of indigenous education in the Northern Territory.* Darwin: NT Department of Education. Retrieved from, file://ad.monash.edu/home/User075/jrennie/Desktop/A-Share-in-the-Future-The-Review-of-Indigenous-Education-in-the-Northern-Territory.pdf

Yarrow, A., Ballantyne, R., Hansford, B., Herschell, P., & Millwater, J. (1999). Teaching in rural and remote schools: A literature review. *Teaching and Teacher Education, 15,* 1–13.

Dr Jennifer Rennie is a senior lecturer in literacy education in the Faculty of Education, Monash University. Prior to working in higher education, she worked as a primary and high school teacher. Her research interests relate to Indigenous literacies, students who are marginalised from mainstream schooling and reading pedagogy for disengaged adolescent readers.

Professor Peter Anderson is from the Warlpiri and Murrinh Patha, First Nations in the Northern Territory. He is a professor at Queensland University of Technology where he is the director of the Indigenous Research and Engagement Unit. His research theorises the understandings of the organisational value of academic freedom in Australian universities and more broadly the polar south. His current research is in the areas of organisational leadership, Indigenous peoples' education and teacher and academic professional development.

Part II
Examining the Systemic: Theory and Practice

Chapter 10
A Long Unfinished Struggle: Literacy and Indigenous Cultural and Language Rights

Janine Oldfield and Joseph Lo Bianco

What counts as bilingual education for Australian Aboriginal people in the Northern Territory (NT) has varied significantly depending on geographical location and temporal context, Indigenous community involvement and the prevailing political environment. This chapter discusses NT bilingual education in relation to national and international cultural ethics, legislative acts and public policies and proclamations and declarations, alongside the effects of value differences and ideologies. It emerges that Indigenous social agents have mostly enhanced literacy education in communities and have been instrumental in the evolution of culturally informed pedagogy and team-teaching practices over the last 40 years. The chapter discusses the educational effects (assessed outcomes and school persistence rates) among Indigenous children through bilingual/biliteracy programming and exposes the recurring failure of bilingual and culturally appropriate pedagogies to attract mainstream legitimacy or consistent funding. Finally, the chapter discusses human rights questions entailed in this pervasive and continuous neglect of Indigenous languages in Australian education.

Introduction

The first volume-length analysis of the turbulent history of bilingual education in the NT (Devlin et al. 2017) identifies the multiple origins of educational responses to the distinctive language and cultural needs of Indigenous Australian students. A

J. Oldfield (✉)
Batchelor Institute of Indigenous Tertiary Education, Batchelor, NT, Australia
e-mail: janine.oldfield@batchelor.edu.au

J. Lo Bianco
Melbourne Graduate School of Education, University of Melbourne, Melbourne, VIC, Australia
e-mail: j.lobianco@unimelb.edu.au

© Springer Nature Singapore Pte Ltd. 2019
J. Rennie, H. Harper (eds.), *Literacy Education and Indigenous Australians*,
Language Policy 19, https://doi.org/10.1007/978-981-13-8629-9_10

major policy breakthrough was achieved under the direct political intervention of the federal labour government of Prime Minister Whitlam, between 1972 and 1975. Yet such political events were belated responses to years of advocacy, research, conceptual innovation and organisational demands at grassroots levels. Much of this agitation was led by Indigenous communities, often in alliance with language professionals, both linguists and educators (e.g. Gale 1990; Lo Bianco and Slaughter 2016). Further momentum for change came from international agencies which supplied the terminology of language and cultural rights and documented instances of international practices that could be emulated (UNESCO 2003).

This chapter examines key points of history and policy implementation in terms of *ideological and implementational spaces* (Hornberger 2005). It aims to account for the persistence and survival of some bilingual programs and Indigenous pedagogies in the face of considerable obstacles and frequent hostility. The chapter explores the forces – intellectual, cultural and political – that have conditioned the politicised, long, unfinished struggle for Indigenous cultural and linguistic rights.

The Research Basis for Bilingual Education in the Northern Territory

Early education for Indigenous people was characterised by colonial hierarchy and conditioned by prevailing ideologies of racial dominance. When combined with largely uncontested social-Darwinist thinking, the result was limited schooling, essentially as preparation for menial or unpaid labour (McKay 2017). Most education for Indigenous people failed to impart control over Western academic knowledge and skills while also excluding their distinctive cultures and languages, thereby entrenching intergenerational inequality and, in remote areas, abject poverty (McKay 2017). The few instances of bilingual education, and isolated attempts at culturally responsive pedagogies, typically relied on benevolent and enlightened individuals (e.g. the late 1800s Hermannsburg school).

By contrast, the education of Indigenous children has long been the subject of international interest, including curriculum reform and program innovation exploring multicultural pedagogies based on incorporation of cultural and linguistic differences. A watershed development were new research protocols from the mid-1960s that dramatically overturned flawed bilingual research which had concluded bilingualism was an educational handicap. By failing to control for variable levels of mother tongue (MT) proficiency among minority populations, early research had found either negative or no correlation between bilingualism and cognitive functioning. More rigorous research designs controlling for proficiency and socioeconomic status have since repeatedly identified a significant independent contribution of MT proficiency on second-language learning and general cognitive performance (Baker 2008; Cummins 2000) producing a long stream of consistently positive research studies on bilingualism.

Bilingual education research often addresses three broad themes, whether bilingualism in education fosters maintenance of the first language, enhances learning of the second and improves general academic performance. Most research endorses strong or robust bilingual models, involving sustained instructional roles for MTs (Baker 2011), in preference to transitional or temporary interventions. Many replicated studies show improved general literacy, better overall academic results and stronger acquisition of official/dominant languages (Bialystok et al. 2014). A strong bilingual model involves active MT instruction for between 3 and 5 years, ideally for substantially longer (Cummins 2000). While full bilingual learning occasionally produces a "lag effect" in which parity with age-appropriate cohorts is briefly delayed, minority language children, whether immigrant or Indigenous, typically achieve what Cummins (2000) has termed *basic interpersonal communication skills* quickly and full *cognitive and academic proficiency* (Cummins 2000) more rapidly than comparable learners taught only in the socially dominant second language. Failure to ensure a strong MT proficiency, or limiting MT roles to cognitively unchallenging superficial tasks (such as rote learning), puts students at risk of never developing the academic language and reasoning abilities for more demanding de-contextualised and literacy-saturated upper levels of schooling.[1]

Cummins (2000) noted, and more recent research in India (Nakamura 2015) confirms, the likely presence of "threshold attainments" in MT literacy to facilitate socially dominant literacy acquisition. Such thresholds typically occur in additive language learning conditions, where the first language and culture are treated as a learning resource and continue to be developed in academically substantive classroom activity. Additive multilingual education ensures children *add* extra language skills, rather than replace their home-acquired linguistic repertoire with socially dominant languages, a condition called *subtractive* bilingualism whereby the child's ultimate language ability is confined only to the replacing language.

The classroom is not immune from the language and socio-economic hierarchies prevalent in wider social environments. School practices which do not contest external subtractive pressures and treat children's MTs as a hindrance to learning collude in social marginalisation, foster poor identity formation, undermine academic language development and create the conditions for long-term social exclusion, resistance to learning and cultural conflict (Cummins 1996, 2000; Oldfield 2016). Alternatively, when learners' MTs are strategically and extensively integrated into well-planned bilingual/bicultural programs, the available styles of learning, stocks of knowledge and resources of information are expanded for all learners (Cummins 2000; Oldfield 2016).

The general neglect of MT development in the mostly monolingual NT education system denies Indigenous children the opportunity to cultivate deeper knowledge of ancestral languages, and compounds social pressures that relegate Australian languages to diglossic inferiority in relation to English, impeding more effective

---

[1] High first-language development is believed to strengthen processing centres in the brain that are used for all languages and hence can allow the transfer of literacy skills and metalinguistic knowledge to other languages (Baker 2011; Cummins 2000).

second-language acquisition and provoking extensive code or language mixing.[2] Language mixes can develop into creoles (new forms using largely English vocabulary with Indigenous grammar and syntax) and new languages (such as Light Warlpiri composed of creole, Warlpiri and English; O'Shannessy 2005) or lead to language shift from standard varieties in traditional languages and failure to acquire standard English.

Ethical International Interest and National Change

International interest in Indigenous education also evolved as a result of ethical as well as scholarly change. Critical was the 1953 publication of a 150-page expert report: *The Use of Vernacular Languages in Education* (UNESCO 1953). This watershed document was intended to help post-colonial African and Asian countries design national education systems. Most newly independent nations continued education practices of the pre-colonial era, including exclusive use of colonial languages for school and university instruction. The report injected new understandings of "vernacular" languages into discussions of educational success and anticipated the emergence of ethically principled language rights. The document contains a famous MT declaration: "We take it as axiomatic that every child of school age should attend school....We take it as axiomatic, too, that the best medium for teaching is the mother tongue of the pupil" (UNESCO 1953).

Since the 1953 declaration, UNESCO has maintained a steady output of research literature supporting the primacy of the MT in immigrant and Indigenous initial education. This has been reinforced with human rights covenants such as the (1966) *International Covenant on Civil and Political Rights* (ICCPR), whose Article 27 (UN 1966) declares that linguistic minorities "*shall not be denied* the right… to enjoy their own culture, to profess and practise their own religion, or *to use their own language*". This was further strengthened with the 1992 *United Nations Declaration on the Rights of Persons Belonging to National or Ethnic or Religious Minorities*, Article 2.1 (UN and OHCHR 1992), which similarly supported the right to "enjoyment" of culture and use of language and stipulated this right should be available in both private and public spheres and without interference or discrimination. This has been further sustained by the 2007 *United Nations Declaration on the Rights of Indigenous Peoples* whose Article 14 (UNDRIP 2008) reaffirmed Indigenous people's "right to establish and control education systems … in their own language…in their own culture".

These examples of the evolution of more explicit language rights in international law shift from conceptions of language rights as freedom to private use of unique cultural practices to more robust affirmation of cultural and linguistic identities in public settings. Similarly, legal instruments now address educational practices in an

---

[2]Teachers who extensively developed the oral first language of their students in bilingual oral and monolingual English literacy programs, however, achieved a higher level of success.

effort to support language rights, removing discrimination against minority-language-speaking communities and, more widely, fostering positive appreciation of the benefits of the world's heritage of linguistic diversity (Skutnabb-Kangas and Phillipson 2017).

Increased attention to Indigenous education also resulted from the *Constitution Alteration (Aboriginals) 1967 Referendum* (voted 27 May but enshrined in law in August) which was endorsed by a large majority and universally regarded as groundbreaking in the political history of Australia's Indigenous people. The changes permitted the federal government to legislate in Indigenous affairs and included Aborigines within the formal record of population, facilitating deeper cultural shifts and permitting policy and resourcing transformation of the position of Indigenous people.[3] While the focus of the referendum was administrative and juridical, its success reflected growing dissatisfaction with prevailing ideologies and assumptions about the long term fate of Indigenous Australians and a sense that the Australian state should centrally engage with their welfare. Thus, the referendum made possible broad cultural acknowledgement of the role of advocacy and led to various forms of federal policy intervention and contestation of assimilation ideology, processes which flowed into the later imaginings of new kinds of Indigenous rights and representation.[4] In the NT, this ferment took the form of advocacy and provision of bilingual/biliteracy education for Indigenous learners (Devlin 2017; Harris 1997; Lo Bianco and Slaughter 2016).

Wider changes in the political landscape extended to removal of race and national origin criteria for immigrant selection as part of a major expansion of the national population. The rapid increase in the non-indigenous but non-British components of the population generated through the recruited immigration scheme launched in the aftermath of World War II radically altered Australian society ethnically and linguistically, fuelling a wider interest in questions of language. During the 1970s, while acknowledging historic primacy of Indigenous people, immigrant and Indigenous interests converged within a new sense of "national reconstruction" (Lo Bianco and Slaughter 2016: 348) around advocacy for attention to issues of "language and culture". As these notions proceeded in debate over the next two decades, the idea of *language* became established as a firm, identifiable object of policy formulation, expanding through various phases. First, language issues were linked to immigrant claims for citizenship and economic participation. Then language questions were taken up in understandings of the nation itself, as a pluralist entity understood as a multicultural rather than British polity. Later language questions were tied to the pragmatic need for facilitating commercial trading relationships

---

[3] Devlin (2017: 12) notes that in 1950, an agreement to provide education to the "natives" also stipulated remote Indigenous children (with strong language and culture) should be provided first-language education.

[4] These rights included the Land Rights Act and the introduction of Aboriginal advisory and representative bodies such as the National Aboriginal Consultative Committee in 1972 and the National Aboriginal Conference 1977 and eventually Australian and Torres Strait Island Commission (abolished in 2003).

with Asian countries. These shifting and often irreconcilable priorities in language policy reflect a tension also present in the main rubrics under which Australian languages are present in policy which today include advancing Indigenous "reconciliation" (Lo Bianco and Slaughter 2016: 348) and effective delivery of schooling to Indigenous children to *close the gap* of school performance compared with non-Indigenous peers.

Because competing visions of Australia's national interest and self-identity have become attached to different visions of language policy it has become a barometer and index of wider cultural change, from assimilation and integration, 1960s to 1980s, to multiculturalism during the 1980s and 1990s (Leitner 2004). These debates culminated in the adoption of a comprehensive *National Policy on Languages* (NPL) in 1987 (Lo Bianco 1987) in which Indigenous cultural policy and educational programming were centrally important in an overarching project of universal multilingual support, the first multilingual declaration and Australia's first formal Commonwealth policy on language. The NPL marked the first formal recognition of the worth and endangerment of Aboriginal languages (Schmidt 1990) and according to McKay (2017: 88) gave "unprecedented recognition" and importance to Indigenous languages justifying their status as "legitimate forms of communication...appropriate for communicating information about government services and programs" in addition to recognising their value in Indigenous struggles for "cultural survival" (Lo Bianco 1987: 13, 14).[5] Significantly, the NPL acknowledged the foreignness of English in remote areas where it may be a fifth or sixth language in the communication lives of young people, and little used outside classrooms.[6]

NT Bilingual Developments

Bilingual education for Indigenous learners evolved from these research, ethical and policy changes. Initially proposed in a 1973 report on innovation in NT education for traditional-language-speaking children – then under federal jurisdiction (Watts et al. 1973) – the report justified bilingual teaching as providing pedagogical scaffolds to increase children's motivation, pride, school attendance, English literacy and numeracy scores. Possibly influenced by the 1953 UNESCO declaration, it linked high oral language fluency with ability to decode texts as elements required for reading success. In response the Whitlam government set up bilingual programs in five sites across the NT, notwithstanding the scarcity of written Indigenous literature, trained teachers and the large number of languages in which such programs could potentially be delivered (Devlin 2017). Despite being a top-down imposition in a small number of sites, the 1973 initiative produced palpable excitement among

---

[5] The NPL in fact sustained bilingual programs in the NT at a time when their legitimation and resourcing were being denuded by the NT government according to Devlin (2009).

[6] Indeed, as noted in a contemporary NT education review, 65% of remote Indigenous children still speak an Indigenous language at home (Wilson 2014: 44).

Indigenous communities who perceived it as the *"first real recognition by Government of the value of Indigenous language, culture and law"* (Collins 1999: 121) and supported the priority given to community involvement.

From this modest start bilingual programming expanded across the NT through the 1980s. Although programs were unique in design and operation, all featured the aim of spoken first-language maintenance and literacy support, but with rapid shift from initial MT instruction to schooling in English (Devlin 2017). Called the *step program*, children began schooling with MT immersion, transferring to either 50:50 MT and English or a higher percentage of English than MT by upper primary (Devlin 2009).

North American precedents influenced NT developments, especially the mid-1970s research of Canadian James Cummins on the interdependence of first and second languages in educational growth and the successful Indigenous-controlled program at Rough Rock Navajo School in the USA. A less tangible early influence came from the language documentation efforts of the US-based Summer Institute of Linguistics, which was very active in language preservation and Bible translation in Southeast Asia, Papua New Guinea and various Pacific Island countries (EWG 1973; Harris 1997). Programs were notable for the extensive involvement of Aboriginal people as teacher staff and teacher support, in professional development, as participants/organisers of excursions and related activities as well as involvement in curriculum innovation and literature production (Harris 1999; Watt 1993). These roles afforded communities socio-economic empowerment, varying according to program type, mode of implementation and literature production and influenced linguistic development as well as evolution towards written-language-literate societies because of the important role of school literacy centres. Community involvement was a clear foundation of program success.

Ideological Space

Until the mid-1980s community activities associated with bilingual schools increased dramatically (Hornberger 2005) worldwide. Hornberger's documentation describes this as emergence and widening of ideological and implementation spaces that are otherwise only implicit, but which overt policy formation and implementation can make explicit and prominent. She argued that these spaces can be examined with critical ethnographic and sociocultural examination of language policy, where all agents (bureaucrats, teachers, community members, principals, politicians and linguists) involved in policy formation, interpretation and implementation can account for micro- and meso-level developments that influence macro-level policy construction (Hornberger and Johnson 2007; Johnson 2010; Johnson and Johnson 2015). According to Hornberger's analysis of Latin and North American settings, settler colonial education systems produce major contraction of the ideological space for bilingual education, but implementation spaces can remain vibrant or be prised open with bottom-up activity which remain

172   J. Oldfield and J. Lo Bianco

community-focused because pragmatic communication realities necessitate bilingual responses and concrete programming. In earlier work addressing this same phenomenon, Corson (1999) also noted a dialectical interaction between policy discourse at different institutional levels that allows minority communities agency to formally create policy texts locally and to informally implement classroom programs for bilingual learners.

When the ideological space for bilingual education in the NT expanded in the 1970s, this allowed the emergence of a considerable number of positive developments. Novel and sophisticated multilingual discourses, pedagogy and Indigenous literacy practices emerged that impacted extensively on the socio-economic outcomes of whole communities. Community members actively teaching in bilingual programs transformed their educational roles from economic dependency and menial tasks to "real jobs with real pay" with acknowledged professional status (Harris 1999: 70). The impact of such change reverberated throughout many communities across the NT and was felt nationally. Assistant teachers, given increasingly responsible positions, including teaching the local language to non-Indigenous teaching staff, exponentially increased their English language skills and began to address wider public audiences, becoming powerful social agents (Oldfield 2016). They received onsite teacher training through Batchelor Institute and Deakin (for their final year) with the commencement of remote teacher training which was delivered entirely by Batchelor by the late 1980s.[7] This resulted in the emergence of new and innovative multicultural Indigenous discourses that stemmed from the wider but related Land Rights movement, the writings on conscience and education transformation of Paulo Freire (1972) and local advocacy within communities.

These discourses consequently impacted on teacher training pedagogy at Batchelor, which designed a "highly Aboriginalised degree" implemented at local sites and entailing participatory action research and community-based teaching (Disbray 2014; Harris and Devlin 1997; Lee et al. 2014; Oldfield 2016: 388; Watt 2017). These innovations impacted on schools as institutions and their associated communities which began to use the same approaches to transform education (Watt 2017).

The success of this program, dwindling by the late 1990s, led Hoogenraad (2001) to comment:

> This is arguably the greatest achievement of bilingual education in the NT to date, and it is the most potent mechanism for the community to exercise its responsibilities and rights to educate its children. (Hoogenraad 2001: 137)

---

[7]Batchelor Institute was specifically set up as an Indigenous-controlled institution for teacher training of remote Indigenous students in 1972 to accommodate the influx of Indigenous trainees (Watt 2017). Originally named the Aboriginal Teacher Education Centre, it was renamed Batchelor in 1979.

10 A Long Unfinished Struggle: Literacy and Indigenous Cultural and Language Rights 173

Whole Communities of Linguists, Readers and Writers

The expansion of Indigenous bilingual implementational spaces that resulted from the opening of an ideological space presented by national bilingual policy extended beyond schools. From the cohort of bilingual teachers and students discussed above, there arose a strong and extremely talented Indigenous leadership, including the 1992 Australian of the Year and international rock musician, Mandawuy Djarrtjuntjun Yunupingu.

Implementational spaces also included the expansion of literacy practices of community members. The literature production centres attached to schools generated large numbers of bilingual publications. School texts, narratives, traditional stories, media texts such as newspapers and magazines (invariably bilingual – English plus a local language), documentation of scientific knowledge of communities (such as local classification systems and meteorological patterns), and vernacular publications on cultural geography, history, mathematics and technology all emerged from a plethora of literature production activities to create highly engaged, active, empowered literate communities (Hale 1999; Harris 1997).

Locally employed workers at literacy centres were trained in applied and descriptive linguistics at the School of Australian Linguistics (later Batchelor's Centre for Australian Languages and Linguistics). These workers were transformed into sought-after experts by established and emerging linguistics academics for correspondence on grammar and lexis (Hale 1999). This eventuated in the emergence of "*standard practical orthographies ... for all the Central Australian languages*" (Hoogenraad 2001: 129). This uptake of literacy and linguistic activity generated from school programs into wider scholarship and policy-influencing knowledge was, by historical standards, both "*rapid and spectacular in the extreme ... despite ... neglect and lack of support*" (Hoogenraad 2001: 129).[8]

Culturally Sustaining Pedagogy

The community empowerment, independence and influence on school-associated Indigenous bilingual education as a consequence of this widening of ideological and implementational spaces, in addition to increased discourses related to multilingualism and multiculturalism, also led to the emergence of culturally sustaining Indigenous pedagogy (CSP) in the NT from the 1980s: *Both Ways* or *Two-Way* schooling.[9] The US practice of CSP involves acknowledging "tribal sovereignty"

---

[8] Hoogenraad (2001) reported that the early Warlpiri work in particular used community resources, including funds from the local shop, as opposed to Education Department resources to fund eminent linguists such as Ken Hale to work with Warlpiri assistant teachers on Warlpiri language and literacy. Warlpiri have retained and continue to use "the technical linguistic discussion of the Warlpiri sound system and grammar taught to them by Ken Hale" (Hoogenraad 2001: 130).

[9] This is not to be confused with the poorly structured Two-Way policy of the early 2000s.

and the effects of colonisation (McCarty and Lee 2014: 102).[10] CSP originates in culturally relevant pedagogy, through forms of teaching that entail cultural competence. These include helping students to identify, celebrate and practice aspects of their own culture while gaining competency in another, "socio-political consciousness" (solving "real-world problems" through critical analysis and problem solving) in addition to academic achievement and "intellectual growth" gained from classroom practices that fuse Indigenous and Western stocks of knowledge, language and education (Ladson-Billings 2014: 75). All this acknowledges that deeper cognisance of both Indigenous and Western concepts can only occur with linguistic engagement of students, participation of community members and heavy reliance on place (Fogarty and Kraal 2011; Oldfield and Willsher 2017).[11] CSP therefore represents a sophisticated culmination of postcolonial ideological discourse that arose from the early bilingual policy (Watt 2017).

Team Teaching

The philosophy of Both Ways extended into all professional operations of Indigenous and non-Indigenous teachers. Both Ways thinking was evident in the division of tasks in classrooms between Aboriginal language and culture teachers and their non-Indigenous counterparts as well as the incorporation of "bush trips" undertaken to gain deeper Indigenous conceptual learning (Disbray 2014; Oldfield 2016). It was also evident in the team-teaching model first advocated in the Watts et al. (1973) report where each class in a bilingual school had one Indigenous and one non-Indigenous teacher who forged close and continuous professional relationships. These professional relationships were "built" from strong personal relationships, requiring co-planning and co-teaching (Graham 2017: 30; Disbray 2014). The mentoring by the non-Indigenous teacher (Batchelor teacher trainers) was offset by their high dependency on the language and cultural skills and knowledge of the Indigenous teacher in lesson preparation and delivery and in ensuring a localised curriculum (Disbray 2014; Graham 2017; Oldfield 2016).

The early bilingual programs were not only noted for their increased Aboriginalisation of schools but for success in securing high attendance of students and much improved academic results (Gale et al. 1981; Hale 1999; Murtagh 1982). These outcomes were not sustained and varied during the history of NT bilingual education, due to how bilingual programs were evaluated (with whole schools, as

---

[10]While in the USA this is constitutionally recognised, as well as being embedded in treaties and laws, this is not the case in Australia (McCarty and Lee 2014). However, Australia is a signatory to United Nations Rights of Indigenous Peoples which encapsulates these USA Federal Indigenous rights of "self-government, self-education, and self-determination" (McCarty and Lee 2014: 101).

[11]The term *Both Ways* originates with the Gurindji people of Kalkaringi, who needed a term to represent their desire to generate an effective pedagogy, a distinctive Indigenous culture and language of education, and to align this with the prevailing practices of schooling.

opposed to actual bilingual classes, being classified as bilingual when bilingual programs were not universally implemented through a school) and the different levels of commitment of principals and non-Indigenous staff to the aims of bilingual teaching (Hoogenraad 2001).[12]

Schools adhering to high standards of bilingual implementation practices with strong principal support, however, could maintain excellent bilingual/biliteracy programs.[13]

Ideological/Implementational Policy Contraction of Aboriginal Bilingual/Biliteracy Education

However, as the chapters in Devlin et al. (2017) reveal, this welcome and innovative experimentation in Indigenous bilingual education has suffered funding contraction, inconsistency, interrupted research efforts, lack of sustained attention to appropriate teacher preparation and interminable chopping and changing in policy settings and assessment regimes. There has been a wide array of forms of provision and departmental or school-based support that vary according to geographic location and community involvement as well as whether local education staff, teachers and administrators alike are personally sympathetic or hostile to the multilingual ecology of Indigenous life.

Instead of steady attention to developing pedagogies and curriculum that incorporate traditional knowledge and cultural practices, especially Indigenous children's forms of communication (multilingual, mixed, domain focused), we have witnessed high levels of fragmentation, absence of guiding policy, contested understandings of the starting points for school learning and their connections to what is known before school and used out of school as well as failure to achieve consensus about desirable arrival points.

In short, Indigenous education has been highly politicised and continually disrupted. The issue of how and what to teach Indigenous children not only stands as an indicator of national confusion and concern about Indigeneity in Australian life, it signifies a deeper national malaise linked intimately to the failure of Australia to acknowledge Indigenous history and sovereignty. This malaise is connected to Australia's status as a settler colonial nation. Settler colonialism, according to Barker (2012: 1), is a "distinct method of colonising involving the creation and consumption of a whole array of spaces by settler collectives that claim and trans-

---

[12] Because of non-Indigenous teacher resistance, a class may not follow an Indigenous bilingual biliteracy program or follow a diluted form of programming in a bilingual school, and this effected the academic performance outcomes for a whole school (Hoogenraad 2001).

[13] This is evidenced by Tiwi bilingual school students in the early 2000s whose very strong MT focus in lower grades achieved literacy rates higher than the Australian average and who won two Australian (English) Literacy Awards in competition with mainstream monolingual students in 2003 (Devlin 2009).

form places through the exercise of their sovereign capacity". Indigenous people pose a problematic and obscured position in these states since they represent a threat to nation state sovereignty given their "difference" and original occupation (Barker 2012). When this is combined with the physical and symbolic violence attached to processes of colonisation, Indigenous people remain largely ignored and invisible in the invention of new sanitised colonial histories with concerted efforts to eliminate traces of cultural and linguistic difference through assimilative education (Barker 2012). In Australia, this began with the myth of "terra nullius" that has continued a construction of Indigenous people as a homogenous group devoid of languages and cultures to the degree that Indigenous language, Indigenous English as a second language and English as a foreign language contexts in remote regions and some urban areas can be completely discounted (Sellwood and Angelo 2013). The invisibility of Indigenous cultural and linguistic difference has led to a normativity of standard dominant forms of language and a deficit discourse consistently applied to the complex linguistic contexts and repertoires so common in remote communities and among remote community children at school (Pajaczkowska and Young 1992).

This failure to acknowledge linguistic and cultural difference is reinforced in the national constitution. While settler colonial counterparts such as New Zealand, Canada and the USA have treaties, bills of rights, laws or acts of parliament recognising language and cultural rights of their Indigenous people, Australia has no such protections, with the exception of anti-discrimination legislation (Behrendt 2000; McCarty and Lee 2014). Regarded as aspirational rather than concrete equality measures, few international declarations have been signed into Australian law (Malezer 2013). This lack of such formalised rights has left Indigenous Australians open to extinguishment of their general human rights as in the NT Intervention of 2007,[14] (a factor predicted by Behrendt in 2000). These conditions have also effectively silenced Indigenous people in relation to language education and inhibited the development of policies conducive to such rights.

The settler colonial process peculiar to Australia's has also been accompanied by ideological change in governance to create poorer conditions for Indigenous language education. Recent decades have seen widespread resource reductions, largely a result of global changes to health and education sectors, arising from the influence of mid-1980s neoliberal economic and social philosophy. Neoliberalism is an approach to the public disbursement of resources and the management of economies which stresses the primacy of free markets, the associated reasoning of individualism, free choice for individuals and small or reduced government responsibility. Originally known in Australia as *economic rationalism*, neoliberal public philosophy and economic management, and its extension into all public sectors, has resulted in the commodification of education and governments relinquishing their welfare role in favour of *enabling* active consumers to achieve their individual goals (Davies

---

[14] A set of reforms that led to the suspension of Indigenous human rights as well as the forced acquisition and government control of Aboriginal lands, housing and assets, including state-supported income.

10 A Long Unfinished Struggle: Literacy and Indigenous Cultural and Language Rights   177

and Bansel 2007; Moore 1996). Neoliberal philosophy is prone to attribute failures of individuals to achieve economic or educational goals as choices or effort differentials between individuals or groups as opposed to structural inequalities or disparities of opportunity and position (Clarke 2012). As applied to Indigenous education, neoliberal reasoning has given rise to normalising standards of comparison between Indigenous learners and other students. Now encapsulated in the term *closing the gap*, neoliberalism has eroded the 1970s innovations and the 1987 NPL moves towards bilingualism, favouring instead a monolingual English ethos, competition between schools for resourcing and students as well as external testing regimes that foster inter-group comparison (Davies and Bansel 2007). The inexorable effect of such developments weakened the case for MT education because the cultural, identity and local benefits that bilingual education affords are not comparable, not compared across groups, and thereby not measured so their esteem declines as a result.

This pattern of erosion has been compounded by NT self-government. In 1978 NT attained the status of *responsible government* and has progressively achieved greater forms and levels of administrative autonomy. While short of full statehood, NT is effectively an independent administration of the Australian Commonwealth. For Indigenous bilingual education this politico-administrative shift has resulted in compromises to programming that include a lack of monitoring or redress to manage resistance by principals, teachers and other NT Department of Education (NTDoE) staff, a significant loss of dedicated department support personnel and resourcing for bilingual/biliteracy programs, including staffing and training (reductions for all language programs, including ESL, to four linguists and one education officer by the mid-1990s and the eradication of this position by 2008). There is also the requirement that (often reluctant) school principals request NTDoE approval for bilingual status, inhibiting their growth (Hoogenraad 2001).

These NT erosions have been exacerbated by diminution of the original federal remit under the NPL as it was replaced by the 1991 *Australian Language and Literacy Policy* (McKay 2017; Moore 1996). The characterisation in this document of English as *central* to Australian cultural and economic life shifted the notion of bilingual complementarity inherent in the NPL into a competitive relationship pitting minority language maintenance against acquisition of prestigious English literacy. The intended effect of this change was felt strongly in the NT, feeding into local political factions that had long "ignored, discounted, misquoted or denied" (McKay 2017: 94) research evidence which categorically showed enhanced academic and English literacy and numeracy outcomes under the bilingual/biliterate model. One low point in this progression of obstructions, reductions and marginalisations was the attempt to close all bilingual programs in 1998. Although this fizzled into a diluted practice of *Two-Way* teaching it effectively contracted the more than 20 bilingual programs of the NPL era to 12 in 2000. However, the all-time low point was reached with the 2008 prohibition on teachers using Indigenous languages to teach morning lessons, under the NT ministerial declaration known as the *Compulsory Teaching in English for the First Four Hours of Each School Day*

(FHHP) which was later mitigated by ideological concessions in the federal arena with the *National Indigenous Languages Policy* (2009) proposals and discursive acknowledgement of Indigenous languages as important for well-being and academic achievement (MCEETYA 2005). This assuagement was reinforced with the 2015 creation of the national *Framework for Aboriginal Languages and Torres Strait Islander Languages* (ACARA 2015).

Some of these recent policy moves and curriculum initiatives have partially re-energised NT Indigenous language education, producing NT institutional initiatives like the 2014 NTDoE reappointment of a bilingual education manager (terminated in the 2009 FFHP) and appointment of a Manager of programs in Indigenous Languages and Culture. More recently, the NT government has developed a general plan for Indigenous language education (NTDoE 2016), and transition to Year 9 Indigenous language curricula (cultural and language awareness, second- and first-language learning) have been completed and were trialled in 2018.

According to Disbray (2016) 29 schools of 97 surveyed had managed to retain Indigenous language support or teaching in 2013, of which 8 had maintained bilingual program funding. Disbray (2016) noted these developments could be a consequence of the impact of expanding ideological spaces through policy that creates increased implementational spaces. There is extensive work and agitation of social agents across the NT: efforts to create independent non-government bilingual schools in remote areas, early childhood programs through philanthropic funding such as Children's Ground, efforts to expand out-of-school programs (Ranger Programs) to afford a means of maintaining local languages and new Batchelor Institute Indigenous language units and specialisations for teaching degrees at Charles Darwin University. These bottom-up activities serve to expand ideological and implementational bilingual spaces (Children's Ground 2018; Fogarty and Schwab 2012; Vanovac 2017).

While the FHHP has been abandoned and positive implementational movement occurs in isolated cases, prejudiced and stigmatising characterisations of Indigenous languages and people continue to deny bilingual schooling respect or opportunity for experimentation and deny any prospect of significant expansion to meet continually expressed community demand. Astonishingly, there is no formal bilingual policy in the NT, home of the vast bulk of the unique and highly endangered languages of the continent. The draft form of a 2014 report commissioned by the NTDoE on future directions in Territory education advocated complete removal of bilingual education citing implementation cost, lack of trained Indigenous staff and low success as the reasons, the latter claim being strongly contested by academic researchers and attributed instead to NTDoE's failure to evaluate programs (Graham 2017; Wilson 2014). The failure to reinvigorate bilingual education policy and significantly expand implementational spaces by resourcing additional programs has led one previous NTDoE staff member to lament:

> Apart from a few brave schools that struggle on in defiance of NT policy, bilingual education, as we knew it is now gone. The evidence for such a program of teaching and learning for Indigenous children of the NT is overwhelming. (Graham 2017: 32)

Positive Moves

There is, however, a potentially deep conceptual change underway, involving a radical reconfiguring of what counts as communication, indeed of what counts as normal communication patterns. Multilingualism is increasingly regarded as the *"default human condition in terms of current worldwide demography...arguably our primal human state"* (Evans 2017: 34).

The naturalness of multilingual societies and multilingual communication norms are increasingly being affirmed in mainstream international declarations, such as the most recent *Salzburg Declaration* issued by the Salzburg Global Seminar and released globally on International Mother Language Day, 21 February 2018 (Salzburg 2017). The body of recent scholarship that has led to such global declarations and to increased pressure on national governments to respond is often resisted by bureaucracies, as the history of bilingual/biliteracy education in Australia amply demonstrates. But pressure continues to percolate through social agent networks of scholars, activists and community representatives. These new scholarly and international developments support the well- attested claim that multilingualism is a positive resource for general cognition, now largely incontestable in academic research. Yet multilingualism remains a source of struggle in the policy settings that shape Australian language and literacy education.

A new policy battleground will likely centre on reinvigorated notions of linguistic human rights now made possible by these new forms of reasoning about the socio-communicative world. Essentially, this reasoning endorses the idea that multilingualism as a social phenomenon is humanistically and scientifically a historical inevitability and a contemporary value. This conception of multilingualism challenges its institutional characterisation as a problem which represents an obstacle for effective literacy learning by minority populations. It is a challenge that education systems must manage, distance or even eliminate. Schooling has classically responded to out-of-school communication complexities by selecting and modelling emblematic (monolingual standardised) language elements and speech registers associated with standard school subject disciplines as well as exemplars (words, grammar, chunks of communication, educated discourse and selected texts and genres) garnered through insights, categories and developments in linguistics and pedagogy. The radical challenge posed by new multilingualism research aims to shift the focus away from how institutional life functions to a closer approximation of the lived reality of multiple, non-separated languages as they appear in the informal conventionalised patterns of daily community life (Heugh and Skutnabb-Kangas 2010).

While national and northern Australian policy lags woefully behind in acknowledging multilingualism as a normative state and the fundamental connection between language and cultural rights and high educational, academic and socio-economic performance, recent planning, policy and practical developments in the NT mentioned above would suggest an incipient expression of this link that could be exploited and captured within Australian educational practice.

Conclusion

The dominant social responses to bilingual programs arising from federal and NT policy has wavered from ideologically supportive to outright hostile. Ethical support for Indigenous bilingual education generally was heralded with UNESCO's 1953, *The Use of Vernacular Languages in Education*. It was reinforced with the 1967 *Constitution Alternation (Aboriginals)* referendum and later human rights agreements that evolved language rights to an issue of cultural and linguistic identity. These proclamations were concurrently supported by a wave of international research that consistently demonstrated cognitive functioning gains resulting from bi- and multilingualism. These developments, in turn, led to positive educational advances such as the emergence of NT bilingual education from the mid-1970s and the NPL that placed community and Indigenous languages at the forefront of public policy. These policy events stimulated creation and expansion of bilingual implementational spaces and practices, resulting in the development of dynamic and highly productive and more literate remote Indigenous communities, the professional and socio-economic development of Indigenous teaching staff and remarkable and nationally renowned Indigenous leadership in schools.

However, this has been tempered by the influence of settler colonial and neoliberal governance ideologies. These have led to a contraction of positive bilingual discourse and educational practices so that successive NT governments have under-resourced bilingual/biliteracy programs and instead implemented policies that have, at times, aimed to extinguish bilingual education in schools.

Contemporaneously, events such as the reappointment of NTDoE staff to manage, research, plan and develop curricula for Indigenous bilingual, language and literacy education programs, and an increase in Indigenous language programs in out-of-school settings, that have evolved from policy, international agreements and developments suggest potential expansion of implementational spaces.

New directions emanating from scholarship, international declarations, continuing positive research findings and civil society innovation with active global linkages tie to the growing global acceptance of multilingualism as normative. From this we can hope for new kinds of mobilisation for policy and education systems to supplant endemic monolingual, mono-dialectical and mono-literate policy settings, early signs of which appear promising. However, for now the long unfinished struggle for Indigenous cultural and language rights, long denied to First Nations peoples because of various manifestations of literacy policy, continues.

References

ACARA–Australian Curriculum, Assessment and Reporting Authority. (2015). *Framework for aboriginal languages and Torres Strait Islander languages*. https://www.australiancurriculum.edu.au/f-10-curriculum/languages/framework-for-aboriginal-languages-and-torres-strait-islander-languages/. Accessed 1 Dec 2017.

Baker, C. (2008). Knowledge about bilingualism and multilingualism. In J. Cummins & N. H. Hornberger (Eds.), *Encyclopaedia of language and education* (pp. 315–327). New York: Springer.

Baker, C. (2011). *Foundations of bilingual education and bilingualism*. Clevedon: Multilingual Matters.

Barker, A. (2012). Locating settler colonialism. *Journal of Colonialism and Colonial History, 13*(3). http://muse.jhu.edu.ezp.lib.unimelb.edu.au/journals/journal_of_colonialism_and_colonial_history/v013/13.3.barker.html. Accessed 13 Mar 2015.

Behrendt, L. (2000). *The protection of indigenous rights* (Research Paper No. 27 1999–2000). Department of the Parliamentary Library Information and Research Services, Canberra: Commonwealth of Australia.

Bialystok, E., Peets, K. F., & Moreno, S. (2014). Producing bilinguals through immersion education: Metalinguistic awareness. *Applied PsychoLinguistics, 35*, 177–191. https://doi.org/10.1017/S0142716412000288.

Children's Ground. (2018). *Make it matter*. http://www.childrensground.org.au/campaign/20/make-it-matter. Accessed 17 Jan 2018.

Clarke, M. (2012). Talkin' 'bout a revolution. *Journal of Education Policy, 27*, 173–191. https://doi.org/10.1080/02680939.2011.623244.

Collins, R. (1999). *Learning lessons*. Darwin: NT Government.

Corson, D. (1999). *Language policy in schools*. Mahwah: Erblbaum.

Cummins, J. (1996). *Negotiating identities*. Ontario: California Association for Bilingual Education.

Cummins, J. (2000). *Language, power and pedagogy*. Clevedon: Multilingual Matters.

Davies, B., & Bansel, P. (2007). Neoliberalism and education. *International Journal of Qualitative Studies in Education, 20*, 247–259.

Devlin, B. (2009, June 26). *Bilingual education in the NT and the continuing debate about its effectiveness and value*. Canberra: AIATSIS Research Symposium Bilingual education in the NT, ANU.

Devlin, B. (2017). A glimmer of possibility. In B. Devlin, S. Disbray, & N. Devlin (Eds.), *History of bilingual education in the NT* (pp. 11–26). Singapore: Springer.

Devlin, B., Disbray, S., & Devlin, N. (2017). A thematic history of bilingual education in the NT. In B. Devlin, S. Disbray, & N. Devlin (Eds.), *History of bilingual education in the Northern Territory* (pp. 1–10). Singapore: Springer.

Disbray, S. (2014). Evaluating the bilingual education program in Warlpiri Schools. In R. Pensalfini, M. Turpin, & D. Diana Guillemin (Eds.), *Language description informed by theory* (pp. 25–46). Amsterdam: John Benjamins.

Disbray, S. (2016). Spaces for learning. *Language and Education, 30*, 317–336.

Evans, N. (2017). Ngûrrahmalkwonawoniyan: Listening here. *The Journal of the Australian Academy of the Humanities, 8*, 34–44.

EWG-Education and Welfare Group Legislative Research Service. (1973). *Bilingual education for Australian aborigines*. Canberra: The Parliamentary Library Legislative Research Service.

Fogarty, W., & Kraal, I. (2011). *Indigenous language education in remote communities*. Canberra: Centre for Aboriginal Economic Policy Research, ANU.

Fogarty, W., & Schwab, R. G. (2012). *Indigenous education: Experiential learning and learning though country*. Canberra: Centre for Aboriginal Economic Policy Research, ANU. http://caepr.cass.anu.edu.au/sites/default/files/docs/WP_80_Fogarty_Schwab_0.pdf. Accessed 25 June 2015.

Freire, P. (1972). *Pedagogy of the oppressed*. Harmondsworth/Middlesex: Penguin.

Gale, M. (1990). A review of bilingual education in Aboriginal Australia. *Australian Review of Applied Linguistics, 13*(2), 40–80.

Gale, K., McClay, D., Christie, M., & Harris, S. (1981). Academic achievement in the Milingimbi bilingual education program. *TESOL Quarterly, 15*(3), 297–314. https://doi.org/10.2307/3586755.

Graham, B. (2017). Reflections on team teaching. In B. Devlin, S. Disbray, & N. Devlin (Eds.), *History of bilingual education in the Northern Territory* (pp. 27–34). Singapore: Springer.

Hale, K. (1999). Remarks on NT bilingual education. *Ngoonjook, 16*, 42–50.

Harris, S. (1997). More haste less speed: Time and timing for language programs in NT aboriginal bilingual education. *The Aboriginal Child at School, 8*(4), 23–43. https://doi.org/10.1017/S0310582200011184.

Harris, S. (1999). The human face of bilingual education. *Ngoonjook, 16*, 70–76.

Harris, S., & Devlin, B. (1997). Bilingual programs involving aboriginal languages in Australia. In J. Cummins & D. Corson (Eds.), *Encyclopedia of language and education* (Vol. 5, pp. 1–14). Dordrect: Springer.

Heugh, K., & Skutnabb-Kangas, T. (2010). *From Periphery to the centre*. New Delhi: Orient Black Swan.

Hoogenraad, R. (2001). Critical reflections on the history of bilingual education in Central Australia. In J. Simpson, D. Lauphren, P. Austin, & B. Alpher (Eds.), *Forty years on: Ken Hale and Australian languages* (pp. 123–150). Canberra: Pacific Linguistics Research School or Pacific and Asian Studies, ANU.

Hornberger, N. (2005). Opening and filling up implementational and ideological spaces in heritage language education. *The Modern Language Journal, 89*(4), 605–609.

Hornberger, N., & Johnson, D. (2007). Slicing the onion ethnographically. *TESOL Quarterly, 41*, 509–532.

Johnson, D. (2010). Implementational and ideological spaces in bilingual education language policy. *International Journal of Bilingual Education and Bilingualism, 13*, 61–79.

Johnson, D., & Johnson, E. (2015). Power and agency in language policy appropriation. *Language Policy, 14*, 221–243.

Ladson-Billings, G. (2014). Culturally relevant pedagogy 2.0: a.k.a. the remix. *Harvard Educational Review, 84*(1), 74–135. https://doi.org/10.17763/haer.84.1.p2rj131485484751.

Lee, P., Fasoli, L., Ford, L., Stephenson, P., & McInerney, D. (2014). *Indigenous Kids and Schooling in the Northern Territory*. Batchelor: Batchelor Press.

Leitner, G. (2004). *Australia's many voices: Ethnic Englishes, indigenous and migrant languages: Policy and education*. Berlin: De Gruyter.

Lo Bianco, J. (1987). *National policy on languages*. Canberra: Australian Government Publishing Service.

Lo Bianco, J., & Slaughter, Y. (2016). Bilingual education in Australia. In O. Garcia, M. Angel, Y. Lin, & S. May (Eds.), *Bilingual and multilingual education* (pp. 347–360). Cham: Springer.

Malezer, L. (2013). Challenges in evaluating indigenous policy. In Productivity Commission (Ed.), *Better indigenous policies*. Canberra: Commonwealth of Australia. http://www.pc.gov.au/research/supporting/better-indigenous-policies/06-better-indigenous-policies-chapter4.pdf. Accessed 25 July 2015.

McCarty, T. L., & Lee, T. (2014). Critical culturally sustaining/revitalizing pedagogy and indigenous education sovereignty. *Harvard Educational Review, 84*(1), 101–124.

MCEETYA-Ministerial Council on Education, Employment, Training and Youth Affairs. (2005). *National statement for languages education in Australian Schools (2005–2008)*. Hindmarsh: Education Services Australia DECS. http://www.curriculum.edu.au/verve/_resources/languageeducation_file.pdf. Accessed 20 Jan 2017.

McKay, G. (2017). The policy framework for bilingual education in Australian indigenous languages in the NT. In B. Devlin, S. Disbray, & N. Devlin (Eds.), *History of bilingual education in the NT* (pp. 85–100). Singapore: Springer.

Moore, H. (1996). Language policy as virtual reality. *TESOL Quarterly, 30*(3), 82–106.

Murtagh, E. J. (1982). Creole and English used as languages of instruction in bilingual education with Aboriginal Australians. *International Journal of the Sociology of Language, 1982*(36), 15–33.

Nakamura, P. R. (2015). *Facilitating reading acquisition in multilingual environments (FRAME) India*. American Institutes for Research. http://www.air.org/project/facilitating-reading-acquisition-multilingual-environments-frame-india. Accessed 12 Jan 2018.

NTDoE–NT Department of Education. (2016). *Keeping indigenous languages and cultures strong*. Darwin: NT Government.

Oldfield, J. (2016). *Anangu Muru Wunka – Talking Black Fella*. PhD, The University of Melbourne, Melbourne.

Oldfield, J., & Willsher, M. (2017, September). Aboriginal worlds in the Western academy. In S. Shore (Ed.), *Traders neighbours and intruders*. Darwin/Canberra: Charles Darwin University and Australian Council for Adult Literacy. http://www.acal.edu.au/conference/wp-content/uploads/2017/10/2017-ACAL-e-proceedings-double_sided-web-min.pdf. Accessed 30 Oct 2017.

O'Shannessy, C. (2005). Light Warlpiri: A new language. *Australian Journal of Linguistics, 25*(1), 31–57.

Pajaczkowska, C., & Young, L. (1992). Racism, representation, psychoanalysis. In J. Donald & A. Rattansi (Eds.), *'Race', culture and difference* (pp. 198–219). London: Sage.

Salzburg. (2017). *Statement for a multilingual world*. Salzburg Global Forum: http://www.salzburgglobal.org/topics/article/fellows-co-create-salzburg-statement-for-a-multilingual-world.html. Accessed 15 Feb 2018.

Schmidt, A. (1990). *The loss of Australia's aboriginal language heritage*. Canberra: Aboriginal Studies Press.

Sellwood, J., & Angelo, D. (2013). Everywhere and nowhere. *Australian Review of Applied Linguistics, 36*(3), 250–266.

Skutnabb-Kangas, T., & Phillipson, R. (2017). *Linguistic human rights, past and present*. Research Gate: https://www.researchgate.net/publication/311452886_Linguistic_human_rights_past_and_present. Accessed 21 Mar 2018.

UN. (1966). *International covenant on civil and political rights* (Vol. 999, pp. 1–14668). United Nations https://treaties.un.org/doc/Publication/UNTS/Volume%20999/volume-999-I-14668-English.pdf. Accessed 15 June 2017

UN & OHCHR. (1992). *Declaration on the rights of persons belonging to National or ethnic, religious and linguistic minorities* (p. 9). New York: United Nations. http://www.ohchr.org/Documents/Issues/Minorities/Booklet_Minorities_English.pdf. Accessed 15 June 2017.

UNDRIP. (2008). *United Nations declaration on the rights of indigenous peoples*. United Nations, p. 7. http://www.un.org/esa/socdev/unpfii/documents/DRIPS_en.pdf. Accessed 16 June 2017.

UNESCO. (1953). *The use of vernacular languages in education*. Paris: United Nations Education, Scientific and Cultural Organisation. http://unesdoc.unesco.org/images/0000/000028/002897EB.pdf. Accessed 18 Jan 2018.

UNESCO. (2003). *Education in a multilingual world* (Position Paper). Paris: United Nations Education, Scientific and Cultural Organisation. http://unesdoc.unesco.org/images/0012/001297/129728e.pdf. Accessed 17 Jan 2018.

Vanovac, N. (2017). *Barker College agrees to launch aboriginal academy for girls in Utopia*. ABC Online. http://www.abc.net.au/news/2017-06-27/barker-college-plans-for-aboriginal-girls-academy-in-utopia/8610654. Accessed 17 Jan 2017.

Watt, R. (1993). *Bilingual education and self determination at Lajamanu in NT*. Dissertation, School of Education Deakin Universit, Geelong.

Watt, R. (2017). *Batchelor Institute's contribution to the maintenance and development of aboriginal languages: 1972–2017*. Batchelor: Batchelor Institute of Indigenous Tertiary Education.

Watts, B., McGrath, W., & Tandy, J. (1973). *Recommendations for the implementation and development of a program of bilingual education in schools in Aboriginal Communities in the NT*. Canberra: Department of Education.

Wilson, B. (2014). *Indigenous education draft report*. Darwin: NT Government.

Dr. Janine Oldfield is a higher education lecturer and researcher for Batchelor Institute of Tertiary Indigenous Education working in conjunction with Charles Darwin University. For the past 18 years, she has been engaged in Aboriginal and Torres Strait Islander education and research in the Northern Territory in Alice Springs, remote communities and Darwin. This included remote community workshop delivery of VET and higher education units, Indigenous project-based work and PhD and other research.

Joseph Lo Bianco is a professor of language and literacy education at the University of Melbourne. He is a specialist in language and literacy education policy analysis, past president of the Australian Academy of the Humanities and author of Australia's first official language policy, the 1987 National Policy on Languages.

Chapter 11
Embedding Evidence-Based Practice into a Remote Indigenous Early Learning and Parenting Program: A Systematic Approach

Louise Cooke and Averill Piers-Blundell

Abstract Engaging and empowering Indigenous families and their young children in quality early learning experiences through increasing parent knowledge and skill is critical to bridging the gap between Indigenous and non-Indigenous disadvantage. To do this, there must be evidence-based programs and approaches that achieve positive child outcomes and meet the needs of families in a myriad of ways. The systematic implementation of the Abecedarian Approach Australia (3a) within the Families as First Teachers (FaFT) program and other Indigenous contexts aims to do exactly this. This chapter outlines why high-quality evidenced-based approaches are necessary in the context of Indigenous academic and social disadvantage. It will also examine early literacy experiences necessary for school learning, linking these to 3a in the FaFT context. Implementation history will be explored and challenges discussed, demonstrating the complexity of systematically implementing an evidenced-based approach in a remote Indigenous parenting support program in the Northern Territory.

Introduction

Early literacy experiences and orientation to school learning are highly privileged and deemed necessary for success in modern Australian society. The Western schooling system as we know it today has evolved over time as a key institution for the transmission of important cultural knowledge and norms relating to a paradigm that encompasses democratic values, rapid industrialisation and urbanisation. Whether one subscribes to this paradigm or not, it is necessary to understand it in an

L. Cooke (✉)
Gunbalanya School, Gunbalanya, NT, Australia
e-mail: louise.cooke@ntschools.net

A. Piers-Blundell
University of Melbourne, Melbourne, VIC, Australia

© Springer Nature Singapore Pte Ltd. 2019
J. Rennie, H. Harper (eds.), *Literacy Education and Indigenous Australians*,
Language Policy 19, https://doi.org/10.1007/978-981-13-8629-9_11

attempt to participate in its systematic constructs such as employment and health services.

Many Indigenous children bring a set of experiences and skills to school which are important in preparing them for life in their family and community; however, they do not provide the same foundations for Western education. Children require specific knowledge, skills and behaviours to flourish in the school environment. Skills and knowledge necessary for children to access the school curriculum include English language and early literacy experiences as well as behaviours and constructs that support children's future school learning. The question is, then, how do Indigenous children and families while living in a context so vastly different from, and sometimes at odds with the Western societal paradigm, gain access and mastery to that paradigm's systematic constructs without losing the cultural practices, skills and knowledge that are so important to them, and indeed to the rest of Australia?

This chapter will outline the use of an evidenced-based proven early learning approach (Abecedarian Approach) within an established parenting support program (Families as First Teachers) in remote Indigenous communities across the Northern Territory. The Abecedarian Approach, one of the most successful early childhood interventions, has provided 30 years of evidence from various methodologies, including randomised controlled trials. In 2010, the approach was adapted for Australia through a collaboration between Professor Joseph Sparling and the University of Melbourne and named the Abecedarian Approach Australia (3a). The implementation of 3a within FaFT sought to bridge the gap between school knowledge and learning, and Indigenous cultural knowledge and skills, and to ultimately improve developmental outcomes for Indigenous children living in remote communities in the Northern Territory.

Background of the Abecedarian Approach and 3a

The Abecedarian Approach is a suite of early learning strategies that were developed for the Abecedarian Studies developed to examine the effects of learning on vulnerable children. The Abecedarian Project, Project Care and the Infant Health and Development Project are the three most comprehensive, and well known, longitudinal investigations using this approach. These studies were designed to examine the influence of high-quality early childhood services in improving academic achievement of children from vulnerable or at-risk families (Ramey et al. 2012). The Abecedarian Studies produced the largest and longest-lasting cognitive and academic achievement gains (measured by standardised tests) ever recorded by any experimental study (Sparling et al. 2007). The Abecedarian Approach has been proven through these studies to build the foundations of literacy and academic achievement from birth to affect lifelong positive outcomes.

The Abecedarian Approach holds at its core the fundamental premise that language plays a pivotal role in a young child's intellectual and social-emotional development (Ramey et al. 2012). Responsive, intentional and frequent adult-child language interactions are seen as the most important things to do in the early years, so all of the key elements of the approach have strategies which embed the kind of language interactions that lead to better outcomes for young children (and their families).

Joint attention is another critical aspect underpinning the Abecedarian Approach. Joint attention refers to the process of sharing the experience of observing an object or event by following gaze, or using pointing gestures, and it is considered important in the development of vocabulary (Dodici et al. 2003; Rogoff 1990; Morales et al. 2000; Tomasello and Farrar 1986). The salience of joint attention is the naming of objects and the elaboration of concepts when the focus of the child and the adult is shared (Dodici et al. 2003; Tomasello and Farrar 1986). It is thought to be particularly effective when the adult follows that child's attention, rather than the adult attempting to refocus their attention by being directive. Early joint attention is a predictor of receptive language development and vocabulary development. Lack of joint attention accounts for a high percentage of later learning problems in school (Morales et al. 2000; Mundy and Gomes 1998).

Further to this, responsivity and sensitivity are seen as parent behaviours that are prompt, contingent and appropriate responses to children's actions or cues and are linked to positive child outcomes (Dodici et al. 2003; Landry and Smith 2006). The Abecedarian Approach applies specific strategies that support adults to use these types of interactional styles when engaging with young children.

The Abecedarian Approach was developed to be preventative in nature, using early intervention strategies with a focus on prerequisite skills and knowledge for later academic success (Ramey et al. 2012). Importantly, the Abecedarian Approach makes explicit the learning behaviours that are necessary for later school success and uses simple but deep strategies to encourage these behaviours through positive, frequent and intentional adult-child interactions. Some of these child behaviours include control over his/her environment; use of expressive and receptive language; independently exploring the environment; being responsive and adaptive to the environment and changes within it; relating strongly to family and identifying with the subculture group (Ramey et al. 2012).

Mastery of language is the aspect of early learning most closely related to later success in school (Sparling et al. 2014a, b, c, d) and therefore is at the core of the Abecedarian Approach. Rich, contextual and intentional language is put into daily practice in programs using the 3a. The idea of making language a caregiver's first priority is referred to as Language Priority in the Abecedarian Approach.

All of the key elements are considered strategies for Language Priority; therefore, this is seen as a wraparound element of 3a. Language Priority, like the other elements, has a specific strategy for use which is easy to learn and remember. This strategy is called Notice, Nudge, Narrate or 3N and is a pattern adults can follow in their interactions with children to support the more spontaneous learning moments throughout the day. The other three elements of 3a are Conversational Reading, LearningGames® and Enriched Caregiving (Ramey et al. 2012).

Conversational Reading involves an adult sharing age-appropriate books with individual children (or a pair for children aged 2 years and up) using the specific

See, Show, Say strategy (or 3S). This element of the approach helps young children and adults coordinate their attention (joint attention). The basic principles underlying this element are:

- It is appropriate at any age (from birth to age 4 years and up).
- It is used with individual or pairs only.
- It uses a specific three-part strategy to ensure the adult-child interaction is conversational and employs elements of input, comprehension and output (Sparling et al. 2014a, b, c, d).

Conversational Reading helps children with the rudiments of literacy learning including development of strong oral language, interest in print and written language conventions, understanding and saying words, linking pictures to print, recognising letters and noticing and manipulating sounds in words (Sparling et al. 2014a, b ,c, d).

LearningGames® focus on adult-child interactions, and each game is an adult-mediated play episode (Sparling et al. 2014a, b, c, d). They are referred to as 'games' because they go back and forth between adult and child, and they are fun. The basic principles of the LearningGames® include:

- The games are simple but deep; the content and learning intentions of these games have deep significance to children's learning and development.
- The games are one-on-one interactions (occasionally small group experiences) which help participants keep focus on back-and-forth adult-child interactions.
- They are flexible and can be made to suit the context (whilst maintaining integrity of the games themselves) (Sparling et al. 2014a, b, c, d).

Enriched Caregiving refers to and supports the idea that using the approach is not an add-on to the daily routine but rather is embedded within it. Education and caregiving are not seen as different activities; each routine throughout the day has caregiving, emotional and educational aspects to it; and attention should be given to all three (Sparling et al. 2014a, b, c, d).

Basic principles of Enriched Caregiving include:

- It is not low-skilled or unimportant work.
- Applies to all routine parts of the day.
- Should be done repeatedly, over and over.

All of the elements and the embedded strategies help support the kinds of interactions needed to achieve literacy success. A study of caregiver behaviours after the implementation of the Abecedarian Approach showed statistically significant increases in rich oral language interactions, support for the development of vocabulary/comprehension and responsiveness to children (Collins and Goodson 2010). Similarly, results from developmental assessments of children engaged in the Abecedarian Approach in a childcare centre in Manitoba, Canada, consistently show positive language development scores linked to total number of Conversational Reading sessions (Santos and Stevens 2014).

Studies examining parent education aspects of the Abecedarian approach have shown that the approach can increase responsiveness to child and parental interactive reading skills, parent behaviours which have been positively and significantly correlated to child literacy outcomes. One randomised controlled trial commissioned by the US Department of Education's Institute of Education Sciences examined 2430 parents across 120 sites using Abecedarian Approach elements in the Even Start program and found that that was indeed the case (Judkins et al. 2008).

An evaluation of childcare subsidy strategies in Massachusetts (Collins and Goodson 2010) shows the Abecedarian Approach positively influences the adults' use of rich oral language, intentional support of children's vocabulary development and their responsiveness to children's cues.

The Necessity for an Evidence-Based Approach to Support Indigenous Children and Families in Remote Northern Territory

Before discussing the social and educative disadvantages of many remote Indigenous children, we believe it is also important to note the strengths with which many of these children first enter early childhood programs, strengths such as physical and emotional resilience, strong kinship ties, cultural knowledge and connection to country to name a few. It is the responsibility of early childhood program providers in remote Indigenous communities to reconcile these strengths with the immense challenges faced to begin to address gaps in literacy and numeracy outcomes for Aboriginal students in remote communities of the Northern Territory.

There is, however, a plethora of evidence that Indigenous children in the NT experience high levels of disadvantage leading to developmental vulnerability and poor educational outcomes. In 2015, there were approximately 4004 registered births in the Northern Territory of which 1355 or 34% were recorded as Indigenous (ABS 2015). These children have an increased likelihood of having lower birth weights, living in socioeconomically disadvantaged households, experiencing involvement with the child protection system and living in remote communities where basic necessities such as housing and nutrition are not always sufficiently met (Silburn et al. 2011a, b, c).

The Australian Early Development Census (AEDC) data indicates that for very remote Indigenous children, there are a complex and compounding set of disadvantage variables. They are remoteness, Indigeneity, low socioeconomic status and language backgrounds other than English. To exemplify this point, we can examine the results for the remote area of Victoria River, NT, where 90.2% of the participants were Indigenous. Nationally, the percentage of children who are vulnerable on two or more domains is 11.1%; in the Northern Territory, the percentage is 23.1%; and in the Victoria River regions, the percentage is 57.1% (Commonwealth of Australia 2015).

In year 3 of school when children first participated in the National Assessment Program Literacy and Numeracy (NAPLAN), we see a strong correlation with their AEDC data. Year 3 reading results for 2017 indicate that 3.1% of children across Australia are below the national minimum standard, whereas in the Northern Territory 26% have not attained it; in very remote Northern Territory, the figure rises to 66.3% (ACARA 2017).

National and international research has consistently demonstrated that low literacy attainment can be linked to disadvantage, including isolation, unemployment, delinquency and low self-esteem (Spedding et al. 2007). In Australia, children from rural and remote areas, and particularly Indigenous children, have been shown to be at considerable risk of low literacy acquisition (ACARA 2017).

Recognised risk factors for poor literacy outcomes include low parental education, minority status and a mismatch between home language and the language of school instruction (Locke et al. 2002; Lucchese and Tamis-Lemonda 2007). In particular, the language gap between lower-income, less educated parents and those with higher-education and high socioeconomic status has been identified as a key factor in the language and literacy trajectory of children (Carey 2013; Perkins et al. 2013).

There is evidence to suggest the number of words spoken at home can influence significantly a child's language development, which can have a long-lasting impact on their overall success in life (Perkins et al. 2013). Hart and Risley (2003) identified a 30 million word gap between children from high and low socioeconomic groups. Children from disadvantaged backgrounds have heard 30 million fewer words than their more advantaged peers by the time they are 3 years of age. These children have an expressive vocabulary of just 50% of that of the children from high SES families. It was also found that these differences in early childhood were highly predictive of reading comprehension at 9–10 years of age.

A number of research studies have focused on the specific nature of these language experiences and in particular the nature of the parent-child interactions (Crawford and Zygouris 2006; Davis-Kean 2005; Dodici et al. 2003; Galindo and Sheldon 2012; Guo and Mullan-Harris 2000; Hoff 2006; Leseman and Van Tuijl 2006; McNaughton 2006). Young children need rich language experiences to enable them to develop language and semantic knowledge, two fundamental components of literacy development (Deckner et al. 2006; Karrass and Braungart-Rieker 2005; Landry and Smith 2006). These studies show that oracy is a strong precursor to literacy achievement.

Key stakeholders in education and social services increasingly understand that high-quality prior-to-school experiences are critical to successful literacy attainment at school and into adulthood (Rose 2004; Wheelahan 2010). Current Australian Government and Non-Government Organisations initiatives focusing on the early years have grown largely from the understanding of the interplay between biology and children's experiences of family, community and early learning and the role it has in shaping future health, learning and behaviour (Gable and Hunting 2000; Silburn et al. 2011a, b, c).

Families as First Teachers Program: The Ideal Host for the Abecedarian Approach Australia

Key to the implementation of 3a in the Northern Territory was the foundations provided by an embedded early learning and parenting program. Families as First Teachers provided a perfect host program for the implementation of 3a. It was a well-developed dual generational model, had significant community take up, was well funded and had a culture of professional learning and continuous improvement. Professor Joseph Sparling, a research partner in the original Abecedarian Studies, was committed to a long-term relationship to support the implementation, and the government at the time (2011) was highly interested in the capacity of 3a to create change for vulnerable families and children. There were teams resident in 21 remote communities across the Northern Territory which included qualified and local Indigenous staff.

The Families as First Teachers (FaFT) program was launched in 2009 in the Northern Territory to address the social and educational disadvantage of Indigenous children living in remote communities. FaFT is an early learning and family support program for remote Indigenous families. The aim of FaFT is to improve developmental outcomes for remote Indigenous children by working with families and children prior to school entry. Parent and carer support and education are seen as keys to the program's success, and it aims to level the playing field so that children will be better prepared to take advantage of the educational opportunities that schooling provides them.

The FaFT model design is holistic in its approach and aims to develop place-based programs to engage families and communities in giving their children the best start in life. FaFT begins from birth and incorporates early learning, parent capacity building, literacy and numeracy at home and transition to preschool strategies. It strives to support healthy development and be respectful of Indigenous child-rearing practices and is strength-based (Department of Education 2013). Parents and carers are important participants in the program and are required to attend with their children to participate in facilitated playgroups and other program activities. The programs are managed through schools and supported by staff within the Darwin and regional offices.

Within 2 years, the program had been established in 21 remote communities, and a mobile model reached a further 24 smaller very remote communities and achieved annual enrolments of 2354 children and 2323 parents in 2012 (Wilson 2014). As there were fewer than 6000 Indigenous children aged 0–4 in the NT at the time, this suggests that approximately 70% of eligible children in serviced communities were involved to some extent in FaFT programs provided (Wilson 2014). Given the historical disengagement of remote Indigenous children and families within Western school systems and programs, this was a very encouraging sign. 'Within one to two years of implementation, principals began to comment on the benefits of the large numbers of parents appearing at their doorstep to attend FaFT programmes. Schools began to look at the program as a key to building community partnerships, developing a culture of attendance at school, increasing school readiness of children, and a way to engage parents in adult education' (Abraham and Piers-Blundell 2012 p. 28).

A process evaluation recommended that the program model required further specification. It was suggested there was a need for an evidence-based early learning pedagogical model within the program in order to support consistency and quality improvement across sites to drive child education outcomes. The Commonwealth funding body also applied pressure to include an evidence-based approach as a requirement of the funding contract.

Fortuitously, Professor Sparling spent some time in the Northern Territory speaking at conferences and to groups of interested people. It was at a meeting of administrators and bureaucrats in 2010 that leadership representatives from the Department of Education first heard Professor Sparling speak about the Abecedarian Approach and pursued a meeting with him. So began a highly productive partnership between Professor Sparling and the Department of Education that spanned the next 7 years. Professor Sparling was keenly interested in learning about how the 3a could be adapted for remote contexts while maintaining program integrity. The Department of Education was very keen to work with such a highly respected international academic and could see the potential benefits for early childhood education in the Northern Territory.

After considerable consultation and deliberation, 3a was selected to support quality improvement of FaFT due to its potential applicability in remote Indigenous contexts. The implementation of 3a within the FaFT program in remote Indigenous communities across the Northern Territory sought to find a balance between the two imperatives of improved school readiness and continued community engagement.

The Abecedarian Approach model is relatively simple and can be used across multiple setting types such as childcare, playgroups, preschool and parenting classes. Steeped in academic research, the approach is not packaged rigidly for financial gain and has been implemented in numerous settings including China, South America, Pakistan, France, Canada and Romania. It has been delivered from orphanages, childcare centres, playgroups, preschools, parenting programs and hospitals. These aspects of the approach made it ideal for implementation in the FaFT program.

Of critical importance is the fact that the Abecedarian Approach can be adapted for the context, can be delivered in first language and is not dependent on adult participants having high levels of literacy. In professional discussions with the authors, Joseph Sparling identified that the method and language of delivery are not critical to ensure positive child outcomes, whereas frequency of access and participation, emphasis on adult-child interactions and use of all elements of the approach are. This type of flexibility in the delivery of an evidence-based approach made it ideal for the FaFT context.

Another potential benefit of implementing 3a within the FaFT program is the pivotal role that parents and carers play in the delivery. The structured adult-child interactions assist parents to build productive and positive relationships through early educational experiences. Parents learn about their child's development, become skilled in facilitating educational activities and feel empowered to support their child's learning. This has become the practical 'learning through play' parent education strategy sought by FaFT leadership at the time of initial implementation.

A Systematic Implementation Approach of 3a in the Northern Territory

In 2011, the FaFT program mandated the implementation of the 3a Conversational Reading element to begin with. The FaFT leadership staff and Professor Sparling agreed that a slow and structured introduction of the elements was most likely to ensure 3a was embedded into FaFT programs with full fidelity. Over the first year, programs worked to learn about Conversational Reading, implement the element and refine their practice. There were two territory-wide and two regional workshops that year to support the learning of Conversational Reading and develop expertise among staff. A continuous improvement cycle of training, supported delivery, supervised practice and coaching and feedback to inform the training needs for the next term simulated the action research cycle (Kemmis and McTaggart 1988).

This strong interconnection between evidence-based practice and practice-based evidence assisted all staff to recognise and value learnings from both the original research and the implementation challenges as they emerged in the field. Each term staff were required to film and document focus areas of practice to share with their colleagues for professional learning. Common issues arose, and practitioners, administrators and researchers worked together to co-construct responsive program strategies and protocols. This very focused and careful model of implementation was followed for the introduction of the subsequent elements of 3a.

As delivery of 3a within FaFT progressed, it became obvious that there was a need for more contextualised training and implementation resources. Children and families bring a range of experiences and knowledge with them, and there is an ongoing need for resources and approaches which value and connect to those experiences. Local examples of parents and children demonstrating each of the 3a elements were inserted into training packages and animations were commissioned which provided information and demonstration in an accessible manner.

The Northern Territory Government invested heavily in the adaptation of the 200 LearningGames® to support implementation. Photoshoots across 15 remote FaFT sites facilitated a largely pictorial version of the original LearningGames®. This was to improve accessibility of the resources due to low literacy levels of many parents. All customisation was supported and approved by the Department of Educations' Indigenous Early Childhood Parenting Reference Group for cultural appropriateness and by Professor Joseph Sparling for program integrity.

Young children in remote Indigenous communities of the Northern Territory grow up in a complex language environment, learning a number of Aboriginal languages as well as English. 'The maintenance and development of children's first home language is essential for developing a child's sense of identity as well as promoting language and cognition' (Scull 2016). Delivery of 3a learning experiences by parents and carers is encouraged in first language while non-Indigenous staff use English. This develops a strong foundation of these language skills and concepts upon which children can later build English language skills, as well as preserve first language knowledge for future generations.

Whenever adaptation is considered to an evidence-based program, caution is raised about the continued veracity of the evidence. Professor Sparling (2015) discussed how beneficial adaptation can be encouraged and harmful adaptations or 'program drift' avoided during the implementation processes in different sites. He concluded that to achieve positive child outcomes frequency of access and participation, emphasis on adult-child interactions and conversations as well as the use of all four elements of the approach must be maintained. However, he accepts that the delivery mode and language, pictures and words to present the Abecedarian elements as well as the sequence and balance of the elements may be altered without significant risk.

Parental Empowerment

For all children, but particularly young children, learning happens in the home or family setting and through interactions with family members (Cohrssen and Niklas 2016). Children affect and are affected by their home learning environment, and because of this multidirectional process, it is increasingly clear that all early childhood programs should support a family-centred approach (Cohrssen and Niklas 2016). Connections between home, school and community are recognised as a key element in achieving literacy success, particularly for vulnerable students (Comber and Kamler 2005).

A fundamental premise of both the Abecedarian Approach and the FaFT program is that they work when there is a change in the behaviours of the adults affected by the approach (in the case of FaFT, this is the parent or caregiver). Abecedarian training and coaching help adults modify their interactions with children and give parents and caregivers simple but deep strategies to engage children in ways that are evidenced to improve academic outcomes.

A strong theme of parent empowerment is evident within FaFT. Parental involvement in the program is viewed as essential for maintenance and development of young children's first language which is fundamental to identity, cultural knowledge as well as strong foundations in cognition and language skills (Silburn et al. 2011a, b, c). Parents are supported and coached to implement the 3a strategies effectively on site and encouraged to use them in the home environment also. The FaFT program makes resources available to families that encourage and facilitate the use of 3a in homes. Families enrolled in the program receive a variety of age appropriate free books to facilitate the use of Conversational Reading at home. Copies of the LearningGames® are available for families to take home or are delivered during home visits. FaFT teams constantly reflect on ways to increase parent use of 3a in the home, and it is often a focus of professional development sessions.

During the initial phase of implementation of 3a into FaFT programs, significant time was spent supporting staff in coaching and mentoring strategies, in particular a focus on coaching methods that were interactive, based on partnerships with families and involved deep levels of reflective practice. FaFT staff were encouraged and supported to reconceptualise their role as 'expert' to that of collaborative partner working alongside families. A focus on sharing of skills, knowledge and experiences between staff and families or learner and coach was frequently encouraged in training and on-the-ground support.

Impacts in the Northern Territory Context

The evidence available so far suggests that 3a impacts positively on children's language development, preschool readiness and adult engagement with children.

Recently, Brookes and Tayler (2016) conducted a small-scale study with young Aboriginal children at an Aboriginal childcare service in the Northern Territory. It showed positive change in adults with increased behaviours that facilitate children's learning as a result of participating in the study and learning critical elements of the Abecedarian Approach. In addition, this study showed that 'significant increase in their expressive and receptive language, and their initiation of joint attention behaviours, illustrates the potential of this intervention to change the language growth trajectories of very young children who live in similar circumstances' (Brookes and Tayler 2016, p. 4).

Anecdotal evidence from on-the-ground FaFT staff and through perception surveys of parents in the program indicate families do see the value of 3a in the children's learning journeys. Dorothy Gapany, a Family Liaison Officer at Galiwinku, recently said 'FaFT and the research project empowered mothers to teach their children'. A perception survey of 585 remote parents of children enrolled in the FaFT program across 21 sites in the Northern Territory was conducted in 2014. In response to the question about Abecedarian strategies, 'Do Conversational Reading and LearningGames® support your child to learn?', 96.24% said *yes*, 0.51% said *no* and 3.25% said they *don't know*.

Results from a case study at one FaFT site focusing on Conversational Reading strategies with parents showed that families were having a positive experience using the approach and were using the strategies to teach children cultural concepts and knowledge such as kinship and relationship to environment and that parents valued the approach as a way to support their young children's school readiness (Cooke 2013). This research also indicated that the high levels of professional development and on-the-ground support were enabling factors in the implementation of 3a (Cooke 2013).

Consistent feedback from a range of stakeholders including principals, preschool teachers and community members indicates that the implementation of 3a has enhanced children's preschool readiness. In 2012, a survey of school principals where 3a was being delivered found that 86% of principals felt the program had been very helpful or helpful in preparing families for school (DECS 2012).

Through the implementation of 3a within the FaFT program, a strong community of practice has evolved in the Northern Territory and beyond. Academics and teachers are engaged in research projects, teaching and learning clusters and presentations of their work. Champions have emerged across the fields of health and social services who value the evidence-based approach and its outcomes which reach far beyond educational attainment. There is strong political and bureaucratic support based on the social impact achieved in the early Abecedarian projects.

The enormous potential of the NT implementation of 3a within its FaFT program has caused strong interest from policymakers and academics. In 2013, an Australian Research Council linkage grant 'Building a Bridge into Preschool in Remote Northern Territory Communities ~ LP130100001' was procured to examine the success of the program in preparing children for preschool. The University of Melbourne continues to lead this work in partnership with the NT Department of Education. Final data collection was completed in 2017/2018 and results will likely be published in 2019.

Implementation Challenges

The implementation of 3a within FaFT meets many of the fundamental principles that support successful literacy outcomes for remote Indigenous children. Principles relating to maintenance of language and culture, connection to community knowledge and experiences, valuing and respecting Indigenous practices, skills and knowledge, high levels of investment in professional development and support and investment in an evidenced-based practice (Scull 2016) are all evident in the systematic implementation of 3a into established FaFT programs across the Northern Territory. Throughout this chapter, many of the positive aspects of delivering an evidence-based approach have been explored; it will now delve into some of the challenges faced.

Implementation of an evidence-based program into very remote, highly complex environments is not straightforward. The impact of the social and cultural contexts on programs must be recognised. 'Early childhood interventions can shift the odds toward more favourable outcomes, but programs that work are rarely simple, inexpensive or easy to implement' (Shonkoff and Phillips 2000. p 4).

Achieving the necessary participation to ensure positive child outcomes has been the most significant challenge during implementation of 3a in FaFT. Families live complex lives with many demands on their time that prevent their daily participation in the FaFT program. While a high proportion of families participate in the program, they do not come often enough to receive the dosage recommended. Wilson (2014) suggests that to achieve success throughout schooling, an attendance rate of more than 80% is necessary. The outstanding results achieved in the early

Abecedarian projects required participation in excess of 26 h per week (Ramey et al. 2012). Families engaged in the FaFT program in the Northern Territory are highly mobile, have many family and cultural responsibilities and often travel extensively when their children are young. The current ARC study will likely shed more light on this challenge by examining the effects of levels of participation on school readiness in the Northern Territory.

The increased focus on a specific pedagogy (3a) has seen improvements in the delivery of the early learning element of FaFT. However, parents have less time to spend in other program areas that they find highly engaging. Families previously used the FaFT program to explore a range of holistic adult learning experiences and community projects of their own choosing such as cultural parenting practices, nutrition, information technologies, family budgeting, keeping kids safe, child health and more. While every effort is made to include community representatives in the program decision-making, 'doing to' rather than 'doing with' families is always a risk to community disengagement.

Quality control of 3a delivery is highly problematic due in most part to the tyranny of distance. The model of implementation is one of training, delivery, supervised practice and coaching. However, due to vast distances and expensive travel requirements such as chartered light aircraft, most sites only have an opportunity for supervised practice and coaching three to four times a year, which is hardly optimal. Regional networks and video coaching work to mitigate this; however, it remains a key challenge.

The implementation model is resource heavy as it requires constant and highly contextualised training as well as ongoing supervised practice and coaching. The development of context-specific training materials and resources required substantial financial investment. Qualified staff in remote communities require additional financial incentives such as remote allowances and subsidised housing to name a few. This ongoing investment depends on continuing political support for an approach which may take a lot longer than the political cycle to produce definitive results. We have provided training to smaller organisations who lacked the structural supports to successfully implement 3a. These programs experienced lower levels of traction and found it challenging to maintain any level of fidelity.

A review of Indigenous education in the Northern Territory (Wilson 2014) acknowledged the early success of the program and recommended that it be provided in urban, regional and additional remote sites. When the implementation of 3a into FaFT programs began in 2011, there were 21 sites in the Northern Territory; as of August 2017, there are 30 remote and 2 urban FaFT programs operating across the region. As the program currently undergoes rapid expansion, there will be ongoing challenges to maintain the quality and the fidelity of 3a.

These challenges are not insignificant; however, the benefits that have been seen over the last 7 years have convinced principals, administrators and politicians that 3a has enormous potential. Families are engaging in early learning programs together, parents are feeling more empowered to support their children's learning, children are showing signs of increased school readiness, and educators are learning to support families and children more effectively.

Conclusion

The implementation of 3a within the FaFT program across 30 remote Aboriginal communities (as well as 2 urban sites as of August 2017) in the Northern Territory marries a highly engaging parenting support program with an evidence-based approach in a way that has not yet been seen in the context. It is ambitious in its goals and strategies, but the evidence of Indigenous disadvantage in remote communities means that we must be ambitious, we must be strategic and we must give programs time to collect sufficient evidence to be used in influencing further implementation actions. Early indications are that largely as a result of the FaFT program, children are more 'school ready' when they commence school (Menzies 2013). We look forward to results from the Australian Research Council linkage grant 'Building a Bridge into Preschool in Remote Northern Territory Communities ~ LP130100001' to enhance our picture of what is happening for children and families engaged in this ambitious and promising approach in the remote Aboriginal communities of the Northern Territory.

References

Abraham, G., & Piers-Blundell, A. (2012). *Early childhood matters – Sharing a vision. ARNEC CONNECTION: Working Together for Early Childhood, 6*, 27–29.

Australian Bureau of Statistics. (2015). *Births Australia.* https://www.abs.gov.au/ausstats%5Cabs@.nsf/0/8668A9A0D4B0156CCA25792F0016186A?Opendocument. Accessed 21 Aug 2017.

Australian Curriculum Assessment and Reporting Authority (ACARA). (2017). *National assessment program, literacy and numeracy, achievement in reading, writing, language conventions and numeracy, national report for 2017.* https://www.nap.edu.au/docs/default-source/default-document-library/naplan-national-report-2017_final_04dec2017.pdf?sfvrsn=0. Accessed 17 Dec 2017.

Brookes, I., & Tayler, C. (2016). Effects of an evidence-based intervention on the Australian English language development of a vulnerable group of young aboriginal children. *Australasian Journal of Early Childhood, 41*(4), 4–15.

Carey, B. (2013, September 25). *Language gap between rich and poor children begins in infancy, Stanford psychologists find* (Stanford report). http://news.stanford.edu/news/2013/september/toddler-language-gap-091213.html. Accessed 24 July 2017.

Cohrssen, C., & Niklas, F. (2016). Partnering with families to promote learning. In J. Page & C. Tayler (Eds.), *Learning and teaching in early years* (pp. 90–104). Melbourne: Cambridge University Press.

Collins, A., & Goodson, B. (2010). *Evaluation of child care subsidy strategies: Massachusetts family child care study executive summary, OPRE 2011-1.* Washington, DC: Office of Planning, Research and Evaluation, Administration for Children and Families, U.S. Department of Health and Human Services.

Comber, B., & Kamler, B. (Eds.). (2005). *Turn-around pedagogies – Literacy interventions for at-risk students.* Newtown: Primary Teaching Association.

Commonwealth of Australia. (2015). *Northern Territory Australian early development census data 2015.* http://www.aedc.gov.au/data/data-explorer. Accessed 10 Aug 2017.

Cooke, J. L. (2013). *Empowered parents: Book reading practices of indigenous parents coached in conversational reading techniques in Galiwin'ku – A case study*. Unpublished Masters Research thesis. Melbourne Graduate School of Education, The University of Melbourne.

Crawford, P. a., & Zygouris-Coe, V. (2006). All in the family: Connecting home and school with family literacy. *Early Childhood Education Journal, 33*(4), 261–267.

Davis-Kean, P. E. (2005). The influence of parent education and family income on child achievement: The indirect role of parental expectations and the home environment. *Journal of Family Psychology, 19*(2), 294–304.

Deckner, D. F., Adamson, L., & Bakeman, R. (2006). Child and maternal contributions to shared reading; effects on language and literacy development. *Journal of Applied Developmental Psychology, 27*(1), 31–41.

Department of Education and Children's Services (DECS). (2012). *Principal survey, transition to preschool strategy*.

Department of Education and Children's Services (DECS). (2013). *2013 Program handbook: Families as first teachers (FaFT)*. Northern Territory Government.

Dodici, S., Draper, D., & Peterson, C. (2003). Early parent-child interactions and early literacy development. *Topics in Early Childhood Special Education, 23*(3), 124–136.

Gable, S., & Hunting, M. (2000). *Nature, nurture and early brain development*. University of Missouri Extension. http://extension.missouri.edu/publications/DisplayPrinterFriendlyPub.aspx?=GH6115. Accessed 20 July.

Galindo, C., & Sheldon, S. B. (2012). School and home connections and children's kindergarten achievement gains: The mediating role of family involvement. *Early Childhood Research Quarterly, 27*(1), 90–103.

Guo, G., & Mullan Harris, K. (2000). The mechanisms mediating the effects of poverty on children's intellectual development. *Demography, 37*(4), 431–447.

Hart, B., & Risley, T. R. (2003). The early catastrophe. The 30 million word gap. *American Educator, 27*, 4–9.

Hoff, E. (2006). Environmental supports for language acquisition. In D. Dickinson & S. B. Neuman (Eds.), *Handbook of early literacy research Vol 2* (pp. 163–172). New York/London: Sage.

Judkins, D., St. Pierre, R., Gutmann, B., Goodson, B., von Glatz, A., Hamilton, J., & Rimdzius, T. (2008). *A study of classroom literacy interventions and outcomes in even start*. Washington, DC: National Centre for Education Evaluation and Regional Assistance, Institute of Education Sciences, U.S. Department of Education. https://ies.ed.gov/ncee/pubs/20084028/pdf/20084028.pdf. Accessed 18 Aug 2017.

Karrass, J., & Braungart-Rieker, J. M. (2005). Effects of shared parent-infant book reading on early language acquisition. *Journal of Applied Developmental Psychology, 26*(2), 133–148.

Kemmis, S., & McTaggart, R. (Eds.). (1988). *The action research planner*. Waurn Ponds: Deakin University Press.

Landry, S. H., & Smith, E. K. (2006). The influence of parenting on emerging literacy skills. In D. Dickinson & S. B. Neuman (Eds.), *Handbook of early literacy research* (pp. 135–148). New York/London: Sage.

Leseman, P., & Van Tuijl, C. (2006). Cultural diversity in early literacy: Findings in Dutch studies. In D. Dickinson & S. B. Neuman (Eds.), *Handbook of early literacy research* (pp. 211–228). New York/London: Sage.

Locke, A., Ginsborg, J., & Peers, I. (2002). Development and disadvantage: Implications for early years and beyond. *International Journal of Language & Communication Disorders, 37*(1), 3–15.

Lucchese, F., & Tamis-LeMonda, C. (2007). *Fostering language development in children from disadvantaged backgrounds*. Published on 2007 – 10-22 16: 13:37 Encyclopedia of Language and Literacy.

McNaughton, S. (2006). Considering culture in research based interventions to support early literacy. In D. Dickinson & S. B. Neuman (Eds.), *Handbook of early literacy research* (pp. 229–240). New York/London: Sage.

Menzies School of Health Research (Menzies). (2013, May). *Strong start bright futures final evaluation report*. Centre for Child Development and Education, Menzies School of Health Research.

Morales, M., Mundy, P., Delgado, C. E. F., Yale, M., Messinger, D., Neal, R., et al. (2000). Responding to joint attention across the 6-through 24-month age period and early language acquisition. *Journal of Applied Developmental Psychology, 21*(3), 283–298.

Mundy, P., & Gomes, A. (1998). Individual differences in joint attention skill development in the second year. *Infant Behavior and Development, 21*(3), 469–482.

Perkins, S., Finegood, E., & Swain, J. (2013). Poverty and language development: Roles of parenting and stress. *Innovations in Clinical Neuroscience, 10*(4), 10–19.

Ramey, C. T., Sparling, J. J., & Ramey, S. L. (2012). *Abecedarian the ideas the approach and the findings*. Los Altos: Sociometric Corporation.

Rogoff, B. (1990). *Apprenticeship in thinking: Cognitive development in social context*. New York: Oxford University Press.

Rose, D. (2004). Sequencing and pacing of the hidden curriculum: How Indigenous learners' are left out of the chain. In J. Muller, B. Davis, & A. Morais (Eds.), *Reading Bernstein, researching Bernstein* (pp. 61–74). London: RoutledgeFalmer.

Santos, R., & Stevens, H. (2014). *Interim report*. Lord Selkirk Park Child Care Centre Evaluation. Healthy Child Manitoba Office.

Scull, J. (2016). Effective literacy teaching for indigenous students: Principles from evidence-based practices. *Australian Journal of Language and Literacy, 39*(1), 54–63.

Shonkoff, J. P., & Phillips, D. (Eds.). (2000). *From neurons to neighbourhoods: Committee on integrating the science of early childhood development* (pp. 39–56). Washington, DC: National Academics Press.

Silburn, S. R., Nutton, G., Arney, F., & Moss, B. (2011a). *The first 5 years: Starting early* (Early childhood series no. 2). Darwin: Northern Territory Government.

Silburn, S. R., Robinson, G., Arney, F., Johnstone, K., & McGuinness, K. (2011b). *Early childhood development in the NT: Issues to be addressed. Topical paper commissioned for the public consultations on the Northern Territory Early Childhood Plan*. Darwin: Northern Territory Government.

Silburn, S. R., Nutton, G., McKenzie, J. W., & Landrigan, M. (2011c). *Early years English language acquisition and instructional approaches for aboriginal students with home languages other than English: A systematic review of the Australian and international literature. The Centre for Child Development and Education*. Darwin: Menzies School of Health Research.

Sparling, J. (2015). *The Abecedarian approach: The implementation and differential effects*. PowerPoint presentation.

Sparling, J., Ramey, C. T., & Ramey, S. L. (2007). The Abecedarian experience. In M. Young (Ed.), *Early child development from measurement to action: A priority for growth and equity* (pp. 103–127). Washington, DC: World Bank.

Sparling, J., Ramey, C. T., & Tayler, C. (2014a). *Language priority 3a Abecedarain approach Australia*. Melbourne Graduate School of Education. University of Melbourne. 3a.education. unimelb.edu.au. Accessed 12 Aug 2017.

Sparling, J., Ramey, C. T., & Tayler, C. (2014b). *Enriched caregiving 3a Abecedarain approach Australia*. Melbourne Graduate School of Education. University of Melbourne. 3a.education. unimelb.edu.au. Accessed 12 Aug 2017.

Sparling, J., Ramey, C. T., & Tayler, C. (2014c). *Conversational Reading 3a Abecedarain approach Australia*. Melbourne Graduate School of Education. University of Melbourne. 3a.education. unimelb.edu.au. Accessed 12 Aug 2017.

Sparling, J., Ramey, C. T., & Tayler, C. (2014d). *LearningGames® 3a Abecedarain approach Australia*. Melbourne Graduate School of Education. University of Melbourne. 3a.education. unimelb.edu.au. Accessed 12 Aug 2017.

Spedding, S., Harkins, J., Makin, L., & Whiteman, P. (2007). *Investigating children's early literacy learning in family and community context: Review of related literature*. South Australia Department of Education and Children's Services.

Tomasello, M., & Farrar, M. J. (1986). Joint attention and early language. *Child Development, 57*(6), 1454–1463.

Wheelahan, I. (2010). The structure of pedagogic discourse as relay of power: The case for competency-based training. In P. Singh (Ed.), *Toolkits, translation devices and conceptual accounts; Essays on Basil Bernstein's sociology of knowledge* (pp. 47–63). New York: Peter Lang.

Wilson, B. (2014). *A share in the future: Review of indigenous education in the Northern Territory*. Darwin: Department of Education.

Louise Cooke has over 12 years of experience working in remote Indigenous early childhood settings, including several years of leadership and advisory roles within the Families as First Teachers program. Louise has a Master of Education degree from the University of Melbourne in which she completed a thesis entitled 'Book reading practices of Indigenous parents coached in Conversational Reading Techniques in Galiwin'ku – a case study'. She has contributed to a number of publications and presentations regarding the FaFT program and 3a.

Averill Piers-Blundell has extensive experience in development and implementation of education programs with specific expertise in complex remote Indigenous contexts. Examples of her work include the development and implementation of Child and Family Centres and the Families as First Teachers programs in the Northern Territory. Averill has published several articles and contributed to national projects such as the Engaging Families in the Early Childhood Development Story and the Longitudinal Study of Indigenous Children. Averill has Master in Education (Early Childhood/ Indigenous Education) and Bachelor of Education degrees. She is an honorary fellow of the Melbourne Graduate School of Education within the University of Melbourne.

Chapter 12
Early Literacy: Strengthening Outcomes Through Processes of Collaboration and Engagement

Janet Scull and Debra Hannagan

Abstract Students who fail to make effective progress with literacy learning during their early years often continue to struggle in the later years of schooling and beyond. Without adequate skills in reading and writing, these students are seriously disadvantaged in a literate society. This pertains to all students and is particularly relevant for Indigenous students as we work to "close the gap" in literacy achievement. This chapter reports on an empirical study that aimed to address the literacy achievement of Indigenous students in the early years of schooling, attending schools in the Kimberley region of Western Australia, through the adaptation of preventive processes involving systematic teaching approaches. Specifically, it details implementation processes at three levels of engagement—with the community, with teacher learning, and with classroom practice.

Introduction

The importance of students' early literacy learning is widely acknowledged, with the challenges of teaching students with cultural and linguistic resources that differ from those of the teacher and classroom also recognised. For these students, the act of going to school can be a "risky business" (McNaughton 2002, p. 18) with concerted effort required to meet the needs of Indigenous students and to close the gap between Indigenous and non-Indigenous school achievement (Department of the Prime Minister and Cabinet 2017). Over time, there have been a number of teaching

---

J. Scull (✉)
Monash University, Melbourne, VIC, Australia
e-mail: janet.scull@monash.edu

D. Hannagan
Waardi Limited, Broome, WA, Australia
e-mail: debra.hannagan@waardi.com.au

© Springer Nature Singapore Pte Ltd. 2019
J. Rennie, H. Harper (eds.), *Literacy Education and Indigenous Australians*,
Language Policy 19, https://doi.org/10.1007/978-981-13-8629-9_12

initiatives to address the issue of early literacy teaching and learning for Indigenous students, and we appreciate the contextual realities and the complexities of work in this area. Cognisant of the challenges and issues of teaching reform efforts, a small-scale project was introduced in the Kimberley region of Western Australia. The project focused on teachers working in the first year of school with the aim to improve the literacy outcomes for children. This chapter reports on the implementation processes and the impact of teacher professional learning on classroom literacy teaching practice.

The Local Context

The challenges related to improving education outcomes are multifarious and are connected to the high levels of disadvantage and vulnerability experienced by Indigenous children in the Kimberley (Save the Children 2010; Steering Committee for the Review of Government Service Provision 2014). The Australian Early Development Census (2015) community profile for the Broome area (comprising 46.8% Indigenous Australian and Torres Strait Islander children) indicated that a large number of children were developmentally at risk or vulnerable across a number of domains. Particular to early literacy, 15.6% were vulnerable to language and cognitive delays, and 9.7% were vulnerable to communication problems (Save the Children 2010). Furthermore, 31.4% of those surveyed were developmentally vulnerable in one or more of the measured domains (Save the Children 2010). Also acknowledged are the complex language environments of young Indigenous students in the Kimberley, including traditional languages, non-standard varieties of English (such as various English-based creoles) or Aboriginal English (AE) and Standard Australian English (SAE) (Wigglesworth et al. 2011). Curriculum responses to address students' literacy learning needs scope a range of theoretical perspectives and also place varying degrees of emphasis and value on students' linguistic and cultural diversity within teaching programs (Berry and Hudson 1997; Department of Education and Training, Western Australia 2005; Rennie 2006; Rose et al. 1999).

Points of contestation remain over conceptualisations of literacy teaching, both within and beyond Indigenous communities. Teaching approaches range from those that describe literacy as a social practice, with the meaning and purposes of activities derived from cultural processes (Street 1997), to the view that defines literacy as derived from a cognitive skills perspective (Purcell-Gates et al. 2004). From a cognitive perspective, literacy acquisition follows specific developmental milestones and involves mastery over specified sets of skills that can be applied across all social and cultural contexts with generally uniform effects (Scull et al. 2012). Literacy processing theory provides another perspective that engages young learners in integrating a number of perceptual, linguistic, and cognitive processes that work together in a mutually facilitative manner to support the construction of messages from text (Clay 2001). Key points of difference lie in approaches to teaching constrained and non-constrained skills (Paris 2005). Stahl (2011) defines "constrained skills as consisting of a limited number of items and thus can be mastered within a relatively short time frame while unconstrained abilities are learned across a lifetime, broad in scope, variable among people, and may influence many cognitive and academic skills" (pp. 52–53).

It is from this range of approaches that schools in the Kimberley select instructional practices and programs to support students' early literacy learning needs. More recently, a number of schools have opted for cognitive skill-based approaches to teaching, which place emphasis on constrained skills through models of direct instruction. Direct instruction, derived from behaviourist approaches to learning, requires teachers to follow a staged, sequenced approach to instruction, which is "tightly paced, linear and incremental" (Luke 2014, p. 1).

In essence, this requires students to build from phonemic awareness and letter knowledge to word recognition to text reading. Importantly, the role of phonological awareness is acknowledged as an essential component of early literacy, as being able to perceive phonemes is a prerequisite for learning letter-sound relationships and acquiring mastery over the alphabetic principles of English orthography (Konza 2016). However, as Paris (2005) states with reference to the features of text orthography and phonics, "skills with narrow scope are learned quickly so the trajectory of mastery is steep and the duration of acquisition is brief" (p. 188). It is now well understood that phonics instruction is necessary but not sufficient and that alongside systematic, direct and explicit phonics instruction, teachers need to provide an integrated approach to reading that supports the development of oral language, vocabulary, grammar, reading fluency, comprehension, and the literacies of new technologies (Konza 2016; Rowe 2005).

Early years literacy program implementation and the impact on students' learning outcomes are also dependent on the quality of the professional development provision for teachers. As Darling-Hammond et al. (2017) state, "professional development is an important strategy for ensuring that educators are equipped to support deep and complex student learning in their classrooms" (p. 23). However, provision of professional learning opportunities varies across and within programs, affecting teacher participation and engagement in reform and implementation processes (Scull and Johnson 2000). As previously acknowledged, the factors contributing to Indigenous educational disadvantage are many and complex, with a commitment to targeted quality professional learning support needed to foster coordinated approaches to improvement efforts (Brasche and Harrington 2012).

Based on an extensive review of empirical literature, Darling-Hammond et al. (2017) identified the design elements of effective professional learning. This study indicated that teachers learn best when the learning opportunities are focused, active, and engage teachers in collaboration, including modelling, coaching, feedback and reflection, and occurring over sustained periods of time. When these factors are related to programs of support for teachers of early literacy, they need to develop understandings of teaching that support young children's early literacy learning and reflect on and critique practice while also building professional collaborative networks within and across schools. Also highlighted is the role of coaching and mentoring support. As Onchwari and Keengwe (2010) state, "mentoring provides the benefit of training teachers in the field, it creates a framework through which a better understanding of teachers' learning needs is achieved; it also offers training that is matched to the individual needs of teachers" (p. 311). Particular to early literacy program reform, a study by Neuman and Cunningham (2009) provides evidence that a combination of coaching and course-based professional development improved the quality of language and literacy practice. Hsieh et al. (2009) also report the benefits of coaching for early literacy. Results of their study indicate that coaching was effective in promoting each teacher's use of emergent literacy teaching strategies, with teachers using more strategies, more consistently, during the coaching period (p. 243).

In our work, which focuses on meeting the needs of Indigenous students, we are drawn to the work of Timperley and Alton-Lee (2008) and their account of what counts as professional knowledge when working with diverse learners. Importantly, they stress the need for systematic attention to groups of learners who are disadvantaged or underserved for equity purposes, with an emphasis on the impact of quality teacher education on students' achievement outcomes. They state that "teachers need to have a problem to solve, to have multiple opportunities to learn relevant pedagogical content and assessment knowledge in ways that integrate theory and practice, and to maintain a constant focus on how teaching affects students" (Timperley and Alton-Lee 2008, p. 359). In addition, McNaughton and Lai (2009) claim that sustainable improvement for linguistically and culturally diverse students can be achieved through a strong emphasis on professional development, with teachers as adaptive experts drawing on local evidence to design effective curriculum. Specific to areas such as early literacy, teacher expertise includes an "understanding of their children's language and literacy practices as these reflect children's local and global cultural identities" (McNaughton and Lai 2009, p. 58).

The Literacy Acquisition Program for Pre-primary Students (LAPS) Program

Within the context of competing approaches to early literacy instruction, five schools in the Kimberley decided to engage in an alternative early years literacy curriculum initiative, the Literacy Acquisition for Pre-primary Students (LAPS) program. This program is jointly funded by Waardi Limited and the Department of Prime Minister and Cabinet, through the Indigenous Advancement Strategy funding program, and was introduced to increase the early literacy attainment levels of Kimberley Indigenous children through a holistic classroom approach involving processes of prevention and early intervention (Pianta 1990). The program targets teachers and teaching support staff, including Aboriginal Teacher Assistants of Pre-primary students, strengthening classroom practices to support young Indigenous learners to reach national and state, and school-based targets and goals. The program has its origins in the Language, Learning, and Literacy (L3) intervention program designed to meet the learning needs of students experiencing vulnerability and disadvantage in New South Wales (NSW Department of Education and Training 1999–2000). L3 provided a strong conceptual base, a range of well-researched assessment tools, alongside respected teaching approaches that formed the basis of the LAPS program. So, while the structural elements remained, implementation processes were revised to fit within the local design. The five project schools were asked to consider the alignment of LAPS teaching approaches and assessment practices to existing routines, with ensuing discussions to consider levels of compatibility. Testing procedures were negotiated to avoid the duplication of existing data collection processes and the scheduling of the professional learning program was discussed. Further, while school administrative teams selected staff to participate in the program, a separate and independent process occurred to enlist staff to the research project, in line with approved ethical protocols.

The LAPS professional learning program engaged teachers in five off-site professional development days over the course of the year and weekly classroom support visits. Both aspects of teachers' professional learning were facilitated by the Professional Learning Facilitator (PLF) employed full time to work in partnership with schools and closely with teachers. The PLF, a qualified teacher with demonstrated expertise in early literacy and supporting students with English as an additional language or dialect (EAL/D), developed and delivered the LAPS training based on the strategies in the L3 program. Onsite support was managed across the five schools so that each classroom teacher received an hour to two-hour block of support once a week during their literacy time. Remote schools received less frequent support, with two, three-day visits per term. In order to gain insight into the effectiveness of the professional development program and review the impact of the LAPS program on students' learning, the program has been carefully evaluated over the first two years of implementation. Data collection tools included interviews with ten teachers, six support staff, and four principals, as well as teacher questionnaires, written feedback from training sessions, and a reflective journal kept by the PLF.

Implementation as a Process of Engagement and Mediation

The approach to the examination of the LAPS program implementation draws on concepts of mediation using Rogoff's (1990) understanding of learning as a process of transformation through participation in shared sociocultural endeavours. To support the analysis of multifaceted activities, Rogoff refers to the personal, interpersonal, and community as three "foci for analysis" (Rogoff 2008, p. 58). The three foci are used to foreground and background different aspects of the activity, and rather than each being seen as separate, hierarchical levels with arbitrary boundaries, they are seen as mutually constituting planes used to consider diverse aspects of the whole activity (Rogoff 2008).

Program Mediation

In the first instance, the approaches to classroom teaching needed to be responsive to community influences. An adaptation of the L3 program enabled LAPS to be contextualised to meet the requirements of Kimberley students while maintaining a clear focus on language development and text reading and writing. Intensive consultation with the selected schools' administrators and pre-primary teaching teams was undertaken before the implementation of the pilot program. Key messages emerged about the schools' desires for LAPS: to be flexible enough to adapt to each school's needs; to complement existing programs and approaches such as synthetic phonics; and to maintain opportunities for play-based learning, an approach valued by many schools. Insights from the pilot program informed the development of the LAPS program and enabled the design of the program to meet the requirements of Kimberley schools. Regular stakeholder meetings throughout 2015 and 2016 maintained the schools' input into the program and contributed to the engagement of participant schools. School leadership support was acknowledged as critical to pedagogic reform within the everyday practices of the school (Bishop 2011).

LAPS includes a range of core teaching strategies designed to engage young Indigenous learners in focused reading and writing experiences. This follows one of the key principles of the program that children have daily opportunities to learn about reading and writing in context. A second principle emphasises the need for individualised instruction, with all children regularly engaged in small-group teaching targeted to their needs. This involves close monitoring of students' learning and resulting adjustments to teaching. A necessary consideration for a literacy program operating in the Kimberley region is the needs of EAL/D learners. Approaches to and research around EAL/D literacy education, including two-way teaching and learning (Malcolm and Education Department of Western Australia 1999), the code-switching stairway (Berry and Hudson 1997) and understanding reschematisation of educational materials by EAL/D students (Sharifian and Department of Education WA 2012) have been integrated into the LAPS training and coaching. This has allowed the adaptation of the strategies of the L3 program to specifically suit the needs of Indigenous students in the Kimberley.

The LAPS teaching procedures are part of a scaffolded approach that includes modelled, guided, and independent learning opportunities (Pearson and Gallagher 1983). Modelled strategies such as reading to students and interactive writing are generally delivered to the whole class but may also be conducted with a group of students with common needs. Interactive writing allows the teacher to model concepts about print, writing strategies, and how to move from talking to writing (Mackenzie 2011). Reading to students follows a gradual progression to support students' developing needs. Initial learning experiences are encouraged as small-group lessons, with a focus on developing students' listening skills. Later lessons foster analytic talk about texts, facilitating students' vocabulary development and comprehension.

The needs of EAL/D learners in the context of reading to students have been emphasised in the LAPS program as an important consideration. Most texts read to students are in Standard Australian English (SAE), which is often a second dialect or language, respectively, for Aboriginal English (AE) or Kriol-speaking Indigenous students. The LAPS training has highlighted the possibility of EAL/D students interpreting these texts differently to the authors' intentions, as shaped by a different set of cultural and linguistic schemas (Sharifian and the Department of Education WA 2012). An example of this was observed by the PLF when an Indigenous student was asked to retell the story *Hattie and the Fox* (Fox and Mullins 1987). Instead of referring the fox as it emerged from the bushes she began talking about "gumbun" (Torres 1987), a being from local mythology said to hide in the mangroves, schematically linking the illustration of the eyes in the bushes with her own cultural knowledge. Reading to students in small groups has allowed for closer observation of students' interpretations of texts and opportunities to unpack the intended meanings of the author. Enlisting the assistance of Indigenous support staff in presenting two-way stories (Education Department of Western Australia, Catholic Education Office of Western Australia & Association of Independent Schools of Western Australia 2000) has been facilitated through LAPS classroom coaching. LAPS teachers have been supported in choosing a range of texts for reading to students, including recommended texts written by Indigenous authors. These strategies have facilitated the adaptation of modelled reading to suit the needs of EAL/D students.

Alongside the modelled strategies of reading to students and interactive writing, LAPS involves guided learning experiences, assisting students in their transition towards the independent application of literacy behaviours. Guided reading and writing procedures are recommended for delivery to groups of three students with like needs. The procedures involve careful observation of and response to students' needs through intentional micro-scaffolding (Dansie 2001). Through guided reading, teachers are able to help students develop their concepts about print and provide opportunities to extend their processing of the information in text (Clay 2016). Through guided writing, students are assisted to develop the skills required for successful independent writing, including composition. Explicit phonics instruction is embedded in the guided procedures, with teachers paying close and systematic attention to phonemes in the context of reading and writing (Emmitt et al. 2013).

Guided reading and writing provide further opportunities for adjustment of teaching to suit the needs of EAL/D learners. In guided reading, students must draw on a range of information sources: semantic, syntactic, and graphophonic information (Hill 2012). Cultural schemas shaping the meaning of a guided reading text may be unfamiliar to EAL/D students, rendering semantic information sources inaccessible. Students who are unfamiliar with the grammatical structures of SAE may have difficulty with the syntactic structures of text. Where phonological differences exist between SAE and AE or Kriol, visual information may also present difficulties for students. The language iceberg/anthill model (Department of Education, Western Australia and Department of Training and Workforce Development 2012) has been used to facilitate teachers' understanding of linguistic and dialectal differences across the different levels of language and how these relate to the information sources. Opportunities to address these differences arise through explicit teaching in the orientation to the text, a strong feature of the LAPS approach. Guided writing provides further opportunities for explicit teaching of identified areas of need across the different levels of language. The adaptation of the guided writing procedure as a two-way approach has also been explored in the LAPS program through work with teachers and Indigenous support staff. The guided procedures, while not specifically designed with the needs of Indigenous students in mind, have been tailored to allow for culturally sensitive explicit teaching of SAE to EAL/D learners.

Regular opportunities for independent reading and writing experiences occur alongside the guided and modelled lessons discussed above. Independent reading involves opportunities to read and retell stories previously read to the students and to independently read familiar texts from guided reading lessons. Independent writing may be facilitated through play and later through formalised writing tasks. These independent learning opportunities allow students to apply skills that they have seen modelled and use the strategies developed through guided support. Students may begin by role-playing what it means to be a reader and a writer, gradually transferring new knowledge and skills into their literacy practices.

A further need to contextualise the program for the Kimberley region emerged in the delivery of teacher professional learning, specifically in videos of teaching strategies. Although teachers appreciated the video examples from NSW, they commented that more local examples of teaching were needed. In examining teachers' responses to viewing videos of teaching as part of their professional learning, Lefstein (2017) describes the phenomenon of radical contextualism: teachers may comment that the approach observed will not work in their own class due to the context being different. In the case of the LAPS program, the context of many Kimberley schools was recognised as significantly different to those featured in the NSW training videos, so this response from teachers was not unexpected. Teachers also expressed a need for videos filmed in authentic, non-staged classroom situations so they could see how the strategies could work for them. As a result of feedback from teachers, efforts have been made in the LAPS program to produce Kimberley-based training videos. This has been well received by teachers and is a continuing area of development for the program.

Professional Collaboration

The teachers' professional collaboration and practice was considered with reference to the interpersonal lens, involving processes of guided participation. The focus of professional learning was on participatory, collaborative learning, with attention to processes that strengthen teacher practice for diverse learners (Timperley and Alton-Lee 2008). An overview of the data revealed two components supporting teachers' learning. The first related to the out-of-school "off-site" training sessions and the opportunities provided for input and collaboration. The second built on aspects of interpersonal learning through processes of on-site modelling and coaching. Using a range of professional learning processes, the PLF encouraged teachers to critique and reflect on existing approaches to teaching and to examine pedagogical practices to enhance the literacy learning opportunities for their students.

Off-Site Professional Learning: Extending Domain and Pedagogical Content Knowledge

The off-site professional learning program focused on developing teachers' understanding of the small-group and whole class literacy teaching approaches used with the program. This provided a context for building teachers' early literacy content knowledge, their understanding of pedagogy, and appropriate assessment tools. Video recordings of teaching were used to introduce each approach to teachers, accompanied by a detailed description and focused discussion of the rationales and purposes of the approaches selected. Teachers were asked to examine and comment on the teaching procedures and to plan lessons to implement in their own classes. In later sessions, teachers shared their own implementation of the approaches, which included the analysis of video-recorded lessons of teaching in their classrooms.

> I really enjoyed watching the videos of the teachers.... They were really helpful for me. Just seeing it in practice and how it works. (Teacher 10, 2015)

Despite the schools' input into the program and the high level of professional support, a number of teachers found the process of change challenging, and we recognise the tensions in pedagogical reform as teachers incorporate new understandings into existing curriculum programs. A number of issues arose when teachers first encountered the program. The combination of establishing classroom routines and time management was initially overwhelming for some teachers. With explicit small-group teaching a key component of the program, teachers were concerned with what the remaining students in the class would be doing while they were working with a small group. Establishing routines that equipped students to work independently was a necessary prerequisite to implementing the small-group teaching. An ongoing challenge is to support teachers through this transition.

> Initially when it was suggested to me about doing LAPS, and I was looking at it and going that will never work, like how are you going to control your class, get your reading done and … the writing done and how are you going to manage the time, so you know initially when you have new teachers coming on board next year they will probably still have those issues but I would appreciate if you told them that it does work. (Teacher 7, 2015)

Teachers were also concerned that they would lose their focus on learning through play, and that as a result they would not provide age-appropriate learning opportunities. Similarly, teachers with existing pedagogies that involved the teaching of discrete literacy skills were concerned with finding time to address all areas of literacy. Both issues were addressed in professional learning sessions as teachers engaged in reflection and discussion, sharing ideas and considering solutions. Ways of integrating play-based learning alongside explicit small-group literacy teaching were explored, with teachers encouraged to include a range of independent play-based activities. Teachers were also encouraged to carefully examine the LAPS approaches and identify where these discrete literacy skills might be developed, allowing for integrated learning. Teachers appreciated these opportunities to collaborate with colleagues and peers, citing them as one of the most valuable aspects of the professional learning program.

> Being able to collaborate with the other teachers on how to do it … being able to see, oh that's how they do it, and being able to see there's different ways of doing the same type of activity. (Teacher 6, 2015)

> The reality of the day-to-day teaching and how do you manage it all so getting through that … just that time management thing is probably the biggest challenge but the opportunity to discuss, you know, those things with other teachers has been good. (Teacher 2, 2015)

A focus on students' learning and assessment was central to the professional learning. Teachers were provided with opportunities to develop and set goals for their class and individual students based on student data and consider how they might use the teaching approaches to support students' learning.

> Highlighting exactly where my class is lacking and being able to work towards those particular goals and students…. To be able to set goals, explicit goals from the data … and then being able to check if I'm actually working towards those goals. (Teacher 6, 2015)

On-Site Professional Learning: Coaching and Modelling

The approach adopted to support teacher learning included modelling and teaching support in classrooms alongside frequent opportunities for collaboration with the PLF. The gradual release of responsibility model (Pearson and Gallagher 1983) embedded in the LAPS instructional approaches was also mirrored in the classroom support provided for teachers. Teachers were initially provided with an opportunity to observe the PLF modelling the literacy strategies. They were then observed using these procedures, with feedback provided by the PLF. Teachers and administrators saw this approach as a strength of the program.

> Having (the PLF) model it and then me sit and watch and then me do it and her watch and give me feedback, I found that really, really helpful as well ... the classroom support was fantastic. (Teacher 9, 2015)

On-site support provided to schools by the PLF was intensive and ongoing. This involved assistance and guidance through all stages of the teaching and learning cycle: planning, teaching, and assessment. The planning sessions, in particular, were perceived as valuable, as teaching staff were informed about students' development, their individual goals, and what needed to be done in order to support students' literacy learning.

> We did receive a lot of support from (the PLF) ... coming in to either support us form our groups or with our planning, our forward planning and our objectives. And also helping us with assessing kids has been amazing. (Teacher 3, 2016)

The level of collaborative support and guidance provided through participation in the program was also acknowledged by school principals.

> Having (the PLF) come into the classroom and provide that extra support after the PL I think is an essential part of the program so they can actually see it in action with their own kids ... that's what makes the difference to their ability to improve. (Principal 1, 2015)

> That level of contact with the staff has been valued ... the opportunity for regular contact in conversations, and to be able to talk about the program and delivery and assessment of the program and the progress the students have been making has been valuable. (Principal 2, 2015)

Transformed Practice

The third focus relates to teachers' personal learning and their appropriation of literacy pedagogies that resulted in transformed classroom practice and improved student learning outcomes.

Over time, teachers reported increased levels of confidence in teaching with this attributed to heightened professional knowledge about the teaching of literacy, the support of the collegiate networks, and from seeing the results of the program in terms of students' learning. In particular, teachers' use of the teaching approaches to facilitate the needs of all students, including those considered at educational risk, was seen as a strength of the program. The small-group teaching procedures were cited as a specific area in which teaching had changed, in particular guided reading. Implementation of this approach became more explicit, informed by an understanding of early reading behaviours and various ways children learn to integrate the information in texts (Clay 2016).

> I think my teaching (of) guided reading has come so far compared to what it was before.... It's evolved. It's a more explicit approach. (Teacher 3, 2016)

My teaching has improved with how to question students with their reading.... So knowing ... what to say when they make a mistake, how to prompt them. (Teacher 6, 2016)

It's very deliberate. It's very thoughtful in the way we are teaching children specific to their needs ... particularly with the Indigenous kids, the instructions are quite crisp. They are short, they're sharp, there's not a lot of language involved in the explicit teaching. (Teacher 4, 2015)

Teachers' enhanced understandings and practice around literacy instruction were accompanied by an increased focus on students' learning needs and careful planning.

I'm more conscious of catering for each individual child.... So I'm more aware of each child and what areas they need to work on, their strengths and their weaknesses, and I think that's given me the power to be able to move each child to where they need to be. (Teacher 10, 2016)

I find that my planning and the way I teach has changed in a positive way ... I find that now it's more child-focused.... It's given me much more structure and guidance in my planning. (Teacher 8, 2015)

(Teachers) engage in more targeted relevant professional dialogue about student achievement (and) effective teaching ... most importantly, how to group students of similar needs based on the data collected. (Principal 2, 2016)

Teachers cited specific improvements in students' reading and writing; this included higher text reading levels and an increased range of strategies for reading and writing. They commented on the significant progress made throughout the year and increased levels of literacy achievement in comparison to previous years. Improvements in learning were attributed to the implementation of teaching approaches that included increased reading and writing opportunities and teaching that was designed to cater for the needs of a diverse range of students.

I've seen huge improvements (from) just having daily practice and having texts that are appropriate to their level ... and having really targeted activities in the lessons has really improved their levels. (Teacher 4, 2015)

We are very happy with the results from this year and it obviously caters well for a variety of learners. (Principal 4, 2016)

Not just Aboriginal children of course but all of the children improved performance or literacy performance at a much higher level ... the simple answer is the evidence, the data shows us that it works. (Principal 1, 2016)

Looking Forward

The level of disadvantage and vulnerability experienced by our Indigenous students provides compelling evidence for continued attention on early literacy learning that enhances students' outcomes. In this case, the focus on professional learning contributed to transforming teachers' understandings to support children's development of a broad range of language and literacy skills. Teachers' appropriation of small-group and whole class approaches facilitated the development of generative strategies and skills available for children's use on novel and/or more complex texts (Clay 2001). In each school site, there was clear evidence of children's language and literacy development as they engaged in reading and writing tasks. Teachers and principals commented that the literacy attainment levels had improved, and importantly, children were reading and writing at levels beyond previous years' cohorts. In an educational environment where there is strong advocacy for synthetic phonics and models of direct instruction (Luke 2014), LAPS is an alternative program that focuses on essential skill development in context, within a comprehensive literacy curriculum.

Our experience also recognises the impact of processes and systems that coordinate efforts of participation and guidance, with teachers as social partners in learning activities (Rogoff 2008). Central to the LAPS professional learning program was the integrated nature of teacher support and opportunities for intensive ongoing learning with close connections to teaching practice, and opportunities for professional dialogue that valued teachers' knowledge. Working alongside teachers to critique existing and new approaches to teaching, we built content knowledge and examined a range of pedagogical practices to enhance students' learning opportunities. The success of the program was largely attributed to the focus on processes of collaboration with participating teachers engaged in reflection and action to meet the local needs of students and schools. Results of the program evaluation highlight principles for professional learning, as identified by Darling-Hammond et al. (2017), that might be applied to enhance students' early literacy outcomes and to overcome the challenge of curriculum and pedagogical reform efforts in Indigenous contexts.

We also acknowledge the need for programs to complement and supplement schools' existing pedagogies and to build strong connections to community. As Luke (2014) reports, schools "making marked progress on 'closing the gap' on conventional measures were using programs that had been selected specifically because of the needs of local students" (p. 4). There is a continual need to examine local evidence to design effective instruction while broadening teacher expertise and effectiveness to better personalise teaching (McNaughton and Lai 2009). As the LAPS program continues, it will be important to consider ways of enhancing teachers' skills and understandings to support early literacy learning alongside developing knowledge of how to engage "Indigenous communities to help Indigenous students" (Bennet and Lancaster 2013, p. 216).

The outcomes of the LAPS program detailed above are particular to the cohort and context described. While the analysis scopes the support processes and the levels of adaptation and appropriation of the teaching approaches, given similar opportunities other teachers may display a different pattern of implementation, and the association between the professional learning provided and students' learning outcomes may vary. In addition, further data collection and analysis are required to examine teachers' learning and students' competence to enable the reporting of patterns of achievement, with greater confidence, across a wider range of participants. However, as policymakers promise to close the achievement gap for young Indigenous learners, this small study contributes to evidence-based practices to improve students' literacy outcomes. For communities looking to improve the literacy outcomes of young Indigenous learners, the results highlight the need for multilevel engagement, involving principals and teachers in conversations that respect their professional expertise while also indicating the level of collaboration and support required to create change. The outcomes also signal the rich potential of programs and approaches that engage children in reading and writing tasks, facilitative of literacy acquisition processes, as a clear, viable substitute to single variable models of reading instruction. The trajectory of our collaborations with teachers provides details of the conditions for effective, ongoing professional learning and classroom practices that can make a difference for children and over time address "the real-world consequences of unequal literacy achievements from school" (Lo Bianco 2016, p. v).

References

Australian Early Development Census. (2015). *A snapshot of early childhood development in Australia AEDC national report 2015*. Canberra: Department of Education and Training.

Bennet, M., & Lancaster, J. (2013). Improving reading in culturally situated contexts. *The Australian Journal of Indigenous Education, 41*(2), 208–217.

Berry, R., & Hudson, J. (1997). *Making the jump. A resource book for teachers of aboriginal students*. Broome: Catholic Education Commission of Western Australia.

Bishop, R. (2011). How effective leaders reduce educational disparities. In J. Robertson & H. Timperley (Eds.), *Leadership and learning* (pp. 27–40). London: Sage.

Brasche, I., & Harrington, I. (2012). Promoting teacher quality and continuity: Tackling the disadvantages of remote indigenous schools in the Northern Territory. *Australian Journal of Education, 56*(2), 110–125.

Clay, M. M. (2001). *Change over time in children's literacy development*. Portsmouth: Heinemann.

Clay, M. M. (2016). *Literacy lesson deigned for individuals* (2nd ed.). Auckland: The Marie Clay Literacy Trust, Global Education Systems Ltd.

Dansie, B. (2001). Scaffolding oral language: "The Hungry Giant" retold). In J. Hammond (Ed.), *Scaffolding: Teaching and learning in language and literacy education*. Sydney: Primary English Teaching Association.

Darling-Hammond, L., Hyler, M. E., & Gardner, M. (2017). *Effective teacher professional development*. Palo Alto: Learning Policy Institute. https://learningpolicyinstitute.org/product/teacher-prof-dev.

Department of Education and Training, Western Australia. (2005). *Aboriginal literacy strategy*. Perth: Department of Education and Training. http://www.det.wa.edu.au/curriculumsupport/eald/detcms/navigation/english-as-an-additional-language-or-dialect-for-aboriginal-students/aboriginal-literacy-strategy/.

Department of Education, Western Australia and Department of Training and Workforce Development. (2012). *Tracks to two-way learning*. Perth: West One Services.

Department of the Prime Minister and Cabinet. (2017). *Closing the gap Prime Minister's report 2017*. Canberra: Department of the Prime Minister and Cabinet.

Education Department of Western Australia, Catholic Education Office of Western Australia, & Association of Independent Schools of Western Australia. (2000). *Deadly ideas: A collection of two-way bidialectal teaching strategies from the deadly ways to learn project*. Perth: Deadly Ways to Learn Consortium.

Emmitt, M., Hornsby, D., & Wilson, L. (2013). *The place of phonics in learning to read and write*. Adelaide: Australian Literacy Educators' Association.

Fox, M., & Mullins, P. (1987). *Hattie and the Fox*. Lindfield: Ashton Scholastic.

Hill, S. (2012). *Developing early literacy: Assessment and teaching* (2nd ed.). Melbourne: Eleanor Curtain Publishing.

Hsieh, W.-Y., Hemmeter, M. L., McCollum, J. A., & Ostrosky, M. M. (2009). Using coaching to increase preschool teachers' use of emergent literacy teaching strategies. *Early Childhood Research Quarterly, 24*, 229–247.

Konza, D. (2016). Understanding the process of reading. In J. Scull & B. Raban (Eds.), *Growing up literate: Australian literacy research for practice* (pp. 149–176). Melbourne: Eleanor Curtain Publishing.

Lefstein, A. (2017). *Relocating teacher professional development: From "learning" to work*. Paper presented at the joint Australian Association of Teachers of English and Australian literacy education association National Conference, Hobart, Australia. http://dialogicpedagogy.com/aate/

Lo Bianco, J. (2016). Understanding growing up literate). In J. Scull & B. Raban (Eds.), *Growing up literate: Australian literacy research for practice* (pp. iii–ivi). Melbourne: Eleanor Curtain Publishing.

Luke, A. (2014). On explicit and direct instruction. *Australian Literacy Association Hot Topics*, 1–4.

Mackenzie, N. M. (2011). From drawing to writing: What happens when you shift teaching priorities in the first six months of school? *Australian Journal of Language and Literacy, 37*(3), 182–191.

Malcolm, I., & Education Department of Western Australia. (1999). *Two-way English: Towards more user-friendly education for speakers of aboriginal English*. Perth: Education Department of Western Australia.

McNaughton, S. (2002). *The meeting of minds*. Wellington: Learning Media.

McNaughton, S., & Lai, M. K. (2009). A model of school change for culturally and linguistically diverse students in New Zealand: A summary and evidence from systematic replication. *Teaching Education, 20*(1), 55–75. https://doi.org/10.1080/10476210802681733.

Neuman, S. B., & Cunningham, L. (2009). The impact of professional development and coaching on early language and literacy instructional practices. *American Educational Research Journal, 46*(2), 532–566.

New South Wales Department of Education and Training (NSW DET). (1999–2000). *Language, learning and literacy (L3)*. http://www.curriculumsupport.education.nsw.gov.au/beststart/lll/general/index.htm

Onchwari, G., & Keengwe, J. (2010). Teacher mentoring and early literacy learning: A case study of a mentor-coach initiative. *Early Childhood Education Journal, 37*(4), 311–317.

Paris, S. (2005). Reinterpreting the development of reading skills. *Reading Research Quarterly, 40*(2), 184–202.

Pearson, P. D., & Gallagher, M. C. (1983). The instruction of reading comprehension. *Contemporary Educational Psychology, 8*, 317–344.

Pianta, R. C. (1990). Widening debate on education reform: Prevention as a viable alternative. *Exceptional Children, 56*(4), 306–313.

Purcell-Gates, V., Jacobson, E., & Degener, S. (2004). *Print literacy development: Uniting cognitive and social practice theories*. Cambridge, MA: Harvard University Press.

Rennie, J. (2006). Meeting kids at the school gate: The literacy and numeracy practices of a remote indigenous community. *Australian Educational Researcher, 33*(3), 123–142.

Rogoff, B. (1990). *Apprenticeship in thinking*. New York: Oxford University Press.

Rogoff, B. (2008). Observing socio-cultural activity of three planes: Participatory appropriation, guided participation and apprenticeship. In P. M. Hall, K. Murphy, & P. Soler (Eds.), *Pedagogy and practice: Culture and identities* (pp. 58–74). London: Sage.

Rose, D., Gray, B., & Cowey, W. (1999). Scaffolding reading and writing for indigenous children in school. In P. Wignell (Ed.), *Double power: English literacy and indigenous education* (pp. 23–60). Melbourne: Language Australia.

Rowe, K. (2005). *Teaching reading: Report of the national inquiry into the teaching of literacy*. Canberra: Department of Education, Science and Training. http://www.dest.gov.au/nitl/documents/report_recommendations.pdf.

Save the Children. (2010). *Situation analysis and recommendations: Dampier Peninsula indigenous parenting support services*. Canberra: Department of Families, Housing, Community Services and Indigenous Affairs.

Scull, J., & Johnson, N. J. (2000). Reconceptualizing a change model: Implementation of the early literacy research project. *Literacy Teaching and Learning: An International Journal of Early Reading and Writing, 5*(1), 43–59.

Scull, J., Nolan, A., & Raban, B. (2012). Young learners: Teachers' conceptualisations and practice of literacy in Australian preschool contexts. *International Journal of Early Years Education, 20*(4), 379–391.

Sharifian, F., & the Department of Education WA. (2012). *Understanding stories my way: Aboriginal-English speaking students' (mis)understanding of school literacy materials in Australia English*. Perth: Department of Education WA. http://www.det.wa.edu.au/aboriginaleducation/detcms/aboriginal-education/aboriginal-education/docs/understanding-stories.en?cat-id=8092822.

Stahl, K. A. D. (2011). Applying new visions of reading development in today's classrooms. *The Reading Teacher, 65*(1), 52–56.

Steering Committee for the Review of Government Service Provision. (2014). *Overcoming Indigenous disadvantage: Key indicators 2014*. Canberra: Productivity Commission. http://www.pc.gov.au/research/ongoing/overcoming- indigenous-disadvantage/key-indicators-2014.

Street, B. V. (1997). Social literacies. In V. Edwards & D. Corson (Eds.), *Encyclopaedia of language and education* (Vol. 2, pp. 133–141). Dordrecht: Kluwer Academic Publishers.

Timperley, H., & Alton-Lee, A. (2008). Reframing teacher professional learning: An alternative policy approach to strengthening valued outcomes for diverse learners. *Review of Research in Education, 32*(1), 328–369. https://doi.org/10.3102/0091732X07308968.

Torres, P. (1987). *Jalygurr: Aussie animal rhymes – Poems for kids*. Broome: Magabala Books.

Wigglesworth, G., Simpson, J., & Loakes, D. (2011). NAPLAN language assessments for indigenous children in remote communities: Issues and problems. *Australian Review of Applied Linguistics, 34*(3), 320–343.

Janet Scull is an experienced language and literacy educator. Her research interests focus on the areas of language and literacy acquisition, literacy teaching and assessment and teaching practices that support the continuity of children's literacy learning across early childhood settings and the early years of schooling. Janet has also contributed to the design, implementation and evaluation of approaches to early literacy teaching, for students from a range of culturally and linguistically diverse backgrounds. She is currently an Associate Professor at Monash University, Melbourne, coordinating and teaching language and literacy subjects across a range of degree programs.

Debra Hannagan is an Early Years Literacy Specialist, delivering the Literacy Acquisition for Pre-primary Students (LAPS) program in the Kimberley region of Western Australia. She is an experienced early years teacher who has worked with Indigenous students in regional and remote settings throughout her career. She has specialised in literacy education through school curriculum leadership and as a consultant with the Western Australian Education Department.

Chapter 13
'Just Teach Our Kids to Read': Efficacy of Intensive Reading Interventions for Both Younger and Older Low-Progress Readers in Schools Serving Mainly Remote Indigenous Communities

Kevin Wheldall, Robyn Wheldall, Alison Madelaine, Meree Reynolds, Sarah Arakelian, and Saskia Kohnen

Abstract Annually, the results released from the National Assessment Program Literacy and Numeracy testing Australia-wide confirm the huge gaps in literacy performance between students from Indigenous and non-Indigenous Australian backgrounds, particularly for those students living in remote communities. Recent research has shown promising results, indicating that one of the major changes that is likely to show positive effects on Indigenous students' literacy levels is the provision of scientific, evidence-based, best-practice reading instruction.

Pilot research in Sydney and Cape York in Far North Queensland showed that Indigenous students made statistically significant and educationally meaningful improvements in reading and related skills (reading accuracy, reading fluency, reading comprehension and spelling) when afforded such instruction. A larger scale project was established to implement two remedial literacy programs with students at four schools located in Cape York. In this chapter, we report the cumulative results for the total sample of students from all sites over the 3-year life of the project, 2008–2010. Results are reported separately for each program; for older low-progress readers and for young struggling readers. Students completed a battery of measures of reading and related skills prior to and following two terms of instruction. For both the older students and the younger students, statistically significant gains were made with very large effect sizes on all measures.

We would like to thank the teachers and students who worked with us in Cape York, our MultiLit instructors and research teams and Cape York Partnership.

K. Wheldall (✉) · R. Wheldall · A. Madelaine · M. Reynolds · S. Arakelian · S. Kohnen
Macquarie University, Sydney, NSW, Australia
e-mail: kevin.wheldall@pecas.com.au; robyn.wheldall@pecas.com.au;
alison.madelaine@multilit.com; meree.reynolds@multilit.com;
sarah.arakelian@multilit.com; saskia.kohnen@mq.edu.au

© Springer Nature Singapore Pte Ltd. 2019
J. Rennie, H. Harper (eds.), *Literacy Education and Indigenous Australians*,
Language Policy 19, https://doi.org/10.1007/978-981-13-8629-9_13

222   K. Wheldall et al.

While it is clear that the programs made a real and substantial difference, we have come to believe that our programs were, in some respects, merely acting as ambulances for the instructional casualties created by the inadequate primary education the children were receiving in their schools. Issues of project implementation, sustainability and future challenges are discussed.

Preamble

In 1990, the first author (Kevin Wheldall) moved from the UK to Australia to become the Director of Macquarie University Special Education Centre in Sydney. It was not long before he became involved in a proposed project in a school in Redfern, also in Sydney, with the aim of improving the reading performance of students from Indigenous backgrounds who were low-progress readers. Being a newcomer and an outsider, he was given a great deal of advice along the lines of Indigenous education being a political minefield and the importance of cultural sensitivity. He also knew that Redfern was sometimes referred to as the political heart of Indigenous Australia.

Consequently, when he first met with parents from the local Koori community to explain his approach to helping older low-progress readers, he tried to incorporate this advice but was very nervous and stumbled through his presentation. The project was saved when a Koori elder put her arm around his shoulders and said, 'Listen Kevin; leave the culture to us and you just teach our kids to read'.

That was a defining moment and has informed much of the approach that we have taken as a group ever since. It aligned with our conviction concerning a non-categorical approach to education. In short, the non-categorical approach posits that effective instruction does not need to be tailored to particular populations, or categories, of students according to background characteristics, or by virtue of a labelling 'condition' (Wheldall 1994). We will return to this concept later in the chapter.

Many years after we first started working with the students from Redfern, Indigenous academic Martin Nakata (2003) offered a view on the seemingly intransigent issue of poor educational outcomes for Indigenous people in this country and suggested that the dual policy goals of cultural maintenance and equal outcomes are essentially oppositional positions. He stated: '...neither the cultural agenda nor the pursuit of equal outcomes can be properly targeted without undermining the other' (p. 9). We believe this comment goes to the heart of being culturally appropriate when we are teaching Indigenous students to become literate in English. This, of course, is not necessarily a popular view but we are unashamedly committed to pursuing equal outcomes for Indigenous Australians by teaching them to read effectively, in English. This is in no way suggesting that students from Indigenous backgrounds should shy away from, or be discouraged from, learning about their culture or learning their Indigenous languages, for example. What we must recognize is that these are *separate* and *different* endeavours. Moreover, the transmission of

Indigenous culture, including the preservation of rapidly disappearing Indigenous languages, may arguably be more successful where individuals are literate in English and can participate in the mainstream of Australian life to provide the important place that Indigenous culture has in our past, present and future in this nation. Prominent Indigenous leader and activist, Noel Pearson, refers to this as 'orbiting in two worlds' (Pearson 2009). We embrace a vision of ensuring Indigenous cultural maintenance and transmission by securing requisite literacy skills in English as part of the solution to the full participation of our first peoples in contemporary Australian society.

This chapter will describe work that we have carried out in Cape York with Noel Pearson and his Cape York Partnership in the years 2005 to the end of 2010 *as a demonstration* of what can be achieved when we are clear about our role as educators and when we use methods that have been scientifically proven to be effective. Many readers will be aware of Pearson's subsequent work in the 'Good to Great Schools' initiative (Good to Great Schools Australia 2013). This is an initiative with explicit and direct instruction at its very core and it was the MultiLit work (discussed in this chapter) in Cape York that prompted Pearson and his colleagues to go down this path. In discussing the thinking behind the formation of the Cape York Aboriginal Australian Academy, in his address to the Centre for Independent Studies (CIS) in Sydney in November, 2016, Noel Pearson reflected:

> …We were guided by Professor Kevin Wheldall from the MultiLit Program here in Sydney. We had had very promising success with MultiLit, remediating students at Coen. …we were so impressed by how the kids were responding to the MultiLit Program, the kind of question occurred to us, well if the teaching in this tutorial room is so good, why isn't it happening down in the main classroom? We had a time of it, trying to break into that classroom. It took us a couple of years. And finally Kevin told us that, in fact, the ancestral program of MultiLit was direct instruction…. (Pearson 2016)

Statement of the Problem

Before describing this work, we should remind ourselves of the difficulties Indigenous people face in becoming literate in English. The problem of poor literacy rates within Indigenous communities sometimes appears to be both enduring and intractable. Annually, the results released from the National Assessment Program Literacy and Numeracy (NAPLAN) testing Australia-wide (National Reports n.d.) confirm the huge gaps in academic performance between students from Indigenous and non-Indigenous backgrounds. These gaps are particularly pronounced for those students living in remote Indigenous communities and, while there is little room for complacency regarding numeracy, it is the pursuit of improved literacy outcomes that has proved to be so particularly challenging and with which we are concerned here.

The report from the latest NAPLAN testing for which results were available at the time of writing (ACARA 2016) showed that Year 3 (see Fig. 3.R3 of the report)

Indigenous students Australia-wide had a much lower mean scale score for reading compared with that for non-Indigenous students, a whole standard deviation difference. Even more telling were the percentages of students performing at or above the national minimum standard (NMS). Ninety-six per cent of non-Indigenous students (Australia-wide) performed at the minimum standard compared with 81% of Indigenous students. In remote communities and very remote Indigenous communities, the percentages were 64% and 47%, respectively, at or above NMS.

For Year 5 (see Fig. 5.R3 in the report; ACARA 2016), the results were broadly similar: the mean scale score for Indigenous students was much lower than for non-Indigenous students. Non-Indigenous students scored 94% at or above NMS compared with 71% for Indigenous students. For remote and very remote Indigenous students, the figures were 52% and 26%, respectively; that is, only a quarter of students in very remote Indigenous communities scored at or above the National Minimum Standard.

In February 2017, the latest report card for the Closing the Gap targets showed that of the six target areas, life expectancy, child mortality, employment, reading and writing, school attendance, early education and Year 12 attainment, only Year 12 attainment had improved significantly (Conifer et al. 2017).

The target for the Reading and Writing dimension is to halve the gap in reading and numeracy for Indigenous students by 2018. While some improvements are occurring, only Year 9 numeracy is on track to meet the target (Conifer et al. 2017). Indigenous 15-year-olds are on average about two-and-a-third years behind non-Indigenous 15-year-olds in reading and maths and worse in more remote areas. We would like to relate how MultiLit came to be on the Cape as part of a possible solution to this enduring problem.

Background to Our Involvement in Cape York

In 2003, Noel Pearson contacted the first author having heard about our work with low-progress readers in the Making Up Lost Time In Literacy (MultiLit) Initiative which had been operating since 1995 within Macquarie University Special Education Centre. Our early work in teaching low-progress readers showed large gains in reading and related skills (reading accuracy, reading fluency, reading comprehension and spelling) in short time periods. (For more detail, see Wheldall 2009; Wheldall and Beaman 2000; and Wheldall and Wheldall 2014.)

Pearson was looking for solutions to the dire educational outcomes for his people on Cape York. In November 2004, he observed the Schoolwise Program, a tutorial centre for disadvantaged children, including 14 Indigenous students, which the MultiLit team were running for the Exodus Foundation in Ashfield, Sydney

(Wheldall 2009). The results for these students are summarized in the following section of this chapter and are reported fully in Wheldall et al. (2010).

Of his visit to the MultiLit Schoolwise Program at the Exodus Foundation in 2004, Pearson (2009) wrote:

> I had never seen teaching like the instruction these MultiLit teachers were delivering at Schoolwise. It was dynamic, the teachers were extraordinarily skilful, the kids were eyes-on-the-teacher attentive, they hardly noticed our presence, no time was wasted, no child was left unattended for long, the teacher kept records of children's performance throughout the class, stopwatches counted words read correctly per minute from prescribed passages, the teacher dispensed positive reinforcement at every turn through their 'a hundred smiles an hour' method. It left me breathless. You could have no doubt about the nutritious nature of the lessons these children were receiving; it was right there in front of you. And no child was missing out on the action. (p. 116)

Pearson was sufficiently impressed by what he saw operating in the program that a collaborative pilot project was planned to establish a tutorial centre in Coen State School, beginning mid-year 2005.

Preliminary Evidence for the Efficacy of Our Programs for Indigenous Students

Our early research showed that one of the major changes that is likely to show positive effects on Indigenous students' literacy levels is the provision of scientific evidence-based, best-practice, reading instruction. (By this term, we mean reading instruction that is based on the methods that scientific research has shown to be the most effective.) Wheldall et al. (2010) showed that a group of Indigenous students attending the Exodus Foundation tutorial centre in Ashfield made statistically significant and educationally meaningful improvements in reading accuracy, reading fluency, reading comprehension and spelling following two terms of intensive remedial instruction. (This was the group that Pearson had seen in the program, described above.)

Moreover, these 14 Indigenous students made *just as much* progress as their 20 non-Indigenous, socially disadvantaged low-progress peers in the tutorial centre (Wheldall et al. 2010). The differences in mean gains for the two groups were small and not statistically significant. These results have subsequently been replicated with much larger samples of students (Wheldall et al. 2012).

So what did we conclude from this study? First, that there were no major differences in gains for Indigenous and non-Indigenous students when offered the same instruction, and, second, that MultiLit is highly effective for Indigenous students. These results gave us the confidence to proceed with the pilot studies in Cape York and confirmed our belief in the non-categorical approach.

The Non-categorical Approach

We, like many other researchers in special education, believe in *a non-categorical* approach to instruction (Wheldall 1994; Wheldall and Carter 1996). As previously stated, the non-categorical approach posits that effective instruction does not need to be tailored to particular populations, or categories, of students according to the label of a 'condition'. What we need to do is to assess what the student needs to know and then to teach them accordingly, using methods of proven efficacy. Another way of thinking about this is to say, 'effective instruction is effective instruction is effective instruction'. It can also be thought of as truly child-centred education, as it is what the student needs to learn that is the focus of the effort, not what characteristics the student brings to the classroom. Translated into the current context, this means that we do not need literacy programs specifically designed for Indigenous students but we do need literacy programs of proven efficacy such as explicit, systematic, synthetic phonics instruction.

Our Work in Cape York

We turn now to our work specifically carried out in Cape York. Figure 13.1 shows the timeline of when we were working in each of four Cape York communities in the years 2005–2010. Figure 13.2 shows the geographical location of the four sites: Coen, Hope Vale, Mossman and Aurukun. We started our work with two pilot studies carried out in Coen: the first over 12 months from July 2005 to June 2006. The second Coen trial took place in 2007 for the full school year. From 2008, Pearson's Welfare Reform Trial commenced in the four Cape York communities. MultiLit in Cape York Schools (MCYS), as it was known, was one element of the Welfare Reform Trial.

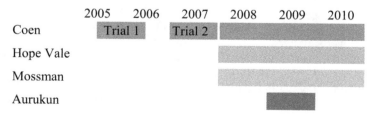

Fig. 13.1 Timescale showing the periods when MultiLit provided instruction in the four communities

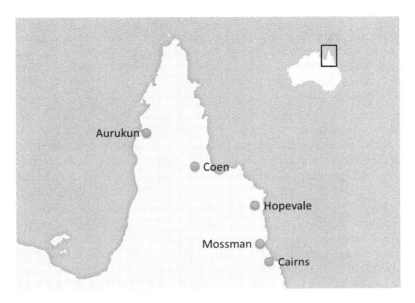

Fig. 13.2 Location of the four communities on the Cape York peninsular

The Interventions

The two remedial reading programs provided to these students, who were young struggling readers and older low-progress readers, were developed by MultiLit ('Making Up Lost Time In Literacy'), led by the first author since 1995. This comprises systematic scientific inquiry into how best to meet the instructional needs of students who are struggling to acquire basic reading and related skills. (For a more detailed description of MultiLit, see Wheldall and Beaman 2000 and Wheldall and Wheldall 2014.)

In an earlier work, Ellis et al. (2007) provided an account of the research locus and conceptual basis for MultiLit, aiming to answer the question 'why we do what we do'. For those less familiar with the MultiLit approach and direct/explicit instruction, we have summarized below our main arguments in this regard.

Our approach to reading instruction is consistent with international research and best practice in the area of literacy instruction as exemplified in the reports from three international reviews (the USA, Australia and the UK) on the teaching of reading (National Reading Panel 2000; Department of Education, Science and Training 2005; Rose 2006). MultiLit employs direct/explicit and systematic teaching approaches and Positive Teaching classroom management techniques (Merrett and Wheldall 1990; Wheldall 1991; Wheldall and Merrett 1984) to ensure that students receive regular praise for effort and achievement.

MultiLit embodies an integrated approach to reading and includes specific emphasis on all five of the pillars of effective reading instruction (sometimes known as the 'five big ideas'): that is, phonemic awareness, phonics, fluency, vocabulary knowledge and text comprehension. The MultiLit approach to reading instruction incorporates both systematic synthetic phonics and the reading of connected text (i.e. we emphasize both code and meaning) to deliver significant and appreciable gains in reading and related skills.

Direct, explicit and systematic instruction is a key feature of our approach. By 'direct instruction' we mean an approach based on the theory that clear instruction eliminating misinterpretations can greatly improve and accelerate learning. Lessons follow a prescribed model-lead-test format, whereby the teacher first models the strategy and guides the students through examples. Specific skills are taught to students in an overt, step-by-step manner, and mastery of each step must be obtained before new learning can be attempted (see also, Ellis 2005). The term 'direct instruction' can be confusing and is often used in different ways. In a recent research note, Wheldall et al. (2017c) have provided a brief overview of what is meant by use of this term.

Phonics is a method of instruction that teaches students correspondences between graphemes in written language and phonemes in spoken language and to use these correspondences to read and spell words. Our approach employs the use of systematic, *synthetic* phonics, as opposed to incidental phonics, when all the major grapheme-phoneme correspondences are delineated and taught in a clearly defined sequence to mastery. Like the term 'direct instruction', 'synthetic phonics' is often misunderstood. In two recent 'explainers', Wheldall et al. (2017a, b) have sought to provide an answer to the question 'what does the term synthetic phonics really mean' and to make clear that 'phonics is not a method of reading, it is a method of learning how to read'.

For Older Low-Progress Readers

The program delivered to the older low-progress readers (mainly in Years 3–7; hereafter referred to as the MultiLit program) was based on the MultiLit Reading Tutor Program (Macquarie University Special Education Centre 1998; MultiLit 2007). Students received intensive, systematic and direct instruction in three key areas of effective literacy instruction (Ellis et al. 2007): MultiLit Word Attack Skills, MultiLit Sight Words and MultiLit Reinforced Reading.

The first key component consisted of the phonics program, **MultiLit Word Attack Skills**. The three elements of MultiLit Word Attack Skills are accuracy, fluency and spelling. A specific sequence is adhered to and presented in hierarchical order of difficulty, where essential pre-skills knowledge is taken into consideration.

The second component was the **MultiLit Sight Words** program. This program was designed to teach 200 of the most frequently occurring words in print by sight, with a high level of automaticity. The basic premise behind teaching a bank of high-frequency sight words is to enable older, low-progress readers, who have previously had very little exposure to text, or, indeed, success in reading, to access text quickly.

The third element of the program was **MultiLit Reinforced Reading**, the text reading component of the program. This was where students put all the sub-skills learning of word attack and sight word knowledge into action in reading connected text, where the generalization of newly acquired skills could take place. Students read instructional level text supported in the process by a tutor who used a variety of prompts. As well as focusing on reading accuracy and fluency, Reinforced Reading had a focus on reading comprehension.

Students were taught mainly in small groups (usually up to six students) for 3 h daily (after which they returned to their regular classroom). This time was divided into eight different activities of various durations from 5 min to a maximum of 45 min (one-to-one instruction plus independent work) including several group lessons. Students were grouped according to their ability for group lessons on each component of the program. Targeted individualized instruction in word attack accuracy and fluency and sight words occurred during one-to-one sessions, as well as daily reading to a supportive and trained 'other' during the MultiLit Reinforced Reading sessions.

In addition to MultiLit lessons, there was also daily group instruction in the highly effective Spelling Mastery (Dixon et al. 1999), a scripted Direct Instruction program that complemented the Word Attack skills component used in the MultiLit program.

For Young Struggling Readers

The second program given to the younger students (mainly in Years 1–3 in this project) at the four participating Cape York schools was the precursor to the now popular MiniLit program (MultiLit 2011) which at this time comprised a modified version of the MultiLit program more suitable for younger low-progress readers. It consisted of four activities: phonemic awareness activities or sight word teaching, word attack skills activities (using a systematic synthetic phonics approach), supported reading of text and storybook reading to enhance vocabulary and comprehension. Each of these group activities lasted for 15 min, totalling a 1h group lesson daily.

Students were taught in two groups of up to four students in each group, according to skill level, with the exception of the storybook reading component which was conducted as a combined activity for the eight students. Students were monitored individually throughout the intervention. Typically, the aim was to deliver approximately 20 weeks of instruction for each intake (two intakes per year) depending on the length of school terms.

Pilot Studies

In June 2005, our MultiLit testing team assessed all students in Years 2–7 attending Coen State School. Two trained and experienced MultiLit Instructors relocated to Coen for 5 months in July 2005, followed by a second team in January 2006, and a MultiLit tutorial centre was established on site in the school from July 2005.

The primary-aged children in Years 4–7 were, on average, over 3 years (40 months) behind their chronological age in reading accuracy and, on average, nearly 4 years (46 months) behind in reading comprehension in June 2005. The younger students tended to score below the norms of the tests we were using and so reading ages, for example, could not be calculated. Two intakes of students were admitted to two programs, MultiLit and MiniLit, for two terms (approximately 20 weeks) each over the 12-month period.

For both intakes of the older students, their gains on measures of reading and related skills were substantial. For the first intake of 10 older students, being those in Years 6 and 7, Fig. 13.3 shows the gains made in months in these key areas: reading accuracy, reading comprehension, single word recognition, phonic decoding and spelling.

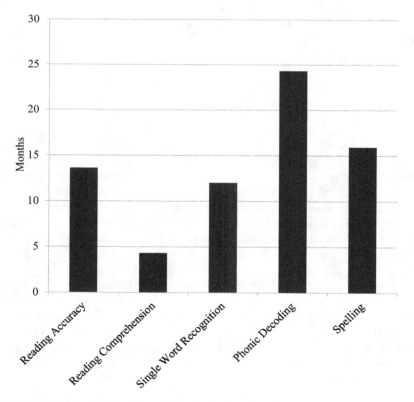

Fig. 13.3 Results from the first Coen pilot study (estimated reading age gains in months)

These results were achieved in less than two school terms, with about 17 weeks of instruction between testing. Phonic decoding was a particularly strong result, yielding more than 2 years of growth. This demonstrated convincingly that this foundational skill could be taught effectively to the students using the MultiLit approach. In the second intake in the first Coen trial, similar strong results were again achieved under two terms, with about 18 weeks between testing. Based on these findings, a second successful pilot study was conducted in Coen in 2007. The detailed findings from these early Coen trials can be found in Wheldall and Beaman (2011).

The Context of the Larger Study: The Welfare Reform Trial

The encouraging results from the Coen pilot studies led to MultiLit subsequently being proposed and trialled as the literacy solution for the four communities involved in Pearson's Welfare Reform Trial 2008–2011: Coen, Hope Vale, Mossman Gorge and Aurukun. Over the course of the trial, MultiLit tutorial centres were established in the State Schools of Coen, Hope Vale, Mossman and Aurukun.

Here, we shall report the results for the small group instruction for students in Years 3–7 after two school terms. For ease of understanding, we are calling this group of older students the 'MultiLit' group who received the same program of instruction as previously described under 'The Interventions' – for older low-progress readers. As already indicated, instruction took place for 3 h daily, and there were typically 12 students from Years 3 to 7 being taught by two MultiLit instructors in each location. We shall also report the results of the small group 'MiniLit' instruction that took place for 1 h daily, typically with eight students from Years 1 to 2 and two instructors, again for two terms. Note that the same instructors delivered both forms of interventions to the groups.

Details of Tests Employed

Standardized and curriculum-based assessments of reading and related skills were carried out before the commencement of the program in each intake for each site and again at the end of students' second term in the program. These assessments were carried out by trained research assistants who were not involved in teaching the students. The assessment battery for the students attending the 'MultiLit' program included measures of reading accuracy and comprehension (Neale Analysis of Reading Ability; Neale 1999), single word reading (Burt Word Reading Test; Gilmore et al. 1981), spelling (South Australian Spelling Test; Westwood 2005), text reading fluency (Wheldall Assessment of Reading Passages or WARP; Wheldall and Madelaine 2013), receptive vocabulary (Peabody Picture Vocabulary Test-IV; Dunn and Dunn 2007) and phonological recoding (Martin and Pratt Nonword Reading Test; Martin and Pratt 2001).

232   K. Wheldall et al.

Students attending the MiniLit program were similarly assessed on measures of single word recognition (Burt Word Reading Test; Gilmore et al. 1981), spelling (Astronaut Invented Spelling Test [in 2008 only]; Neilson 2003a; and the South Australian Spelling Test; Westwood 2005), phonological awareness (Sutherland Phonological Awareness Test-R Neilson 2003b), word reading fluency (Wheldall Assessment of Reading Lists or WARL; Wheldall et al. 2015), receptive vocabulary (Peabody Picture Vocabulary Test-IV; Dunn and Dunn 2007) and phonological recoding (Martin and Pratt Nonword Reading Test; Martin and Pratt 2001).

Details of Students Involved in the Studies

The Older Students (Years 3–7): The 'MultiLit' Group

During the period 2008–2010, complete pre- and post-test data were available from 146 students (79 males and 67 females) attending their *first two terms* of MultiLit instruction at the four Cape York school sites, three of which were very remote. The students were in Years 3–7 and were aged between 6 years 3 months and 13 years 1 month ($M = 122$ months, 10 years and 2 months). All students identified as being of Aboriginal ethnic background. While the mean age of the students at the time of initial assessment was 10 years and 2 months, the initial mean reading age calculated using the Neale reading accuracy measure was 6 years 7 months and the mean age calculated using the Neale reading comprehension measure was 6 years 5 months. Students were over 3.5 years behind typical age peers in reading accuracy and almost 4 years behind in reading comprehension, very similar to what we found in the earlier Coen pilot studies.

The Younger Students (Years 1–2): The MiniLit Group

Complete data were also collected for 103 students (59 males and 44 females) attending for their *first two terms* of MiniLit instruction at the four sites. Their mean age at the time of initial assessment was 7 years and 6 months. At pre-test, their mean age for reading accuracy was less than 6 years 1 month (<73 months), as measured by the Burt Word Reading Test. This is below the lowest reading age equivalent for the test. Given this, the gains for these students could not be presented in months as they would not accurately reflect the gains that were made. Again, all students identified as being of Aboriginal ethnic background.

Results

Older Low-Progress Readers

Repeated measures t-tests were carried out for all measures comparing pre- and post-test raw scores and partial eta squared values were calculated as measures of effect size. Partial eta squared calculates the amount of variance explained and is typically considered as small, at least 0.01 or 1%; medium, 0.06 or 6% or above; and large, 0.138 or 13.8% or above.

The results for all students attending their first intake of MultiLit instruction are shown in Table 13.1. Following an average of 18 weeks of instruction, the students made statistically significant mean gains ($p < 0.0005$) with very large effect sizes (partial eta squared ≥ 0.138) on all seven measures, as may be seen from the table.

Fig. 13.4 represents the gains of MultiLit students in terms of estimated *reading age* in months. These students made estimated gains of about 8 months in reading accuracy, about 4 months in reading comprehension, about 9 months in single word reading, about 10 months in spelling, about 13 months in phonological recoding, about 7 months in receptive vocabulary, and could read about 50% more words correctly per minute.

Although most gains are large, the students were still behind in their literacy skills, especially in reading comprehension. So, while students made large and significant gains in quite a short time, following the end of the program there was still a lag between their chronological ages and reading ages. In other words, they were not yet fully fluent readers. (It is, arguably, unrealistic to expect average gains of

Table 13.1 Raw score means (and standard deviations) and the resultant gains on literacy measures from six intakes of MultiLit students during 2008–2010 in the four sites in Cape York

Literacy variable	N	Pre-test (SD)	Post-test (SD)	Gain (SD)	t	p	Effect size[a]
Neale accuracy	146	20.37 (14.88)	30.19 (16.99)	9.82 (7.70)	15.41	<0.0005	0.62
Neale comprehension	146	5.84 (3.83)	7.91 (4.61)	2.07 (2.72)	9.19	<0.0005	0.37
Burt word reading	146	32.34 (14.77)	41.01 (16.08)	8.68 (6.54)	16.04	<0.0005	0.64
SA spelling	146	21.84 (9.57)	28.05 (8.00)	6.21 (4.08)	18.38	<0.0005	0.70
WARP (wcpm)	146	38.45 (31.71)	57.40 (38.38)	18.96 (13.89)	16.49	<0.0005	0.65
Peabody Picture Vocabulary Test	146	94.67 (19.86)	105.34 (19.53)	10.66 (12.28)	10.50	<0.0005	0.43
Martin and Pratt	146	14.02 (9.64)	21.84 (10.75)	7.82 (6.49)	14.56	<0.0005	0.59

[a]Partial eta squared (large effect 0.138 or greater)

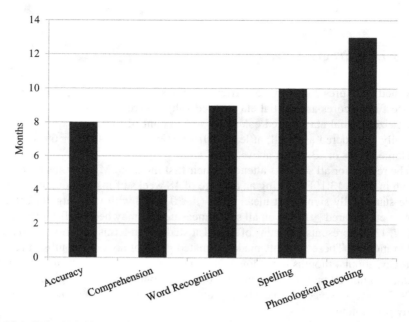

Fig. 13.4 Estimated gains of MultiLit students (in months)

4 years in 18 weeks of instruction.) Nevertheless, the students were now progressing at a greater than typical rate and certainly at a greater rate than they were making prior to the intervention program.

Young Struggling Readers

The results for all students attending for MiniLit instruction are shown in Table 13.2. After an average of 18 weeks of instruction, the students made average *raw score* gains of 9.42 in single word reading, 6.29 in spelling, 9.41 in invented spelling, 11.09 in phonemic awareness, 6.40 in phonological recoding (reading non-words), 11.69 in receptive vocabulary, and could read 13 (116%) more words correctly per minute. These translate to statistically significant gains on all seven measures ($p < 0.0005$), all with very large effect sizes (≥ 0.138). Note that at pre-test, the students' mean crude reading age could not be estimated because the mean raw score fell below the figure for the lowest reading age equivalent, as measured by the Burt Word Reading Test. All we know is that the reading age estimate would be well below 6 years. Consequently, we are unable to provide estimates of growth in months of reading age for this group.

Table 13.2 Raw score means (and standard deviations) and the resultant gains on literacy measures from six intakes of MiniLit students during 2008–2010 in the four sites in Cape York

Literacy variable	N	Pre-test (SD)	Post-test (SD)	Gain (SD)	t	p	Effect size[a]
Burt word reading	103	11.71 (11.31)	21.13 (11.01)	9.42 (5.77)	16.56	<0.0005	0.73
SA spelling	103	7.90 (8.31)	14.19 (8.54)	6.29 (4.53)	14.09	<0.0005	0.66
SPAT-R	102	20.22 (11.67)	31.30 (11.21)	11.09 (7.99)	14.02	<0.0005	0.66
Astronaut invented spelling	71	19.25 (14.50)	28.66 (12.24)	9.41 (8.16)	9.71	<0.0005	0.57
WARL (wcpm)	102	11.57 (14.97)	24.91 (18.79)	13.34 (10.89)	12.37	<0.0005	0.60
Peabody Picture Vocabulary Test	102	73.81 (21.12)	85.50 (19.68)	11.69 (12.90)	9.15	<0.0005	0.45
Martin and Pratt	103	5.08 (6.21)	11.48 (8.22)	6.40 (5.28)	12.30	<0.0005	0.60

[a]Partial eta squared (large effect 0.138 or greater)

Discussion and Implications for Practice

Indigenous students in remote and very remote communities responded to MultiLit instructional approaches in the same way as their 'city peers' had done in our pilot work. This is not surprising, as the basic processes for learning to read in English are universally applicable. For low-progress and at-risk readers, what varies is the intensity and duration of the instruction that is required to close the gap. The magnitude of the gains was impressive, particularly for reading accuracy and reading fluency, spelling and phonological recoding, with very large effect sizes. The two areas where the effect sizes were lower were reading comprehension and receptive vocabulary skills, although the gains made in these two areas were still impressive with large effect sizes.

We turn now to a consideration of why we have been more successful in teaching these Indigenous students to decode successfully than we have in improving their reading comprehension, as our results have shown. The widely accepted 'simple model of reading', originally proposed by Gough and Tunmer (1986), is helpful here. The simple model proposes that reading comprehension is the product of decoding and listening comprehension. If one cannot decode the text in the first place, there is no opportunity for understanding to take place. Similarly, if skill in listening comprehension is limited, then being able to decode alone will not be sufficient for understanding what has been decoded: the child will indeed be merely 'barking at print'.

Phonological Ability (PA)

		High	Average	Low
	High	High progress readers	Above average readers	Hidden and classic dyslexic readers
Quality of Literacy Learning Environment (QLLE)	**Average**	Above average readers	Average readers	Regular dyslexic readers
	Low	Below average readers	Below average readers	Doubly disadvantaged dyslexic readers

Fig. 13.5 A simple model of reading disability

The first author has proposed a model whereby reading difficulties may be seen as arising from two, not necessarily discrete, factors: phonological (processing) ability and the language and literacy learning environment (Pogorzelski and Wheldall 2005; Wheldall and Beaman 2011) (see Fig. 13.5). This model has important implications for understanding the problems that many Indigenous students from socially disadvantaged backgrounds will face in learning to read: 'there will be those whose difficulties are largely environmental and those whose difficulties are due to both the environment and intrinsic, poor phonological processing ability' (Wheldall and Beaman 2011). The environment, once such children reach school, obviously also includes the quality of the reading instruction they receive.

As Wheldall and Beaman (2011) explained:

If reading is critically dependent upon the ability to segment and blend the component sounds within words, then an inability or reduced ability to do so is likely to lead to difficulties in learning to read. … It is important to recognise and to accept, however, that not all reading difficulties will necessarily be predicated upon inherent underlying phonological processing problems. The language and literacy learning environment is also critically important and plays a powerful role in determining how readily a child will learn to read. Children who have enjoyed a linguistically rich and stimulating environment and whose parents have read to them consistently from an early age will begin school with a huge advantage when it comes to learning to read.

While we may readily teach the essential skills of decoding text relatively quickly in short periods of time (in the present study, two school terms), it may be asking too much to expect that the many years of missed quality language learning experiences in English for most of these children can be 'remediated' in this time period. For the vast majority of low-progress readers from more advantaged backgrounds (whose language comprehension skills will be well developed as a result of having enjoyed quality language learning environments), once they have been taught to decode effectively and efficiently, they should now be able to make sense of the texts they can now read aloud. But this is not the case for children from socially disadvantaged backgrounds who have received an impoverished language and literacy learning environment.

It is for these reasons that we supported Pearson's move to a more intensive curriculum for students from remote Indigenous communities so that a structured, quality language and literacy learning environment is provided from Prep onwards (and preferably before in the preschool environment).

We went into the work in Cape York with two 'remedial' or Tier 2 small group programs for low-progress and at-risk young readers in a Response to Intervention framework; MultiLit (which has become MacqLit) and MiniLit. What is required to address the significant disadvantage that is experienced by Indigenous children living in remote and very remote locations in particular is a fully articulated and consistent program of reading instruction that commences the day students begin their formal schooling. Not only that, a great deal of input is required in the early childhood years so that solid foundations for learning to read and speak in English can be laid.

There were a number of key findings that we consider have implications for working in the area of redressing Indigenous disadvantage through education, outlined below.

Evidence-Based Instruction in Literacy Is Effective: What and How It Is Taught Matters

It is clear to us from the results of these studies that explicit and systematic instruction is effective for teaching Indigenous students to read in the sense of being able to decode text. Decoding text is a necessary, but not sufficient of course, condition for students to become successful readers. But we know that without this skill, students will never be able to read and write in English. We also know from other studies that employing a synthetic phonics approach is more effective than other methods (like analytic phonics; Johnston et al. 2012). The approaches we use in highly disadvantaged populations are even more important than in the general populace. Pearson (2009) has noted that:

> In Aboriginal communities, the approach to literacy must be qualitatively different because the majority of students are in the bottom quartile. It is not sufficient to modify the mainstream formula. Explicit, phonics-based reading instruction is imperative for Aboriginal students. (pp. 81–82)

We would argue that *all* students require this approach to ensure that all children learn to read but it is certainly the case for students from socioeconomically disadvantaged backgrounds.

Timing Is Important

Evidence-based methods to teach reading are required as soon as Indigenous children enter the school system. Informed by our work in Cape York, as well as elsewhere, we have developed a whole class program of instruction in the initial teaching of reading, called InitiaLit, recently released for wider use (MultiLit 2017). InitiaLit is a Tier 1, that is, universal tier, program of literacy instruction for all children entering school, that covers the first 3 years of formal schooling.

There needs to be a sense of urgency in this endeavour to get Indigenous children off to a good start in reading, and this sense of urgency needs to be maintained. Every hour of instruction is critical when we are dealing with disadvantaged populations. There is a great deal of focus on school attendance in the Indigenous education space. And while attendance is clearly important – how can a child learn if she/ he is not there – what happens in the classroom is critically important. Too often having Indigenous students in the classroom is a squandered opportunity. Attendance should not be an end in itself.

Start Much Earlier: 'Reach Down' into the Early Childhood and Preschool Years

We also need to 'reach down' to the preschool years. It became very clear to us that these students were coming to school 'well behind the eight ball' and the prospect of them catching up seems improbable. A focus of teaching the prerequisite skills for learning to read is a pressing priority. Addressing phonological awareness and oral language skills is a good place to start, as well as checking for hearing impairments which we know are rife in remote Indigenous communities and will hamper a child's ability to learn to read. (As a result of observing the poor prerequisite skills of children coming to school in the pilot phases of this project, the authors initiated the development of a preschool literacy preparation program, subsequently published as PreLit [MultiLit 2012].) We would wholeheartedly agree with Wolf et al. (2016) when they say that 'the first five years of a child's development are crucial for the next five years' (p. 146). It is imperative that we focus our efforts on these early childhood years as well as the school years if we have any chance of closing the gap.

Sustained Effort Is Required

There is also the need for sustained effort. The size of the task is huge. As is evident from both our own and NAPLAN data, the large gaps between chronological age and reading performance in Indigenous students mean that these students will need intervention over a long period to close the gap. Pearson (2009) notes that Geoff Masters from the Australian Council for Educational Research has indicated that by Year 9 in very remote parts of the state of Queensland (which include parts of Cape York), the gap between Indigenous and non-Indigenous students is, on average, equivalent to 6 or 7 years of schooling. This shows how the gap becomes increasingly wide as children get older, thereby effectively excluding them from further education once high school has finished. While it is possible to reduce the achievement gap, the efforts required are enormous and should not be underestimated. Sustained effort with individual students will be the norm, not the exception, if we are to create any kind of equity for Indigenous young people.

Avoid Short-Termism

We need to avoid the 'short-termism' of many approaches to closing the gap. Because the task is difficult, there is sometimes a temptation to 'chop and change' interventions or approaches in the desperate scramble to demonstrate that our efforts are being successful. While there is a clear need for accountability for the millions of taxpayer dollars that are spent in this area, bureaucrats and policymakers should be realistic about the timeframes for improvement. This is an endeavour that is likely to take a generation to resolve, not 3 or 4 years. We need literate young people becoming the parents of tomorrow, being able to provide the kinds of early childhood language experiences that more privileged children typically experience. We need to build intergenerational literacy skills.

More Intensive Approach for Comprehension and Vocabulary Skills

A more intensive approach is required for comprehension and vocabulary skills as indicated by the results of this project. This is, of course, one of the difficulties of students from lower socioeconomic backgrounds (Hart and Risley 1995). Children from these backgrounds typically come to school with far fewer words in their oral vocabulary (Buckingham et al. 2014), as we have alluded to above. This in turn has a negative impact on the speed at which children acquire reading skills (Wegener et al. 2017). There is also the issue that for many of these children, English will not necessarily be their first or home language. Having said this, having English as a second language (ESL) is not necessarily a barrier to proficiency in learning to read in English, as demonstrated by Lesaux and Siegel (2003). NAPLAN data also show that ESL students can successfully learn to read in English when the instruction is sound. Having English as an additional language is often used as a reason why students may struggle to learn to read but it is more likely that it is an instructional issue rather than a home language issue.

Alongside the often varying language backgrounds that are evident, the compounding impact of the Matthew Effect (Stanovich 1986) has a negative influence on the acquisition of world knowledge. The Matthew Effect is a commonly referred to metaphor referring to the gospel of St Matthew whereby the rich (in this instance the language rich) get richer and the poor get poorer. These are cumulative effects that play havoc with the acquisition of reading skills and, in turn, knowledge, as children are unable to access information that is mediated by text. In this heavily text-dependent age, this constitutes a real disability. Realistically, it takes longer for improved reading skills to translate fully into improved vocabulary and comprehension skills. It takes time for these skills and knowledge to be acquired. The importance of the *amount* of time spent reading cannot be underestimated.

Remain Committed to a Non-categorical Approach

We must remain committed to a non-categorical approach and not be seduced by faulty reasoning that suggests that Indigenous students need a 'special' program for Indigenous instruction. Here and elsewhere (Wheldall et al. 2010, 2012), we have demonstrated that Indigenous children can make progress at the same rate as their non-Indigenous peers on the same instructional programs. Hence, it is not clear why a 'special' program should be required for teaching these students as is sometimes suggested. Only if it were shown that such a 'special' program produces significantly higher gains than demonstrated here, would it be reasonable to advocate for such an approach? In the face of continuing poor literacy outcomes for Indigenous students, it is tempting to engage in novel programs in an attempt to get better outcomes more quickly. The reality is that we need to remain committed to

13 'Just Teach Our Kids to Read': Efficacy of Intensive Reading Interventions for Both... 241

approaches that have scientific evidence for their efficacy, or at least, are based on the science of effective literacy instruction. We should resist efforts that try to tailor programs based on characteristics of the learners, where such approaches have no empirical base.

Need for Quality Instruction

The need for quality instruction is manifest. A focus on improving teaching quality is critical. As we know, the most powerful factor in the classroom is the teacher (Buckingham 2003). One of the perennial challenges of teaching Indigenous students in remote and very remote areas is that they are notoriously hard to staff. High staff turnover in hard-to-staff areas is often a barrier to consistent quality teaching. Our experience over the 6 years that we had a presence on the Cape was that often teachers came and went with monotonous regularity. Our experience in the second Coen trial (2007), where we were attempting to pass on the instructional approaches that had been successful in the MultiLit tutorial centres through professional development (PD) and coaching support, was that no sooner had we 'trained' a teacher than she/he would leave the community and another fresh face was there in their place. This meant that the PD had to be conducted continuously. This is obviously less than ideal and far short of the experience that students would typically experience in less remote areas. Students typically benefit from stable staffing in a school (if effective instruction is delivered) and this is even more important where the students come from disadvantaged backgrounds. The net result of high staff turnover is that it is very difficult to be able to guarantee high-quality and consistent instruction for all students. Without a coordinated and rigorous program of instruction, students are more likely to get piecemeal approaches that will not foster highly developed readers.

Be Realistic About High Rates of Staff Turnover in Hard-to-Staff Areas

High staff turnover has a huge impact on the quality of instruction in the schools that serve many of our Indigenous children. One gets the impression that we are being successful if we manage to get teachers to relocate to these remote areas. There are many factors militating against this including isolation, lack of fresh food supplies, access in and out of the community in times of flooding, to name a few. The lack of suitable and sufficient housing can be a perennial problem in some communities. We need to be realistic about the likelihood of a high turnover of staff and put measures in place to have a solid instructional framework with consistent approaches to instruction. The instructional framework can then provide the continuity that more unstable staffing might not.

Committed School Leadership

As in any venture that we undertake in the school system, the need for a committed school leadership is essential. Principals and their executive need to make sure that adequate resources (human and material) are made available and that learning to read (and the time taken to teach it effectively) is a priority for the school. A school may have a really effective teacher or a great program of instruction occurring in single classrooms but without the support from the top, this is likely to have a short-term or limited impact. School leaders need to be clear about what it is that they are hoping to achieve, how they are going to do it and what they require from their staff to make this happen. Where there is entrenched disadvantage, the need for evidence-based approaches is more pressing than in any other school environment. There is one opportunity to redress the educational aspects of disadvantage in these locations, and this needs to be seized with vigour and determination. Being literate in English, being able to participate in the mainstream of Australian life, is the most important job our schools should be engaged in. Protecting instructional time in the evidence-based teaching of reading should be the single most important thing that a school principal should guarantee for our Indigenous students. This may not be a popular statement when we consider all of the pressures of the curriculum, but we must not lose sight of the fact that being literate in English is essential for our Indigenous children and young people to be successful in our society, to have the choices that other young people have as Australians.

Conclusions: Were We Successful in Our Work in Cape York?

If we ask the question 'was MultiLit successful in achieving its aims in Cape York?', the answer can reasonably be given in the affirmative. But if the question is followed up with 'but was MultiLit successful enough?', we are on less secure ground. Clearly, as the empirical results presented for these studies show, a great many children from the four Cape York schools are better readers as a result of the project. Very large and statistically significant average gains were made by the students attending our programs and the effect sizes for the gains made were very large. The programs made a real and substantial difference. But we have come to believe that our programs were, in some respects, merely acting as ambulances for the instructional casualties created by the inadequate primary education the children were receiving in their schools.

While we provided reading intervention (i.e. remedial) support, what is needed is effective literacy instruction from the outset. Moreover, we want to reiterate that a heavy focus on the preschool years is critical to enable these young children to be ready to benefit from explicit and systematic instruction from their first day of school. It is not enough to *Make Up Lost Time In Literacy*, we have to commit to a fully articulated Response to Intervention framework with exemplary universal whole class instruction being the norm in every classroom from the first day a student enters the school, and appropriate supports at Tier 2 and 3 for the students who are not making adequate progress. A commitment to *effective evidence-based whole class instruction* is the first critical step in the solution to this intractable problem, with effective Tier 2 and 3 programs, like the MultiLit programs, providing more intensive instruction for those who are not making adequate progress.

References

Australian Curriculum, Assessment and Reporting Authority. (2016). *NAPLAN achievement in Reading, persuasive writing, language conventions and numeracy: National Report for 2016.* Sydney: Author. Retrieved from https://www.nap.edu.au/results-and-reports/national-reports.

Buckingham, J. (2003). Class size and teacher quality. *Educational Research for Policy and Practice, 2*, 71–86. https://doi.org/10.1023/A:1024403823803.

Buckingham, J., Beaman, R., & Wheldall, K. (2014). Why poor children are more likely to become poor readers: The early years. *Educational Review, 66*, 428–446. https://doi.org/10.1080/0013 1911.2013.795129.

Conifer, D., Leslie, T., Tilley, C., & Liddy, M. (2017). *Closing the gap: Australia is failing on indigenous disadvantage goals.* Retrieved from http://www.abc.net.au/news/2017-02-14/closing-the-gap-report-card-failing/8268450

Department of Education, Science and Training. (2005). *Teaching reading: Report and recommendations.* Canberra: Department of Education, Science and Training.

Dixon, R., Engelmann, S., & Bauer, M. M. (1999). *Spelling mastery.* Columbus: SRA McGraw Hill.

Dunn, L. M., & Dunn, D. M. (2007). *Peabody picture vocabulary test* (4th ed.). Minneapolis: NCS Pearson Inc.

Ellis, L. A. (2005). Balancing approaches: Revisiting the educational psychology research on teaching students with learning difficulties. *Australian Education Review* (No. 48). Camberwell: Australian Council for Educational Research.

Ellis, L., Wheldall, K., & Beaman, R. (2007). The research locus and conceptual basis for MULTILIT: Why we do what we do. *Australian Journal of Learning Disabilities, 12*, 61–65.

Gilmore, A., Croft, C., & Reid, N. (1981). *Burt word reading test – New Zealand revision.* Wellington: New Zealand Council for Educational Research.

Good to Great Schools Australia. (2013). *Effective instruction – The keystone to school reform.* Cairns: Author. Retrieved from https://goodtogreatschools.org.au/effective-instruction-keystone-school-reform/.

Gough, P. B., & Tunmer, W. E. (1986). Decoding, reading and reading disability. *Remedial and Special Education, 7*, 6–10. https://doi.org/10.1177/074193258600700104.

Hart, B., & Risley, T. (1995). *Meaningful differences in the everyday experience of young American children.* Baltimore: Paul H. Brookes Publishing.

Johnston, R., McGeown, S., & Watson, J. (2012). Long term effects of synthetic versus analytic phonics teaching on the reading and spelling ability of 10 year old boys and girls. *Reading and Writing, 26*, 1365–1384. https://doi.org/10.1007/s11145-011-9323-x.

Lesaux, N., & Siegel, L. (2003). The development of reading in children who speak English as a second language. *Developmental Psychology, 39*, 1005–1019. https://doi.org/10.1037/0012-1649.39.6.1005.

Macquarie University Special Education Centre. (1998). *The MultiLit reading tutor program (revised).* Sydney: Macquarie University Special Education Centre.

Martin, F., & Pratt, C. (2001). *The Martin and Pratt nonword reading test*. Melbourne: Australian Council for Educational Research.

Merrett, F., & Wheldall, K. (1990). *Positive teaching in the primary school*. London: Paul Chapman.

MultiLit. (2007). *The MultiLit reading tutor program (revised)*. Sydney: MultiLit Pty Ltd.

MultiLit. (2011). *MiniLit early literacy intervention program*. Sydney: MultiLit Pty Ltd.

MultiLit. (2012). *PreLit: Early literacy preparation program*. Sydney: MultiLit Pty Ltd.

MultiLit. (2017). *InitiaLit foundation: Whole class initial instruction in literacy*. Sydney: MultiLit Pty Ltd.

Nakata, M. (2003). Some thoughts on literacy issues in indigenous contexts. *The Australian Journal of Indigenous Education, 31*, 7–15. https://doi.org/10.1017/S1326011100003641.

National Institute of Child Health and Human Development (NICHD). (2000). *Report of the national reading panel: Teaching children to read: An evidence-based assessment of the scientific research literature on reading and its implications for reading instruction* (NIH Publication No. 00-4769). Washington, DC: U.S. Government Printing Office.

National reports. (n.d.). Retrieved from https://www.nap.edu.au/results-and-reports/national-reports

Neale, M. (1999). *Neale analysis of reading ability* (3rd ed.). Melbourne: Australian council for educational research.

Neilson, R. (2003a). *The astronaut invented spelling test*. Jamberoo: Language, Speech and Literacy Services.

Neilson, R. (2003b). *Sutherland phonological awareness test* (Rev. ed.). Jamberoo: Language, Speech and Literacy Services.

Pearson, N. (2009). Radical hope: Education and equality in Australia. *Quarterly Essay, 35*, 1–105. Retrieved from https://www.quarterlyessay.com.au/essay/2009/09/radical-hope.

Pearson, N. (2016, November). Direct instruction works: Evidence and experience of direct and explicit teaching. In Centre for Independent Studies (CIS). *Direct instruction event*. Public lecture conducted from Sydney. Retrieved from https://www.youtube.com/watch?v=oBBQbixVK74

Pogorzelski, S., & Wheldall, K. (2005). The importance of phonological processing skills for older low-progress readers. *Educational Psychology in Practice, 21*, 1–22.

Rose, J. (2006). *Independent review of the teaching of early reading: Final report*. Retrieved from http://www.standards.dfes.gov.uk/rosereview

Stanovich, K. (1986). Matthew effects in reading: Some consequences of individual differences in the acquistion of literacy. *Reading Research Quarterly, 21*, 360–407. https://doi.org/10.1598/RRQ.21.4.1.

Wegener, S., Wang, H., de Lissa, P., Robidoux, S., Nation, K., & Castles, A. (2017). Children reading spoken words: Interactions between vocabulary and orthographic expectancy. *Developmental Science, 21*, e12577. https://doi.org/10.1111/desc.12577.

Westwood, P. (2005). *Spelling: Approaches to teaching and assessment* (2nd ed.). Camberwell: Australian Council for Educational Research Press.

Wheldall, K. (1991). Managing troublesome classroom behaviour: A positive teaching perspective. *International Journal of Disability, Development and Education, 38*, 99–116. https://doi.org/10.1080/0156655910380202.

Wheldall, K. (1994). Why do contemporary special educators favour a non-categorical approach to teaching? *Special Education Perspectives, 3*, 45–47.

Wheldall, K. (2009). Effective instruction for socially disadvantaged low-progress readers: The Schoolwise program. *Australian Journal of Learning Difficulties, 14*, 151–170. https://doi.org/10.1080/19404150903264294.

Wheldall, K., & Beaman, R. (2000). *An evaluation of MultiLit: 'Making up lost time in literacy'*. Canberra: Commonwealth Department of Education, Training and Youth Affairs.

Wheldall, K., & Beaman, R. (2011). Effective instruction for older low-progress readers: Meeting the needs of indigenous students. In C. Wyatt-Smith, J. Elkins, & S. Gunn (Eds.), *Multiple perspectives on difficulties in learning literacy and numeracy*. New York: Springer.

13 'Just Teach Our Kids to Read': Efficacy of Intensive Reading Interventions for Both... 245

Wheldall, K., & Carter, M. (1996). Reconstructing behaviour analysis in education: A revised behavioural interactionist perspective for special education. *Educational Psychology, 16*, 121–140. https://doi.org/10.1080/0144341960160203.

Wheldall, K., & Madelaine, A. (2013). *The Wheldall assessment of reading passages (WARP) manual*. Sydney: MultiLit Pty Ltd.

Wheldall, K., & Merrett, F. (1984). *Positive teaching: The behavioural approach*. London: Allen and Unwin.

Wheldall, K., & Wheldall, R. (2014). The MultiLit story: Effective instruction for low-progress readers. *Perspectives on Language and Literacy, 40*(3), 32–39. Retrieved from https://dyslexi-aida.org/perspectives/.

Wheldall, K., Beaman, R., & Langstaff, E. (2010). Mind the gap': Effective literacy instruction for indigenous low-progress readers. *Australasian Journal of Special Education, 34*, 1–16. https://doi.org/10.1375/ajse.34.1.1.

Wheldall, K., Beaman, R., Madelaine, A., & McMurtry, S. (2012). *Evaluations of the efficacy of MultiLit and MiniLit programs for aboriginal students at the various exodus tutorial centre sites over a three year period, 2009–2011*. Unpublished research report submitted to the Exodus Foundation. Sydney: MultiLit Research Unit.

Wheldall, K., Reynolds, M., & Madelaine, A. (2015). *The Wheldall assessment of reading lists*. Sydney: MultiLit Pty Ltd.

Wheldall, K., Snow, P., & Graham, L. (2017a). Explainer: What does the term 'synthetic phonics' really mean*? Learning Difficulties Australia Bulletin, 49*(1), 6–7.

Wheldall, K., Snow, P., & Graham, L. (2017b). Explainer: Phonics is not a method of reading, it is a method of learning how to read. *Nomanis, 4*, 18–19.

Wheldall, K., Stephenson, J., & Carter, M. (2017c, October). What is direct instruction? *Nomanis Notes, Issue 2*. https://docs.wixstatic.com/ugd/81f204_9c9551a55dfb410b993fbdf29532e912.pdf

Wolf, M., Ullman-Shade, C., & Gottwald, S. (2016). Lessons from the reading brain for reading development and dyslexia. *Australian Journal of Learning Difficulties, 21*, 143–156. https://doi.org/10.1080/19404158.2016.1337364.

Emeritus Professor Kevin Wheldall, AM BA, PhD, C.Psychol, MAPS, FASSA, FBPsS, FCollP, FIARLD, FCEDP Prior to his retirement in 2011, Emeritus Professor Kevin Wheldall, AM, served as Professor and Director of Macquarie University Special Education Centre (MUSEC) for over 20 years. He is Chairman of MultiLit Pty Ltd. and Director of the MultiLit Research Unit and is the author of over 300 academic books, chapters and journal articles. In 1995, he established the MultiLit (Making Up Lost Time In Literacy) Initiative, to research and develop intensive literacy interventions. He is a Fellow of the Academy of Social Sciences in Australia and in 2011 was made a Member (AM) in the Order of Australia.

Dr. Robyn Wheldall (formerly Beaman), BA, PhD, was a Research Fellow at Macquarie University until her retirement in 2011 and now continues as an Honorary Fellow. She is a founding director of the University spin-off company MultiLit Pty Ltd and is the Deputy Director of the MultiLit Research Unit. She jointly authored 'An Evaluation of MultiLit' (2000) (commissioned by the Commonwealth Government) and has published numerous articles in peer-reviewed journals. Robyn has extensive experience in the establishment and implementation of intensive literacy programs in community settings. In 2005, she was awarded a Macquarie University Community Outreach Award for her MultiLit work.

Dr. Alison Madelaine, BA, Dip Ed, Grad Dip Spec Ed, PhD, was a Lecturer in Special Education at Macquarie University Special Education Centre until 2017 and is currently the Clinical Director of the MultiLit Literacy Centres with MultiLit Pty Ltd. She is also a Senior Research Fellow within the MultiLit Research Unit. Her publications and research interests are in the areas of effective reading instruction, curriculum-based measurement of reading, effective vocabulary instruction, preschool literacy, and teachers' knowledge and skills in teaching reading. She provided consultation to the delivery of MultiLit's literacy programs in Cape York.

Dr. Meree Reynolds, BA, MA, PhD, has extensive experience working in primary schools as a class teacher and support teacher for students with learning difficulties. She has also worked as a special education consultant and/or administrator in the state and independent school systems in NSW. Her doctoral research included investigating the effectiveness of the *MiniLit early literacy intervention program* for young struggling readers and establishing benchmarks of progress in reading for students in Years 1 and 2 in NSW schools. She is a Consultant and Senior Research Fellow within the MultiLit Research Unit.

Sarah Arakelian, BA Psych (Hons), is the Manager of the MultiLit Research Unit where she coordinates research in effective literacy instruction and assessment. She has an honours degree in psychology and has also completed a Postgraduate Certificate in Research Preparation. She has been involved in several research projects on early and initial reading instruction with Kindergarten children, trials with older low-progress readers and assessment and assisted with community programs involving low-progress readers from disadvantaged and Indigenous backgrounds.

Dr. Saskia Kohnen, MA, PhD, holds a degree in Linguistics and Speech-Language Pathology and completed a PhD in 2008 at Macquarie University and is Deputy Director of the Macquarie University Reading Clinic. Her current research interests include the assessment of the underlying causes of reading and spelling difficulties in children, conducting intervention trials for children and adults with developmental and acquired reading and spelling difficulties and the investigation of reading acquisition in typically developing children. She also previously worked as an instructor in the MultiLit tutorial centre established in Coen, in Cape York and as a Research Fellow in MultiLit.

Chapter 14
A Case Study of Controversy: The Cape York Aboriginal Australian Academy

John McCollow

Abstract The Cape York Aboriginal Australian Academy (CYAAA) is a partnership between the Queensland Department of Education and Training (DET) and Good to Great Schools Australia (GGSA). The CYAAA has operated in the remote Queensland communities of Coen, Aurukun and Hope Vale. While Aurukun is no longer a campus, the CYAAA continues to operate at Coen and Hope Vale, where it uses Direct Instruction (DI), a standardised pedagogical and curriculum program. This chapter addresses the questions: What is the nature of the CYAAA reform? How has its implementation played out? What is the evidence of its success/failure? What conclusions should be drawn from the CYAAA experience? All of these questions have had significant relevance to literacy education in the three communities discussed here. Because the CYAAA is a high-profile, contested reform that embodies a particular approach to remote Indigenous education, these questions are important, not only to the communities involved but in considerations concerning literacy education for Indigenous communities in general.

Introduction

The Cape York Aboriginal Australian Academy (CYAAA) operates as a partnership between the Queensland Department of Education and Training (DET) and Good to Great Schools Australia (GGSA),[1] a not-for-profit organisation headed by Noel

---

I acknowledge the traditional owners of the lands on which the CYAAA operates. I also acknowledge the helpful comments from anonymous reviewers of the drafts of this chapter and the patience of the editors.

---

[1] Technically the partner is "The Cape York Academy", a registered business name of the GGSA.

J. McCollow (✉)
TJ Ryan Foundation, Brisbane, QLD, Australia

© Springer Nature Singapore Pte Ltd. 2019
J. Rennie, H. Harper (eds.), *Literacy Education and Indigenous Australians*,
Language Policy 19, https://doi.org/10.1007/978-981-13-8629-9_14

248   J. McCollow

Pearson, founder of the Cape York Institute for Policy and Leadership.[2] This case study covers the years 2010 through 2017. CYAAA began operation at Coen and Aurukun in 2010 and in the following year expanded its operations to Hope Vale. Previously, the schools in these communities had operated as systemic state schools. From the start of the 2017 school year, following disturbances in the community and a review conducted by the School Improvement Unit of DET in 2016, the Aurukun campus was excised from the Academy and returned to being a systemic state school. As of 2017, the CYAAA continues to operate at Coen and Hope Vale where it uses Direct Instruction (DI), a standardised pedagogical and curriculum program developed and promoted by the US-based National Institute for Direct Instruction (NIFDI).

This chapter examines questions about literacy education that arise from reforms implemented by the CYAAA. First, the nature of the CYAAA reform and its implementation is interrogated. This is followed by a discussion of evidence of the success/failure of the reform, particularly in relation to the literacy component of Direct Instruction. Finally, some conclusions are drawn from the CYAAA experience. Because the CYAAA is a high-profile, contested reform that embodies a particular approach to remote Indigenous education, these questions are important, not only to the communities involved but in considerations – including public debate and policy-formation – concerning literacy education for Indigenous communities in general.

The Cape York Aboriginal Australian Academy: Some Background

Coen, Hope Vale and Aurukun are remote communities located on the Cape York Peninsula in the state of Queensland. Coen is a small inland town in the Cook Shire. "The Indigenous people of the region comprise several language groups including the Kaanju, Umpilla, Lama Lama, Wik Munkan and Ayaputhu" (CYAAA 2017). Aboriginal English is the most commonly spoken language variety and is shared throughout the community (Dow 2011). In 2011 Coen was home to 310 people, 85% of whom identified as Aboriginal (ABS 2017b). In 2016, the Coen campus of the CYAAA had an enrolment of 57 (GGSA 2016a).

Hope Vale, the home community of Noel Pearson, had an estimated population of 1125 in 2015, of whom 94% identified as Aboriginal (ABS 2017c). It is located about 45 kilometres north-west of Cooktown in eastern Cape York. It is home to

---

[2] Pearson has been described as "undoubtedly the most influential person in Indigenous policy making in Australia today" (Altman 2011). Establishment of the CYAAA predates establishment of GGSA. It was originally a project of Cape York Partnerships (CYP), an Indigenous policy reform and leadership organisation also headed by Noel Pearson. While the CYAAA is its flagship program, GGSA also supports "40 schools in rural and remote communities across Western Australia, the Northern Territory and Queensland" (GGSA 2017a, p. 3).

several clan groups of the Warra peoples. It was a Lutheran mission until 1986 when it received a "Deed of Grant in Trust". Native title was recognised in 1997. In 2016 the Hope Vale campus of the CYAAA had a student population of 114 (GGSA 2016b).

Aurukun had an estimated population of 1424 in 2015, 92% of whom identified as Aboriginal (ABS 2017a). The community was originally a mission station, being reconstituted in the late 1970s as a local government (shire) council. The area was the subject of the successful Wik Native Title case in the High Court in 1996. The main language spoken in the community is Wik-Mungkan. In 2016, the last year of its operation as a campus of the CYAAA, the school had an enrolment of 208 (DET 2017).

According to the My School website (2017), the three CYAAA campuses had a total enrolment of 370 in 2016, 98% of whom were Indigenous. Combined enrolments at Coen and Hope Vale in 2017 were 166 (DET 2017).

The Wicked Problem of Remote Indigenous Schooling

As several writers have observed, in remote Indigenous education, numerous policies and initiatives have been implemented that continually come up "short of the mark" (McKinley 2017, p. 192; see also, e.g. Dreise and Thomson 2014; Gillan, et al., 2017). The concept of a "wicked problem" (Rittel and Webber 1973; Australian Public Service Commission 2007) is now well-established in policy analysis and research. As Dreise and Thomson (2014, p. 3) note, "Indigenous education easily fits the definition of 'wicked public policy problems'". Features of a wicked problem include that it is socially complex with multiple causes; that it eludes definitive description; that it is perhaps incapable of final resolution; and that there are no universally agreed criteria for determining whether solutions are "right" or "wrong". Further, every implemented solution has consequences (often unintended) that affect the nature of the problem and of future interventions.

There are many exogenous factors that impinge on the education of remote Indigenous children, most of which apply in the cases of the CYAAA communities. These include geographical isolation; cultural and language barriers; poverty; poor health; substance abuse; lack of employment opportunities; and racism and the legacy of neo-colonialism. Aurukun has occasionally suffered from outbursts of lawlessness and violence. Factors such as the inexperience of teaching staff and high levels of staff turnover can significantly affect the "fidelity" with which any particular program is implemented and render definitive assessment of the program itself problematic. Furthermore, key educational issues such as the aims of schooling, the nature of quality teaching, and the best means of sustaining it remain contested.

As Luke et al. (2013, pp. 13–16) note, while a commitment to social justice is a feature of all approaches to Indigenous education, views on how equity should be defined, how it is to be achieved and how it should be measured differ. Following Fraser (1997), Luke and his colleagues distinguish between the pursuit of "redistributive social justice" which entails "a fairer, more equitable distribution of conventional educational goals" and "recognitive social justice" which seeks to include and recognise "those cultures and histories, knowledges and skills that have been previously been marginalised" (Luke et al. 2013, p. 14).

Curriculum that focuses on acquisition of mainstream knowledge and skills may have redistributive effects but ignore or exacerbate features of mainstream ideology that distort and marginalise non-mainstream cultures. Conversely, it can be argued that:

> ... empowerment consists of direct and transparent access not to minority, diasporic and marginalised knowledge, but to mainstream codes and canon, the ... disciplinary knowledge of dominant societies. (Ibid., p. 16)

Many of these general observations about Indigenous education apply to the specific case of the CYAAA. Education in Hope Vale, Coen and Aurukun is a socially complex phenomenon for which there is no universally agreed path forward. Debates about this path and the means of travelling it – including how the redistributive and recognitive dimensions of social justice are best balanced – are marked as much by ideological predilections, political considerations and rhetorical assertions as by the weighing of evidence. Numerous exogenous factors affect the implementation of the educational program and thus make valid assessment of the evidence difficult.

Finally, as Osborne (2016, p. 3) notes, Indigenous education tends to be "ordered and resourced by government policy, informed by research, and enacted largely by non-Aboriginal and Torres Strait Islander educators". While the chief instigator of the CYAAA, Noel Pearson, is Aboriginal – and local to one of the CYAAA communities – his approach is top-down, informed by theories developed, research conducted and practices enacted by non-Indigenous people.

Social and Educational Foundations of the Approach Used at the CYAAA

The CYAAA initiative is embedded in a wider program of Indigenous social reform, the Cape York Welfare Reforms (CYWR; see FRC 2011), and reflects the principles and approaches to Indigenous social and education reform outlined by Pearson (2007, 2009), Pearson et al. (2009), CYP (2009) and McCollow (2012a). In his writings Pearson has developed a critique of current Indigenous social and education policy and sets out an alternative approach.

Pearson's critique of left/liberal social theory is based on what he sees as the malignant effects of its focus on the structural causes of social problems such as racism, poverty and inequality. The problem, according to Pearson, is that the focus on structural causes has acted to absolve Indigenous people from accepting responsibility for improving their own situation and cultivated a culture of victimhood and dependency (Pearson 2007, pp. 52–53). In a structural analysis, Indigenous Australians are projected as weak and incapable of achieving advancement on their own, and the solution is for them to be rescued through the coordination of services. Furthermore, according to Pearson, structurally based social policies operate in a dynamic in which, despite the ongoing failure of successive interventions – which not only do not work but create a whole new set of secondary problems – the "progressive" premises on which policy is based are immune to challenge.

Further, in Pearson's view the left has romanticised traditional Aboriginal culture and ignored or glossed over its features that make the exercise of "self-determination" in current political and economic contexts problematic. In particular, Pearson believes that left/liberal social policy has ignored "deeply entrenched destructive behaviour that tolerates excessive alcohol abuse, domestic violence and school absenteeism" (Altman 2011, p. 2). As an alternative, Pearson "decided to champion the Indigenous responsibility agenda" (Pearson 2007, pp. 54–56).

The Cape York Welfare Reforms (CYWR), negotiated between the federal and Queensland governments and the Cape York Institute and of which Pearson may be described as the architect, aim to "restore positive social norms and re-establish local Indigenous authority; move communities and individuals from welfare dependence to productive engagement in the 'real' economy" (Altman 2011, p. 2).

For Pearson, progressive education is a specific manifestation of left/liberal social policy. He has depicted it as the prevailing orthodoxy in schooling, and his critique takes as its starting point the egregious failure of schooling to provide remote Indigenous students with outcomes anywhere near those provided to non-Indigenous students. In his view, one reason for this failure is that progressive approaches draw on structural analyses of disadvantage; the effect in schools is a "soft bigotry of low expectations" (Pearson 2009, p. 16). Pearson takes particular issue with what he sees to be the progressive "aversion to focusing on skills" (Ibid., p. 74).

Pearson is also concerned that mass education assumes a standard distribution of academic aptitudes: mainstream instruction is supplemented by remedial programs for "low-progress" students. In remote Indigenous schools, however, the "academic tail" constitutes the majority of students. In these settings a mainstream program supplemented by remedial programs is not appropriate.

For Pearson, the "education establishment", including teacher education institutions, teacher unions and state education bureaucracies, is implicated in the failure of remote Indigenous education in at least two significant ways. First, all are bastions of the prevailing progressive education orthodoxy, which they vigorously defend. Second, in Pearson's view, as manifestations of a centralist welfare state, they embody state-imposed visions of social good and operate outside of, and restrict, the corrective disciplines of the market. For this reason, he is drawn to the to the American charter school model where schools are funded by the government but have considerable autonomy when it comes to matters of staffing, curriculum and pedagogy. This allows these schools, in Pearson's view, to encourage and reward excellence from both teachers and students, pursue innovative approaches, engage authentically with their clientele and avoid the "dead hand" of educational bureaucracy.

GGSA (2017a, p. 7) claims that its model of school improvement is based on the influential 2010 McKinsey & Company report, *How the World's Most Improved*

School Systems Keep Getting Better (Barber et al. 2010). McKinsey & Company is a major global management consulting firm that undertakes qualitative and quantitative analyses across a wide range of business and policy issues for private corporations and government. The McKinsey report categorises systems as operating at one of five stages, poor, fair, good, great and excellent, and identifies a set of interventions that allows systems "to successfully traverse from one stage to the next" (Ibid., p. 18).

Of particular relevance to the CYAAA is the report's finding that systems overseeing a successful transition from "poor" to "fair" performance exercised "tight control over teaching and learning processes" (Ibid.). This stands in contrast to systems moving their schools' performances from "good" to "great", which provided only loose guidelines, encouraging creativity and innovation from school leaders and teachers. The implication is that introducing flexibility too early in the improvement process may be counter-productive. According to the McKinsey research, in moving schools from the "poor" to the "fair" category, the emphasis should be on "achieving the basics of literacy and numeracy" by "providing motivation and scaffolding for low skill teachers", "getting all schools to a minimum quality level" and "getting students in seats" (Ibid., p. 28). Specific features of such an approach could include "scripted teaching materials", direct coaching and oversight of teachers, data collection linked to assessment against performance targets, an extended school day and incentives (for schools and staff) for high performance (Ibid., pp. 28–34). This approach is compatible with Pearson's critique of progressive approaches to teaching and aligns with the Academy's use of the highly scripted DI program.

The McKinsey Report has been criticised. Coffield (2012, p. 136) claims that:

> … it has an impoverished view of teaching and learning; its evidential base is thin; its central arguments are implausible; its language is technocratic and authoritarian; it underplays the role of culture in education and it omits any mention of democracy.

There can be no argument with Pearson's depiction of the failure of remote Indigenous education nor with his assertion that current remedial measures are inadequate to address the gap in educational outcomes between remote Indigenous students and "mainstream" Australian students. Other aspects of Pearson's analysis are, however, open to contestation. In particular, he has overstated the degree to which modern educational theory and practice rejects explicit instruction and skills acquisition (see discussion below).

DI and Its Critics

Direct Instruction (DI) is one specific commercial manifestation – developed by Siegfried Engelmann and his colleagues – within the broader category "explicit instruction", which refers to a range of teacher-centred approaches that are focused on making clear to learners the behavioural and cognitive goals of instruction.[3] In the "literacy wars" (see Snyder 2008), these approaches are often juxtaposed in binary, either-or, opposition to "student-centred" approaches. This is despite numerous research reports (e.g. Chall 1967; May et al. 2016; Paris 2005; Snow et al. 1998) recommending a mix of instructional strategies relating to literacy. One of the difficulties of dealing with this phenomenon is that identifying the binary nature of the debate tends to instantiate and therefore proliferate the binaries so identified.

DI involves explicit teaching of a curriculum based on sequenced sets of knowledge and skills and ability grouping. "The literacy model [of DI] is skills-based, focusing on five major print literacy components: phonemic awareness, phonics skills, fluency, vocabulary and comprehension" (Dow 2011, p. 55). Learning is broken down into a hierarchy of discrete skills and tasks, the teacher controls the learning environment, lessons are highly scripted and typically involve students responding in unison, and student work is regularly assessed and corrected. Students progress to a higher level only when they have mastered the skills and tasks of the preceding level. One feature of DI, which distinguishes it from some other forms of explicit instruction, is the detailed and prescriptive way that it sets out the role of the teacher: "the teacher is trained to precisely deliver the script, hand gestures, corrections and behavioural modification techniques" (Dow 2011, p. 55). All materials (lesson plans, activity sheets, workbooks and reading materials) are supplied by DI, and the content is exclusively North American.

Luke (2014, p. 2) notes that debates about DI have both "philosophic and empirical" dimensions. Philosophical objections to DI include that it conceives education as "neutral, passive and one-way process, with knowledge transmitted from expert to student" (Martin, et al. 2017, p. 1164); that it fails to recognise that comprehension is not just a cognitive but also a social phenomenon[4]; and that its narrow understandings of comprehension are insufficient for the literacy education of diverse and marginalised students. Further, Luke et al. (2013, p. 11) argue that the function of curriculum materials should be to enhance teacher professionalism and are critical of approaches (such as DI) that "prescribe and dictate pedagogic method, style and instructional interaction", as these are "optimally the domain of school and teacher professional judgement".

For Blades (2007), DI's widespread use in disadvantaged school settings creates a pedagogy and curriculum divide where "poor kids get behavio[u]rism and rich kids get social constructionism … that means skills for the poor and knowledge for the rich". On the other hand, Delpit (2006) contends that explicit instruction can provide students of minority cultures a clarity about rules of communication and discursive practice that may be lacking in child-centred approaches. She argues that

---

[3] Generic explicit instruction and various specific approaches that are informed by its principles are also sometimes referred to as "direct instruction" (as, e.g. in Rowe 2006). As Ryder et al. (2006, p. 181) comment, "DI … is confused often with the more general approach to classroom instruction referred to as direct or teacher-directed instruction". Detailed information on DI as promoted by NIFDI is available on that organisation's website: https://www.nifdi.org/

[4] That is, it ignores the "recognitive" dimensions of teaching marginalised groups.

254   J. McCollow

the failure of child-centred approaches to provide this knowledge can lock students out of the culture of power.[5]

Empirical issues revolve around questions of DI's effectiveness, characterised by "over three decades of claims, counter-claims, and debates amongst empirical researchers about the conventionally-measured educational outcomes and effects of DI" (Luke 2014, p. 2). According to its proponents, DI was assessed as being the most effective literacy intervention program in use in US schools by *Project Follow Through*, a massive US Department of Education study (see Engelmann 2007). The efficacy of DI is also supported by Hattie's influential synthesis of research on achievement (Hattie 2009, pp. 204–207).

The findings of *Project Follow Through* have been contested, notably by House et al. (1978), who identified numerous classification, methodological and interpretive problems and concluded that it did not provide a basis for preferring any one model of instruction over another. Similarly, Ryder et al. (2006, p. 181) identify numerous issues with *Project Follow Through* that render general conclusions about the efficacy of DI versus other methods problematic. They also review subsequent studies (see in particular pp. 188–190) and conclude that these (and their own empirical research on DI) provide little evidence to prefer DI to alternative approaches to teaching literacy.

Advocates of DI ascribe the failure to "adopt" the findings of *Project Follow Through* to a wilful refusal to accept the evidence, to "parochial vested interests that work to either maintain the status quo or to advance self-serving models" (Watkins, quoted in Rowe 2006, p. 7; see also Hattie 2009, pp. 258–259).

As noted above, the weight of the research literature over a number of years has recommended a mixture of instructional strategies and approaches, and this is reflected in education policy documents and professional association publications (e.g. Education Queensland 2000; Ludwig 2003).[6] Luke (2014) argues that it is unhelpful for the debate to develop in a way in which the choice is between polarised "pro-DI" and "anti-DI" positions. There is evidence supporting explicit teaching and highly formalised literacy strategies to provide a strong grounding in "the basics". However, there are potential problems: such an approach could lead to a deskilling of teachers, and it might not provide the necessary means by which students can broaden and extend their knowledge and develop analytical and critical skills.

Dow (2011), who taught DI at Coen, gives examples from her own classroom experience of how the scripted procedures for curriculum delivery failed to deal with student responses and behaviours that fell outside of the ambit of responses

---

[5] Delpit makes specific reference to "Distar" (Direct Instruction System for Teaching Arithmetic and Reading), which is an earlier version of DI. See Delpit, pp. 27–28, for her analysis of how Distar provides a clarity about discursive conventions lacking in at least some "progressive" programs. Delpit's position is not that of unqualified support for explicit instruction but for a mix of instructional strategies.

[6] It can also be noted that, far from discouraging explicit approaches, another model of explicit instruction is mandated for all state schools in the Far North Queensland Region.

and behaviours predicted by the program writers, something that happened not infrequently in the context of dealing with students from non-mainstream cultural backgrounds whose first language is not standard Australian English. In such cases of misunderstanding, the teacher is forbidden to go "off script" and must repeat the lesson as scripted, rather than addressing the unanticipated issues that have led to confusion.

Dow's depiction of the rigidity and cultural inappropriateness of DI ring true. Nevertheless, the DI lessons observed for this case study were well constructed and interesting, and students were enthusiastically engaging with the tasks. This stood in contrast to lessons observed in some other settings where remote Indigenous students were too "shamed" to respond actively.

Establishment and Operation of the CYAAA

Pearson's rejection of "progressive" educational and social policy and practice and his attempt to establish an alternative approach that emphasises personal responsibility and skill acquisition has been debated by educationalists and those working in the area of Indigenous social policy. Simultaneously, his message – or particular aspects of it – has been enthusiastically embraced and supported by "cultural warriors" in the mass media (e.g. Devine 2010; Albrechtsen 2012; Mitchell 2016) and by think tanks such as the Centre for Independent Studies. This has made it difficult to disentangle arguments about Pearson's social and educational agenda or the CYAAA from wider political and cultural "wars" and the posturing and manoeuvring that accompany them.

Pearson has been adept at garnering support from the major political parties for his social and educational projects, but he has also accumulated opponents from the left and right of politics. Amongst Indigenous public intellectuals and academics, views about Pearson and his programs are also mixed. A prominent supporter has been Marcia Langton (e.g. 2012); however, Waters (2014) claimed that Pearson has "no followers in our [Indigenous] communities" and accused him of pursuing an agenda designed to appeal to white Australians. Chris Sarra, who gained renown as principal of Cherbourg State School (an Indigenous school located in rural south-eastern Queensland) and who has developed his own "Stronger, Smarter" program for Indigenous schools, has been a prominent critic of the CYAAA, primarily for its use of DI – which he sees as demeaning both students and teachers (see, e.g. ABC 2016).

A significant limitation of research on and analysis of the CYAAA to date is the lack of a thorough examination of the experiences and views of local community members. A recent paper produced by ACER, concluded:

> The CYAAA was not an original part of the CYWR … which meant that not all of the Aurukun, Coen and Hope Vale communities were formally involved in the decision-making process for the set-up of the educational program … in this case the communities appear to

have largely, and possibly by default, delegated the governance of the CYAAA, to its Chair – Noel Pearson. (Gillan et al. 2017)

The DET review of schooling in Aurukun reported that "many community members reported that they feel they have been excluded from the school and are not consulted in relation to the school curriculum, teaching practices and the school's overall direction" (DET 2016b, p. 7).

The CYAAA (2016b) argued that the criticisms of its community engagement ignore the complexities of navigating politics and tensions within the communities. In Aurukun, there are five clan groups with a history of rivalry. The late Neville Pootchemunka, mayor of Aurukun at the time of the establishment of the CYAAA, was a strong supporter of the academy. His successor, Dereck Walpo, is a critic and opponent. The CYAAA response to the Aurukun review (Ibid., p. 14) claims that the DET review "elevated the opinion of one group over the others", ignoring, for example, the grassroots Wik Womens' Group (which includes Aurukun elder Phyllis Yunkaporta), which was very supportive of the academy and of DI as an instructional strategy.

It is true to say that, other than Noel Pearson, there are no community representatives on the Board of GGSA and that community engagement as defined by the CYAAA tends to ignore issues of governance. It is not true to say, however, that there was no consultation with the communities in laying the groundwork for the academy. In relation to Aurukun, for example, the CYAAA (2016b, p. 14) reports that:

In 2009 the Academy undertook extensive community consultation in Aurukun about the implementation of the CYAAA model. Over 95 members of the Aurukun community were closely consulted, and over 77% of Aurukun residents demonstrated commitment to the model.

Not all of the people of Aurukun, Coen and Hope Vale support the CYAAA, but there are groups within these communities who strongly support it.

Critics have claimed that the costs of the program run at the CYAAA are exorbitant (ABC 2016; Luke 2014). However, data from the My School website indicates that recurrent expenditure at the CYAAA is comparable to that at other remote Queensland Indigenous schools (see Fig. 14.1).[7]

Pearson's original proposal for the CYAAA, as set out in 2009 Business Case, envisaged an extended school day and a curriculum divided into three domains: "class", "club" and "culture".[8] The class domain was "delineated as an English language domain dedicated to western learning" (CYP 2009, p. 19) with a heavy emphasis on basic literacy and numeracy (using DI). There were to be no cross-cultural or bilingual dimensions to the class domain. The club domain was to incorporate activities such as physical education, sports, science and music. The culture

---

[7] The degree to which the My School data captures all expenditure is uncertain.

[8] The number of domains has expanded to six, with the addition of the "childhood" "civics" and "community" domains (GGSA 2017b).

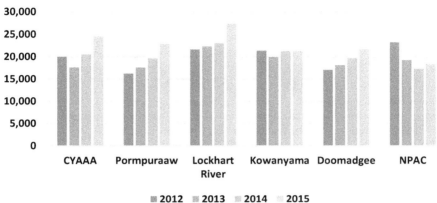

Fig. 14.1 Recurrent expenditure ($) per student (all sources) NPAC = Northern Peninsula Area College. (Source: My School website, https://www.myschool.edu.au/)

domain would include subjects in the humanities, social sciences, business, technology and language (Western and Indigenous).

More recently the CYAAA has also used a program called Explicit Direct Instruction, developed by Hollingsworth and Ybarra (2013), which has been aligned with the Australian curriculum. Explicit Direct Instruction is less prescriptive, has less frequent testing and data analysis, allows greater teacher flexibility and is delivered in age-based class groupings rather than ability groupings. It can be argued that the introduction of Explicit Direct Instruction addresses some (but not all) of the concerns about the rigidity of Direct Instruction.

The three (now six)-domain model of schooling is a holistic approach that recognises the importance of building social capital, community engagement, inquiry-based learning and critical thinking. Criticism of DI at the Academy has tended to ignore the potential for activities undertaken in other curriculum domains to address the concerns about its limitations.

In the wake of community violence in Aurukun in 2016, a review of schooling in Aurukun was carried out by DET.[9] The DET review made recommendations that fell under "four central themes": governance and operational arrangements; engagement of the Aurukun community; secondary education provision; and Direct Instruction (DET 2016b, p. 7).[10]

---

[9] A more detailed discussion of the developments in Aurukun in 2016 is provided in McCollow 2016. The DET report did not examine the other two CYAAA campuses.

[10] The issue of whether the CYAAA should provide secondary education at Aurukun will not be considered in this paper.

While the report found that DI "has provided a consistent language and focus for teachers in a school where a high turnover of staff exists" (Ibid., p. 9), it concluded that an over-reliance on DI to the exclusion of other strategies had led to many aspects of the Australian curriculum being ignored or inconsistently taught.

The club and culture domains, which should have provided opportunities for a range of learning experiences beyond basic literacy and numeracy, had been mainly relegated to the period between 2.30 pm and 4 pm in the extended school day – attendance during this time was voluntary, though strongly encouraged. The DET reviewers found that "student engagement during this part of the program varies considerably" (Ibid., p. 41).[11] Additionally, the pressure to deliver improved literacy and numeracy outcomes in an atmosphere of staff shortages, irregular attendance and disruption led to more and more emphasis on DI.

The CYAAA response contests the DET report's findings that only DI was used in the school and that the school was not providing the full Australian Curriculum, stating that "the Academy has a comprehensive set of custom-designed Club and Culture curriculum resources and materials developed by expert Queensland teachers … customised to the local context through extensive consultation with the community" (CYAAA 2016b, pp. 17–18). It drew attention to the participation of students in instrumental music and art programs. It acknowledged, however, that "the school deliberately has additional time devoted to literacy and numeracy … whilst providing an extended school day to fully address other areas of the Australian Curriculum" (Ibid., pp. 18–19) and that teacher shortages had created problems in the delivery of the club and culture domains.

The review (DET 2016b) also identified issues relating governance and administration. It found that there was a lack of clarity about the respective roles and responsibilities of the CYAAA and DET partners, leading to confusion about who is driving the future direction of the school. The partnership arrangement between GGSA and the Department of Education falls considerably short of establishing the autonomy of an American charter school that Pearson admires. Tensions between GGSA and Education Queensland about the nature of the authority of each party and the direction and operation of the CYAAA have been ongoing.

The report recommended that DET and the CYAAA negotiate a new service agreement, in which the former would "strengthen its support for the governance and day-to-day operation of the school" (DET 2016b, p. 7). The CYAAA would retain responsibility for professional development, curriculum and pedagogy. The CYAAA (2016b) response expressed concern about the report's recommendation that DET "strengthen its support for the governance and day-to-day operation of the school", interpreting it as relegating "the Academy to the role of a contracted service provider … in direct contradiction to the Memorandum of Understanding between the Academy and DET", which positions them as "partners" (Ibid., p. 5). Suspicion that the DET review prefigured a significant reassertion of DET control over the campus was one of the factors that scuppered renegotiation of the DET/CYAAA MOU for Aurukun.

---

[11] Dow (2011, p. 59) expressed similar concerns in relation to Coen.

14   A Case Study of Controversy: The Cape York Aboriginal Australian Academy   259

What Is the Evidence of the Effectiveness of the CYAAA Reform?

For evidence of the performance of the CYAAA, data are available on student attendance, parent/student satisfaction and student NAPLAN results; but in none of these
areas are the data comprehensive or unambiguous. Further, conversations with
teachers and former teachers at the CYAAA reveal a variety of views.

As in many remote Indigenous schools, regular attendance has been a persistent
problem. The 2016 DET review of the Aurukun campus observed that low levels of
attendance were seen as "a major factor in the inability of the teachers and school
leaders to enact the intended curriculum" (DET 2016b, p. 29). However, Hattie
(2016, p. 8) reports that for 2016, the "Coen and Hope Vale [campuses] … recorded
the highest attendance of remote-based indigenous Queensland schools". Table 14.1
shows student attendance rates for the CYAAA in comparison to some other remote
Indigenous schools in far north Queensland for the period 2012–2016. When the
Aurukun campus is excluded, the CYAAA attendance rate for 2014 was 83%; for
2015 was 88%; and for 2016 was 82% (CYAAA 2016a, p. 12). Table 14.2 shows the
proportion of students attending 90% or more of the time for selected remote
Indigenous schools in semester one, 2016.

Table 14.3 shows trends for the three CYAAA campuses for 2008 to 2016. It
shows that there was a dramatic improvement in attendance at Aurukun in the first
year of its operation as a campus of the CYAAA in 2010,[12] that this attendance rate
was sustained through 2013, but that thereafter attendance rates fell, reaching a
comparable level to the pre-CYAAA period from 2015. Attendance rates for Coen
and Hope Vale are comparable before and after their inclusion as campuses of the
CYAAA (in 2010 for Coen; in 2011 for Hope Vale).

Table 14.1 School attendance rates

School	2012	2013	2014	2015	2016
CYAAA	73.7	71.1	71.0	71.9	64.0
Doomadgee	54.1	48.3	64.4	57.9	57.8
Kowanyama	74.8	76.5	78.7	74.2	73.2
Lockhart	72.1	79.1	69.2	67.6	72.3
Mornington Island	74.7	66.6	74.1	75.9	71.3
NPAC[a]	68.3	65.7	72.3	72	71.6
Pormpuraaw	73.4	76.9	81.9	85.3	82.3
Indigenous students – all schools in far North Queensland Region[b]	82.8	82.4	82.9	83.6	83.4

Source: Queensland DET 2017
[a]Northern Peninsula Area College
[b]Includes Indigenous prep and primary students in schools in city (Cairns), rural town and remote
settings

---

[12]Though enrolment rates were trending upwards prior to 2010

Table 14.2 Proportion of students attending 90% or more of the time

School	Proportion of students
CYAAA	25
Doomadgee	11
Kowanyama	22
Lockhart River	26
Mornington Island	28
NPAC[a]	38
Pormpuraaw	37

[a]Northern Peninsula Area College
Source: My School website, https://www.myschool.edu.au/

Table 14.3 Attendance rates % (Term 1)

School/Campus	2008	2009	2010	2011	2012	2013	2014	2015	2016
Aurukun	50.2	60.8	71.3	75.4	70.0	69.7	59.6	62.1	52.4
Coen	91.3	93.6	94.9	93.5	91.5	86.8	92.8	96.5	92.0
Hope Vale	80.6	88.2	87.3	89.9	83.1	73.9	81.5	89.3	77.7

Figures in red font indicate period before incorporation into the CYAAA (Color figure online)
Source: Queensland DET (2016a)

Queensland schools conduct annual parent opinion surveys. The results for the CYAAA (over the period 2012–2016) show relatively high levels of satisfaction; however, the results should be treated with caution as participation is voluntary and response rates (which are not identified) can be low.

Since its inception in 2010, there have been several reviews of and reports on the CYAAA that have considered student outcomes. McCollow (2012b) examined 2012 NAPLAN results (mean scores) in reading, writing and numeracy for the three CYAAA campuses in comparison to other Indigenous Cape York schools. He found that, while student performances at the Coen campus were consistently amongst the best of these schools, the results for Aurukun and Hope Vale were consistently amongst the worst. An evaluation conducted by the Australian Council for Educational Research (ACER) in 2013, noted that "school staff and community members at Aurukun, Coen and Hope Vale report that the CYAAA Initiative has had a wide range of positive outcomes" (ACER 2013, p. 10). However, the report stated, "it is not possible to conclude from the available test data … whether or not the CYAAA Initiative has had an impact on student learning" (Ibid., p. 9). Another review undertaken in 2013 by Grossen, who is associated with NIFDI and used DI data, was far more positive, concluding that student literacy outcomes had increased in each year.

Hattie (2014, 2016) examined NAPLAN data from the three campuses for 2008, 2010 and 2012 and concluded that CYAAA students demonstrated impressive

14 A Case Study of Controversy: The Cape York Aboriginal Australian Academy

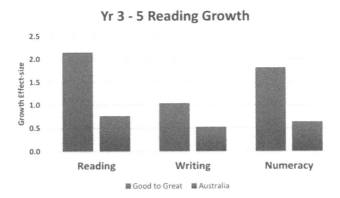

Fig. 14.2 Year 3–5 reading growth. (Source: Hattie 2016, p. 9. While the blue lines are labelled in the chart as depicting growth effect-sizes for "Good to Great" schools, it appears from the text that they specifically depict the growth effect-sizes for the CYAAA) (Color figure online)

growth in performance over this period (see Fig. 14.2), providing "every confidence to continue the current DI programs" (2014. p. 4). He comments, "this is the good news: the program is truly making a difference; but the sobering news is that the students have to make 3+ years growth in a year to catch up [with the performance of mainstream Australian students]" (2016, p. 8). Hattie concludes that "the naysayers want to destroy an evidence based program because it has not performed magic" (Ibid.).

However, Hattie also notes "quite considerable missing data" which allowed him to calculate growth for less than "a quarter of all students" (2014, pp. 1 & 5). In a similar vein, the 2016 DET review, which focused specifically on Aurukun, rather than on the CYAAA as a whole, noted that the NAPLAN participation rate at Aurukun in 2015 was "one of the lowest of any Queensland state school" (DET 2016b, p. 20) and that in 2016 Aurukun students did not sit for the NAPLAN exams at all, due to "instability within the school community at the time" (Ibid., p. 24). On the basis of low participation and missing data, the report concludes that "extreme caution should be taken in relation to the use of Aurukun campus' NAPLAN data as a basis of judgements regarding the school" (Ibid., p. 22).

The performance of the CYAAA in the reading, writing and numeracy domains in comparison to "like schools" and "all schools" is summarised in Table 14.4.[13]

The views of current and past teachers at the CYAAA vary. Some are enthusiastic proponents of DI and the CYAAA model. Others are fierce in their criticism. The majority fall somewhere between these positions. While some teachers bristled under what they perceived as the inflexible nature of DI, others welcomed the guidance and structure that DI provided in a setting that was unfamiliar and challenging. Some

---

[13] NAPLAN also tests "spelling" and "grammar and punctuation". The CYAAA performed "above" similar schools in Year 3 grammar and punctuation, 2014, and Year 3 spelling, 2016. The CYAAA performed "substantially above" similar schools in Year 5 spelling, 2014, and Year 3 grammar and punctuation, 2016.

Table 14.4 Cape York Aboriginal Australian Academy – NAPLAN mean scores in comparison to other schools[a]

	Reading		Writing		Numeracy	
	In comparison to "similar schools"[b]	*In comparison to all schools*	*In comparison to "similar schools"*	*In comparison to all schools*	*In comparison to "similar schools"*	*In comparison to all schools*
Year 3, 2013	'close to'	'substantially below'	'below'	'substantially below'	'below'	'substantially below'
Year 3, 2014	'above'	'substantially below'	'above'	'substantially below'	'above'	'substantially below'
Year 3, 2015	'close to'	'substantially below'	'close to'	'substantially below'	'close to'	'substantially below'
Year 3, 2016	'above'	'substantially below'	'substantially above'	'substantially below'	'above'	'substantially below'
Year 5, 2013	'below'	'substantially below'	'below'	'substantially below'	'below'	'substantially below'
Year 5, 2014	'close to'	'substantially below'	'close to'	'substantially below'	'close to'	'substantially below'
Year 5, 2015	'below'	'substantially below'	'substantially below'	'substantially below'	'substantially below'	'substantially below'
Year 5, 2016	'close to'	'substantially below'	'below'	'substantially below'	'below'	'substantially below'

[a]Source: My School website: https://www.myschool.edu.au/. The font colour code in the table reflects the colour code used on the My School website (Color figure online)
[b]Schools "serving students from statistically similar backgrounds"

acknowledged that DI was delivering improvements in basic literacy and numeracy but expressed concern about its incapacity to provide advanced critical skills.

It is perhaps noteworthy that amongst the strongest supporters of DI are some of the Indigenous teachers and teacher aides. Cannon (2010), a local Indigenous teacher who was head of campus at Coen in 2010 and, as of 2017, has taught at the Hope Vale campus, remains an enthusiastic supporter of DI. Another local Indigenous teacher at Hope Vale, who trained through the Remote Area Teacher Education Program (RATEP), an alternative teacher education program that allows Indigenous teachers to gain their teacher qualification in their home communities, said that DI had given her more confidence in teaching and classroom management and that as a result the community now saw her as a "real teacher", not just a token Aboriginal face on staff.

Conclusion

The Nature of the CYAAA Reform

The CYAAA can be characterised as a top-down reform driven by the ideas of Noel Pearson, negotiated by him and his organisation with governments and relevant agencies and managed, jointly with the Queensland Department of Education, by Good to Great Schools Australia (of which Pearson is the founder and co-chair). The CYAAA is also a high-profile, high-stakes reform. Pearson is a prominent and influential participant in debates about Indigenous social policy, with strong views about the failures of that policy to date and the directions it should now take. These evoke equally strong responses. The CYAAA's alleged success or failure will be weighed as evidence of the soundness of Pearson's ideas and methods of operating.

The use of DI at the CYAAA has been depicted as an example of a search for a quick-fix, "off-the-shelf" solution to a complex problem (e.g. ABC 2016; Adoniou 2016). DI is, of course, an off-the-shelf curriculum package. Yet, such a depiction is partial and potentially misleading, ignoring the fact that the program at the CYAAA, including its use of DI, is embedded in a broader and carefully elucidated educational and social philosophy that seeks to promote individual responsibility and achievement, acquisition of basic skills, restoration of positive social norms and productive engagement in the economy.[14] The debate about the CYAAA is as much about this underlying philosophy as it is about the curriculum as enacted.

DI itself has long been the subject of debate. It has been criticised for constituting the learning process almost entirely as a one-way transmission of knowledge and skills, its rigid scripted lessons, and its failure to engage with the specific social and cultural situation of students. In remote Indigenous settings, this latter feature means that it ignores the recognitive dimensions of social justice. On the other hand, there is evidence that explicit approaches to education (such as DI) can provide students from minority cultures with clarity about mainstream modes of discourse (and thus enhance redistributive social justice). The recent trend is for increased use of explicit teaching in Australian classrooms, including in "mainstream" contexts. While the weight of literacy research argues for a mix of instructional strategies, there has been a tendency for debates to be carried out in binary, either-or, terms. This is reflected in the fact much of the critical commentary on the CYAAA has ignored its "club" and "culture" domains, which do not utilise DI and seek to provide opportunities for creative expression, critical thinking and engagement with local culture.

---

[14] Examination of data relating to these wider aims is important but beyond the scope of the present study.

Implementation

Implementation of educational reform in remote Indigenous settings is beset with factors that have the capacity to impact on the fidelity with which a reform is realised. These can make assessment difficult, for example, in determining the degree to which problems derive from the nature of the reform itself or to failures to implement it properly or, indeed, to extraneous factors.

The degree of consultation and engagement with the local communities remains a point of contention. A significant limitation of research on and analysis of the CYAAA to date is the lack of a thorough examination of the experiences and views of local community members. The CYAAA claims that it engaged in extensive consultation with the local communities in setting up the academy and continues to emphasise community engagement (albeit around issues of attendance, homework and academic progress rather than governance). The DET review of schooling in Aurukun, on the other hand, reported that "many" community members felt that they have been excluded from the school. In the case of Aurukun, community relations were complicated by tensions and divisions in the community.

Staffing is a perennial problem in remote Indigenous schools, which are characterised by difficulties in recruiting, staff shortages, high proportions of inexperienced staff and high rates of staff turnover. All of these applied in the case of the CYAAA in the period 2010–2016. While one of the rationales for implementing DI was that it provided continuity and structure in a situation marked by instability – and some staff felt that it was useful in this regard – in the case of Aurukun, staff shortages and turnover contributed to a situation where club and culture activities were de-emphasised and the curriculum became more and more centred around DI.

Implementation of the extended school day proved far more problematic than was anticipated. It was intended to allow for extended time to be devoted to basic skills instruction (via DI) without sacrificing time for activities in the club and culture domains. However, the relegation of these activities to late afternoon sessions meant that students were either less than fully attentive or had absented themselves from school.

In conceiving of the CYAAA, Pearson was drawn to the American charter school in which publicly funded schools enjoy autonomy in relation to staffing, curriculum and pedagogy. The CYAAA is not, however, a charter school. The Department of Education is responsible for school finance and administration. Teachers are departmental employees. The hybrid management of the CYAAA, combining features of charter schooling and systemic state schooling, created ambiguities and tensions. Interpretations of the memorandum of understanding by the Department of Education and the GGSA clearly differed leading to accusations of "interference" by and from each party. Teachers, particularly in the context of staffing shortages and turnover, were caught in the middle. In the case of Aurukun, the inability to reconcile these tensions resulted in the withdrawal of the site from the CYAAA.

14 A Case Study of Controversy: The Cape York Aboriginal Australian Academy 265

Finally, as a high-profile reform, implementation of the CYAAA has received considerable coverage in the mass media, where it has been both championed and harshly criticised. This increased the stakes for all parties. The review of schooling in Aurukun in 2016, for example, took place in the context of intense media scrutiny, including of the conduct of Noel Pearson, education minister Kate Jones and senior education department officers.

Evidence of Its Success/Failure?

Data on student attendance, parent/student satisfaction and student NAPLAN results for the CYAAA are incomplete and ambiguous.

Attendance rates at Aurukun initially improved with the commencement of the CYAAA but deteriorated from 2014 and were significantly down in the troubled 2016 school year. Attendance at Coen and Hope Vale, on the other hand, has remained high relative to other remote Indigenous schools.

Annual surveys conducted by the school show high levels of parent satisfaction, but these are not a reliable indicator of parental views because response rates are not known.

Despite enthusiastic reporting of performance growth on tests by CYAAA students by Hattie (2014, 2016) and Grossen (2013), the data analysed by these authors is, at best, incomplete. NAPLAN results, as reported by the Australian Curriculum, Assessment and Reporting Authority, show that the CYAAA is not outperforming other remote Indigenous schools generally. The Coen campus, however, appears to be performing well in comparison to other remote Indigenous schools.[15]

Teachers and former teachers at the CYAAA hold a variety of views about its operation and success.

What Conclusions Should Be Drawn from the CYAAA Experience?

Evaluation of an educational reform that occurs in the context of polarised ideological debate and in a setting complicated by significant social, historical and geographic factors requires ongoing, close, systematic and patient data collection (extending well beyond the use of standardised tests). The evidence reviewed here does not provide a basis for a definitive assessment of the CYAAA. Its operational history has been troubled and evidence of its effectiveness is, at best, incomplete and ambiguous.

---

[15] The My School website does not disaggregate NAPLAN results by campus, but Hattie (2014, 2016) and McCollow (2012b) had access to disaggregated data.

The use of DI at the CYAAA has featured prominently in critiques of its operation. The review of schooling in Aurukun, for example, found that DI was being used to the exclusion of other strategies that foster creativity and critical thinking. Whether the club and culture domains can be invigorated and, if so, whether this will sufficiently address concerns about the use of DI remain to be seen. Certainly, however, a concerted effort to improve delivery in these domains is warranted.

Indigenous education is a "wicked problem"; the durability of its challenges should not be underestimated. No reform can be expected to achieve clear-cut, immediate success. Approaches to Indigenous education are based on social, cultural and political as well as educational assumptions. The CYAAA presents as an instance where these assumptions have been explicitly expressed. The CYAAA is also an example of a top-down reform linked to a high-profile participant in the political and media debates about Indigenous social policy. Its development has been influenced not only by an ideological orientation but by the activities of an influential and articulate individual and his colleagues and supporters and in turn by the reactions to these activities by decision-makers, commentators, and the media.

While there is no such thing as an ideology-free position on Indigenous education, the CYAAA case suggests that a less polarised debate should be sought in which parties acknowledge that there is no single "correct" answer to the challenges faced. This should include work to develop a common ground across various philosophical orientations on the uses and abuses of empirical evidence.

This case study demonstrates that local circumstances matter. Conflict in the community and divergent views about the academy brought CYAAA involvement in Aurukun to an end. Staffing difficulties have been ongoing, significantly affecting the capacity of the academy to implement its program as envisioned. This suggests that an important feature of any reform in remote Indigenous education must be the capacity to adjust, revise and adapt as implementation proceeds and as evaluations are conducted and acknowledged. It also emphasises the need for professional conversations with teachers that go beyond instructional methodology and for ongoing community engagement that goes beyond matters of school attendance, homework completion and academic performance. The case study also demonstrates that community engagement may be no simple matter. Reform in Indigenous education tends to be debated and enacted from the top down, with teachers reduced to the role of implementers and communities reduced to the role of recipients. These groups need to be given greater voice. This presents as both an ethical responsibility and as a prerequisite for operational success.

Acknowledgement Figure 14.2 and quotes from "Some preliminary analyses of the three Cape York schools on NAPLAN", unpublished paper (Hattie 2014) are reproduced with the permission of Professor John Hattie.

References

Australian Bureau of Statistics (ABS). (2017a). *Aurukun.* http://stat.abs.gov.au/itt/r.jsp?RegionSu mmary&region=30250&dataset=ABS_REGIONAL_LGA&geoconcept=REGION&datasetA SGS=ABS_REGIONAL_ASGS&datasetLGA=ABS_REGIONAL_LGA&regionLGA=REGI ON&regionASGS=REGION. Accessed 7 July 2017.

ABS. (2017b). *2011 census community profiles: Coen.* http://www.censusdata.abs.gov.au/census_services/getproduct/census/2011/communityprofile/UCL322029. Accessed 7 July 2017.

ABS. (2017c). *Hope Vale.* http://stat.abs.gov.au/itt/r.jsp?RegionSummary&region=33830&dat aset=ABS_REGIONAL_LGA&geoconcept=REGION&datasetASGS=ABS_REGIONAL_ ASGS&datasetLGA=ABS_REGIONAL_LGA&regionLGA=REGION&regionASGS=REG ION. Accessed 7 July 2017.

Adoniou, M. (2016, July 8). What went wrong at Aurukun school? *The Conversation.* https://the-conversation.com/what-went-wrong-at-aurukun-school-62175. Accessed 12 Feb 2018.

Albrechtsen, J. (2012, June 23). Chris Sarra stretches the gap on credibility. *The Australian.* http:// www.theaustralian.com.au/opinion/columnists/chris-sarra-stretches-the-gap-on-credibility/ news-story/0c3409c701652e29624b8ff2845e882c. Accessed 21 Aug 2017.

Altman, J. (2011, August 9). Noel Pearson's policies embraced by white Australia, but how effective are they? *The Conversation.* https://theconversation.com/noel-pearsons-policies-embraced-by-white-australia-but-how-effective-are-they-2226. Accessed 21 Aug 2017.

Australian Broadcasting Corporation (ABC). (2016, May 29). *Noel Pearson's program part of problem in Aurukun, Indigenous educator Chris Sarra says.* http://www.abc.net.au/news/2016-05-29/pearson-program-part-of-problems-in-aurukunchris-sarra-says/7456902. Accessed 21 Aug 2017.

Australian Council for Educational Research (ACER). (2013). *Evaluation of the Cape York aboriginal Australian academy initiative: Final report.* Brisbane: Department of Education Training and Employment Queensland. http://research.acer.edu.au/cgi/viewcontent.cgi?article =1036&context=indigenous_education. Accessed 15 May 2017.

Australian Public Service Commission. (2007). *Tackling wicked problems: A public policy perspective.* Canberra: Commonwealth of Australia.

Barber, M., Chijioke, C., & Mourshed, M. (2010). *How the world's most improved school systems keep getting better.* London: McKinsey & Company. http://www.mckinsey.com/industries/ social-sector/our-insights/how-the-worlds-most-improved-school-systems-keep-getting-better. Accessed 15 May 2017.

Blades, M. (2007). *Jim Cummins demolishes NCLB's ideology and practice.* http://walktalkteach. com.au/news/154-using-direct-instruction-methods-to-teach-english-as-an-additional-language. Accessed 9 Sept 2017.

Cannon, C. (2010). *Cape York Australian Aboriginal Academy: Coen campus.* Paper presented at the Queensland Teacher's Union Aboriginal and Torres Strait islander educators conference, September, Brisbane, Australia.

Cape York Partnership (CYP). (2009). *Cape York Aboriginal Australian Academy: Business case.* https://goodtogreatschools.org.au/wp-content/uploads/2017/05/CYP_Cape_York_Aboriginal_ Australian_Academy_Business_Case_V1.7-2.pdf. Accessed 9 Sept 2017.

Chall, J. (1967). *Learning to read: The great debate.* New York: McGraw-Hill.

Coffield, F. (2012). Why the McKinsey reports will not improve school systems. *Journal of Education Policy, 27*(1), 131–149.

Cape York Aboriginal Australian Academy (CYAAA). (2016a). *Annual report.* https://cyaaa. eq.edu.au/Supportandresources/Formsanddocuments/Annual%20reports/annual-report-2016. pdf. Accessed 7 July 2017.

CYAAA. (2016b, August). *Farrago: Response to the Review of School Education in Aurukun.* https://goodtogreatschools.org.au/wp-content/uploads/2017/05/CYA-Farrago-Response-to-Aurukun-School-Review.pdf. Accessed 14 Nov 2016.

CYAAA. (2017). *Coen Campus*. https://cyaaa.eq.edu.au/Campuses/Coen/Pages/Coen.aspx. Accessed 7 July 2017.

Delpit, L. (2006). *Other people's children: Cultural conflict in the classroom*. New York: The New Press.

Department of Education and Training (DET). (2016a). *Student attendance rate summary for term 1, 2008 to term 2, 2016*. http://www.frcq.org.au/files/DET%20School%20Attendance%20for%20the%20web.pdf. Accessed 9 Sept 2017.

DET. (2016b). *Review of school education in Aurukun*, School Improvement Unit. http://statements.qld.gov.au/Content/MediaAttachments/2016/pdf/Review%20of%20school%20education%20in%20Aurukun.pdf. Accessed 14 Nov 2016.

DET. (2017). *Reports and statistics: Full-time enrolment counts February collection 2013–17*. Strategy and Performance Branch. http://education.qld.gov.au/schools/statistics/pdf/enrolments-by-school-february.pdf. Accessed 9 Sept 2017.

Devine, M. (2010, May 29). Scripted lessons start a classroom revival. *Sydney Morning Herald*. http://www.theage.com.au/opinion/society-and-culture/scripted-lessons-start-a-classroom-revival-20100528-wlba.html. Accessed 7 July 2017.

Dow, L. (2011). Spiders are mammals: Direct Instruction in Cape York. *Literacy & Numeracy Studies, 19*(1), 50–65.

Dreise, T., & Thomson, S. (2014). Unfinished business: PISA shows Indigenous youth are being left behind. In *ACER occasional essays*. Camberwell: Australian Council for Educational Research. file:///F:/CYAAA%20chapter/indigenous%20pedagogy/driese%20and%20thomson%20.pdf. Accessed 3 Dec 2017.

Education Queensland. (2000). *Literate futures: The report of the literacy review for Queensland state schools*. Brisbane: Department of Education.

Engelmann, S. (2007). *Teaching needy kids in our backward system: 42 years of trying*. Eugene: ADI Press.

Family Responsibilities Commission (FRC). (2011). *Our communities*. http://www.frcq.org.au/. Accessed 7 July 2017.

Fraser, N. (1997). *Justice interruptus*. New York: Routledge.

Good to Great Schools Australia (GGSA). (2016a). *2016 Report Card: Coen School*. https://goodtogreatschools.org.au/wp-content/uploads/2017/05/MS-CYA-321-Annual-Report-Coen-20161202-V0.11.pdf. Accessed 9 Sept 2017.

GGSA. (2016b). *2016 report card: Hope Vale School*. https://goodtogreatschools.org.au/wp-content/uploads/2017/05/MS-CYA-321-Annual-Report-Hope-Vale-20170207V0.12.pdf. Accessed 9 Sept 2017.

GGSA. (2017a). *Our story: Supporting schools to meet the needs of all Australian children*. Cairns: Good to Great Schools Australia. https://goodtogreatschools.org.au/wp-content/uploads/2017/05/Updated_GGSA_OURSTORY_01232017_V1.11.pdf. Accessed 9 Sept 2017.

GGSA. (2017b). *6C education model*. Cairns: Good to Great Schools Australia. https://goodtogreatschools.org.au/our-products/6c-education-model/. Accessed 9 Sept 2017.

Gillan, K., Mellor, S., & Krakouer, J. (2017). The case for urgency: Advocating for Indigenous voice in education. In *Australian Education Review*. Camberwell: Australian Council for Educational Research. http://research.acer.edu.au/cgi/viewcontent.cgi?article=1027&context=aer. Accessed 11 July 2017.

Grossen, B. (2013). *Evaluation of the academic progress of children served by the Cape York Aboriginal Australian Academy*. Hillsboro: Centre for Applied Research in Education.

Hattie, J. (2009). *Visible learning: A synthesis of 800+ meta-analyses on achievement*. Oxford: Routledge.

Hattie, J. (2014). *Some preliminary analyses of the three Cape York schools on NAPLAN* (unpublished paper).

Hattie, J. (2016). *Shifting away from distractions to improve Australia's schools: Time for a reboot*. Jack Keating Memorial Lecture, University of Melbourne. http://education.unimelb.

edu.au/__data/assets/pdf_file/0008/1993904/Deans-lecture-June-2016-Jack-Keating-lecture. pdf. Accessed 7 Aug 2017.

Hollingsworth, J., & Ybarra, S. (2013). *Explicit direct instruction for English learners*. Thousand Oaks: Corwin Press.

House, E. R., Glass, G. V., McLean, L. D., & Walker, D. F. (1978). No simple answer: Critique of the follow through evaluation. *Harvard Educational Review, 48*, 128–160.

Langton, M. (2012). Why I continue to be inspired by Noel Pearson. *The Australian*, 5 May. http://www.theaustralian.com.au/national-affairs/opinion/why-i-continue-to-be-inspired-by-pearson/news-story/faf2c70474faca378e07c8b32adea768. Accessed 21 Aug 2017.

Ludwig, C. (2003, February). Making sense of literacy. *Newsletter of the Australian Literacy Educators' Association*. https://www.alea.edu.au/documents/item/53. Accessed 11 July 2017.

Luke, A. (2014, May). On explicit and direct instruction. *ALEA "Hot Topic"*, Australian Literacy Educators' Association. https://www.alea.edu.au/documents/item/861. Accessed 11 July 2017.

Luke, A., Woods, A., & Weir, K. (2013). Curriculum design, equity and the technical form of the curriculum. In A. Luke, A. Woods, & K. Weir (Eds.), *Curriculum, syllabus design and equity: A primer and model*. New York: Routledge.

Martin, G., Nakata, V., Nakata, M., & Day, A. (2017). Promoting the persistence of Indigenous students through teaching at the cultural interface. *Studies in Higher Education, 42*(7), 1158–1173.

May, H.; Sirinides, P.; Gray, A., & Goldsworthy, H. (2016). *Reading recovery: An evaluation of the four-year i3 scale up*. Consortium for Policy Research in Education. http://www.cpre.org/reading-recovery-evaluation-four-year-i3-scale. Accessed 13 Feb 2018.

McCollow, J. (2012a). A controversial reform in Indigenous education: The Cape York Aboriginal Australian Academy. *The Australian Journal of Indigenous Education, 41*, 97–109.

McCollow, J. (2012b). *The Cape York Aboriginal Australian Academy three years on: What is the evidence? What does it indicate?* Conference Paper, Australian Association for Research in Education Conference. Retrieved from.: https://www.aare.edu.au/publications-database. php/6839/the-cape-york-aboriginal-australian-academy-three-years-on-what-is-the-evidence-what-does-it-indicat. Accessed 8 May 2017.

McCollow, J. (2016). *Schooling in Aurukun*. TJ Ryan Foundation, Research Report 49. http://www.tjryanfoundation.org.au/_dbase_upl/McCollow_RR49_Cape_York_Academy.pdf. Accessed 8 May 2017.

McKinley, E. (2017). From inequality to quality: Challenging the debate on Indigenous education. In T. Bentley & G. C. Savage (Eds.), *Educating Australia: Challenges for the decade ahead* (pp. 191–205). Carlton: Melbourne University Press.

Mitchell, C. (2016, August 20). Direct interference: Cape York Academy's good work under threat. *The Australian*. http://www.theaustralian.com.au/news/inquirer/direct-interference-cape-york-academys-good-work-under-threat/news-story/172ed7e62c8f2a717d300efe9f0d938b. Accessed 21 Aug 2017.

My School. (2017). *Cape York Aboriginal Australian Academy*. Cairns QLD. Retrieved from: https://www.myschool.edu.au/. Accessed 7 July 2017.

National Institute for Direct Instruction (NIFDI). (2015). *Web site*. https://www.nifdi.org/. Accessed 7 July 2017.

Osborne, S. (2016). *Power and pedagogy in remote Aboriginal and Torres Strait Islander education – Why families and communities matter in pursuing educational justice*. Remote education systems lecture #11. UniSA, Magill Campus, 27 November. http://www.catconatus. com.au/ebook/lecture_series/11_151127_Power%20and%20Pedagogy%20in%20remote%20 Aboriginal%20and%20Torres%20Strait%20Islander%20education.pdf. Accessed 7 Dec 2017.

Paris, S. G. (2005). Reinterpreting the development of reading skills. *Reading Research Quarterly, 40*(2), 184–202.

Pearson, N. (2007). White guilt, victimhood and the quest for a radical centre. *Griffith Review, 16*, 13–58.

Pearson, N. (2009). Radical hope: Education and equality in Australia. *Quarterly Essay, 35*, 1–105.

Pearson, N., Denigan, B., & Götesson, J. (2009). *The most important reform: Position paper*. Cairns: Cape York Partnership.

Rittel, H. W., & Webber, M. M. (1973). Dilemmas in a general theory of planning. *Policy Sciences, 4*(2), 155–169.

Rowe, K. (2006). *Effective teaching practices for students with and without learning difficulties: Constructivism as a legitimate theory of learning AND of teaching?* Australian Council for Educational Research. http://research.acer.edu.au/learning_processes/10. Accessed 9 Sept 2017.

Ryder, R. T., Burton, J. K., & Silberg, A. (2006). Longitudinal study of direct instruction effects from first through third grades. *The Journal of Educational Research, 99*(3), 179–191.

Snow, C. E., Burns, S., & Griffin, P. (Eds.). (1998). *Preventing reading difficulties in young children*. Washington, DC: National Academy Press.

Snyder, I. (2008). *The literacy wars: Why teaching children to read and write is a battleground in Australia*. Crows Nest: Allen & Unwin.

Waters, W. (2014, November 15). Pearson, Langton, Mundine are not our leaders. *The Stringer*. http://thestringer.com.au/pearson-langton-mundine-are-not-our-leaders-9078#. Wi4TTExuLIU. Accessed 9 Sept 2017.

Dr. John McCollow, now retired, was a (non-Indigenous) research officer with the Queensland Teachers' Union. In this capacity he provided support for the union's Aboriginal and Torres Strait Islander Education Committee, Gandu Jarjum. In his teaching career, he worked with Indigenous students in rural and remote settings. He is currently a Visitor at the Queensland University of Technology.

Chapter 15
Good Theory, Good Systems: An Instance of Accelerated Literacy Pedagogy Implementation

Bronwyn Parkin

Abstract Accelerated Literacy pedagogy was implemented in many places in Australia in the 1990s and 2000s in remote Indigenous and other educationally disadvantaged school sites. The pedagogy has been evaluated many times, with mixed outcomes. Evaluation methodologies have varied widely, and student apparent growth data have proved difficult to collect. This chapter argues that a program so implemented in such varied contexts cannot be judged without due and separate regard to the theories that underpin the pedagogy and to the implementation processes in each context. The chapter offers the South Australian Accelerated Literacy Program (SAALP) as one example of an implementation site, managed by the author. After explaining the theoretical basis and intent of the pedagogy, I use criteria for effective implementation proposed by two McKinsey Reports and Fullan to analyse the implementation processes used in SAALP. I use NAPLAN effect size data for Reading and Writing, and Reading Comprehension growth data to demonstrate the effect of the program in mainstream South Australian schools across 3 years. The data show how the implementation strategies used in this context were able to show a sustained positive effect.

Introduction

This chapter begins with a personal reflection. I began working in Indigenous education in a remote desert community in the 1980s, in a bilingual instruction school. Our methods of teaching literacy were eclectic. One teacher taught English through recitation of nursery rhymes, others by getting students to write recounts of their weekend. I focused on transactional English, using role plays of the clinic and the store, with trips to a regional centre a 6-h drive away for consolidation. We worked

---

B. Parkin (✉)
University of Adelaide, Adelaide, SA, Australia
e-mail: bronwyn.parkin@adelaide.edu.au

© Springer Nature Singapore Pte Ltd. 2019
J. Rennie, H. Harper (eds.), *Literacy Education and Indigenous Australians*,
Language Policy 19, https://doi.org/10.1007/978-981-13-8629-9_15

so hard, and the outcomes were so poor. Later I moved to a low socio-economic metropolitan primary school with a high Indigenous enrolment. This cohort spoke Aboriginal English as their first dialect. We were a strong team: the principal, some classroom teachers, two Aboriginal Education Workers and me as the Aboriginal Education Teacher, all with extensive experience working with Indigenous students and community. We explicitly taught about dialect differences (Berry and Hudson 1997) and introduced standard Australian English, yet whatever we did, we struggled with teaching students the academic English, and particularly writing, that they needed to be successful at school and to be literate, fully participating citizens of Australia.

It was at this stage, in the late 1990s, that the principal and I were introduced to the next iteration of Brian Gray's work, Scaffolding Literacy (Gray et al. 2003; Rose et al. 1998). A group of teachers began to implement the pedagogy with their classes, as best we could. After 6 months, we had begun to see remarkable changes in Indigenous students: a growth in confidence, success in spelling, improvements in reading and a new willingness to write. So we persevered. Other teachers in the school felt the excitement and became involved. We won a national literacy award (APA 2000). Principals and teachers in other metropolitan schools heard the stories and began to visit to see the pedagogy in action. They too were motivated by their observations of marginalised students engaged confidently in literacy learning in the classroom.

At that point, there was positive evidence of effect from pilot programs simultaneously running in some remote Indigenous schools, but not from any scaled-up program. The results came from the small-scale implementation of what became known as the 'Scaffolding Literacy Program' (and subsequently the 'National Accelerated Literacy Program') in remote Indigenous schools (Gray and Cowey 2001, 2002; Gray et al. 2002). Quantitative evidence of the effectiveness of the pedagogy in metropolitan mainstream schools was not available at that time, apart from the short-term, small-scale data from our school (Parkin 1999, 2000, 2001). The imperative for the initiative to be 'evidenced based' (e.g. Mitchell 2013) was problematic because we were in the vanguard. We were creating the evidence. The motivation, therefore, for schools and individual teachers to take up the program developed by word of mouth and from observations of the pedagogy in action. Teachers implementing Accelerated Literacy (AL) pedagogy first noticed the positive effect on student confidence, rather than quantitative data from national assessment tools. A groundswell of support grew, and from this small, personal beginning, the South Australian Accelerated Literacy Program (SAALP) developed.

Two sets of factors contribute to the effectiveness of any literacy intervention. The first are the theoretical underpinnings and intentions of the program itself: that is the knowledge base that underpins the literacy program and its aims. In schools with educationally marginalised students, it might seem more practical and realistic to simply aim for students becoming proficient decoders through an off-the-shelf phonics program, but I argue that this is a social justice issue: we need to aim for a level of literacy that supports participatory citizenship in the twenty-first century (UNESCO 2006). The second set of factors is the program implementation model and how it supports and sustains teacher and school fidelity to the program. Not only is it a waste of the effort of all participants to partially implement a program, but without teacher adherence to a program's principles and processes, no assessment can be fairly made about the effectiveness of any literacy program.

In this chapter, I address both factors in relation to the South Australian Accelerated Literacy Program (SAALP), which I managed for several years. The underpinning theories of the Accelerated Literacy approach are documented elsewhere (Gray 1998, 2007), so here I explain how they contribute to the potential of a robust and thorough literacy program for educationally marginalised students, including Indigenous students. I argue that, while poor implementation of education programs for Indigenous students is identified as a factor of failure (e.g. Wilson 2013), developing a program implementation model that is sustained and works relentlessly to maintain rigour in difficult contexts is complex. SAALP provides an example of an implementation model previously undescribed. It maintained rigour and built capacity, taking the local context into account, and managed to do so for several years. To reflect on and evaluate this implementation model, I draw on the research findings of the McKinsey Report (Mourshed et al. 2010) and Fullan (2006, 2011). The findings identified a number of principles and drivers required to achieve sustained educational change. SAALP predominantly addressed the needs of rural and metropolitan Indigenous students in mainstream schools, rather than remote Indigenous schools, but I argue that a broader but carefully controlled and systematic implementation such as this is needed to develop sufficient program capacity to also support literacy education in remote Indigenous communities. Finally, I discuss current issues with data collection and make some recommendations about assessment processes that might contribute to more robust, reliable data.

The Theoretical Underpinnings of the Accelerated Literacy Program

The Accelerated Literacy program had its first iteration in the 1980s as *Concentrated Language Encounters (CLE)* (Gray 1984, 1990, 2014b; Gray and Cazden 1992). CLE was developed at Traeger Park Primary School, where Dr. Brian Gray was researching literacy pedagogy with students from the fringe camps of Alice Springs. He developed two distinct teaching and learning sequences at that time. The first supported the teaching of language and literacy through science; the second was pared down, designed to support the teaching of language and literacy through literature (Gray 2014a, b). The second version became *Scaffolding Literacy pedagogy*, with Gray working in collaboration with colleague Wendy Cowey in the Schools and Community Centre at Canberra University (Gray et al. 2003). Finally, after a name change prompted by the then federal minister of Education, who wanted a catchier title, it became the *National Accelerated Literacy Program* (e.g. Cresswell et al. 2002). In some respects, this was an unfortunate name change. It is true that there is often an exciting acceleration in student engagement in literacy as the pedagogy is introduced, but it also requires a significant shift by teachers to slow, systematic and painstaking work to capitalise on that initial change and consolidate early gains. Moreover, to attract funding, the pedagogy had to become an entity. What had been developed as a principled teaching and learning process was now labelled a 'program', a sequence of activities expected to reliably produce results, regardless of the user or the method of implementation.

Gray's 'scaffolding pedagogy' has solid theoretical foundations. His training as a psychologist grounded the pedagogy in cognitive developmental theories, such as the importance of attunement and alignment between adult and child (Stern 1985; Siegel 2001); the concept of cognitive load and the effect that has on learning (Kirschner et al. 2006); and the importance of maintaining positive affect between teacher and learner so that students are not marginalised and identify as members of the learning social group (Siegel 2001; Trevarthen 1998). These influences were followed by Vygotskian sociocultural theory (Vygotsky 1978; Wertsch 1985), Bernsteinian sociology (Bernstein 2000) and Hallidayan systemic functional linguistics (Halliday 1993; Hasan 2005). These theoretical fields provide complementary perspectives on pedagogy. Significantly, they recognised the cultural and social nature of learning and the importance of teachers making visible the cultural intent and purpose of what happens in the classroom, as well as teaching the powerful language of each learning area.

With the recognition that language development is central to successful learning, these theories led to the imperative for a more ambitious literacy program that not only taught reading, writing, phonics and vocabulary but reached beyond to explicitly teach the cultural subjectivities behind texts, grammar and vocabulary, i.e. language resources. Accelerated Literacy pedagogy works to develop a critical perspective so that students grow to understand the circumstances that influence language choice and to expand their language repertoire and literate perspectives for participation in many contexts.

The question then turns to how we might achieve those ambitious educational goals with AL pedagogic strategies. Bernstein classified different pedagogic approaches into four paradigms which take differing perspectives on the role of the teacher, the learner and the curriculum (1990, p. 72). Teaching can be explicit or implicit; that is, the curriculum goals and processes can be stated up front or left for students to discover. In some paradigms, students are expected to take responsibility for learning outcomes; in others it is the teacher, or accountability is shared between teacher and learners. The theories introduced above direct us to a pedagogy which is explicit, with responsibility negotiated between teacher and learner and with control gradually handed over to the learner (Gray 1998). This paradigm is described by Martin as 'subversive', because of its commitment to sharing powerful language and knowledge with educationally marginalised students, thereby challenging the social order (Martin 2011, p. 39).

Within the subversive language-focused pedagogic paradigm resides the notion of 'scaffolding': the process of handing over new learning to novices with the support of an 'informed other'. While the concept of the progressive sharing of consciousness between adult and child originated in the work of Vyotsky (1962), the term 'scaffolding' was first used by Wood, Bruner and Ross to describe the child-parent interactions in child development (Wood 1989; Wood et al. 1976). It was taken up by socioculturally influenced educators, particularly in the field of teaching English as a Second Language (Gibbons 2002; Hammond 2001). Central to this pedagogy is the principle of handover. Handover refers to the expectation that the teacher will provide a contingent level of support and that the child will eventually take control and successfully articulate the new learning (Bruner and Watson 1983). It is observable in the classroom as a pedagogic 'shuffle', as the teacher decreases and increases support moment by moment as students take over learning or alternatively begin to falter. There is sometimes confusion between the goal-oriented practice of scaffolding and the practice of 'piloting' (Lundgren 1981) or 'shepherding' (Sugrue 1997, p. 8) where the educator involves the student with a task in a way that only achieves the short-term goal of getting them to completion with no control and limited understanding and maintains dependence. In contrast, the subversive nature of scaffolding involves a shared understanding between teacher and students of the purpose and goals towards which learning activity is leading.

Situating literacy pedagogy for Indigenous students in the subversive, language-focused paradigm means that as teachers, we need to be able to articulate to students the social purpose and learning goals for every topic and every lesson. We also need to be knowledgeable about the powerful language for academic discourses so that students can take on new roles, and can appropriate and take control of *power texts, power language, power grammar* in each learning area (Martin 2013).

Because of the history of Indigenous communities and their place in Australia as the first nations, there is a strong commitment by many teachers to affirm students' home 'ways of knowing' Martin (2005), and an ambivalence about teaching new language and expanding their world view. This has led in the past to well-intentioned attempts to explicitly teach about dialect differences between Aboriginal English and standard Australian English. Gray argued that this was problematic:

> The result of constructing difference at the level of dialect for educators is that any attempt to promote change or development can only be seen in terms of 'trading off' one dialect for another. For this reason it is proposed that framing questions to do with the provision of access to mainstream education in terms of contrast between the linguistic constructs of Aboriginal English and standard English is inadequate. (Gray 1998, p. 45)

Gray's argument is one important reason to deflect attention from dialect differences. When two dialects, Aboriginal English and standard Australian English, are juxtaposed in the classroom, the teacher's appreciation for home language can sound hollow. The inference can be made that home language is somehow insufficient for the task of school learning and that is why they have to learn standard Australian English. A second reason is that teaching dialect differences does not account for the powerful discourse-specific language required for operating successfully in the learning areas. Many standard Australian English speakers would not sound authoritative when speaking about science or mathematics or literature without learning discourse-specific language. The subversive paradigm does not overlook students' existing cultural practices, but affirms their home experience, and commits to expanding repertoires of cultural practice, including being literate, so that they are able to make choices in the future.

The theories so far introduced provide a broad and united perspective on the principles and purposes of a literacy program. However, they don't address the fine detail of literacy teaching in the classroom, that is, how to teach discourse-specific listening and speaking, reading, writing and spelling to low socio-economic and ESL learners. A further theoretical paradigm had to be called on in developing Accelerated Literacy pedagogy, and that was the teaching of reading, writing and spelling. To do this, Gray and Cowey engaged with the findings of the influential US National Reading Panel (NRP 2000), drawing on, for example, Pressley (2002), Stahl (2002), Nicholson (1984) and Pearson (Pearson and Hiebert 2010), as well as the work of Kemp at the Schools and Community Centre in Canberra (1987). One response to the NRP findings is the 'Big Six' at the centre of literacy instruction: Phonics, Comprehension, Vocabulary, Oral Language, Spelling and Writing (Konza 2010, 2011). Isolating each aspect of literacy instruction as a separate category has often led teachers to teach them as separate, unconnected elements. To teach literacy in this siloed way does not explicitly show the interrelationship between each category and does not contribute to a coherent literacy program. This was one of the challenges faced as Gray and Cowey developed the program. The solutions will be explained below.

From this broad theoretical base, Gray and Cowey developed a systematic yet flexible teaching and learning routine which can be used in primary and secondary classrooms, along with a carefully refined questioning sequence (Gray 2007; NALP 2008a, b, c). They have provided a framework that acts as a macro-scaffold for literacy instruction, inside which the teaching and learning can take place in a consistent way. The routine centres the teaching of literacy around literature, beginning with the reading of a high quality, age-appropriate book, often well beyond the independent reading ability of the students. Before the class begins to read the book together, the teacher constructs a literate orientation, introducing the text type and its purpose, explaining themes, introducing the author and providing any necessary background knowledge. She/he will then read the book to the students, stopping to explain important inferences, as well as developing a literate orientation to images. Once they have listened to or read the text, the teacher then selects one or more passages for close study, underlining chunks of text to build meaning and begin decoding, and talking about the purpose and effect of the author's choices. By the end of this stage, most students can read the passage fluently and have a good understanding of the intent and messages of the passage. From there, the focus changes from a reader to a writer, from a decoder to an encoder. Parts of the text are displayed so that they can be manipulated, either written onto strips of cardboard or displayed on the interactive whiteboard. The literate resources identified during the close reading, such those used to build imagery or suspense, are isolated and named and practised so that students can use them in their own writing. This stage becomes the launching point for the spelling program. Words are selected from the passage to teach phonics, letter patterns and morphemes, as well as high frequency words (NALP 2008a). Using a literate text as a launching point for spelling does not conflict with more traditional teaching of decoding skills, but provides a means through which students can see the point of learning those skills, rather than viewing phonics and spelling as an abstract and isolated exercise.

Finally, when the language resources and spelling skills have all been practised, the students move into writing. The class first reconstructs the passage using the author's own words as an opportunity to combine spelling practice and discussion about the purpose of language, before jointly composing and producing a piece of text together, drawing on the literate resources provided in the original text. Some students then move to write independently, while others continue to write as a group using 'shared pen' with the teacher.

Phonics, comprehension, vocabulary, oral language, spelling and writing are all addressed but in a coherent, carefully staged sequence that systematically shifts from meaning to include decoding and encoding and develops student reading skills before using the same text resources to develop spelling and writing skills. Oral language and the development of a meta-language saturate every part of the teaching sequence through classroom dialogue. Interestingly, this routine preceded but is consistent with the framework and principles of the recently introduced Australian Curriculum English (ACARA).

There is sometimes a misconception that the AL teaching sequence is sufficient on its own to develop readers and writers, but of course time must be made for practice and consolidation of skills and knowledge in phonics, spelling, reading and writing once they have been introduced in the AL teaching sequence. Without practice, the new learning remains unstable.

The teaching sequence is not intended to be 'teacher-proof' but to support the quality of teaching. It is certainly not a quick-fix formula that produces literate students as the guaranteed outcome. Rather it is a careful, systematic routine that enables teacher and students to *give their attention less to choreographing the activity and more to the academic content* (Cazden 2001, p. 101) and proved, in the research phase (Cresswell et al. 2002), to be reliable and robust.

The principles of Accelerated Literacy pedagogy were applied in many different political and social contexts in Australia, with varying funding resources and with widely varying outcomes. I have explained why the theory and the teaching sequence are robust, cohesive and comprehensive and carry great potential for Indigenous students. However, to realise that potential requires an awareness and management of educational change processes. Understanding how to bring about sustained change is as important to success as the literacy and pedagogic principles. If teachers cherry-pick, teaching once a week or in an ad hoc way without attention to the classroom dialogue and questioning within each stage, no claim can be made about program effectiveness or failure. Only when the teaching sequence is implemented with fidelity can a valid evaluation of its effectiveness be carried out.

As an example of one implementation of Accelerated Literacy pedagogy, I introduce the South Australian Accelerated Literacy Program (SAALP), the program in which I worked from 2006 to 2014. I describe the implementation and management strategies that contributed to the program running for 9 years, an unusually long period of time at a time when *(C)ontemporary patterns of educational change*

278   B. Parkin

present educators with changes that are multiple, complex and sometimes contra-dictory (Hargreaves 2005, p. x) and when the imperative for innovation tends to encourage schools and systems to lurch from one direction to another, often too impatient to wait for a result.

Learning from the Implementation of the South Australian Accelerated Literacy Program (SAALP)

The South Australian Accelerated Literacy Program (SAALP) evolved from a short-term, federally funded Indigenous Literacy intervention: the Deadly Writin', Readin' and Talkin' (DWRAT) Project in one low socio-economic school (Parkin 1999, 2000, 2001). As 'Scaffolded Literacy', it moved to the Aboriginal Education Unit and later, as SAALP, was managed as part of the Curriculum section in the head office of the South Australian Department for Education and Child Development (DECD). It was a program for disadvantaged schools, mostly at primary school level, rather than a solely Indigenous-focused program, offered to state schools in Index of Disadvantage categories 1–4,[1] with priority given to schools with high Indigenous enrolments. In South Australia, 89% of Indigenous students speak Aboriginal English as their first dialect and are enrolled in the regional and metro-politan schools which were the program's target client group. In this way, the pro-gram commitment to Indigenous students continued.

Before I describe the program implementation model, I introduce the relevant educational contexts and the theoretical approach to educational change that was reflected in the model.

Understanding Educational Change

Educational change is notoriously difficult to sustain, particularly in the schools with which we worked. They were all low socio-economic. Many program schools had poor student attendance and high transience of students and were hard-to-staff with high teacher turnover, a frequent change of principals and a high proportion of new and inexperienced teachers and school leaders. Many had self-selected because their school literacy results were low, even when compared with similar schools. 25% were regional schools, ranging from a 2 to 10 h drive from Adelaide, the capi-tal city. Some schools had high enrolments of Indigenous students, while others

---

[1] In South Australia, schools are categorised using an Index of Disadvantage, ranging from 1 (high-est level of disadvantage) to 7 (lowest level of disadvantage.) The formula is similar to the national Index of Community Socio-Educational Advantage.

catered for high enrolments of English as a Second Language or Dialect (EALD) students. We also had a group of more stable metropolitan schools: while still low socio-economic status schools, they had stable and experienced staff and strong, stable and experienced leadership.

The McKinsey Report of 2010 identified different stages of educational change: there were schools and systems moving from poor to fair; fair to good; good to great; and great to excellent (Mourshed et al. 2010). Many SAALP schools began at poor or fair, with a small proportion of good or great. Despite McKinsey's argument that the school's stage of development requires different change strategies, SAALP had to support schools at all stages.

Accelerated Literacy pedagogy is not simple. It requires commitment, effort and discomfort as familiar teaching practices are unsettled and consciously replaced by new, more complex ones, providing consistent and systematic practice to support marginalised students from year to year. To commit to this change was difficult for some teachers in a system where most were accustomed to using their own, familiar pedagogic practices. Change was even more difficult in more challenging schools where teachers grappled with so many pressures in their day-to-day work. One important feature of the program was that, in building capacity, we were able to draw on the good and great schools to support the others.

The McKinsey Report of 2010 analysed successful interventions undertaken by 20 education systems. McKinsey contended that, to successfully change, three aspects of the school system must be considered. The first is the performance stage of the school as previously discussed. The second aspect is the intervention cluster. Successful schools select and *maintain the integrity of the implementation and... implement them with fidelity* (2010 p. 20). The third aspect is contextualising: *learning how to navigate the challenges of their context* (ibid). These factors were all under consideration in the development of SAALP.

Fullan (2011) extends this understanding by identifying four important drivers for school change, contrasted in Fig. 15.1 below with four commonly used but ineffective drivers:

Wrong	Right
Accountability	Capacity building
Individualistic solutions	Collaborative effort
Technology	Pedagogy
Fragmented strategies	Systemness

Fig. 15.1 Wrong vs right drivers for educational change (Fullan 2014)

280   B. Parkin

In analysing SAALP's implementation strategies, I have combined McKinsey's factors and Fullan's drivers to create the following principles:

1. *Rigorous pedagogy implemented with fidelity*: the challenges here were that many teachers believed in eclecticism; *I just choose the best bits and incorporate them into what I already do.* SAALP consultants asserted that it took 2 years for most teachers to use the pedagogy rigorously, and that was difficult, particularly in schools with high teacher turnover. Early on we recognised a one-term 'hump', where teachers were tired of feeling unsettled, where they had to be conscious of what they said at every point and nothing was stable. It was important that we could support teachers beyond the initial training through to competence. This was a particular challenge for regional and remote schools, where distance complicated matters.

2. *Capacity building* (recruitment, scaling up and capacity building at school and program level): in contexts such as those SAALP worked in, building capacity meant working at all levels of competence. We had to have highly competent AL consultants to build teacher competence, and we had to have competent school leaders. The inexperience of some school leaders proved to be high risk for the program; leaders who wanted to be the teachers' friend, in comparison with those who had the strength to support teachers through moments of challenging and unsettling pedagogic change.

3. *Collaborative effort* (intra- and inter-school and intra-program): for the pedagogy to be effectively implemented in all school sites, the SAALP consultant team had to work collaboratively with leaders and teachers. In addition, strong school leaders had to support less experienced ones to establish a collegiate but professional culture in their schools.

4. *Building systematic support responding to local contexts*: SAALP had to balance the maintenance of systematic, rigorous support with the imperative to scale up. We also had to meet the varying needs of all program schools, regardless of their stage of development.

5. *Accountability and data collection*: despite Fullan's argument that accountability is not a useful driver for initiating educational change, SAALP operated within a culture where NAPLAN, the national literacy and numeracy test (ACARA 2008), had become the only measurement that mattered for accountability. Despite SAALP's unusual 'grass-roots' foundation, for the program to continue, there had to be evidence of outcomes. The effort required to collect reliable data was much greater than we could have imagined. The issues we faced at teacher, school and system level would resonate with any educational intervention, particularly in schools at the poor-to-fair stage of development.

Rigorous Pedagogy Implemented with Fidelity

Part 1 of this chapter has introduced the theoretical basis and rigorous nature of the pedagogy as developed by Gray and Cowey. The 4 days of professional development workshops, using National Accelerated Literacy Program materials (NALP

2008a, b, c) provided an intense but nationally consistent basis for classroom implementation.

The challenge of ensuring fidelity to the program in schools was ongoing. Students, especially educationally marginalised students, need redundancy of information to support learning (Hammond 2001), and the high absentee rate of students in many SAALP schools made this even more crucial. A piecemeal approach was a waste of precious resources: a waste of consultant and teacher time and a waste of funds for the principal who had to pay for the training and consultant support. Minimum program requirements were basic: the teacher attended the 4 days of workshops; they planned and implemented the AL teaching sequence at least 4 days per week, working towards an hour per day; and they agreed to work with a consultant, planning, team teaching, being observed and receiving feedback. Any less time or effort than this had little chance of success.

In other jurisdictions, schools were given a grant to establish Accelerated Literacy pedagogy in their school. In South Australia, the grass roots development of the program meant that for some time, no grant funds were available. If schools wanted to be involved, they had to pay. Ironically, this proved to be a great advantage. Because school principals had invested their own school funds into the program, they had greater ownership and a greater interest in ensuring that they got value for money.

Schools interested in joining SAALP committed to a minimum of 2 years. This was the time we estimated was needed to develop teachers to a minimum level. A maximum of six teachers were nominated to be trained and supported by a SAALP consultant who visited the school 1 day per fortnight. We accepted teachers on the terms listed above to maintain fidelity, perhaps not sufficient in all cases but the best we could do. After those first 2 years, school commitment and fidelity were reviewed by the SAALP team. If schools or teachers could not demonstrate commitment to program implementation, an exit was negotiated if necessary.

The SAALP consultants played a pivotal role in ensuring program fidelity. Their planning and observation of teachers in their classrooms provided detailed information on teacher quality and effort, and they negotiated with the principal each year on the level of consultant support required to develop and maintain quality teaching and learning.

Early in the program, a researcher was engaged to find correlations between the conditions we thought were important for school implementation of AL, and LAN (Literacy and Numeracy) test results. This was a small-scale research project, looking at the literacy outcomes of the 25 SAALP schools at the time (Westhorp 2008).

The findings were consistent with the factors identified by the McKinsey report for bringing about school improvement. Most significantly, the 4-lesson guideline correlated with a 1 point or 4-month improvement in LAN scores. Other important conditions included the provision and organisation of adequate teaching and learning resources; support for teachers to attend professional development workshops; and the attendance by the school principal at AL workshops. It should not be a surprise that there was also a correlation between increased LAN outcomes and reduced interruptions during AL lessons, such as withdrawing students, holding excursions and events during literacy time as well as loudspeaker and phone interruptions during lessons.

Teacher volunteerism also correlated with improved outcomes. Volunteerism occurred at two levels. Firstly, teachers already in the school had to volunteer to be part of the program. Secondly, agreeing to be trained in and use AL pedagogy and to be supported by a consultant could be made a condition of employment for new teachers, and this level of volunteerism also showed a positive correlation.

Finally, structural factors, such as keeping AL implementation on the staff meeting agenda and having organised systems for data collection, also had an impact. Westhorp's 2008 conclusion was that there was not one 'magic bullet' but good implementation overall (ibid).

Westhorp's conditions for effective implementation became the basis for the 'Effective School Rubric' (SAALP 2013) which supported schools to reflect on their motivations, school structures, people and resourcing. The rubric alerted principals to the level of effort required for effective implementation; it was used by schools to review their implementation processes and make plans for the following year; and the SAALP team used the rubric when deciding whether a school would continue with us in the following year.

Capacity Building

The SAALP professional learning pathway was the core work of the SAALP team: manager and consultants together. Its quality and scope were essential for building system-wide and school capacity. The pathway provided learning opportunities for novices, to competent teachers to curriculum leaders. Our funding model encouraged teachers to keep on learning: schools paid a considerable sum for their nominated teachers to attend the initial, non-negotiable training. We used those funds to pay for additional professional development workshops and programs which were offered at no cost for potential lead teachers and curriculum leaders.

In addition to the 4-day *Introduction to Accelerated Literacy,* we offered a 2-year *SAALP Accreditation* process. Teachers engaged with theory and practice, videoing and critiquing their own lessons. AL accreditation assisted teachers with job applications for other SAALP schools, serving as a quality marker for school principals.

Our *Curriculum leaders' days* each term provided an opportunity for AL consultants to share their own theoretical and practical understandings and for teachers to engage further with, and articulate the principles of the teaching sequence. All workshops offered on that day were available for curriculum leaders to offer at their own sites.

SAALP offered a number of scholarships to South Australian teachers each year to undertake the *Graduate Certificate in Accelerated Literacy* designed and coordinated by Gray and offered through Charles Darwin University. Over the 8 years of the program, more than 50 South Australian teachers gained their Graduate Certificate. These teachers had a depth of understanding of the theory and practice of AL and a good working knowledge of systemic functional linguistics (Halliday

1993) that assisted them in applying for, and carrying out, curriculum leadership roles, including our consultant role.

Open classrooms: SAALP's strongest schools, those who might be labelled by McKinsey as moving from good to great, opened their classrooms for demonstrations of best practice for visiting teachers and principals. Teachers with Accreditation or a Graduate Certificate were expected to be able to demonstrate and talk about the teaching sequence to other educators. Open classrooms strengthened the capacity of each of those schools, as well as strengthening the program. Talking principal to principal and teacher to teacher played an important role in presenting the program as it was enacted in a school site.

Collaborative Effort

The success of the program was due, not just to rigorous pedagogy, but to the combined, relentless work of the SAALP team, school principals and teachers. An important initiative was the SAALP Steering committee, comprised of principals of SAALP schools from different regions. They became a powerful lobby group, establishing implementation policy and liaising with curriculum leaders in head office. Importantly, they offered themselves as mentors for principals new to the program, on top of their existing responsibilities. Changes in school leadership were a risk point for the program, and contact with other principals helped with induction.

It became quickly apparent that the strength, vision, commitment and determination of school leaders had the greatest influence on program implementation. The strongest principals recognised that increasing teacher capacity and competence was a priority. They attended the initial workshops with their teachers. They implemented the program initially with volunteer teachers and allowed the enthusiasm to spread, rather than force all existing staff to comply. They did not use consultant classroom support as a punishment for underperforming teachers, but offered it as a privilege to teachers who were committed to improving their practice. They offered release time to teachers doing further study, in recognition of their effort. They expected a weekly teaching and learning plan from their teachers. They anticipated the implementation slump after a few weeks, when teachers new to the program had unsettled their old routines and had not re-established new routines, and they supported their teachers through that phase, while holding firm. They did not try to implement a suite of new educational initiatives all at once, but allowed teachers to focus their attention on Accelerated Literacy pedagogy until they were confident. When they recruited new teachers, they stipulated that Accelerated Literacy was the school literacy pedagogy and that attending the workshops and being supported by a consultant, including classroom observations, was a condition of employment.

The role of the SAALP-accredited teachers and Graduate Certificate graduates was also important in demonstrating and articulating best practice to visiting teachers. It was difficult for teachers in hard-to-staff schools to observe experienced AL teachers in action in their local settings, and these more experienced teachers showed what was possible.

Building Systematic Support

The most important aspect of SAALP's systematic support was the role of the SAALP consultants. They played a pivotal role in supporting all the drivers of educational change: they helped to maintain rigour and fidelity to the program, they built capacity, and they worked collaboratively with principals and teachers. Their quality, consistency and commitment cannot be overstated. Most had completed the Graduate Certificate in Accelerated Literacy through Charles Darwin University and had been implementing AL pedagogy in their own schools for a minimum of 2 years but usually much more.

The consultant planned, demonstrated lessons, shared the teaching, observed lessons and provided feedback to teachers. Deprivatisation of the classroom has been shown to strongly contribute to change in teacher practice (Vanblaere and Devos 2016) and was initially very difficult for some teachers. However, without that strategy, we could not effectively support teachers in improving their practice. Over time, this became normalised.

The schools with the greatest need, with high numbers of inexperienced staff, high absenteeism and high teacher and leader turnover, and therefore the least capacity for bringing about change, were those in regional and remote areas. To ensure that they could receive quality support, all our consultants had a travel component and worked with some regional schools. The strategy of providing external, regular long-distance support was expensive and slowed down our scale-up. We would not overload any consultant with too much travel, and we would not take on a regional school unless we could provide consultant support.

The consultants continued to refine their own practice and deepen their theoretical understanding as part of their role, and shared the delivery of the 4-day *Introduction to Accelerated Literacy* state-wide each year. They developed and maintained professional relationships with hundreds of classroom teachers, walking the fine line between maintaining rigour and being sympathetic to teacher needs. The degree to which we expanded each year was determined by the number of available quality consultants.

Accountability and Data

While accountability and data may not be the most important drivers to initiate educational change (Fullan 2011), student improvement is of course an important driver for continuing and developing a program. We included for data collection, only students whose teachers demonstrated fidelity to program implementation:

simply teachers who had completed all 4 days of the introductory workshops, had been supported by a consultant and were planning thoroughly and teaching literacy using the AL teaching sequence at least 4 days per week.

Small-scale interventions like SAALP share issues with data collection. Comparing SAALP students with non-SAALP students in like schools proved unreliable, particularly with schools moving in and out of the program, with students moving in and out of AL classes and with highly transient student populations. After a number of attempts at systematic data collection, the most rational solution was to use two assessment tools. The first was the National Assessment – Literacy and Numeracy (NAPLAN). The second was TORCH, the Test of Reading Comprehension, a rigorous reading comprehension test developed by the Australian Council for Education Research (ACER 2003). Our TORCH results were independently analysed by ACER psychometricians each year. With both tools, we measured the change in individual student scores so that we could track growth.

SAALP NAPLAN Results

Because students participate in NAPLAN every 2 years in May, we collected data for students who had been with an AL teacher for a minimum of 6 months prior to a NAPLAN test. This gave us student results in Reading, Writing, Spelling, Grammar and Punctuation spanning the influence of at least two AL teachers (the year of the test and the previous year).

We calculated effect size, which takes into account growth plus standard deviation, that is the range of student performance in any cohort (Hattie 1992). It avoids the bias of a small group of high- or low-performing students skewing average performance:

> 'Effect size' is simply a way of quantifying the size of the difference between two groups. It is easy to calculate, readily understood and can be applied to any measured outcome in Education or Social Science. It is particularly valuable for quantifying the effectiveness of a particular intervention, relative to some comparison. It allows us to move beyond the simplistic, 'Does it work or not?' to the far more sophisticated, 'How well does it work in a range of contexts?' Moreover, by placing the emphasis on the most important aspect of an intervention - the size of the effect - rather than its statistical significance (which conflates effect size and sample size), it promotes a more scientific approach to the accumulation of knowledge. For these reasons, effect size is an important tool in reporting and interpreting effectiveness. (Coe 2002)

Each year, for students in Years 5, 7 and 9 who had completed two consecutive NAPLAN tests 2 years apart, we compared the 2-year effect size for SAALP students with the effect size for Years 5, 7 and 9 for the SA Education Department (DECD) in NAPLAN. For the sake of brevity, only data from Reading and Writing are shown here. All SAALP NAPLAN data can be found in Parkin (2014).

In Reading, across the years 2010–2013, SAALP showed a greater effect size than DECD in 9 out of 11 possible test instances. SAALP Year 5 and Year 7 averaged

126% and 125%, respectively, of the DECD effect size in Reading across the 4 years of data collection. SAALP Year 9 students averaged 121% of DECD effect size across 3 years.

In Writing, across the years 2010–2013, SAALP students showed a greater effect size when compared with DECD in 10 out of 11 possible test instances. SAALP Year 5 and Year 7 averaged 115% and 127%, respectively, of the DECD effect size in Writing across the 4 years of data collection. SAALP Year 9 students averaged 324% of DECD effect size in Writing across 3 years. (The effect on Year 9 Writing can be explained because secondary schools used SAALP as a remedial program for their lowest performing students who could therefore show significant gain when compared with other competent Year 9 writers. This fact does not diminish the value of the effect size.) Unfortunately, almost all secondary schools had exited the program before our final year because of issues with fidelity of implementation.

SAALP NAPLAN Results for Indigenous Students

Aboriginal and Torres Strait Islander (ATSI) student data was disaggregated and analysed separately each year. The cohorts of Indigenous students in SAALP schools were small; ranging from 77 to 23 in each NAPLAN year level. (Effect size becomes unstable when calculated with small cohorts, so the results should be seen as encouraging but treated with caution.) The performance of SAALP Indigenous students was compared with the disaggregated cohort of DECD Indigenous students each year.

In Reading across the years 2010–2013, SAALP showed a greater effect size than DECD for Indigenous students in seven out of eight possible test instances. SAALP Indigenous Year 5 students averaged 157% and Indigenous Year 7 students 143% of the DECD effect size in Reading, across the 4 years of data collection.

In Writing across the years 2010–2013, SAALP showed a greater effect size than DECD for Indigenous students in eight out of eight possible test instances. SAALP Indigenous Year 5 students averaged 166% and Indigenous Year 7 students 178% of the DECD effect size in Writing, across the 4 years of data collection.

While the size of Indigenous cohorts for whom we had two consecutive tests is small, averaging 35 students per test, we are nevertheless encouraged by the sustained positive gap between DECD effect size and the effect size for SAALP Indigenous students, particularly in Writing, an area of consistent underperformance in NAPLAN by Indigenous students.

These positive results from the final 4 years of the program are understandable because they came from SAALP schools with sustained commitment and with teachers who were implementing the program with fidelity. They were not all experts, but they were trying their hardest to implement AL pedagogy in a rigorous way, and the improved effect size appears to be cumulative.

SAALP TORCH Results

The second assessment tool was TORCH, a rigorous assessment tool for reading comprehension (ACER 2003) which was administered at the end of each year to understand the impact of SAALP on students' reading comprehension over 1 year. Our annual data were analysed externally by TORCH psychometricians (ACER 2011, 2012, 2013).

SAALP students demonstrated growth in reading comprehension greater than the ACER normed cohort in 14 out of 17 test instances. These changes in student outcomes are statistically significant with 95% confidence (ACER 2011, 2012, 2013). SAALP Indigenous students demonstrated growth in reading comprehension greater than the ACER normed cohort in eight out of ten test instances (ACER 2011, 2012, 2013).

Good Theory, Good Systems

Accelerated Literacy pedagogy and the teaching sequence, when well implemented, proved in the South Australian context to be a thorough and reliable teaching method for teaching literacy. It teaches reading, spelling and writing in a cohesive and coherent manner, working cumulatively and iteratively to build understanding and skills. However, it takes time and support for teachers to develop and take control of the methodology as an inservice intervention. Wilson stated in his recent report into literacy education in remote Northern Territory schools, *the experience of AL and other programs is that complex programs requiring high fidelity in implementation are at greater risk of failure* (Wilson 2013, p. 124). Conversely, SAALP has shown that a well-implemented quality program requires effort but has a chance of sustained success.

A perpertual issue in 'hard-to-staff' schools is that of teacher and leader turnover which means that upskilling teachers to work with marginalised students is expensive but will never stop. This is a given, and not impossible in a wealthy country like Australia. The McKinsey Report emphasised the need for tight control of teacher practice in poor-to-fair schools, but we have to use that control to develop quality teachers of comprehensive programs rather than 'teacher-proof' programs if our efforts are to lead to long-term improvement. Because the poor-to-fair schools in SAALP were part of a bigger system, we were able to strengthen those schools by systematically building capacity in the good-to-great schools and sharing it. We created a community of reflexive teachers who passed on their enthusiasm to others. It will never be easy to support remote schools, but expectations of 'giving back' from high quality teachers and leaders can be built into a program plan.

SAALP was founded as a grass roots program, the impetus to scale up coming from the schools already involved. The great advantage of this was school buy-in and commitment and the fact that we were not required to scale up so fast that rigour and fidelity were reduced. We scaled up according to capacity. The disadvantage was the system-wide discomfort with the program. The pedagogy was deemed too hard, labelled as 'boutique'. I assert that if the level of rigour and effort demonstrated here produces quality teachers for educationally marginalised students, then we have no choice but to keep working towards this in a slow, rigorous and sustained way.

I began with a personal reflection, and I end with another. After more than 30 years working in Indigenous education, I know there is no quick fix. Australia is a context where, for many marginalised students, success at school may appear to have little connection to work and futures, and there is no compelling economic driver to attend school or become literate. Nevertheless, without literacy, participatory citizenship is unlikely. That means that every moment of our interactions with students counts. Each moment has to maintain positive affect and move towards academic success. Drawing on good theory and developing good systems gives us our best chance to achieve positive outcomes.

References

ACARA (2008). *National Assessment Program, Literacy and Numeracy (NAPLAN)*. Melbourne: Australian Curriculum, Assessment and Reporting Authority. https://www.nap.edu.au/

ACER. (2003). *Test of reading comprehension (TORCH)*. Melbourne: Australian Council of Education Research.

ACER. (2011). *SAALP Test of reading comprehension (TORCH) growth analysis*. Camberwell, Victoria: ACER.

ACER. (2012). *SAALP Test of reading comprehension (TORCH) growth analysis*. Camberwell, Victoria: ACER.

ACER. (2013). *SAALP Test of reading comprehension (TORCH) growth analysis*. Camberwell, Victoria: ACER.

APA. (2000). *Excellence in leadership in Indigenous education award*. Sydney: Australian Principals' Association Professional Development Council.

Bernstein, B. (1990). *Class, codes and control No 4: The structuring of pedagogic discourse*. London/New York: Routledge.

Bernstein, B. (2000). *Pedagogy, symbolic control, and identity: Theory, research, critique*. Maryland: Rowman & Littlefield.

Berry, R., & Hudson, J. (1997). *Making the jump: a resource book for teachers of Aboriginal students*. Broome: Catholic Education Office.

Bruner, J. S., & Watson, R. (1983). *Child's talk: Learning to use language*. Oxford: Oxford University Press.

Cazden, C. B. (2001). *Classroom discourse: the language of teaching and learning*. Portsmouth: Heinemann.

Coe, R. (2002). *It's the effect size, stupid: What effect size is and why it is important*. Paper presented at the annual conference of the British Educational Research Association, University of Exeter, UK.

Cresswell, J., Underwood, C., & Withers, G. (2002). *Evaluation of the scaffolding literacy program with Indigenous children in school*. Melbourne: ACER.

Fullan, M. (2006). The future of educational change: System thinkers in action. *Journal of Educational Change, 7*(3), 113–122.

Fullan, M. (2011). *Choosing the wrong drivers for whole system reform*. Melbourne: CSE.

Fullan, M. (2014). *The principal: Three keys to maximizing impact*. San Francisco: John Wiley & Sons, Incorporated.

Gibbons, P. (2002). *Scaffolding language, scaffolding learning. Teaching second language learners in the mainstream classroom*. Portsmouth: Heinemann.

Gray, B. (1984). *Helping children to become language learners in the classroom*. Darwin: Northern Territory Department of Education.

Gray, B. (1990). Natural language learning in aboriginal classrooms: Reflections on teaching and learning style for empowerment in English. In C. Walton & W. Eggington (Eds.), *Language maintenance and education in Australian aboriginal contexts* (pp. 105–139). Darwin: NTU Press.

Gray, B. (1998). *Accessing the discourses of schooling*. Dissertation, University of Melbourne.

Gray, B. (2007). *Accelerating the literacy development of Indigenous students: The National Accelerated Literacy Program (NALP)*. Darwin: Charles Darwin University Press.

Gray, B. (2014a). *The accelerated literacy program: Developmental outline*. ALPAA. http://www.alpaa.com.au/resources/publications

Gray, B. (2014b). *The Traeger Park project: Developmental outline*. ALPAA. http://www.alpaa.com.au/resources/publications

Gray, B., & Cazden, C. B. (1992). *Concentrated language encounters: International biography of a curriculum concept*. Paper presented at the 26th annual TESOL Convention, Vancouver.

Gray, B., & Cowey, W. (2001). *University of Canberra accelerated literacy program: First report to the Northern Territory department of education and training*. Melbourne: University of Canberra.

Gray, B., & Cowey, W. (2002). *University of Canberra accelerated literacy program: Third report to the Northern Territory department of education and training*. Canberra: University of Canberra.

Gray, B., Gray, P., & Cowey, W. (2002). *University of Canberra accelerated literacy program: Second report to the Northern Territory department of education and training*. Canberra: University of Canberra.

Gray, B., Cowey, W., & Axford, B. (2003). *Scaffolding literacy with Indigenous children in school. Final report to the Indigenous education branch, DETYA*. Canberra: University of Canberra.

Halliday, M. A. K. (1993). Towards a language-based theory of learning. *Linguistics and Education, 5*(2), 93–116.

Hammond, J. (2001). *Scaffolding: Teaching and learning in the language and literacy classroom*. Newtown: PETAA.

Hargreaves, A. (2005). *Extending educational change*. Dordrecht: Springer.

Hasan, R. (2005). Semiotic mediation, language and society: Three exotropic theories – Vygotsky, Halliday and Bernstein. In J. J. Webster (Ed.), *Language, society and consciousness: Ruqaiya Hasan*. London: Equinox.

Hattie, J. (1992). Measuring the effects of school. *Australian Journal of Education, 36*(1).

Kemp, M. (1987). *Watching children read and write*. Victoria: Deakin University.

Kirschner, P. A., Sweller, J., & Clark, R. E. (2006). Why minimal guidance during instruction does not work: An analysis of the failure of constructivist, discovery, problem-based, experiential and inquiry-based teaching. *Educational Psychologist, 41*(2), 75–86.

Konza, D. (2010). *Understanding the reading process*. Adelaide: DECS.

Konza, D. (2011). *Phonological awareness*. Adelaide: DECS.

Lundgren, U. (1981). *Model analysis of pedagogical processes*, 2nd edn, Stockholm: CWK Gleerup.

Martin, K. (2005). Childhood, lifehood and relatedness: Aboriginal ways of being, knowing and doing. In J. Phillips & J. Lampert (Eds.), *Introductory Indigenous studies in education: The importance of knowing*. Frenchs Forest: Pearson Education Australia.

Martin, J. R. (2011). Bridging troubled waters: Interdisciplinarity and what makes it stick. In F. Christie & K. Maton (Eds.), *Disciplinarity: Functional linguistic and sociological perspectives*. London: Continuum.

Martin, J. R. (2013). Embedded literacy: Knowledge as meaning. *Linguistics and Education, 24*(1), 23–27.

Mitchell, D. (2013). *What really works in special and inclusive education: Using evidence-based teaching strategies*. London: Routledge.

Mourshed, M., Chikioke, C., & Barber, M. (2010). *How the world's most improved school systems keep getting better*. McKinsey Report. McKinsey & Company.

NALP. (2008a). *AL teaching sequence*. Melbourne: Curriculum Corporation.

NALP. (2008b). *Practitioner guide: Lesson observation and classroom support*. Melbourne: Curriculum Corporation.

NALP. (2008c). *Questioning techniques*. Melbourne: Curriculum Corporation.

Nicholson, T. (1984). *The process of reading: An introduction to theory and practice in the teaching of reading*. Cammeray: Martin Educational.

NRP. (2000). *Report of the national reading panel: Teaching children to read*. Rockville: NRP.

Parkin, B. (1999). *Deadly readin' writin' and talkin' project annual report: We're on to something*. Adelaide: Salisbury North R-7 School. http://www.alpaa.com.au/resources/publications

Parkin, B. (2000). *Deadly readin' writin' and talkin' project annual report: On the move*. Adelaide: Salisbury North R-7 School. http://www.alpaa.com.au/resources/publications

Parkin, B. (2001). *Deadly readin' writin' and talkin' project annual report: Getting somewhere*. Adelaide: Salisbury North R-7 School. http://www.alpaa.com.au/resources/publications

Parkin, B. (2014). *South Australian accelerated literacy program: Final report*. Adelaide: DECD. https://www.alpaa.com.au/resources/reports/parkin-b-2014-saalp-final-report-adelaide-saalp

Pearson, P. D., & Hiebert, E. H. (2010). National reports in literacy. *Educational Researcher, 39*(4), 286–294.

Pressley, M. (2002). *Reading instruction that works: The case for balanced teaching*. New York: Guildford Press.

Rose, D., Gray, B., & Cowey, W. (1998). Providing access to academic literate discourse for Indigenous learners. *Ngoonjook, 15*, 62–70.

SAALP (2013). *Effective school Rubric' DECD*. Adelaide: SAALP. https://www.alpaa.com.au/sites/default/files/downloads/fs10_effective_school_rubric_2013.pdf

Siegel, D. J. (2001). Toward an interpersonal neurobiology of the developing mind: Attachment relationships, mindsight, and neural integration. *Infant Mental Health Journal, 22*(1), 67–94.

Stahl, S. (2002). *Phonics they really use: Phonics in a balanced literacy program*. Paper presented at the CIERA, Georgia.

Stern, D. (1985). Affect attunement: Mechanisms and clinical implications. In J. Call, E. Galenson, & R. Tyson (Eds.), *Frontiers of infant psychiatry* (Vol. 2). New York: Basic Books.

Sugrue, C. (1997). *Complexities of teaching: Child-centred perspectives*. London: Falmer Press.

Trevarthen, C. (1998). The child's need to learn a culture. In M. Woodhead (Ed.), *Cultural worlds of early childhood*. London: Routledge.

UNESCO. (2006). Why literacy matters. In *Education for all: Global monitoring report*. Paris: UNESCO.

Vanblaere, B., & Devos, G. (2016). Exploring the link between experienced teachers' learning outcomes and individual and professional learning community characteristics. *School Effectiveness and School Improvement, 27*(2), 205–227.

Vygotsky, L. S. (1978). *Mind in society: The development of higher psychological processes*. Cambridge: Harvard University Press.

Vyotsky, L. S. (1962). *Thought and language*. Cambridge: MIT Press.

Wertsch, J. V. (1985). *Culture, communication, and cognition: Vygotskian perspectives*. Cambridge: CUP.

Westhorp, J. (2008). *Effective contexts for accelerated literacy*. Adelaide: DECD. http://www.alpaa.com.au/resources/publications

Wilson, B. (2013). *A share in the future: The review of Indigenous education in the Northern Territory*. Darwin: NTDETE.

Wood, D. J. (1989). Social interaction as tutoring. In M. H. Bornstein & J. S. Bruner (Eds.), *Interaction in human development*. Hillsdale: L. Erlbaum Associates.

Wood, D. J., Bruner, J., & Ross, G. (1976). The role of tutoring in problem solving. *Journal of Child Psychology and Psychiatry, 17*(2), 89–100.

Dr. Bronwyn Parkin is an adjunct lecturer in Linguistics at the University of Adelaide and a literacy consultant with a long history of working in literacy education with Aboriginal and low socio-economic students. For many years, she was a Literacy Development project officer in the Literacy Secretariat, South Australian Department of Education, and managed the South Australian Accelerated Literacy Program. Together with Dr. Helen Harper from the University of New England, New South Wales, she was a recent recipient of a PETAA research grant, with a project called *Scaffolding academic language with educationally marginalised students*.

Chapter 16
'A Strong Belief in the Possibility of a Better Life': The Pedagogy of Contingency and the Ethic of Solidarity in the *Yes, I Can!* Aboriginal Adult Literacy Campaign

Bob Boughton and Frances Williamson

Abstract The widespread social and economic inequality between Aboriginal and non-Aboriginal Australia is unlikely to change unless the people who are most marginalised themselves become more able to intervene effectively in the economic, social and political processes and practices which continue to reproduce this situation. For a number of reasons, this requires a level of English language literacy which a large proportion of those most in need have so far been unable to acquire. While the current focus in Indigenous education policy is almost solely on children's literacy, this chapter suggests a different approach. *Yes, I Can!* (Yo, Si Puedo) is a Cuban mass literacy campaign model that is currently being deployed for the first time in Australia in north-western NSW in the Murdi Paaki Region. We report on the first 4 years of the campaign, which is led by an Aboriginal organisation, the Literacy for Life Foundation (LFLF). Between 2012 and 2015, four communities joined the campaign, enrolling 150 participants in 6 months of literacy instruction and practice provided by locally recruited facilitators, who were supported by a small team of professional advisers. Having achieved a successful completion rate of 69%, which is several times greater than comparable formal courses, the campaign has now extended into three more communities. Through our analysis of qualitative data gained through interviews with participants, staff and local agencies who took part between 2012 and 2015, we highlight two aspects of the campaign model which help explain this success, namely, a pedagogy of contingency and an ethic of solidarity.

B. Boughton · F. Williamson (✉)
University of New England, Armidale, NSW, Australia
e-mail: rboughto@une.edu.au; fwilli20@une.edu.au

© Springer Nature Singapore Pte Ltd. 2019   293
J. Rennie, H. Harper (eds.), *Literacy Education and Indigenous Australians*,
Language Policy 19, https://doi.org/10.1007/978-981-13-8629-9_16

Introduction

There is almost total unanimity among educators, politicians and policymakers that low levels of literacy seriously impact on people's life chances. The main policy response, over recent decades, has been to concentrate on achieving improvements through schools. This focus has only increased with the introduction of national and international measurement, assessment and benchmarking regimes, such as NAPLAN and PISA. To date, there has been very little shift in the pattern of inequality in English language literacy outcomes between Indigenous and non-Indigenous school students. NSW Aboriginal education academic Kevin Lowe cites a 2012 Report of the NSW Auditor General:

> Notwithstanding gains and losses at individual schools, there has been no significant improvement in the overall performance of Aboriginal students in national and State tests— either in terms of absolute performance or in terms of the gap between Aboriginal and non-Aboriginal students. Despite efforts to close the gap, it has shown no signs of diminishing. (NSW Auditor General 2012, p. 2; cited Lowe 2017, p. 37)

Meanwhile, very little attention has been paid to the gap in adult literacy rates. This is a serious omission, for several reasons. Parental literacy activities have been repeatedly shown to be an important influence on children's literacy and school success (OECD 2012). Beyond that, low adult literacy is associated with a range of problems including reduced employment prospects, poor physical and mental health, higher rates of incarceration and substance abuse (Reder and Bynner 2008), which all, in turn, impact on families' ability to engage with education in a multitude of ways.

Previous research has strongly emphasised the role of parents and extended family in home literacy practices and intergenerational learning in facilitating children's transition to school as well as supporting their literacy and numeracy development (Brooks et al. 2008; Carpentieri et al. 2011). This is particularly so in indigenous communities in which there is a strong culture of families and communities learning alongside each other (ALA 2014; Hanson 2012). However, supporting children's early cognitive, linguistic and preliteracy development can be challenging for parents and caregivers who themselves experience difficulties with reading and writing. Extended family structures also mean that there are many more significant adults in a child's life beyond biological parents and grandparents whose own education and literacy levels will potentially have an impact on those of the next generation. For this reason alone, a stronger focus on adult literacy would be warranted.

However, adult family members with poor English language literacy almost invariably experience a whole raft of other disadvantages, misfortunes and subtle and not-so-subtle forms of racism and oppression – in relation to their incomes and employment (Shomos and Forbes, 2014), their housing, their interactions with the police and justice system (Hunter et al. 2006) and their physical and emotional health (Biddle 2006). This in turn impacts on the ability of children from those households to attend and engage in schooling. In these circumstances, the lack of attention to adult literacy virtually guarantees the continued reproduction of educational inequality.

Conservative estimates suggest no less than 40% of Aboriginal and Torres Strait Islander adults have low levels of English language literacy, a figure which rises much higher in many rural and remote communities (Boughton 2009b). This is not a new discovery. In 1988, the Aboriginal Education Policy Task Force, chaired by Aboriginal educator Paul Hughes, recommended that the Commonwealth Government negotiate with the states and territories to:

> develop and implement a national Aboriginal literacy strategy aimed to significantly increase the opportunities available to Aboriginal adults to improve their literacy skills … as a result of the lack of education provided for Aboriginal people it can be assumed that at least one half of the Aboriginal population is illiterate or functionally illiterate. The need for a national strategy is vital (Hughes, 1988, p. 33).

Thirty years on, there remains no such strategy. Adult literacy does not appear, for example, in the Close the gap targets. Instead, funding and programs created to support adult literacy development in the general population remain the only and quite ineffective option. Mainstream approaches to adult literacy have mostly taken the form of pre-vocational training, delivered via the accredited Certificate One and Certificate Two level courses offered through public and private registered training organisations (RTOs) in the national vocational education and training (VET) system. Some places in these courses are funded for registered Aboriginal jobseekers with low literacy, through the Commonwealth Skills for Education and Employment program. Despite relatively high participation rates, retention and post-training outcomes for Aboriginal and Torres Strait Islander adults from these courses remain extremely poor, especially in remote communities (Guenther and McRae-Williams 2015). For Indigenous students in remote and very remote locations (the sites where the LFLF campaigns were run), the average completion rate for Certificate One and Certificate Two qualifications is less than 20% (Windley 2017).

Notwithstanding recognition of the need to make education more 'culturally and locally relevant' (Dunbar and Scrimgeour 2007, p. 147), many adult education programs delivered through the formal education system remain unwilling or unable to tailor learning to the needs and realities of many Aboriginal people living in rural and remote communities. The result is often a one-size-fits-all pedagogy so that learners in inner-city Sydney receive the same program and delivery as learners in remote Aboriginal communities. Moreover, what constitutes successful outcomes in adult literacy is often measured narrowly through the productivist framework in which vocational education and training in Australia tends to be located, that is to say, the main measure of success is an employment outcome in the mainstream economy. While employment outcomes are indeed important, there are many adults for whom such an option is unrealistic, not only because of limited job opportunities but because many other issues in their own and the families lives are a barrier to obtaining and keeping a full-time job. For many, building better English language literacy is just the first step on a much longer path, one which may take a generation to traverse.

In this chapter, we report on the outcomes of the first 4 years of an alternative approach, driven by a relatively new national Aboriginal organisation, the Literacy for Life Foundation (LFLF). LFLF has developed a successful but highly unusual partnership with the government of the Republic of Cuba to roll out the *Yes, I Can!* Adult Literacy Campaign across seven rural and remote communities in north-western New South Wales. The mass campaign model for building adult literacy has been a feature of development efforts in many countries over several hundred years and most recently in countries of the Global South (Arnove and Graff 2008). *Yes, I Can!* (or Yo Si Puedo) is one such model which has operated in 30 countries, almost all in the Global South. This Cuban-designed version of the campaign model sets out to achieve population-level change (Boughton and Durnan 2014) by requiring that communities themselves take on responsibility for addressing the issue of low literacy in their adult populations. Following a period of preparation, in which the national structure and resourcing is laid down, the campaign rolls out at a community level in three interlinked phases. Phase One, called *Socialisation and Mobilisation*, seeks to engage the whole community in addressing the problem of low levels of literacy. It is characterised by extensive community consultation and education including training local leaders and staff in the model, visits to every household by local staff to discuss the issue of literacy and the engagement of local organisations and agencies as campaign partners. Phase Two comprises 13 weeks of basic literacy lessons delivered by specially trained local facilitators. Finally, Phase Three, called *Post Literacy*, engages the partner organisations working with the campaign team to provide opportunities for the new graduates to consolidate their literacy in structured activities and work experience, with the aim of building pathways into further education, employment and socially useful community work. The campaign continues until everyone who has expressed a need has had the chance to participate or until the organisation leading the campaign has achieved the target reduction in 'illiteracy'.

Yes, I Can! was first introduced in Australia in 2012. After successful pilots of the first two intakes in Wilcannia, the campaign extended to Bourke and Enngonia and has now completed four intakes in Brewarrina. Building from a recent case study of *Yes, I Can!* undertaken as part of a broader investigation into models of successful vocational education and training (Guenther et al. 2017), this chapter presents the outcomes of *Yes, I Can!* from 2012 to 2015. By examining impacts at both individual and community levels, our explanation for the success of this model moves beyond recognition of the value of community-controlled initiatives. Instead, our focus here is on how a pedagogy of contingency and an ethic of solidarity contribute to the significant impacts *Yes, I Can!* is having in these remote Aboriginal communities.

Background to the Study

While the mass literacy campaign model is designed to operate at a national scale, every community brings its own history and context to the process, and an understanding of the local context is essential for its success. The communities in which *Yes, I Can!* has run since 2012 are part of the Murdi Paaki region. This area of western NSW has an 'identity' based on a long history of its 16 communities working together, initially under ATSIC, and more recently via the Murdi Paaki Regional Assembly (MPRA) (Urbis Keys Young 2006). Aboriginal people comprise over 17% of the total population of this region, making them a very significant minority. However, in 2011, only 48% of the Murdi Paaki region Aboriginal teenagers aged 15–19 were in education, compared with 66% of non-Aboriginal teenagers. There is also a significant and growing gap, as in NSW more generally, in Year 12 completions, with only 14% of the Murdi Paaki region Aboriginal adults having completed 12 years of school, compared with 30% of non-Aboriginal adults. Similar gaps exist in TAFE and higher education participation (AANSW 2014). Given this backdrop, it is estimated that a significant proportion of this population have very low English language literacy (Boughton 2009b).

Methodology

This chapter draws on a range of quantitative and qualitative data collected through a participatory action research program which began with the first pilot intake of students into *Yes, I Can!* in Wilcannia in 2012 and has continued with each subsequent intake. This current study stops at the end of 2015.

The quantitative data reported on here draws on surveys of households in their community at the outset of the campaign, information obtained via enrolment process and weekly attendance reports and literacy assessments of students at the outset and completion of their participation, using the Australian Core Skills Framework (ACSF). Additional data on the local community is taken from the 2011 Australian Bureau of Statistics Census, and from other Commonwealth and State government agencies, including Aboriginal Affairs NSW community profiles. The qualitative data is obtained via participant observation in campaign launches, lessons, graduations and other campaign activities; through in-depth interviews with students, local staff and community stakeholders; and through examination of campaign documents including student work examples, internal LFLF reports to its Board and its external reports to donors. Data reported in this chapter also comes from a case study of the campaign in 2013–2014, which was one of five case studies of 'best practice' in a national project funded by the National Centre for Vocational Education Research (Guenther et al. 2017).

Outcomes

Enrolments and Retention

One of the most obvious outcomes of *Yes, I Can!* has been the high participation and completion rates. The literacy campaign targets approximately 40% of the adult population (aged 15 years and over) in each community based on the proportion of adults estimated as having low literacy (Boughton 2009a). This target population is reached through an extensive door-to-door household survey administered as part of Phase One. Expressions of interest obtained at the end of the visit give an indication of the level of demand, that is, of self-assessed literacy need. Table 16.1 summarises the progress of the campaign, outlining numbers of adults surveyed in each community and the resultant expressions of interest to participate and eventual enrolments.

Summary of Progress of *Yes, I Can!* **2012–2015**
As can be seen from Table 16.1, out of a total of 434 adults contacted via the household survey, 240 or 55% went on to give a formal expression of interest in participating. This indicates a significant level of awareness of the campaign at a grass-roots level, as well as indicating a high level of need. Of those expressions of interest, 150 adults of the target population started classes, representing an uptake of 62.5%. This uptake is a function of the ongoing socialisation and mobilisation activities of Phase One of the campaign, of which the household survey is a crucial component. However, the uptake also reveals how the campaign model of *Yes, I Can!* leverages the connectivity of the various communities of the Murdi Paaki region using word of mouth as an integral tool for the mobilisation of support and interest ahead of actual classes commencing. Even before campaigns formally began in Bourke, Enngonia and Brewarrina, news of the campaign had spread from Wilcannia, the pilot site and so by the time the campaign reached Brewarrina, it was eagerly anticipated. This suggests there is a high degree of alignment between the mass campaign approach to adult literacy and the close family and cultural relationships in Aboriginal communities such as those along the Darling River.

Table 16.1 Progress of *Yes, I Can!* 2012–2015

	Dates	Intakes	Target adult pop	Surveyed	EoI	Enrolments
Wilcannia	February 2012–August 2013	3	279	103	41	39
Bourke	September 2013–April 2015	4	505	125	98	70
Enngonia	September 2013–December 2013	1	52	48	24	21
Brewarrina	September 2015–December 2015	1	415	158	77	19
Total		9	1251	434	240	149

16 'A Strong Belief in the Possibility of a Better Life': The Pedagogy of Contingency... 299

Table 16.2 Retention rates over four sites of *Yes, I Can!*

	Starters	Graduates	Overall retention (%)
Wilcannia	39	23	58.90
Bourke	70	51	72.80
Enngonia	21	15	71.40
Brewarrina	19	14	73.60
Total	150	103	68.60

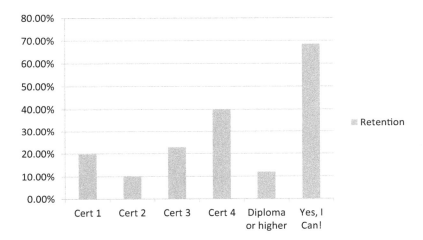

Fig. 16.1 comparison of TVA retention rates for Aboriginal students in Bourke-Brewarrina region and *Yes, I Can!* 2012–2014. (NCVER does not publish Indigenous qualification completion rates for specific regions. These are apparent retention rates, comparing commencements and completions over a 3-year period 2012–2014. However, we do know that in 2014, the 'official' Certificate One and Certificate Two qualification completion rates for Indigenous students were 13.2% and 23.2% and that completion rates of all qualifications tend to be lower in remote and very remote areas.)

After uptake, retention is seen as a key measure of the success of an educational intervention. In the case of *Yes, I Can!*, retention is defined as successful completion of the 13-week literacy component (or Phase Two) of the campaign. Table 16.2 shows the relatively high retention rate across the four sites and over the nine intakes between 2012 and 2015.

Summary of Retention Rates of *Yes, I Can!* 2012–2015
This success of *Yes, I Can!* in terms of retention becomes even more apparent when compared to the total VET activity (TVA) figures for Aboriginal students in Bourke and Brewarrina. Figure 16.1 reveals that retention rates for *Yes, I Can!* are between double and three times the average for Aboriginal students in TAFE programs in the same region.

Comparison of Retention Rates

Expressed another way, the overall attrition rate of Aboriginal students in Bourke and Brewarrina in VET courses is 84.2% compared with 31.3% for *Yes, I Can!* This ability of *Yes, I Can!* to attract and then retain participants is a function of several key aspects of the campaign model, not the least of which is the flexible delivery of the Phase Two lessons. For example, the days and times the literacy classes are held are determined by each community. Typically, classes run for 2–3 h, 3 days per week with one additional day reserved for catch-up lessons. The timetabling of catch-up time each week means that students do not fall behind, despite missing some lessons. It also represents an acknowledgement of the environment beyond the class including the priority that family takes in Aboriginal culture. Examples of how the flexible delivery of *Yes I Can!* classes contribute to the support and ultimate retention of participants were common in the data and indicate a key difference between the *Yes, I Can!* model and conventional adult education programs. As one facilitator explained, 'we've had someone that couldn't come to class stuck home with the grandkids. I visited them and did a lesson'.

Indeed, the ongoing need that many of the participants of *Yes, I Can!* have for high levels of support is clearly understood by the local staff, as are the likely consequences of the withdrawal of that support:

> When someone doesn't turn up, come to class, we go and check on why they didn't come to class. If you don't keep going back and showing your support and you're there for them, they'll just back off and won't come. [Aboriginal trainer, Bourke/Enngonia]

This indicates that the flexible delivery and pedagogy of *Yes, I Can!* takes account of the exigencies of the participants' lives. Moreover, it is also evident from the extract above that this flexibility is more than a matter of pragmatics. Because staff are themselves community members, the level of investment and care for participants inside and outside the classroom is striking.

Literacy Development

Beyond participation and retention rates, *Yes, I Can!* results in significant post-training outcomes for participants. Chief among these is literacy development. Participants typically commence the literacy classes at or below Level One on the Australian Core Skills Framework (ACSF) in the three domains of reading, writing and learning (McLean 2012 cited in Boughton et al. 2013). Throughout the latter part of the classes, participants undertake a series of tasks to demonstrate competence in reading comprehension and writing, culminating in the production of a simple letter to a friend including description and opinion. As part of the Wilcannia pilot study, these tasks were mapped by a qualified ACFS consultant, at the equivalent of Level Two ACSF (McLean 2012 cited in Boughton et al. 2013). The administration of ACSF assessments has not been possible with all students in all intakes, both at the beginning and end of the YIC campaign. For example, no assessments were done in Engonnia, which was one of the communities in this case study. Since then, funding has been obtained to conduct these assessments more systematically, and results will be reported in future publications.

In formal educational terms, therefore, successful completion of the Phase Two lessons constitutes a modest literacy attainment, with participants typically achieving a Level One or Two on the ACSF. However, expressed in real terms, the literacy gains achieved as a result of attending *Yes, I Can!* were far more significant. By concentrating on everyday literacy skills, *Yes, I Can!* enabled graduates to take more control of their lives as this comment from an employment services provider illustrates:

> For lots of providers, in order to complete, you have to gain a qualification but *Yes, I Can!* was more personalised and tailored. It was about developing the skills that people could use in their everyday life like reading to their grandkids, reading the bills, reading the medicine bottle. [Non-Aboriginal employment services, Dubbo]

The value in prevocational training supporting graduates to participate more effectively in domestic and community text-based encounters has been highlighted elsewhere (Kral 2012; Kral and Falk 2004; Kral and Schwab 2012). Our data further suggests that the desire to engage in family literacy practices such as reading to grandchildren is symptomatic of a more general sense that becoming literate will lead to a better future for families as this comment reveals:

> They [the literacy students] say things like we can help at the school but when you drill down, what they really mean is we can feel more confident to go into the school. We feel more confident to talk to the school. A lot of it is people think that literacy is a secret tool and once you're literate you can do all sorts of things. [Non-Aboriginal trainer, national]

It is clear then that for many of the participants, their literacy achievement impacted not only their lives but also their families. However, particularly as a result of Aboriginal kinship structures, these literacy outcomes extend beyond the family. A fundamental tenet of the campaign model of adult literacy is the notion the literacy is a community issue. It was apparent from interviews with a range of community representatives that there was a strong understanding and acceptance of this connection between individuals' literacy levels and the functioning of communities as a whole. This comment from a community representative in Brewarrina illustrates this well:

> I believe that a community's functionality relies on the capacity of individuals. Communities are more than likely to be dysfunctional if individuals have low levels of literacy and capacity in general. [Aboriginal community leader, Brewarrina]

In this way, it is clear that the relevance of the literacy skills developed in *Yes, I Can!* combined with an understanding of the interconnectivity between the literacy of individuals, their families and their communities means that the literacy outcomes of *Yes, I Can!* are significant.

Work Skills and Experience

As outlined earlier, Phase Three of the *Yes, I Can!* campaign model, also known as 'post-literacy', aims to continue the gains of Phase Two (the literacy classes) by giving participants the opportunity to use their newly acquired skills and knowledge. Across the nine intakes reported on here, 30% of graduates participated in work experience at various local businesses and services. While not compulsory, many of those who did participate gained valuable insights into the world of work as well as greater familiarity with agencies and services with which they routinely come into contact. Importantly, the work experience component of the post-literacy phase also provides participants with opportunities to imagine different futures for themselves and their families. For example, one young female participant in Bourke developed an aspiration to become a paramedic following her work experience at the Bourke Aboriginal Medical Service over several weeks. While this has yet to be acted on, the significance of *Yes, I Can!*'s post-literacy activities lies in the fact that the future often has to be seen to be imagined (Burton and Osborne 2014).

Summary of Further Training Outcomes

Another outcome of *Yes, I Can!* is engagement in further training. Table 16.3 indicates the numbers of campaign graduates who went on to further training in the Bourke and Brewarrina cohorts.

The experience of participating in *Yes, I Can!* built students' confidence to attempt accredited training, and many were able to complete one or two modules of training 'bought in' from RTOs as part of the post-literacy phase. As an employment service provider commented: 'people were more receptive to new training and courses like the White Card and Barista course. They seemed more confident in approaching it and on the first day, weren't as shy with the trainer as they would have been'. Participation in *Yes, I Can!* also provided knowledge and skills to understand the expectations and conventions of formal adult education as one participant stated: 'if I hadn't gone to *Yes, I Can!*, I wouldn't have understood most of the things in the TAFE course program'.

Table 16.3 Details of further training outcomes across all two sites of *Yes, I Can!*

	No. of graduates	Percentage in further training	Qualifications enrolled in
Bourke intake 3	2/17	11.7	Cert 3 in children's services
Bourke intake 4	2/8	25.0	n/a
Brewarrina	8/15	53.3	Year 10 (at TAFE) (1)
			Cert 3 (at Tranby) (7)

Self-Esteem and New Identities

The confidence to attempt further training is characteristic of wider psychosocial outcomes of *Yes, I Can!* As with other research which reports on the enhancement of self-esteem as a result of participation in adult literacy programmes (see, e.g. Prins 2008), many people interviewed described the transformation of low-literate adults into confident and engaged members of the community. This was most directly witnessed at the graduation ceremonies held in the communities, an important public recognition of the achievements of the *Yes, I Can!* students and an integral part of the campaign model. The following extract refers to the graduation ceremony held in Bourke in 2014:

> The confidence and the ability to simply stand there and make an acknowledgement of what they've learnt, what their accomplishments in one hit is a huge outcome in itself. Some people probably look at that and go you're just standing up and talking to people. But these people who I've worked with for thirteen years have difficulty. Standing up in front of a group is not easy, you're lucky to get them to come to appointments. [Non-Aboriginal employment service provider, Bourke]

The development in confidence was apparent amongst those most marginalised in the community, as a community leader in Brewarrina signalled:

> Especially with some of the elders, people of very few words. Now they're not scared to walk out the front and read a piece of paper or express their feelings and ask questions and things like that but also like younger people that have been locked away feeling worthless, seeing them also come forward and speak and tell their stories and things like that. [Aboriginal community leader, Brewarrina]

Attending *Yes, I Can!* also provided many with a sense of purpose. According to the national trainer, many students attributed their motivation for continuing with *Yes, I Can!* to the sense of purpose that the campaign gave to their lives:

> What they always say is it's a sense of purpose. You get up and you shower and you get yourself nice because you're going out and you're going to something. So you know, that's a little thing but it's about dignity; it gives people a sense of dignity. They really believe that reading and writing is going to change their life so they start doing things that reward that belief. The way I term it is there is a strong belief in the possibility of a better future and I think that is what the literacy campaign gives its students. [Non-Aboriginal trainer, national]

The transformations that result from simply having a place to go were not only physical. As with the transformation witnessed in those participants who found the courage and confidence to speak at graduation ceremonies, the simple act of coming to the front of the classroom to write on the board becomes a hallmark of personal empowerment, as a trainer from Bourke and Enngonia argued:

> First of all, you hardly have anyone who walks up. It's the shame factor but then seeing someone who was too afraid to get up to the board go and write on the board. Even that empowers them. [Aboriginal trainer, Bourke and Enngonia]

Capacity Building

Another key outcome of *Yes, I Can!* is the degree to which it genuinely builds capacity in the communities in which it is delivered by investing in the ongoing training and support of a local workforce. Apart from the national campaign coordinator, the onsite Australian advisor and the Cuban advisor, all staff employed on the campaign are local Aboriginal people. Most of these local staff have had little or no experience with paid employment prior to joining *Yes, I Can!* and so require significant ongoing training, support and encouragement from the campaign leadership as well as from the community as a whole. This was certainly the case in Brewarrina as this comment indicates:

> It took a little bit of time I think to empower the leadership of the program which was the facilitators and the coordinator to really realise that they were put into a position where they would be making decisions and they would be the ones who would actually be teaching in those positions. [Aboriginal community leader, Brewarrina]

In fact, the local staff were very much co-learners in *Yes, I Can!* Interviews revealed a marked overlap in the kinds of outcomes mentioned by participants and local staff. That is, those individuals engaged as classroom facilitators (two per campaign) and coordinator (one per campaign) underwent a similar process of growth and empowerment, as one of the trainers from the Bourke and Enngonia campaigns articulated:

> I didn't even speak up much the way I do now for Enngonia. I didn't do it before the *Yes, I Can!* I guess it's like a blind person being able to see again. You just see things differently and not only does it do that, it also opens you up to be able to speak to all these other organisations around. It's the confidence that it gives you. [Aboriginal trainer, Bourke and Enngonia]

Local Advocacy and Leadership

The development of a strong, local workforce has led to further outcomes of *Yes, I Can!* at both the individual and community level. Through their own personal growth and empowerment, pivotal staff members have become effective advocates for their people. And these empowered individuals have become leaders in their community, attending a recent young leadership forum and playing a key role in the region's leadership renewal strategy. In this way, the impact of *Yes, I Can!* on community capacity and empowerment is far-reaching. This impact is also being felt in individual communities as the school principal from Enngonia explained:

> The program [*Yes, I Can!*] gave M the confidence to be a leader in the community. Previously, I always used the AEO employed by the school as the liaison between us and the community but M took on the liaison role. [Non-Aboriginal government employee, Enngonia]

16 'A Strong Belief in the Possibility of a Better Life': The Pedagogy of Contingency...   305

Greater Community Engagement

As is clear from the comment above, the leadership shown by the local staff involved *Yes, I Can!* has a flow-on effect to others in the community. This can be seen most clearly in greater participation and engagement with the local community and its services. For example, participation rates in locally run organisations such as land councils have also improved. A local facilitator, now a community leader, reported that where previously they struggled to achieve the quorum, now many locals are attending Land Council meetings. This indicates the power of having role models in the community. This greater participation described above has not only benefited local Aboriginal organisations but has also had a positive impact on local support services, as this comment illustrates:

> Other agencies and other NGOs are getting on with life because this program is making a difference...because it's allowing agencies to have better relationships with clients. [Aboriginal community leader and government employee, Bourke]

Community Healing

The changed participation patterns in local agencies and organisation stem from another key outcome of *Yes, I Can!* In recent times, many local Aboriginal organisations in the Murdi Paaki region, as elsewhere, have struggled with problems of internal conflict and alleged mal-administration. *Yes, I Can!* brought different factions and clans together, something many people chose to comment on. For example, a community leader in Brewarrina said that *Yes, I Can!* was:

> Bringing communities together. Maybe a few months before [the campaign], people hadn't even congregated in the same room or spoke to each other. [Aboriginal community leader, Brewarrina]

These outcomes are not serendipitous but rather a carefully considered aspect of the campaign. In the first instance, local staff receive training and mentoring in the management of conflict sensitive environments as the national trainer explained:

> Part of the training with the staff, before I start *Yes, I Can!* is talking about working in a conflict-sensitive way, not exacerbating conflict, not becoming part of conflict, leaving your rubbish or your conflicts at the gate. [Non-Aboriginal trainer, national]

The strong principle of solidarity that underpins popular education models and *Yes, I Can!* resonated with the communities. Both Aboriginal and non-Aboriginals from within and outside the campaign volunteered observations of solidarity:

> We had young people, mothers and grandmothers sitting in one space on a common ground and working towards the same goal. They were encouraging each other to get out of bed. [Non-aboriginal employment services provider, Bourke]

The solidarity that emerged from the campaign was seen as one of the reasons participants were able to successfully complete the Phase Two lessons:

Solidarity is a key theme of *Yes, I Can!* We talk about it in class and people know what it means, they're really onto it because that's the only way Aboriginal society really has survived, by acting in solidarity with each other, even with people that they don't particularly like but they have the goal that we've got to survive this, the shared goal I mean. We're the literacy campaign people and we've made it [the classroom] pretty and we're doing the garden and this and that and there's a sense of belonging. [Non-aboriginal trainer, national]

As the comments above suggest, the solidarity which the popular education model of *Yes, I Can!* encourages can be seen to align closely with the culture and values of remote Aboriginal communities. The importance of this connection between local cultures and adult training has been highlighted elsewhere and is arguably one of the key factors that contributes to the positive outcomes of *Yes, I Can!* reported here.

Why *Yes, I Can!* Works: A Pedagogy of Contingency and an Ethic of Care

The importance of culturally and locally relevant training is well understood and there are many examples of community-controlled education programs having positive impacts in Aboriginal and Torres Strait Islander communities. Here, however, we want to suggest that there are additional factors that may be in part responsible for significant positive impacts of *Yes, I Can!* in north-western NSW. In the first instance, we argue that *Yes, I Can!* is effective because it is based on what Astrid Von Kotze calls a 'pedagogy of contingency' (Kotze 2013), which she defines as:

A pedagogy that responds assertively to the conditions they seek to improve – and those are conditions of contingency. Contingency means 'dependence on chance or on the fulfilment of a condition; uncertainty; fortuitousness'. (Oxford dictionary).... A 'pedagogy of contingency' is an approach that responds to uncertainty, chance, conditionality; it reflects the dynamics and dynamism of micro-differentials within the forces of macro power environments.

While Von Kotze is writing about workers in the informal economy of the townships of South Africa, 'contingency' is just as much a fact of life for the 'surplus' Aboriginal populations of rural and remote NSW towns, whose labour in no longer required and whose livelihoods, therefore, are dependent for their survival on a 'welfare economy' over which they exercise very little control. The LFLF campaign participants, and the local staff who work with them, have to respond every day to the uncertainty and unpredictability shaped by the very conditions the campaign aims to change, including extreme poverty, an oppressive justice system, high morbidity and mortality and the family and community distress and conflicts which such circumstances produce. These issues are not outside the class or the campaign but a key aspect of the reality with which they must deal. And, as Von Kotze writes:

The really useful knowledge that people need in order to survive not just physically but also emotionally, creatively, spiritually, convivially, demands a pedagogy that responds to the particular conditions of the participants' location and their livelihood rhythms.

Most adult education programs delivered through the formal education system employ a one-size-fits-all pedagogy, which simply cannot do this. Such conditions do not even rate a mention in standard VET system training packages. In contrast, despite being a highly structured program emanating from Cuba, *Yes, I Can!* is contextualised to each distinct community it operates in, taking account of the socio-economic, political and community environments outside the classroom and their likely impact inside the classroom. In practice, a pedagogy of contingency in *Yes, I Can!* is a function of the careful and ongoing balance between high support and high autonomy.

Emblematic of *Yes, I Can!*'s pedagogy of contingency is the highly scaffolded pedagogy that moves in a steady, predictable pace from the elementary to the more complex with frequent opportunities for practice and consolidation. Each lesson follows the same pattern which is established and continually modelled on-screen by the 'actor-teacher', 'Lauren' and her class. Despite this highly structured pedagogy, the is considerable flexibility as mentioned earlier in terms of the lesson pacing with ample opportunities to stop the DVD for catch-up, discussion and consolidation. Lessons have even been conducted in participants' homes when necessary. In addition, the starting level of *Yes, I Can!* is realistic, as is the timetabling around cultural events and the embedding of 'catch-up' days into the weekly timetable. The campaign is also highly pragmatic in terms of providing transport and refreshments and creating class groups that take into account clan/family/gender and other dynamics so as to minimise potential conflicts. This indicates a pedagogy that takes careful consideration of the exigencies of participants' lives in these communities.

And while such a highly structured and even scripted learning environment might appear at first glance to clash with notions of progressive pedagogy, or even with the principle of self-determination, this very structure creates a space where people are not only capable but comfortable and therefore willing to take on responsibility for the campaign in their community:

> I think this method gives students the safety of being able to return to learning when learning in 99% of the cases was absolutely horrific. That's how people view the education, with that fear, in trepidation and anger and what a bloody waste of time. This here gives the facilitators the confidence because it's really structured and they learn how to be a teacher; they learn how to be a facilitator in a very safe way. Then they have this lovely little lesson plan structure and they repeat everything all the time so they repeat it and they gradually get confidence and they start to see that they can do things and say things. Meanwhile, the students are learning to be students by modelling themselves on the class in the DVD. [Non-aboriginal trainer, national]

In other words, this highly supportive structure allows the local workforce, themselves often struggling with the same daily challenges as the students in their classes, to gain in confidence and, therefore, develop the skills that are crucial to the sustainability of the outcomes observed in each community. At the same time, this high support is offset with high degrees of autonomy, which the local trainers say is a key to the campaign's success:

It's us. D and B and J [*Yes, I Can!* leadership], it's community-run and that's the one thing that was so, that's why it works because they [*Yes, I Can!* leadership] let the community run it. They're just in the background and keeping us on track at the same time. It's community-run; that's why it works. You've got to have the respect, the trust. [Aboriginal trainer, Bourke]

The community-controlled nature of *Yes, I Can!* ensures not only trust and respect in the campaign but also ensures that it has the high degree of relevance, accessibility and appropriateness that constitutes a pedagogy of contingency.

The trust and respect held for the local facilitators and coordinators also emanate from their classroom practice, a direct result of the pedagogy of contingency that characterises *Yes, I Can!*. This first-hand observation comes from a local community leader in Brewarrina:

To see people for the first time be able to be in a situation or an environment where they were interested in the learning and were feeling valued for what they knew or what they know in there. Seeing people that were probably every other day of the week involved in alcohol and drugs and things like that but now, having a purpose and being supported in an environment where they were listened to and were able to pick up on their educational processes that they missed out on when they were going to school. [Aboriginal community leader, Brewarrina]

A pedagogy of contingency, therefore, can be seen to build on the existing strength and capacities of participants, 'working holistically and relationally, aiming to strengthen rather than substitute existing capabilities and structural capacities' (Kotze 2013). While such a strength-based learning approach is a principle that underlies andragogy in general, in the case of *Yes, I Can!*, the valuing and building upon individuals' strengths took place at a far more fundamental level and in full recognition of the legacy of generations of marginalisation in Aboriginal communities, as this comment from the Bourke trainer illustrates:

I remind the students all the time that regardless of who we are and where we come from, how drunk we are, how drugged up we are or whatever, in each and every one of us, there's something special. We can do it. I don't know what it is, you've got to find it. [Aboriginal trainer, Bourke]

Here it is clear that the students are being nurtured. This is what we consider to be an ethic of care which we see operating in parallel with a pedagogy of contingency; and both are occurring within an overall model which emphasises community solidarity. The campaign model invites the community to come together, to take responsibility to act together to improve the circumstances of its most marginalised members. This is expressed on Literacy for Life Foundation leaflets and posters in the slogan: *Literacy. Everyone's Right. Everyone's Business.*

An ethic of care and concern, which is key to building this solidarity, is one of the principles underpinning the *Yes, I Can!* model. Such an ethic also works hand-in-hand with the gendered nature of the campaign workforce. As is often the case in 'caring' professions (Abbott and Meerabeau 1998), the majority of positions in *Yes, I Can!* are filled by women with the local facilitators, coordinators, the national trainer and onsite advisor all being female. Furthermore, historically, the role of carer has tended to fall to women not only in the wider world but also in these

Aboriginal communities. This care and concern produces a reciprocal commitment to *Yes, I Can!* that contributes to the high retention and completion rates. While it is often not feasible for adult education providers to follow up non-attenders in the ways described above, the small, flexible and, most significantly, community-led nature of *Yes, I Can!* means that this level of support is possible. Moreover, in the communities that *Yes, I Can!* operates in, a culture of mutual support or solidarity can be seen as a product of the historical experience of oppression and marginalisation. As one participant expressed, 'our philosophy is no one wants to be left behind, we don't want anybody to be left behind, we don't want people on the fringes left behind' [Aboriginal community representative and government employee].

Conclusion

Adult literacy is often seen as a panacea for a range of issues, from unemployment, ill health, social and economic disengagement to crime and recidivism and generations of educational disadvantage (e.g. Griffin et al. 1997; Hanemann 2015; Hartley and Horne 2006). But beyond these social indicators, 'literacy skills are fundamental to informed decision-making, personal empowerment, (and to) active and passive participation in local and global social community' (Stromquist 2005, p. 12).

This chapter has sought to show that there is ample evidence from the first 4 years of the *Yes, I Can!* campaign in western NSW to argue that, with the right national and community leadership and with sufficient resources, the mass campaign model which LFLF uses can raise the literacy levels of a significant number of people in a community in a relatively short time. There is also ample evidence from staff and participants that the work of improving adult literacy in a community is a significant step along the road towards changing the appalling circumstances in which Aboriginal people with low and very low literacy are forced to cope on a daily basis. That said, not everyone benefits, as retention rates show; and the number of people who have joined and succeeded is still far short of what would be hoped from a mass campaign. There is also evidence, which is now being followed up in an Australian Research Council longitudinal study, that while many campaign graduates continue to experience the benefits several years after the campaign is over, others have been unable to sustain the changes they have begun to make, not just in literacy practice but in other aspects on their lives.

It is important, therefore, to distinguish individual impacts from population impacts. Certainly, literacy can be seen as an individual capacity or skill. More importantly, however, it is a characteristic of populations, of communities, which underpins, in modern societies, the collective capacity to plan, organise and carry out specific projects and activities. Faced with an increasingly highly literate settler economy and political system, the majority of Aboriginal people in rural and remote NSW are forced to the margins, unable to participate effectively as citizens in the institutions which are meant to guarantee their rights. Low levels of literacy are therefore a problem, not just for those who lack it, but just as much for those who have it, since it creates divisions within a community or population which must be transcended before the community can exercise its full power. Literacy, in the words of the Literacy for Life Foundations' own materials, is 'Everyone's right, and everyone's business'. In the context of this book, the benefits of raising community adult literacy might be the power that the community can then exercise over its schools, through institutions such as Aboriginal Education Consultative Groups; but it applies equally to the power that can be exercised over every domain of modern life.

Beyond the grass-roots nature of *Yes, I Can!*, we have argued here that the impacts of this approach to Aboriginal adult literacy are a function of a pedagogy of contingency and an ethic of care. Both of these characteristics are in turn a function of the fundamental principles of solidarity and equality that underpin the mass adult education campaign model. However, this is still only the beginning, or one small step. The social benefits of literacy will only truly be felt in these communities when broader rights and development frameworks are in place and operating effectively, so that social transformation, both individual and community, can be sustained (UNESCO 2009).

References

AANSW. (2014). *Community portrait. The Murdi Paaki Alliance*. Prepared using ABS data by The Public Practice, for NSW Office of Aboriginal Affairs. (Copy provided by AANSW Bourke Office).

Abbott, P., & Meerabeau, L. (Eds.). (1998). *The sociology of the caring professions*. London: UCL Press.

Adult Learning Australia. (2014). Indigenous intergenerational learning. ALA: Sydney

Arnove, R., & Graff, H. (Eds.). (2008). *National literacy campaigns and movements. Historical and comparative perspectives*. New Brunswick/London: Transaction Publishers.

Boughton, B. (2009a). Challenging donor agendas in adult & workplace education in Timor-Leste. In L. Cooper & S. Walters (Eds.), *Learning/work. Critical perspectives on lifelong learning and work* (pp. 74–87). Cape Town: Human Science Research Council Press.

Boughton, B. (2009b). Popular education for adult literacy and health development in indigenous Australia. *Australian Journal of Indigenous Education, 38*, 103–109.

Boughton, B., & Durnan, D. (2014). Cuba's "Yes, I Can" mass adult literacy campaign model in Timor-Leste and Aboriginal Australia: A comparative study. *International Review of Education, 60*(4), 559–580.

Boughton, B., Ah Chee, D., Beetson, J., Durnan, D., & LeBlanch, J. (2013). An aboriginal adult literacy campaign pilot study in Australia using yes I can. *Literacy and Numeracy Studies, 21*(1), 5. Retrieved from https://epress.lib.uts.edu.au/journals/index.php/lnj/article/view/3328.

Biddle, N. (2006). The association between health and education in Australia: Indigenous/non-Indigenous comparisons. *The Economic and Labour Relations Review, 17*(1), 107–141.

Brooks, G., Pahl, K., Pollard, A., & Rees, F. (2008). *Effective and inclusive practices in family literacy, language and numeracy: A review of programmes and practice in the UK and internationally*. UK: CfBT.

Burton, R., & Osborne, S. (2014). Kuranyu-kutu nyakula nyaan nyanganyi? Imagining the future. *AlterNative: An International Journal of Indigenous Peoples, 10*(1), 33–44.

Carpentieri, J., Fairfax-Cholmeley, K., Lister, J., & Vorhaus, J. (2011). *FamilyliteracyinEurope: Using parental support initiatives to enhance early literacy development (EAC/16/2009)*. London: NRDC, Institute of Education.

Dunbar, T., & Scrimgeour, M. (2007). Social determinants of Indigenous health. In B. Carson, T. Dunbar, R. D. Chenhall, & R. Bailie (Eds.), *Education* (pp. 135–152). Crows Nest: Allen & Unwin.

Griffin, P., Pollock, J., Corneille, K., & Fitzpatrick, M. (1997). Skilling me softly: The impact of adult literacy classes. Longitudinal Study of the Destination of Adult Literacy Students. Final Report. At https://eric.ed.gov/?id=ED417614

Guenther, J., & McRae-Williams, E. (2015). *The training and employment challenge of remote communities: Is collaboration the solution?* Paper presented at the AVETRA 18th Annual Conference, Melbourne. http://avetra.org.au/wp-content/uploads/2015/04/50.docx

Guenther, J., Bat, M., Stephens, A., Skewes, J., Boughton, B., Williamson, F., Wooltorton, S., Marshall, M., & Dwyer, A. (2017). *Enhancing training advantage for remote Aboriginal and Torres Strait Islander learners*. Adelaide: NCVER.

Hanson, S. (2012). Skilling Aboriginal Parents in Home Literacy Practices. Retrieved from https://www.yumpu.com/en/document/view/26316879/skilling-aboriginal-parents-in-home-literacy-practices-susan-hanson

Hartley, R., & Horne, J. (2006). Social and economic benefits of improved adult literacy: Towards a better understanding. : Adelaide: National Centre for Vocational Education Research.

Hanemann, U. (2015, April). 'Concepts of Literacy' seminar ELINET Conference, Budapest.

Hughes, P. (1988). *Report of the aboriginal education policy task force*. Canberra: Commonwealth of Australia.

Hunter, B., Snowball, L., & Weatherburn, D. (2006, October). The economic and social factors underpinning indigenous contact with the justice system: results from the 2002 NATSISS survey. *Crime & Justice Bulletin, 104*. At http://www.bocsar.nsw.gov.au/Documents/cjb104.pdf

Kotze, A. (2013). *A pedagogy of contingency for precarious work*. Paper presented at the 4th Bonn Conference on Adult Education and Development (BoCAED), Bonn. http://www.dvv-international.de/files/ipe_68_gb_web.pdf

Kral, I. (2012). *Talk, text and technology: Literacy and social practice in a remote Indigenous community*. Bristol: Multilingual Matters.

Kral, I., & Falk, I. (2004). *What is all that learning for? Indigenous adult literacy practices, training, community capacity and health*. Retrieved from Adelaide: https://ncver.edu.au/research-andstatistics/publications/all-publications/what-is-all-that-learning-for-indigenous-adult-english-literacy-practices,-training,-community-capacity-and-health

Kral, I., & Schwab, R. (2012). *Learning spaces: Youth, literacy and new media in remote Indigenous Australia*. Canberra: ANU E Press.

NSW Auditor General. (2012). *Improving the literacy of aboriginal students in NSW public schools: Department of Education and Communities*. Sydney: Audit Office of New South Wales. Retrieved from http://www.audit.nsw.gov.au/ArticleDocuments/244/01_Aboriginal_Literacy_Full_Report2.pdf.

Lowe, K. (2017). Walanbaa warramildanha: The impact of authentic Aboriginal community and school engagement on teachers' professional knowledge. *The Australian Educational Researcher, 44*(1), 35–54.

Organisation for Economic Cooperation and Development. (2012). *Let's read them a story! The parent factor in education*. Retrieved from http://www.oecd-ilibrary.org/education/let-s-read-them-a-story-the-parent-factor-in-education_9789264176232-en

Prins, E. (2008). Adult literacy education, gender equity and empowerment: Insights from a Freirean-inspired literacy programme. *Studies in the Education of Adults, 40*(1), 24–39. https://doi.org/10.1080/02660830.2008.11661554.

Reder, S., & Bynner, J. (2008). The need for longitudinal studies in adult literacy and numeracy education. In S. Reder & J. Bynner (Eds.), *Tracking adult literacy and numeracy skills: Findings from longitudinalresearch* (pp. 1–23). Florence: Taylor and Francis.

Stromquist, N. P. (2005). *The political benefits of adult literacy*. Background paper prepared for the Education for All Global Monitoring Report 2006. Literacy for Life Retrieved from www. unesco.org. 2006/ED/EFA/MRT/PI/93.

Shomos, A., & Forbes, M. (2014). *Literacy and numeracy skills and labour market outcomes in Australia*. Canberra: Productivity Commission.

UNESCO. (2009). Harnessing the power and potential of adult learning and education for a viable future. Belém Framework for Action. CONFINTEA VI. In: Sixth international conference on adult education, Belem, Brazil, December 2009. Paris: UNESCO

Urbis Keys Young. (2006). Evaluation of the Murdi Paaki COAG Trial. Retrieved from http://www.mpra.com.au/uploads/documents/MP%20Final%20Report%2030%20August.pdf

Windley, G. (2017). *Indigenous VET participation, completion and outcomes: change over the past decade*. Adelaide: NCVER.

Bob Boughton is an Associate Professor in the School of Education at the University of New England in Armidale, NSW. His research focuses on the role of popular education in development in marginalised and impoverished communities. Since 2012, he has been researching and evaluating the Literacy for Life Foundation (LFLF) adult literacy campaign in Aboriginal communities in NSW. He is currently the project leader on an Australian Research Council Linkage Project, a longitudinal study of the impact of the campaign on health and well-being in remote communities of north-western NSW.

Frances Williamson is an early career researcher at the University of New England. Her work synthesises sociological and linguistic perspectives in the study of adult language and literacy development. She is currently a member of the ARC Project team investigating the impacts of the Literacy for Life Foundation's Aboriginal adult literacy campaign on health and well-being in remote communities of north-western NSW.

Chapter 17
Afterword: Being Literate in 'Australian': The Future Can

Peter Freebody

Where are the laws and the legends I gave?
Tell me what happened
from 'The first-born', Jack Davis, Noongar, 1970

Abstract This chapter summarises some of the issues raised by the preceding chapters, and comments on the future of research and practice in the literacy education of Indigenous and Settler Australians. Outlined first are the categories of characters that appear across the course of this book, the actions and agency attached to those various characters, and the implications of those categorisations for our interpretation of the projects reported here. The chapter proceeds to draw out three general developments that might improve the efficacy and durability of educators' efforts: more detailed conceptualisations of 'community' and more central engagement with individual communities; long-term research and development projects; and the integration of Indigenous cultural and linguistic knowledge in literacy education for both Indigenous and Settler learners.

Introduction and Background

As an afterword this chapter needs first to recognise the mostly English-based nature of the literacy programs discussed in this volume and to acknowledge that literacy in Indigenous Australian languages, as raised later, remains underrepresented in the work reported here. It is only since 2006 that has there been any substantial, sustained, system-level effort put into teaching Indigenous Australian languages and their literacies in public schools (Purdie et al. 2008; Morgan et al. forthcoming). The exception is the bilingual education programs in the Northern Territory which were established and supported by multidisciplinary teams from the

P. Freebody (✉)
School of Education, The University of Wollongong, Wollongong, NSW, Australia

© Springer Nature Singapore Pte Ltd. 2019
J. Rennie, H. Harper (eds.), *Literacy Education and Indigenous Australians*,
Language Policy 19, https://doi.org/10.1007/978-981-13-8629-9_17

1970s, but which have enjoyed considerably less government support over the past 20 years. Nonetheless, by 2008 there were about 16,000 Indigenous Australian students and 13,000 Settler society students in 260 schools participating in Indigenous Australian language and literacy programs (e.g. Buckskin et al. 2009; Gray 2007; Rigney 2011; Sellwood and Angelo 2013; Siegel 1999; Wigglesworth et al. 2011).

The rationale and conduct of these plurilingual efforts assume particular importance in light of the UNESCO's decades-long work on endangered languages. UNESCO has estimated that about half of the world's 6000 languages will be gone in two generations unless decisive and effective steps are taken:

> With the disappearance of unwritten and undocumented languages, humanity would lose not only a cultural wealth but also important ancestral knowledge embedded, in particular, in indigenous languages. (UNESCO 2018)

This stark conclusion draws our attention to the connection between documenting and teaching written forms of an endangered language and its chances of appearing in next-generation educational policies and practices. So while literacy in English is the main focus of the chapters collected here, for many Indigenous Australians, and for many from Settler societies that work with them, this focus is by no means the entire challenge. To think otherwise is to consider the efforts of English-literacy educators merely as acts of beneficence, charity work for a group that needs help 'closing a gap', rather than in helping secure and preserve a culture's heritage as it prepares its youngsters for the future.

Contributors to this book have written about improving the literacy learning of Indigenous Australian people, in and around schools and other institutional and community settings. They have given us a view of the growing body of evidence that arises from intellectual, cultural, and practical efforts of literacy educators, from Indigenous Australian and Settler backgrounds. Whatever criticisms or qualms readers will have about these chapters – and there is much here to react to – and however unfinished the program of Indigenous Australian literacy education remains, this book documents increasing levels of collaboration and intent in that program. Here I provide a sketch of some themes that arise as I read these contributions – from my perspective as an educator from Settler society, Generation: Baby-boomer – and of some general ways forward that the chapters suggest.

Motifs

The contributions here are so varied – conceptually, methodologically, geographically, culturally, and in terms of their closeness to policy formation and daily practice – that a straight-up summary of common elements would likely miss some of the serious lessons. The commonalities themselves would end up being so common as to obscure the novelty and urgency that drive the projects, or so abstract as to be at the one time irrefutable and unhelpful. So the scaled-down aim is to sketch some of the chapters' less overt ideas and dispositions. I do this by trying to answer

17 Afterword: Being Literate in 'Australian': The Future Can   315

some simple questions so that some ideas about productive ways forward might come into view.

Who are the people here, and who does what? The term 'Indigenous' in the title of this book draws attention to the category of people who started inhabiting this continent sometime before between 60,000 and 100,000 years ago, at least 59,770 years before another category of people, the first Settler societies, arrived from Europe. At the same time, the title shows us how decades of troubled political history can load categorisations with 'attitude', with troubled baggage. Categorisations of people are not just neutral descriptions. How we use categorisations of people in daily exchanges is not only descriptive work: 'the practical, the conceptual, and the moral are laminated together in the organisation of situated action and discourse, and in their very intelligibility' (Jayyusi 1991, p. 242). Categorisation work is 'entwined with moral ordering whereby behaviour and actions, thoughts and opinions are made normatively sanctionable' (Fitzgerald and Housley 2015, p. 100). Our practical activities in understanding one another are simultaneously descriptive and moral, and it is this moral organisation that holds everyday norms of behaviour in place, as well as the power differentials those norms embody.

Categorisations are choices that give us practical ways of acting in various settings of use – public, national, cross-community debates versus informal, local, within-community negotiations. So we can ask questions such as: In which forums is 'Indigenous' a standard or preferred reference? By whom? In what contexts does that term adequately perform the work at hand, the work of, for example, distinguishing the groups to which a policy or program might refer from the 'others'? In which other settings is this categorisation not preferred, perhaps precisely because of its connection to bureaucratic, non-local usage, or because of its troubling national breadth – perhaps in favour of 'Aboriginal' or 'Aboriginal and Torres Strait Islander' or 'First Australians', or others? We also find, especially in the chapters by Djabibba, Auld and O'Mara, and Davis and Woods, that what is preferred is categorisations that refer to particular clans, nations, or peoples, in these cases, Kunibídji and Durithunga. These variable levels of categorisation get different descriptive-moral work done at different times, in different places; they have histories of use that are brought to bear on those occasions.

A question is also raised about how we categorise the 'others', the not-Indigenous Australians? In an everyday, practical way, a categorisation provides its contrast category – Indigenous, Aboriginal, First Nations versus non-Indigenous, non-Aboriginal, invaders, Settler societies/communities, Settler colonials, and so on (as, e.g. in Mills and Dooley and Ma Rhea and Anderson). Again, these have histories of use for different occasions. In this case, because they refer to majority, 'mainstream' collections of people, even their mention, let alone their use, can introduce political and moral trouble.

Contributors collected here use a variety of ways to distinguish between, on the one hand, those categorisations with agency and, on the other, those acted upon or acted with: Who's here and who does what to and with whom? Even a cursory view across the chapters shows that patterns of agency are attached not only to a variety of individuals and collectives but also to institutions, programs, packages, and even tests (NAPLAN 'does' things).

Here is a sketch of the cast of agent characters: Oldfield and Lo Bianco invest agency in 'policy and the work of social agents'; Djabibba, Auld and O'Mara invest agency in young Kunibídji people; for Shinkfield and for Cooke and Piers-Blundell, it is young children and their parents; in the piece by Scull and Hannagan, it is early-years Indigenous Australian students; Wheldall and colleagues show the agency of programs, drawing an analogy between the relationship of a program and students and the relationship of an ambulance and casualties; chapters by Mills and Dooley, Parkin, and Parkin and Harper largely invest agency in text-oriented programs in the hands of students and teachers in remote Indigenous Australian schools; for McCollow and for Boughton, it is formal organisations, such as The Cape York Aboriginal Australian Academy, Queensland Department of Education, the Good to Great Schools Australia program, and Literacy for Life Foundation, that administer reform through particular approaches to teaching and are variously supported or critiqued by influential individual community leaders.

Davis and Woods show the effects that can emerge from 'communities brokering relationships with other systems, approaches, and researchers' on pre-service teachers, community members, and school personnel, while Rennie and Ma Rhea and Anderson provide the two individual close-ups of the collection, showing us the agency and accommodations of Millie and her two educator-coaches and of a supervisor and doctoral scholar.

Conceptual and methodological differences aside, variations in the 'width of the lens' and its 'depth of field' are impressive when it comes to the categorisations that have agency. 'Schooling' and 'governing' provide the frameworks for much of the categorisation work here, but one of the characteristics that distinguishes this collection from comparable anthologies on literacy education in general is an alertness, even across such diverse pieces, to the importance of community; community is taken to be both a source of support for literacy teaching and learning and itself a setting that can be enhanced by more effective work in schools. Throughout, the potential for initiatives by communities, networks, and culturally based organisations stands out.

Where have the people here been; what is the 'story so far'? The stories of past educational efforts to provide literacy education to Indigenous Australian people that we find in these chapters show us historical challenges, obstacles, and sticking points among the various agents. Some contributors place a protracted series of neglected aspirations and recommendations at the centre of their narratives. One discernible line here is that it is inaccurate and probably unproductive to proceed – including with a research project – as if constructing better literacy education for Indigenous Australians is a new idea, an activity that takes place in a previously unpopulated zone, another *terra nullius*, with little to build on. As Oldfield and Lo Bianco note, even the policy initiatives of the Whitlam government were 'belated responses to years of advocacy, research, conceptual innovation, and organisational

17 Afterword: Being Literate in 'Australian': The Future Can

demands at grassroots levels', an observation reworked by Boughton in his description of unheeded adult literacy programs and recommendations.

A recurring motif also emerges of a combination of urgency, haste, and short-termism in policy formation (e.g. in Davis and Woods), including a failure to work patiently on developing coherence between the community and educational policy and practice (e.g. in McCollow). Oldfield and Lo Bianco name what seem, at first glance, to be the almost perverse about-turns in policy and the absence of long-term commitments and interventions that allow time for realistic evaluation. These authors also set out obstructions to that commitment, most prominently the ongoing resistance to formalising the rights of Indigenous Australians, the marketisation of educational provision, and an unorganised array of targeted literacy programs and commodities – a 'pattern of erosion'. Consequences of oscillating policies at the school level are made evident in the chapter by Davis and Woods, where we are shown haphazard accumulations, 'a variety of isolated "programs" and new – or old – approaches that layer on top of each other'.

Considering these hesitations and reversals, it is not surprising that the collection presented here – like the variety of educational sites it shows us – is neither built on nor itself builds a coherent, programmatic set of criteria for evaluating different approaches and outcomes. One message is that this patchwork is a product of the history of Indigenous-Settler relations as those relations have acted out in educational settings.

What do these chapters show us about what literacy education is for? More so than any other educational domain, literacy has been taken to signal development, civility, community well-being, economic productivity, and most other desirable social attributes. These attachments to literacy lead educational authorities to assert their commitment to progress in the literacy learning of youngsters. They have also often led systems away from the contexts of everyday literacy activities and capabilities, toward a functionally autonomous, unidimensional skill, mobile, measurable, and unmoored from the times, places, and bodies of knowledge in which it has been put to work (Street 2012).

Literacy is the communication medium on which Australian schooling is almost entirely dependent at this point in its history. Most chapters here assume that it should be part of preparing individual youngsters and communities to be citizens; part of accessing and developing their heritage, especially via their use of mobile online technologies, and connecting with international heritages and movements, as well as hobby, leisure groups; they can learn how to act effectively to preserve and enhance their own freedoms of participation and choice.

As historians of literacy across the ages have found, however, literacy can do other, darker things too. Here is Thomas on a 'fascinating tension' in the use of literacy in the ancient Mediterranean region:

> ...different potentials are seized upon by different communities. In some, writing means bureaucracy, control and oppression by the state, in others an enabling skill that frees an individual's creative potential. (Thomas 2009, pp. 13–14)

Here is Eisenstein on the contradictory effects, a millennium later, of the invention of the printing press:

We still seem to be experiencing the contradictory effects of a process which fanned the flames of religious zeal and bigotry while fostering a new concern for ecumenical concord and toleration, which fixed linguistic and national divisions more permanently while creating a cosmopolitan Commonwealth of Learning. (Eisenstein 2012, p. 311)

And here is Graff on what motivated twentieth century literacy campaigns:

...a relatively low level of mass literacy contributed more to social order, cultural cohesion, and political stability ... the dominance of a single standard of language, heritage, history, values, and personal characteristics ... in the face of the diversity of society divided by class, race, ethnicity, national origins, and gender ... mass literacy required social and individual controls. (Graff 2010, p. 644)

Whatever components and consequences of literacy learning are to be assessed, prior questions include 'what kinds of literacy? what kinds of capabilities?'

Chapters by Boughton and by Cooke and Piers-Blundell name the literacy-dependence of both contemporary schooling, and in broader civic and economic life, as the key to understanding effective participation in Australian society. As Boughton puts it, in a 'highly-literate settler economy and political system' the majority of Indigenous Australian people are 'unable to participate effectively as citizens in the institutions which are meant to guarantee their rights'. And for Cooke and Piers-Blundell, the 'paradigm' on which Australian schooling is based is key: 'Whether one subscribes to this paradigm or not, it is difficult to dispute the need to understand it, in an attempt to participate in its systematic constructs such as employment and health services'.

Subscribing to the 'paradigm' brings with it a precarious dialectic, knowing, as the participants do, that, historically, its ongoing core project has been assimilation. Ma Rhea and Anderson assert that a more overt 'sovereign rights-based pedagogy needs to underpin the learning theories'. This statement is one of the moments in the volume where the 'lamination' of descriptive, moral, and political activities onto the organisational and procedural details of daily teaching and learning is made explicit. Ma Rhea and Anderson challenge the view that teachers and researchers are neutral agents in the delivery of the neutral technology of literacy. Some researchers here have used literacy as a device to deepen community-pedagogy connections and partnerships. This broader-based educational use for literacy has implications for our understanding of schooling and its effects on the production of a citizenry.

What kinds of projects are reported? One continuum on which these literacy scholars can be spread has, at one end, a focus on literacy policy formation and, at the other, an inquiry into what occurs in the settings that are the targets of those policies. From among the chapters, we find a distinction between scholarship aimed at demonstrating efficacy, at capitalising on and developing diversity, and at reshaping policy.

Contributors might have all of these aims in mind at once, but the design of a study necessarily brings with it a distinctive set of priorities; method is choice – of people, practices, and horizons of outcomes and timing. We can see research aimed

17 Afterword: Being Literate in 'Australian': The Future Can   319

at improving literacy education for Indigenous Australian communities as a paradigm case of the need to think hard about the tension between site-specific and scalable, 'legislate-able' literacy education. How specific do the directives of policy – national, state/territory, or regional – need to be in order to remain evidence-informed? versus politically useable? How deep does, and should, the 'leverage' of policy reach? Research and development on any area relating to language and literacy in contemporary Australia necessarily encounter deep and longstanding patterns of diversity; but the connections surrounding institutionalised literacy education for and with Indigenous Australian communities present additional, highly localised layers of challenge, not only to teachers on site but to the policymakers and curriculum designers charged with supporting them.

Second, many of the contributions here centre-stage the relational aspects of research and development in literacy education for Indigenous Australians. Ways of communicating, knowing, and 'weaving' appear as three versions of a strong motif about strengthening partnerships through knowledge of communities: Boughton's 'ethics of solidarity and care' in adult literacy education, Rennie and Anderson's 'paramount importance' of 'the need for pre-service teachers to have a level of cultural competence', and networking and weaving in Davis and Woods' chapter on Durithunga, where the 'weave' strengthens the sustainability of practices and processes across various networks.

Some contributors treat partnership with the community as an already-known feature of the work, a resource to be worked with. For others, it is a set of locally variable processes to be discovered, documented, and analysed in the here-and-now, not only as framing the project but as an integral part of the project's workings. In some descriptions, the site-specific qualities of Indigenous Australian communities are highlighted, and others assume some generic features of 'community' as part of the setting. As with the categorisation and naming issue, the strategic deployment of the diversity-commonality contrast operates to remind us of the extent to which standard macro-policy in education has long been built on a determined reliance on the mirage of Australia's monolingual monoculture (Clyne 2005); however, much it has been accompanied by acknowledgements of the need for responsive educational practice.

Third, while several chapters refer to the significance of Indigenous Australian languages, few directly recruit local languages as part of a program of literacy education. Shinkfield's piece stands out here, with Ngaanyatjarra parents teaching in the mother tongue as a way of preparing their children for school. There is now a substantial research literature supporting the value of parent-child reading in the early years and of the development of youngsters' sense of story structure (see, e.g. the volume edited by Wasik 2012). For Shinkfield, 'it is only when experiences are embedded in family and community practices that they can become part of a young child's daily experiences within their family'.

The relevance of family and first languages appears only rarely. Similarly, while storytelling is not highlighted in Scull's review of the literacy programs, her 'first principle' is 'maintain children's Indigenous languages and ensure opportunities to become proficient speakers of English to build dual language competence as a strong foundation' (and see Scull 2016, p. 57). In Indigenous Australian communities, with adults who speak a local language, or a version of Aboriginal English, 'mother-tongue' is about sustaining that language and about the respect paid by the school to its local Indigenous Australian clients. Further, Davis and Woods show how developing and spreading Indigenous Australian language, in this case Yugambeh, can form part of a coherent, locally embedded, patient initiative, largely independent of the vicissitudes of government funding, and built instead on local community support.

But the concept of a plurilingual nation, so unproblematic in many contemporary countries, seems a distant aspiration in the Australian policy setting. That distance persists despite more widespread recognition not only of Indigenous Australian languages but of the many languages spoken and even taught at the present time in Australian educational institutions.

Finally, rarely do we find here studies that focus on multimodal aspects of how Indigenous Australians have and might put a variety of semiotic resources to educational work. Mills and Dooley draw our attention to the opportunities that arise if educators give 'priority to the sensorial dimensions of the body and its role in communication in literacy practice', reminding us of the degree to which conventional curriculum is language-saturated and abstract (Freebody et al. 2013; McKee and Heydon 2015).

Almost every chapter folds back onto questions about encounters with the people – an array of individuals, cultures, and communities. A fundamental element of these encounters is literacy as a mode of presenting, sustaining, and passing on their knowledge, beliefs, and moral and social orders. The 'kinds of projects' becomes effectively inseparable from the 'kinds of people' in them, as communities, teachers, and learners, and often as all three.

What is the conceptual reach of these projects? Recurring across these chapters, generally in the background, is a sense that literacy has, for individuals and communities, a significance beyond fluency in the activities of reading and writing, however multilingual or multimodal those activities might be. We encounter frequent references to ways of knowing, to a sense of identity and belonging, and to individuals or communities maintaining themselves and learning to flourish, within their own cultural heritage and as those heritages interact with neighbours. Djabibba, Auld, and O'Mara comment that the youngsters they worked with brought literacy knowledge from home 'but also an ontological sense of what it is to be and become a member of the Kunibídji community. This membership carries responsibilities of integrating knowing and being'.

There is further 'reach': As Djabibba, Auld, and O'Mara show, the local, day-to-day realities of teaching and learning, when closely observed, can exercise assimilative work over the learning events. In their chapter, we meet students who 'were repeatedly demonstrating that literacy learning for them was underscored by relationships with country, food, family, and peers', rather than, say, 'underscored' by test results; the assimilation tables can be turned.

17 Afterword: Being Literate in 'Australian': The Future Can   321

So one accomplishment of the chapters collected here is to invite the Australian community and its educators – parents, teachers, school leaders, professional learning support staff, policymakers and advisors, teacher educators, and researchers – to reflect on the challenges presented by improving Indigenous Australians' literacy learning, conceived broadly as providing a comprehensive view of literacy's effects on individuals, cultures, and nations. They also invite us to ask how well equipped Indigenous and Settler educators are to meet those challenges either through their own professional preparation (see Young et al. 2010) or in light of the policy pressures on them to focus on constrained skills in literacy at the expense of other necessary components (Luke et al. 2013; Paris 2005). This in turn leads back to questions about reliable, patiently acquired knowledge from research and development projects.

Futures: Concluding to Continue

These words are my last stand
The past can't be changed, but the future can
Nooky with The Herd, Radical Son & Sky'High, Reconciliation Week, 2012

What ways forward do these contributions offer teachers, researchers, policymakers, and the community? However significant the work reported here, and however broad the range of approaches, engaging with Indigenous Australian literacy education makes possible some lines of productive thought and work that, I believe, have received less attention than they deserve. Here I suggest three general directions that such an engagement might offer, framed here as revisions: the first is a revision of literacy as a set of resources that help us access the contemporary *communication environment* as it is reshaped by languages, cultures, and communities in digital, online, and mobile environments; the second is a revision of current approaches to *research and development* on literacy for Indigenous Australians to highlight the need for projects that use more extensive, patient, and diverse methods and methodologies; and the third is a revision of literacy education that calls for a more overt conceptual *integration of communities, cultures, and learning*. One aspect of this third revision is the suggestion that educators help the Australian community at large acknowledge the need to 'Close The Gap' but also that 'The Gap' works both ways: Indigenous Australian languages, literature, music, dance, and art are not only sophisticated and intriguing; they are also unique to our country and part of Settler heritage. For the most part, however, we Settlers have been either distracted or resolutely looking the other way. Over the generations, Settler societies have developed and inherited powerful institutionalised, standardised ways of teaching literacy; but that literacy need not be only a print-based, technical challenge, a module of skill uncoupled from learners' individual and collective daily experiences in and out of school.

The Communication Environment

Understanding is replaced by books
Technology replaces timelessness
from 'Your way – our way – the truth', Zelda Quakawoot, Bailai, 2012

Educating with Indigenous Australian communities, teachers, and students helps us rethink literacy as a way of engaging traditional, dominant, and emerging communication settings. Two aspects of these settings are mentioned here: plurilingualism and the digital, online, mobile environment – the DOME.

The value to policy, pedagogy, curriculum, and assessment of recognising the importance of the plurilingual and multi-dialect environment of Indigenous Australia extends to Settler Australians. Dhunghutti-Biripi man Craig Ritchie, the Chief Executive Officer of AIATSIS, recently outlined the three objectives of the AIATSIS Indigenous Languages Strategy: 'documenting every Australian language for use by current and future generations; building the capability of every language community to strengthen their language; and providing opportunities for every Australian to learn and take pride in an Australian language' (Ritchie 2018).

The language-education realities, official and informal, that have been in place in many countries suggest that a research-based understanding of the value of plurilingualism is now widespread (Bialystok and Barac 2012). So too is the practice of educating in a range of official languages along with a widespread acceptance of a common national or state language (Heugh et al. 2017). The extent to which the AIATSIS objectives seem aspirational is a measure of Australia's troubled reaction to the idea of plurilingualism.

We are reminded often that the digital, online, mobile environment continues to reshape social experience. Some affordances of the DOME (Carrington 2017; Dagenais et al. 2017; Leung 2009) speak directly to Indigenous Australian learners and their teachers, including accessibility, anywhere, anytime; portability; personalisation, including multimodality and real-time translation possibilities; and immersion in real or augmented or virtual reality, fictionalised or fantasised. Clearly the collection of network and software products the DOME provides has educational potential for people living in remote settings, including new translation-supported, multimodality-based connections to online or blended learning opportunities for school students and their teachers and parents, to affinity and leisure groups, and to nearby or distant cultural and employment opportunities (see, e.g. J.P. Gee 2005; Gee and Gee 2017; Pellegrino 2018). But these features, and the DOME more generally, have surprisingly little visibility in the selection of literacy education projects reported here.

The DOME can present its users with challenges and threats – sexual exploitation, the attachment of young users to commodity brands, and fake news. There is a growing body of evidence that supports some of these anxieties. Vosoughi et al. (2018), for example, analysed, fact-checked, and tracked about 126,000 stories tweeted by about 3 million people more than 4.5 million times. They found that

17 Afterword: Being Literate in 'Australian': The Future Can

falsehood diffused significantly further, faster, deeper, and more broadly than the truth in all categories of information. The effects were most pronounced for false political news than for false news about terrorism, natural disasters, science, urban legends, or financial information. Further, they established that it was humans rather than robots that were responsible for this wildfire spread of 'the fake'.

So what would be a curricular, pedagogical response to these potentially dystopic features of the DOME for Australian Indigenous learners and their teachers? There is a knowable 'system-logic' to the DOME, even if we cannot capture it via any single popular examples, or somehow 'average' its features across providers and users. The basic algorithms used in search engines, advertising programs, charity drives, crowdsourcing, and the rest are not impenetrable; they are, in fact, well-known, widely discussed in alcoves within the DOME and available in accessible publications.

What this means is that educators can become informed about the key features of this body of specialised knowledge relating to system-logic and use that knowledge to help learners understand how for-profit, not-for-profit, and political provider groups, and others, use and misuse that logic. Needless to say, it is also a rapidly evolving body of knowledge, but it is only through engaging literacy as the DOME is reshaping it that practicable educational responses can be developed to the challenges that DOME literacy itself presents. The need for ongoing research and development for and with teachers, and for regularly updated teachers' development programs, is clear. The digitisation of social, commercial, economic, and curricular communication is expanding its reach, so the resources of literacy – breaking the codes, participating in the meaning patterns, using a variety of social applications, and analysing the critical demands of communications – are evolving. Avoiding the exclusionary effects of the 'digital divide' in this environment is about more than providing equipment and 'signal'; it is about educators helping communities capitalise on the DOME's advantages in their daily social activities, including their school-based activities (Warschauer 2003) to ensure that Indigenous Australians, particularly those in remote communities, are not marginalised but can participate in these rapid evolutionary processes – not left with the literacy basics of the 1960s.

Approaches to Educational Research and Development

So listen very carefully now
As you walk upon our land
from 'Songlines', Nola Gregory, Kija (2017)

Educating with Indigenous Australian communities, teachers, and students helps us appreciate that research and development projects in literacy take place in cultural and linguistic settings that are diverse, complex, and changing. That appreciation is growing partly because of documented classroom innovations (e.g. Chelsea et al. 2018; Stevenson and Beck 2017). If we take this collection of contributions to

324   P. Freebody

be representative of research and development work in the area, then we find literacy education for Indigenous Australians to be a topic in search of programmatic conceptual and methodological ways forward, ways that can permit some cumulative build-up of conceptual and methodological know-how. This is a statement about the current state of affairs – conceptual, methodological, and practical; it is intended to raise questions about the 'scaling up' of research and development findings in educational environments that are diverse in ways yet to be described and understood, ways not adequately addressed front-on in the chapters here. 'Scalability' itself needs to become a topic for inquiry, case-by-case, rather than an imperative in the policy-pedagogy relationship.

There are current international parallels to this concern. In concluding their detailed review of the hundreds of studies comprising the US Department of Education's *What Works Clearinghouse* (WWC), Malouf and Taymans (2016) documented deep flaws in the logic and the reporting of generalisability in the studies summarised in the WWC. They concluded that educators, including policymakers, should re-examine their reliance on experimental impact research as the basis for gauging effectiveness. This policy tends to perpetuate the chronic weakness of the evidence base as well as endorsing evidence with questionable relevance to practice (p. 458).

Over a third of the studies included in their review concerned literacy education, more than for any other topical area. But how has a long-established, rigorously constructed evidence base relating to the teaching and learning of reading and writing such as WWC get accused of having 'chronic weaknesses' and 'questionable relevance to practice'? Malouf and Taymans emphasise the importance of local educational conditions and 'building collaborative partnerships', not just for differentiated practice but also for research and development projects' basic design validity, to be 'better suited to typical school settings': 'Experimental impact evidence might better be viewed as one component of an overall "effectiveness argument" that provides a logical framework for considering disparate general and local elements in making meaningful predictions of effectiveness' (p. 458).

Deutsch's landmark study of the significance of theory in scientific inquiry amounts to a plea for prioritising the search for better explanations, rather than the mere collection of unconnected empirical demonstrations:

> There is no such thing as a purely predictive, explanation-less theory (p. 15) … one must also be seeking a better explanation of the relevant phenomena. That is the scientific frame of mind (pp. 22–23) … The difference between humans and other species is in what kind of knowledge they can use (explanatory instead of rule-of-thumb) and in how they create it. (p. 58)

So we can ask of the collection here: Do these reports of projects offer a collection of 'rules of thumb' or better explanations of how teaching and learning literacy to and with Indigenous Australians? Do they set out to improve how we explain what was there before and how it was improved? Do the studies' designs prioritise the delivery of a better explanation? Or a proof of concept in the here-and-now? Or a truthful description of a series of events?

The combination of more intensive calls for evidence-based educational practice with concerns over diversity in schooling has recently led prominent educational researchers such as Anthony Bryk to call for closer, more patient collaboration and valid, effective, explanation-oriented educational research and development. One focus (and see Snow 2015) has been on collaborations in research design:

> …networked improvement communities are inclusive in drawing together the expertise of practitioners, researchers, designers, technologists, and many others … The point is not just to know what can make things better or worse; it is to develop the know-how necessary to actually make things better. (Bryk 2015, p. 467)

The point applies with force in cross-cultural settings that have been shaped by centuries of substantial and stubborn economic, cultural, linguistic, and political differentials.

The comments by Malouf and Taymans and by Bryk are also about time: As the project described in Davis and Woods indicates, and as reflected in Ma Rhea and Anderson's chapter, the value of sustained program development 'beyond the systemic focus on the 4-to-5-year improvement cycle, instead in many cases marking a decade or generational shift within the reform processes'. Collaborations on that timescale hold a promise of increasing educators' appreciation of alternative understandings of relationships; the workings of language, power, and identity; and a reparative approach to both Australia's history and its future. Taken together, these directions, whatever else they do, speak strongly to a reassessment of the logic of current funding models for research in Indigenous Australian literacy education.

Integrating Curriculum, Community, Cultures, and Learning

Embattled by national educating
Impatient implications.
These are to half our future.
from 'Waste or worse', Lionel Fogarty, Murri, 1990

Educating with Indigenous Australian communities, teachers, and students helps us integrate more strongly and overtly communities, cultures, and learning into the practice and study of literacy. As Boughton reminds us in his chapter, unevenly distributed literacy problems are problems for the whole society because they can create and entrench community divisions that need to be overcome before that society can develop more fully; and as Djabibba, Auld, and O'Mara suggest, 'the schooling system might open itself to learn from the thousands of generations of connectedness to place'.

These are two moments in the collection that recall Levinson's (2007) detailed study of the educational experiences and aspirations of English Gypsies. He found many instances of their active resistance to school-based literacy education, and his encounters led him to reflect on the value and uniqueness of their knowledge:

Against a background in which fissures are evident between pedagogical structures/beliefs and actual literacy practices, and in which (non-school) community-based knowledge has been marginalized, one might speculate as to the alternative literacies that we have all forfeited. (p. 33)

Some ideas 'forfeited' by many Settler and post-colonial societies revolve around the need for stronger alignments among three elements:

- What is to be learned? Communities' general priorities for how one generation educates the next – about heritage, economic participation, social-cohesion, individual expression and aspirations, and pastoral care of the young
- How will teaching and learning take place? The pedagogies developed within the informal or formal programs that are put in place
- How will progress be monitored? How students' and teachers' progress can be evaluated to improve curriculums and pedagogies

It is not hard to see how literacy education has become so prone to misalignments on these counts. Having become a stand-alone, portable object, and a political hot-spot, it is prone to institutionalised detachment, not only from the languages that many learners speak but also from the ends to which literate technologies are put even by people with appropriate monolingual literate resources, in societies that depend upon or are saturated by literacy activities in their vocational, intellectual, artistic, civic, and political endeavours.

Also forfeited in many sectors of urbanised Australia is an existentially charged relation to 'country'. For Indigenous Australians, the word *country* carries with it 'all the values, places, resources, stories and cultural obligations associated with that area and its features', covering the entirety of an Indigenous Australian group's ancestral domains (Reconciliation Australia 2018). For Australian Settler societies, in contrast, the most durable origin narratives centre on expatriate beginnings, often celebrating pioneer explorations, the appropriation of natural resources for rapid population growth, and post-colonial rites of national 'passage'.

So one challenge that arises in studies of language and literacy in Indigenous Australian settings involves the relationship of language, and therefore necessarily of literacy education, to nationality and nationhood. From 1788 to the present, the 250 languages spoken on the continent have been taken by the Settler society to add up to neither a nation, nor a federation of states, nor 250 regions, nor any other collection of clans, communities, or peoples manageable by centralised colonial or governmental policy. These chapters show us that one of the understandings that we have forfeited is the cultural fluidity of 'the nation' and the ways in which that fluidity can be sustained and enriched through varied, more locally derived and managed language and literacy education – in the shadow of, but not under the operational direction of, policies and material supports from a central jurisdiction.

More durable forms of knowing, remembering, inscribing, and interpreting are also at stake: Much has been written about the complexity and significance of visual arts, music, and dance in Indigenous Australian communities, but not so much about how these might enrich the Settler society. Anthropological linguist Allan Marett, for instance, spent years with the Wangga people. His and his colleagues' studies show how their songs and dances enact key Aboriginal convictions about the nature of the universe, about what it is to be human, about how people should and do relate to one another, and about the nature of causality, fundamental convictions that are radically different from those of the Australian or Western mainstream (Marett 2010, p. 255; and see Marett 2005).

Marett analysed how features of the music-dance embody the relationships among the living, the dead, and the landscape. It has also been recognised that Indigenous Australian song traditions have 'documentary' status when it comes to such basic issues as the legalities of land ownership (Koch 2013). So Indigenous Australian music-dance ceremonies are, and not merely metaphorically, enacted literacies with pedagogic intent and moral purpose.

Comparable findings have been documented for the visual art traditions of Indigenous Australians by Luke Taylor, former Senior Curator at the National Museum of Australia and Director of Research at the Australian Institute of Aboriginal and Torres Strait Islander Studies. He studied the bark painting traditions of the Kunwinjku people of Western Arnhem Land. One of his conclusions was that:

> Paintings reinforce belief in the powers of the Ancestral beings by giving visible form to key transformations. Kunwinjku artists create figurative representations which condense a multitude of abstract conceptualisations into tangible images … paintings continue to help Kunwinjku to understand the fundamental connections between individuals and the social and Ancestral order. (Taylor 1997, p. 207 and p. 257)

Again, it is clear that Indigenous Australian paintings document core educational experiences for growing Kunwinjku, including knowledge about their own particular rights and responsibilities to know, and to transfer that knowledge across generations. These are forms of educational experiences, with varying forms of literacy, that Australian Settler society has 'forfeited' along the way.

Coda: Good for Us All?

Let us try to understand the white man's ways
And accept them as they accept us
from 'Let us not be bitter' Oodgeroo, Noonuccal/Kath Walker (1966)

In 1992, the then new Prime Minister Paul Keating addressed an audience in Redfern Park to mark the Australian launch of the International Year of the World's Indigenous Peoples:

> It will be a year of great significance for Australia. It comes at a time when we have committed ourselves to succeeding in the test which so far we have always failed … it is a test of our self-knowledge. Of how well we know the land we live in. How well we know our history. How well we recognise the fact that, complex as our contemporary identity is, it cannot be separated from Aboriginal Australia. How well we know what Aboriginal Australians know about Australia … There is everything to gain … they have shaped our knowledge of this continent and of ourselves. (Keating 1992)

328   P. Freebody

Clearly the 'gap' in literacy education is generally heard as locating Indigenous Australia on the 'in-the-red' side of the ledger. It is also clear, from this volume and many other efforts, that many Settler and Indigenous Australians have done important work to narrow inequalities in health, employment, and education. Keating, however, pointed to the need to 'close' the other 'gap' as well, a cultural gap in the knowledge of Settler Australia. Respect for a culture, a community, or an intellectual, emotional, or aesthetic tradition cannot be conjured up out of a vacuum. To pay respect to a people, a culture, or a heritage, while at the same time admitting to knowing nothing about it and having no interest in finding anything out about it, is gestural. Gestures not only provide nothing actionable to work on; gesturing can be mistaken for acting. (Sutton (2011) presents a fiercely argued case for the dangers of this mistake in the current policy management of Indigenous Australia.)

Similarly, practical reparations and resolutions need to follow promises and apologies; but sustained practical actions themselves will be the results of Settler Australians' recognising, understanding, and prizing the still-lively emotional, social, artistic, and cultural assets that characterise Indigenous Australian experience. In the case of Settler societies, the moral urge to declare respect for Indigenous Australians brings with commitment to a program of finding out about, in Keating's words, 'what Aboriginal Australians know about Australia' and about what it means to be literate in Australian.

Postscript: The Gift of the Dayiwul

In September 2013, on a flight from Paris, I was seated near an elderly Aboriginal lady. She was friendly, quiet, and soft-spoken. She said she thought Paris was 'just beautiful'. She slept most of the way.

A few weeks later, I saw her picture in a media outlet and found that she was Lena Nyadbi, a 77-year-old Gija elder from the Kimberley. For almost the entire first half of her life, Nyadbi was an 'indentured labourer' on a cattle station that incorporated her ancestral land. When she was 32 an industrial commission ruled that cattle station owners pay their Indigenous workers at the same rate as their other workers. One result was that many Gija people, including Nyadbi, were forced to leave their ancestral land and move to the neighbouring Warmun land. Warmun was then an active Aboriginal artist community, and Nyadbi spent years apprenticing with artists there. She took up painting seriously when she was 62.

Nyadbi was in the media because staff at the Paris Musée du Quai Branly, next to the Eiffel Tower, had enlarged her charcoal and white ochre painting 'Dayiwul Lirlmim', or 'Barramundi Scales', to cover the 720 square metre roof of the Musée. It is a permanent installation, viewable only to the seven million people a year who climb the Eiffel Tower, from Google Earth, and from space.

The painting tells the dreaming story of three women who catch a barramundi that escapes. It jumps across the water, rocks, and land with the women in pursuit.

17 Afterword: Being Literate in 'Australian': The Future Can

In the process its scales are scattered across Gija land, near where the biggest diamond mine in the world, the Argyle, is now located; it is the scales that 'reflect' the diamonds.

The media reported that when she first saw her work from the Eiffel Tower, she said 'When I get home, I will tell them I saw my barramundi beside the river, ready to jump into the Paris river. That dayiwul, he can swim all through that whole city, all over, all the way, but that dayiwul he's really in my country', and 'I was very emotional and full of pride. At the same time, I had tears in my eyes. When I looked down, I felt sorry for my country. The landscape has been changed, but the dreaming hasn't'.

(Sources: https://www.gg.gov.au/speech/custodianship-ceremony; "Aboriginal artist gets high-profile Paris display" The Japan Times. Paris. Agence France Presse/Jiji Press. 8 June 2013;

https://www.webcitation.org/6QvEkqq7g?url=http://www.japantimes.co.jp/news/2013/06/08/asia-pacific/aboriginal-artist-gets-high-profile-paris-display/; https://en.wikipedia.org/wiki/Lena_Nyadbi)

Note

Sections of this chapter draw substantially on the piece by Morgan et al. (forthcoming) and in particular on the contribution of Associate Professor Nick Reid. I also gratefully acknowledge the assistance of Dr. Nathan Crevensten and Professor Peter Reimann in the preparation of this chapter.

References

Bialystok, E., & Barac, R. (2012). Bilingual effects on cognitive and linguistic development: Role of language, cultural background, and education. *Child Development, 83*, 413–422.

Bryk, A. S. (2015). 2014 AERA Distinguished Lecture: Accelerating how we learn to improve. *Educational Researcher, 44*, 467–477.

Buckskin, P., Hughes, P., Price, K., Rigney, Ll., Sarra, C., Adams, I., & Hayward, C. (2009). *Review of Australian directions in Indigenous education, 2005–2008*. Ministerial Council for Education, Early Childhood Development and Youth Affairs Reference Group on Indigenous Education, Government of Western Australia. https://catalogue.nla.gov.au/Record/4729883. Accessed 29 July 2018.

Carrington, V. (2017). How we live now: "I don't think there's such a thing as being offline". *Teachers College Record, 119*, 1–24.

Chelsea, N. K., Keehne, M. W., Sarsona, M., Kawakami, A. J., & Au, K. H. (2018). Culturally responsive instruction and literacy learning. *Journal of Literacy Research, 50*, 141–166.

Clyne, M. (2005). *Australia's language potential*. Sydney: University of New South Wales Press.

Dagenais, D., Toohey, K., Bennett Fox, A., & Singh, A. (2017). Multilingual and multimodal composition at school. *Language and Education, 31*, 263–282.

Davis, J. (1970). *'The first-born' and other poems*. Sydney: Angus & Robertson.

Eisenstein, E. (2012). *The printing revolution in early modern Europe* (2nd ed.). Cambridge: Cambridge University Press.

Fitzgerald, R., & Housley, W. (2015). *Advances in membership categorization analysis*. London: Sage Publishing.

Fogarty, L. (1990). Waste or worse. In *Jagera*. Coominya: Cheryl Buchanan. Available at https://redroomcompany.org/poem/lionel-fogarty/waste-or-worse/. Accessed 20 Aug 2018.

Freebody, P., Chan, E., & Barton, G. (2013). Curriculum as literate practice: Language and knowledge in the classroom). In K. Hall, T. Cremin, B. Comber, & L. Moll (Eds.), *International Handbook of research on children's literacy, learning, and culture* (pp. 304–318). Oxford: Wiley-Blackwell.

Gee, J. P. (2005). Semiotic social spaces and affinity spaces: From the age of mythology to today's schools. In D. Barton & K. Tusting (Eds.), *Beyond communities of practice: Language, power and social context* (pp. 214–232). Cambridge: Cambridge University Press.

Gee, E., & Gee, J. P. (2017). Games as distributed teaching and learning systems. *Teachers College Record, 119*, 1–22.

Graff, H. J. (2010). The literacy myth at thirty. *Journal of Social History, 43*, 635–661.

Gray, B. N. (2007). *Accelerating the literacy development of Indigenous students*. Darwin: Charles Darwin University Press.

Gregory, N. (2017). Songlines. *Australian Poetry Journal, 7*, 27.

Heugh, K., Prinsloo, C., Makgamatha, M., Diedericks, G., & Winnaar, L. (2017). Multilingualism(s) and system-wide assessment: A southern perspective. *Language and Education, 31*, 197–216.

Jayyusi, L. (1991). Values and moral judgement: communicative praxis as moral order. In G. Button (Ed.), *Ethnomethodology and the human sciences* (pp. 227–251). Cambridge: Cambridge University Press.

Keating, P. (1992). Redfern Speech Launching the International Year of the World's Indigenous People, Redfern Park, 10 December https://antar.org.au/sites/default/files/paul_keating_speech_transcript.pdf. Accessed 17 Aug 2018.

Koch, G. (2013). *We have the song, so we have the land: Song and ceremony as proof of ownership in Aboriginal and Torres Strait Islander land claims* (AIATSIS Research Discussion Paper #33). Canberra: AIATSIS Research Publications.

Leung, L. (2009). User-generated content on the internet: an examination of gratifications, civic engagement and psychological empowerment. *New Media & Society, 11*, 1327–1347.

Levinson, M. P. (2007). Literacy in English Gypsy communities: Cultural capital manifested as negative. *American Educational Research Journal, 44*, 5–39.

Luke, A., et al. (2013). *A summative evaluation of the Stronger Smarter Learning Project, vols. 1 and 2*. Canberra: Department of Employment, Education and Vocational Training. http://eprints.qut.edu.au/statistics/eprint/59535/.

Malouf, D. B., & Taymans, J. M. (2016). Anatomy of an evidence base. *Educational Researcher, 45*, 454–459.

Marett, A. (2005). *Songs, dreamings and ghosts: The Wangga of North Australia*. Middletown: Wesleyan University Press.

Marett, A. (2010). Vanishing songs: How musical extinctions threaten the planet. *Ethnomusicology Forum, 19*, 249–262.

McKee, L. L., & Heydon, R. M. (2015). Orchestrating literacies: Print literacy learning opportunities within multimodal intergenerational ensembles. *Journal of Early Childhood Literacy, 15*, 227–255.

Morgan, A.-M., Reid, N., & Freebody, P. (forthcoming). Literacy and linguistic diversity in Australia. In To appear in L. Verhoeven, K. Pugh, & C. Perfetti (Eds.), *Cross-linguistic perspectives on literacy education*. Cambridge: Cambridge University Press.

Nooky with The Herd, Radical Son & Sky'High (2012). *Like a Version*, cover of Sam Cooke "Change is gonna come". Reconciliation Week, triplej. https://www.youtube.com/watch?v=4ACBU_DyYMw. Accessed 04 Aug 2018.

Oodgeroo, Noonuccal (Kath Walker). (1966). Let us not be bitter. In *From The dawn is at hand*. Brisbane: Jacaranda Wiley.

Paris, S. G. (2005). Reinterpreting the development of reading skills. *Reading Research Quarterly, 40*, 184–202.

Pellegrino, J. W. (2018). Assessment of and for learning. In F. Fischer, C. E. Hmelo-Silver, S. R. Goldman, & P. Reimann (Eds.), *International handbook of the learning sciences* (pp. 410–421). London: Routledge.

Purdie, N., Frigo, T., Ozolins, C., Noblett, G., Thieberger, N. & Sharp, J. (2008). *Indigenous language programs in Australian Schools: A way forward* (Australian Council for Educational Research Report). http:/research.acer.edu.au/indigenous_education/18/. Accessed 09 Oct 2016.

Quakawoot, Z. (2012). *Your way – Our way – The truth*. www.CreativeSpirits.info. Accessed 29 July 2018.

Reconciliation Australia. (2018). https://www.reconciliation.org.au/wp-content/uploads/2018/03/welcome_acknowledgement_v4.pdf. Accessed 07 Aug 18.

Rigney, L.-I. (2011). Action for Aboriginal social inclusion. In D. Bottrell & S. Goodwin (Eds.), *Schools, communities and social inclusion* (pp. 38–49). South Yarra: Palgrave Macmillan.

Ritchie, C. (2018). *Keynote address*. Gold Coast: National Indigenous Languages Convention. http:/aiatsis.gov.au/publications/presentations/national-indigenous-languages-convention-keynote-address. Accessed 25 June 2018.

Scull. (2016). Effective literacy teaching for Indigenous students: Principles from evidence-based practices. *Australian Journal of Language and Literacy, 39*, 54–63.

Sellwood, J., & Angelo, D. (2013). Everywhere and nowhere: The invisibility of Indigenous Australian and Torres Strait Island contact languages in education and indigenous language contexts. *Australian Review of Applied Linguistics, 36*, 250–266.

Siegel, J. (1999). Creoles and Minority dialects in education: an overview. *Journal of Multilingual and Multicultural Development, 20*, 508–531.

Snow, C. E. (2015). Rigor and realism: Doing educational science in the real world. The 2014 Wallace Foundation Distinguished Lecture. *Educational Researcher, 44*, 460–466.

Stevenson, A., & Beck, S. (2017). Migrant students' emergent conscientization through critical, socioculturally responsive literacy pedagogy. *Journal of Literacy Research, 49*, 240–272.

Street, B. V. (2012). Society reschooling. *Reading Research Quarterly, 47*, 216–227.

Sutton, P. (2011). *The politics of suffering: Indigenous Australia and the end of the liberal consensus*. Melbourne: Melbourne University Publishing.

Taylor, L. (1997). *Seeing the inside: Bark painting in Western Arnhem Land*. Oxford: Clarendon Press.

Thomas, R. (2009). Writing, reading, public and private literacies: Functional literacy and democratic literacy in Greece. In W. A. Johnson & H. N. Parker (Eds.), *Ancient literacies: The culture of reading in Greece and Rome* (pp. 13–45). Oxford: Oxford University Press.

UNESCO. (2018). *Languages matter!* http://www.unesco.org/new/en/communication-and-information/wsis-10-review-event-25-27-february-2013/feature-stories/languages-matter/. Accessed 09 Aug 2018.

Vosoughi, S., Roy, D., & Aral, S. (2018). The spread of true and false news online. *Science, 359*, 1146–1151.

Warschauer, M. (2003). *Technology and social inclusion: Rethinking the digital divide*. Cambridge, MA: MIT Press.

Wasik, B. H. (2012). *Handbook of family literacy* (2nd ed.). New York: Routledge.

Wigglesworth, G., Simpson, J., & Loakes, D. (2011). NAPLAN language Assessments for Indigenous children in remote communities: issues and problems. *Australian Review of Applied Linguistics, 34*, 320–343.

Young, M., Chester, J.-L., Flett, B., Joe, L., Marshall, L., Moore, D., Paul, K., Paynter, F., Williams, J., & Huber, J. (2010). Becoming 'real' Aboriginal teachers: Attending to intergenerational narrative reverberations and responsibilities. *Teachers and Teaching: Theory and Practice, 16*, 285–305.

Peter Freebody is a Fellow of the Academy of the Social Sciences in Australia and an Honorary Professorial Fellow at the University of Wollongong and The University of Sydney. He was most recently a Professorial Research Fellow in the Faculty of Education and Social Work at The University of Sydney. Before that, he held various positions including at Griffith University and the University of New England. He was Deputy Dean/Research and co-founder of the Centre for Research in Pedagogy and Practice at the National Institute of Education, Singapore. He has conducted research and published in the areas of literacy education, educational disadvantage, and educational research methods. He has been a member and Chair of the Literacy Research Panel of the International Reading Association and the 2014 recipient of that Association's W.S. Gray Citation of Merit for outstanding international contributions to literacy education.

Printed in the USA
CPSIA information can be obtained
at www.ICGtesting.com
CBHW062310131024
15794CB00004BA/215